DIGITAL IMAGE CREATION
Insights into the New Photography

Digital Image Creation
Insights into the New Photography

Edited by Hisaka Kojima
Book concept and design by Takenobu Igarashi

Peachpit Press
2414 Sixth Street
Berkeley, CA 94710
510/548-4393
510/548-5991 (fax)

Find us on the World Wide Web at:
http://www.peachpit.com

Peachpit Press is a division of Addison-Wesley Longman.

Translators: David Howarth and Chiaki Hikasa
Printing: Toppan Printing Co. (Singapore) Pte., Ltd.
Coordination: Seiki Okuda

Special thanks to Ken Tanaka

ISBN 0-201-88660-X

9 8 7 6 5 4 3 2 1

DIGITAL IMAGE CREATION
Insights into the New Photography

Edited by
Hisaka Kojima

Book Concept and Design by
Takenobu Igarashi

Peachpit Press

ontents

oreword

gital Photography: The State of the Art
/ Hisaka Kojima

gital imaging represents the biggest breakthrough in the 150-year story of photography. Digital technology has been progressing at unprecedented rate during the 1990s. Photographers who were uick to take up the challenge of the digital medium have mastered rious electronic tools, and fully used their creative energies to oduce outstanding photographic works. A keen observer of this gnificant trend in photography, Takenobu Igarashi proposed the ea of this book, and it was at his request that I gathered material the state of the art of digital photography in the U.S. today.

gital photography can be regarded as two main processes: one volves image capture with a digital camera and input of the image rectly into the computer as digital data; the other concerns image nthesis using image-correction technology, graphical and special fects and other techniques to produce photographs from digital ata. In the latter process, photographers typically use application ftware such as Adobe Photoshop, Live Picture and Barco Creator.

here are two types of digital camera: the purpose-built digital amera, and the hybrid form comprising a conventional camera uipped with a digital camera back containing a CCD image sensor. either type uses traditional silver halide film, but each allows the hotographer to view the images as they are taken. Over the past w years, camera manufacturers have been introducing new models nd making technological improvements rapidly. However, the digital amera has so far been limited in its scope of application to still-life udio photography and fields such as journalism, where there is gh priority on the rapid transfer of information. Because of this, ose practitioners we call digital photographers are not using the gital camera exclusively, but usually in tandem with the onventional camera.

roadly speaking, this volume takes digital photography to mean e conversion of negative or positive film to digital information using scanning device, and the manipulation of that information in the omputer to produce works of photographic art. The book is devoted works of high artistic merit that have been produced with the aid digital technology. It does not take as its starting point descriptions of the ways in which particular digital functions are used, but rather, puts the images first, and touches on the essence of the photography, so that we might catch a glimpse of upcoming trends.

Digital Image Creation presents the works of nine individuals and two groups of photographers, and introduces the artists by way of interviews and examples of their work in progress. The practitioners of digital photography represented here are forceful individuals with persuasive ideas. They are engaged in a variety of fields, including commercial photography, fine-art photography, special effects critical for the photographer, and printing. Every one of them is a pioneer in the field of digital imaging, well versed in all aspects of the medium and bubbling with creative ideas.

Digital photography offers the possibility of more freedom of artistic expression, while from the rational viewpoint it also exerts an enormous influence on the photographic community. In commercial photography or stock photograph business is thriving, and the graphic arts are beginning to eschew analog in favor of a wholly digital process, from photographing through design to printing. The chemical darkroom is being consigned to the past. Photographers are also taking advantage of network communications to transfer image data quickly over long distances.

Developments in digital photography continue apace. Changes have occurred even during the time taken between the initial and the final editing of this book. In this climate of rapid technological progress, there is anxiety that today's innovations will become obsolete tomorrow. But the artistic debate over digital photography is just beginning. The human imagination is without limits. The messages conveyed by the photographers represented here are offered in the hope that what is gained from them leads to an even wider range of possibilities for the future of digital photography.

Jody Dole

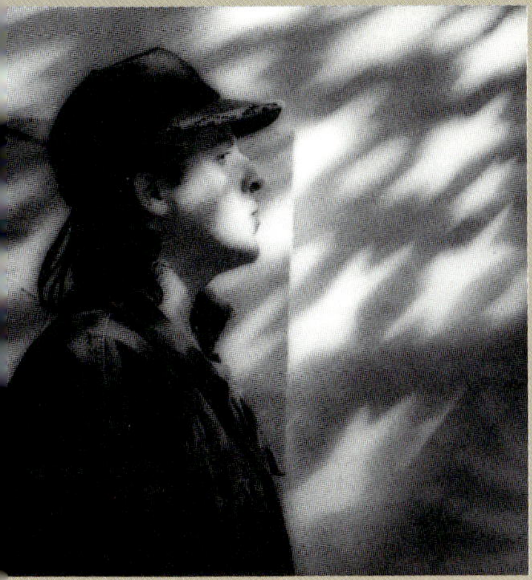

Jody Dole is a fine-art and advertising photographer and a pioneer in fine-art digital production. He first gained commercial success in 1989 with a highly original worldwide advertising campaign for Smirnoff Vodka by McCann-Erickson-New York. In just five years he has become one of the design world's fastest rising stars, earning international recognition for his still life photography.

He has received a host of awards, including those from *Communication Arts,* the Art Directors Club of New York, *PDN/Photo Design, American Photography,* the Clio's, APNY and the *Graphis Photo Design & Poster* annuals. Dole's work has been profiled in numerous publications including *Nikon World, The Commercial Image, Camera & Darkroom, Step By Step Graphics, Applied Arts, Advertising Age* and a cover feature in *American Photo*.

In a feature on Jody Dole in the *New York Times,* John Durniak described his images as "masterpieces of photography, design and printing." Dole photographs ordinary objects so that they transcend themselves with incredible beauty. He simply takes photography to a whole new level and breathes beauty into form with style and taste.

Known for Iris proofing and pre-press color control, Jody Dole Studio is equipped with the latest high-resolution digital systems and state-of-the-art pre-press equipment.

Jody Dole

What was it that got you started in digital imaging? When did you start?

I'm not exactly "in" digital imaging per se although I utilize digital technology along with many other techniques. I brought digital imaging technology into my studio four years ago. What got me interested was the ability to fly without wings. The total freedom that this process provides in imaging caught my attention early on.... The ability to stand up on a magic carpet and fly in the air... that's pretty much what digital imaging is like. The ability to control a visual — to the millionth degree of accuracy — this is what got me started. As a full-time photographer one also needs to be a full-time perfectionist in an effort to solve client needs and being able to make perfect, more perfect, which comes in very handy. Being able to make something that is a hundred-percent sharp, a thousand-percent sharp or whatever you like after the image has been executed is an impressive ability.

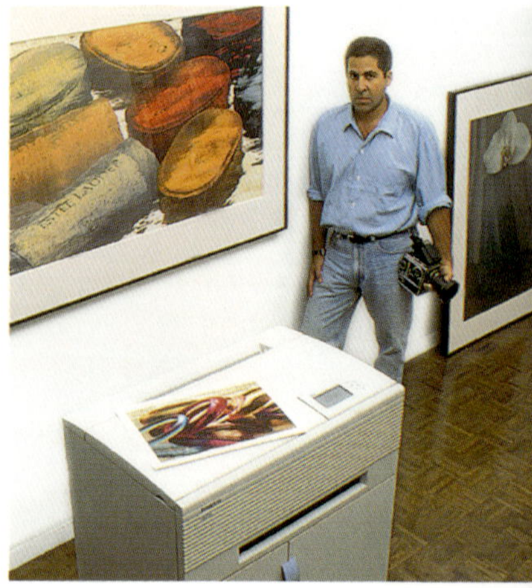

Studio

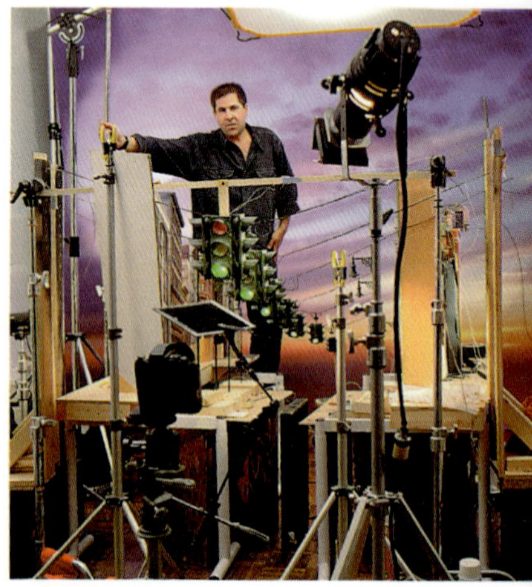

Jody Dole on set in NYC studio

I had been watching this process occur from afar on a greater scale with advertising clients that I had worked with for several years. I admired what could be done on a Quantel Paintbox at the early stages and as I watched this magic being performed I knew that adjusting the "genetics" of film dot by dot, pixel by pixel could play an important role in my work. There was only one drawback... the cost at the time was staggering to pursue it yourself.

I can remember this one project for a hotel ad campaign.... I had to shoot from a 15th-story rooftop balcony, looking straight down at a couple exiting their Jaguar convertible as the porter was removing luggage from the trunk. The semicircle cobblestone entrance made for a wonderful graphic but the driveway was covered with oil and grease stains when seen from so far above. I actually had a crew with buckets of detergent and hard brushes scrubbing four thousand square feet of cobblestone for two days to make it presentable. Clearly, this would have been a 30-minute job for a Mac 8100 and Photoshop.

So I knew what I needed to do with this technology before I actually started using it. I see many users of the technology inventing as they go along, but if you have limited experience and don't know what you need and someone presents you with this

a. Photophase Screen

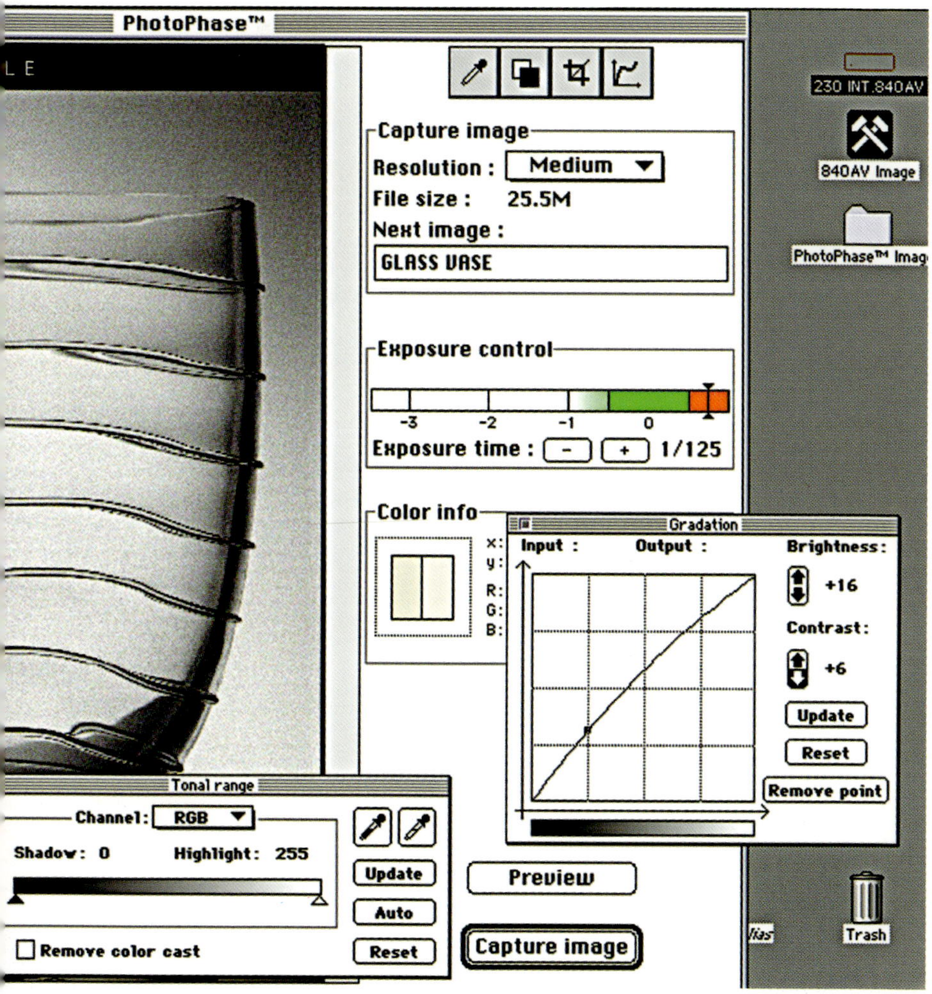

:edure

steps involved in digital photography capture include:

Set up and light the visual
Attach IR filter and open the camera shutter
Select F stop (F16 is a good start)
Set exposure time on PhotoPhase control screen
Take Preview scan
Evaluate and Adjust the image
Crop the image
Name the image
Select the Resolution
Capture the final image
nspect the final image by selecting Open from the file menu or through Photoshop

a. Main Window of user interface for PhotoPhase digital camera back shows:

Tonal Range Button (Pop-up Tonal Range window seen at lower middle area of screen) includes controls for defining the range of tones or ***levels of gray*** contained in the image. The application enables the user to define the tonal range of the image, causing the brightest points to appear pure white and the darkest points to be pure black assuring that the image will show maximum contrast and detail at all points in between.

Gradation Control Button (Pop-up Gradation window to the lower right of the screen).
Gradation refers to the ***distribution of gray levels within the tonal range of the image.*** The gradation window contains the controls that enable the user to control this distribution to affect the image ***brightness*** and ***contrast*** overall, or for specified brightness values.

Resolution / File-Size Windows
Resolution refers to the number of pixels in an image. The more pixels you have, the larger the file will be, and the larger the image that can be printed. High-quality prints or separations require higher resolution; however, large files take longer to scan and take up more room on the hard disk.

Exposure Control Display will indicate the brightest point in the image.

Exposure Time Control Buttons
Adjusting the ***Exposure Time*** is similar to selecting the shutter speed when using film. Increasing the exposure time is like decreasing the shutter speed; it will increase the time that the CCD is exposed, and therefore lighten the image. The Photophase camera's "ASA" speed is equivalent to approximately ASA 200 film with the necessary IR filter attached. Equivalent exposure-time settings range from 1/60 to 1/250 of a second.

Color Info Display Window reads out:
(a) New Pixel color (adjusted) indicated with the color picker on right half and the area on the left showing original pixel color.
(b) R,G,B displays showing the red, green, and blue component values of the pixels under the color picker. Three numbers are shown for each color including old value, new value and captured value.
(c) Pixel Location, which shows the x and y coordinates of the pixel indicated with the color picker.

Preview and Image Capture Buttons
Another important feature of the software includes built-in ***Unsharp Masking,*** which allows for automatic electronic image sharpening during exposure. This control is accessed under the camera pop-up menu at the top of the screen.

Jody Dole

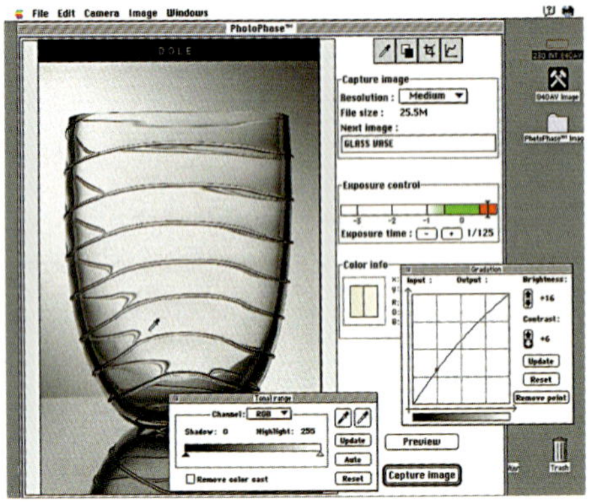

b.

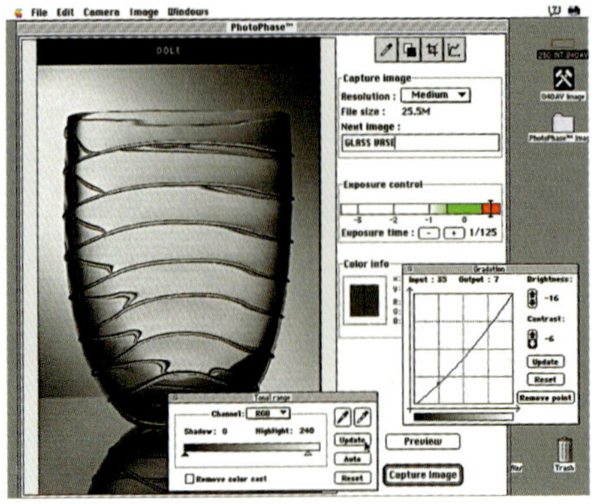

c.

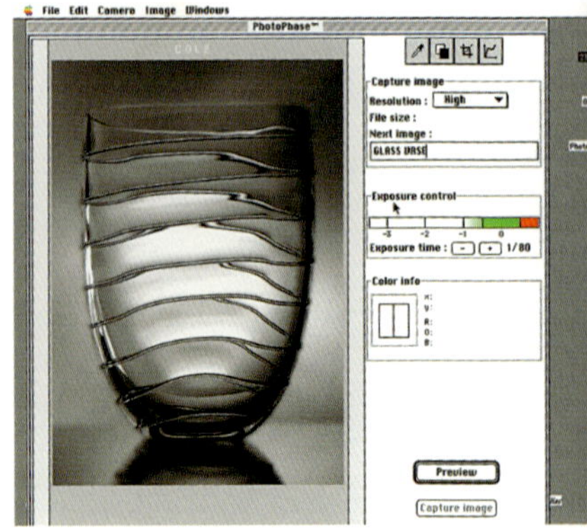

d.

PhotoPhase user-interface screen captures basic exposure controls and lighting variations. All elements of lighting, composition and exposure can be reviewed and adjusted instantly after preview scan.

b. **Screen #1** Shows effect of lighten exposure and raising contrast with tonal range and gradation controls.

c. **Screen #2** Shows effect of darkening exposure and lowering contrast with tonal range and gradation controls.

d. **Screen #3** Shows effect of revised lighti vase reposition and camera angle adjustm combined with wider F-stop setting (more o for shorter depth of field) and exposure con adjustment. Note that this is actually a co image of a monochromatic subject.

b. Photophase #1 lighter
c. Photophase #2 darker
d. Photophase #3 darker
e. Gray Vase

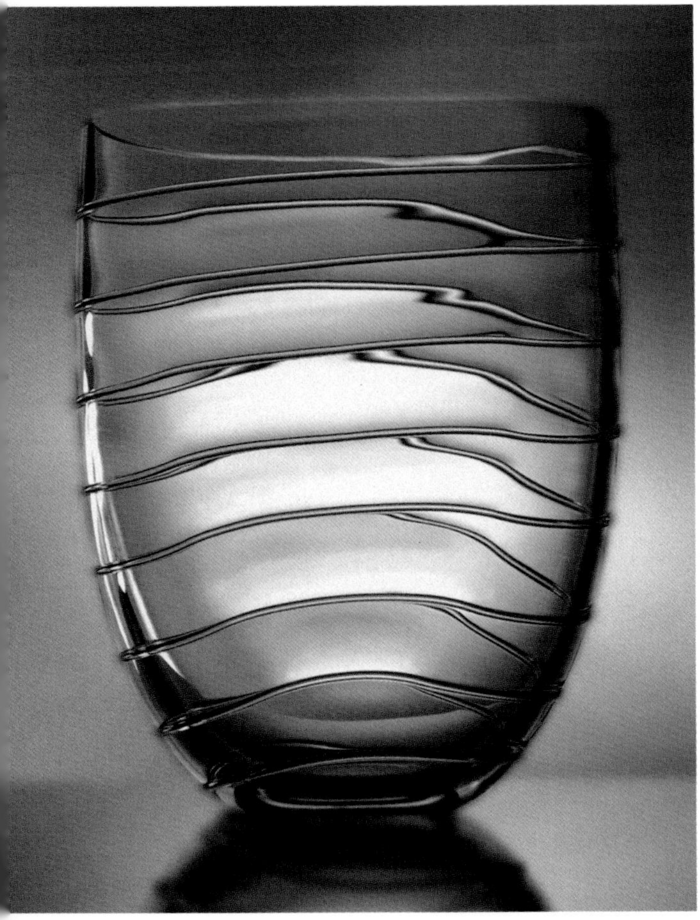

magnificent genie that can give you anything you want, but you don't know what to ask...you are lost. So one quickly starts inventing things from what is "available," limited or not. And we have all seen some pretty weird stuff created from this, sometimes good, most times not. The last thing needed is too much of enough. Unless, that is, you are in the business of selling the expensive equipment to the budding creators. It was crystal clear to me what I wanted to achieve before I started out, and high-resolution digital imaging technology enabled me to reach many goals.

Do you use a digital camera for most of your work? What models do you use? Could you tell us about their performance?

I use the digital back when it is appropriate for a particular project or visual idea I may have, but much of my advertising work is still made with film which is later scanned. There are, however, many examples of my digital capture that simply can't be told from film.

The digital camera back I prefer at this time is made by a firm in Copenhagen called Phase One. In the U.S., Phase One is located in Northport, New York, which is in Long Island, right on the water. It is a marvelous company and offers excellent technical support. The people understand photography and make no false claims about what the product is capable of. For the money, it's great. The 4 x 5 Phase One camera that I use will capture up to a one-hundred-megabyte file and is as sharp, if not sharper than high-res scanned film. The smaller 2 1/4 Photophase back will create up to a 45-megabyte file and simply clips on the back of my Hasselblad just like any other film back except that it connects to a computer via SCCI cable. Both offer very high resolution and highly accurate color control.

What about 35 mm?

For 35 mm, I have been using Nikon and Leica since I started, but I don't use the digital 35 mm format camera because the quality is unacceptable for my work at this moment. I have used the Kodak DCS 420 but it's still low res and for me not really useful. For many other applications, it is probably very useful...casting, location scouting, propping jobs, etc. But for these uses, I still just use the

Jody Dole

one-hour photo, it's much less time consuming and more economical.

Performance-wise, everything with digital capture boils down to resolution and color management. That is, converting a sharp, high-resolution capture from RGB to CMYK format. Once you've got this process down, all one needs is a lot of talent and lots of clients (laughs). For as many people as there are utilizing digital photography, there are as many different solutions of getting from RGB to CMYK, some more reliable than others. I use Adobe Photoshop and my customized look-up tables for much of my fine-art work. When I have a larger commercial project and many images to convert for separation quickly and easily, I may use our Kodak PCS 100 color management system. It does the conversion accurately and creates individual files for the separations in minutes.

A very critical aspect of the digital photography process or any photography process is lighting. Even the best digital camera backs simply do not have the dynamic range of film, and a great deal of care must be given to balancing highlight and shadow areas. It's much easier to lose detail in the shadows and burn out the highlights with digital capture than with film which has a wider latitude. For most of my work, I use electronic flicker-free HMI lights by LTM. They are the best period. The lamps have a very high volume of consistent rich and saturated light output. They are the same lights utilized in high-end film production. I've been using these lights for the past seven years prior to digital photography so I was quite used to their particular quality. When digital photography came along, all we had to do was upgrade the older magnetic ballasts (transformers) to the flicker-free electronic kind. The reason for this is that when you are making a picture via high-resolution scan, it takes a few minutes and below 2,000 watts the lighting must be consistent, no flicker, otherwise you get noise or, simply put, poor quality.

Basically, it's still a science experiment (laughs).

What do you feel about the differences between working with the computer monitor and the conventional optical viewfinder?

This is a good question as obviously, there is a big difference between peering through a small hole or viewing an image upsid down and backwards, which was never really easy for me, a opposed to viewing a big crisp image on a high-resolution colc monitor. In most cases, I prefer the color monitor. However, I st like to compose my image through the camera's optics. And the we put the digital back on, make the preview exposure and view on this big beautiful screen. What's not to like? It's as different a telling time with a sundial, when you have to go outside everytim to tell what time it is, and waiting for the sun to be bright, or usin a wrist watch. You can study the image with much greater clarit of detail on a computer monitor, right while creating the imag which is fantastic. This is now a common way in which I work but I coul see how for the newcomer it could be a liability. So for the most part get an idea in my head first, and whether I'm using a pinhole in a sho box or a view camera or a Hasselblad or a digital back and comput monitor or whatever, it's all the same. What counts is the content.

What are the advantages of the digital camera? What kind o improvements would you like to see in digital cameras?

There are certain projects that I accept where the digital camer has an incredible clear-cut advantage over film, and certai projects where film has the advantage over digital. I recentl completed an assignment that involved photographing a hundre or so very mundane objects that needed to be included in a catalo in a hurry. Some of the merchandise consisted of just plai cardboard boxes with a label! I had worked with the client befor on some very exciting jobs and had a close relationship with them They needed my help and to turn the job away would have bee insulting to the client. I suggested shooting the materia electronically all in a very similar direct way silhouetted on white We managed to produce 35 sharp, high-key shots a day, cleane up, converted, saved to optical disk, pre-press ready to go. Thi is much more than I could ever have done with film, what wit checking Polaroids, loading backs, the processing, scanning, dus busting and all would have been prohibitive aside from driving m

nuts. We put all his merchandise down in a certain position, lit i just right...kept the camera running all day and switched th merchandise as fast as we could scan and BANG! right into th

1. Arlow Rock Stack

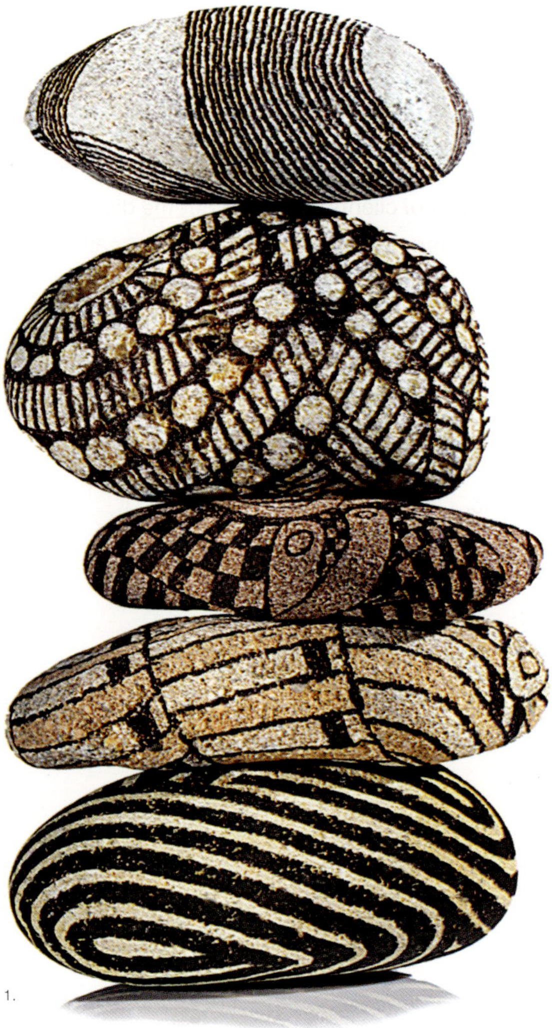

1.

Jody Dole

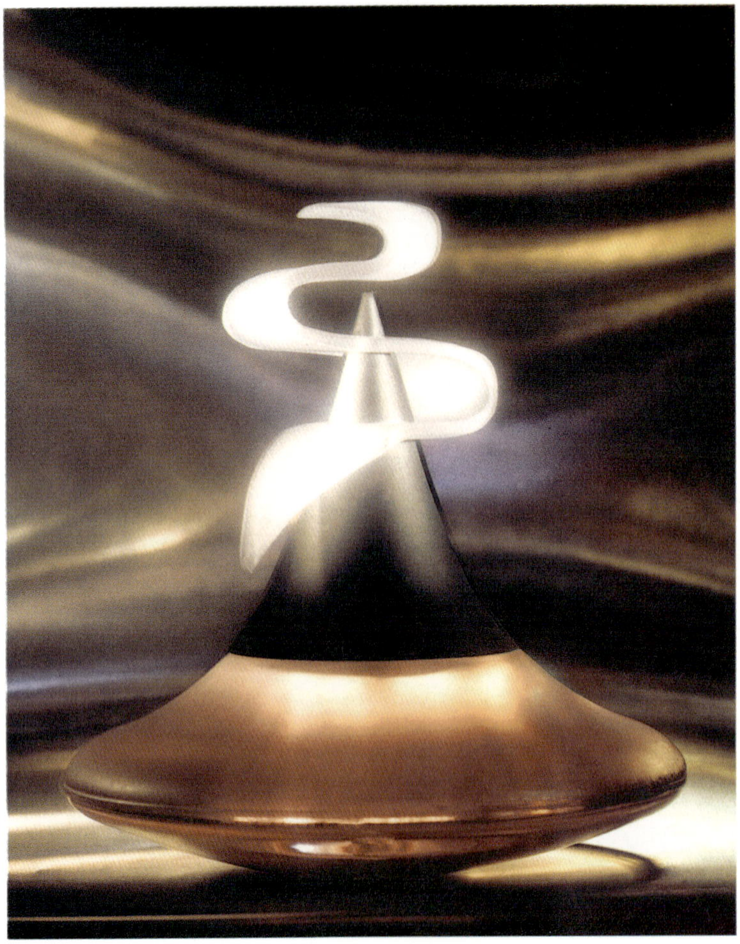

2.

mputer...right through our conversion tables and straight to tical disk and right on out to the client. We completed 100 shots three days' time and the client was on press the following week. d they didn't have to scan film; they simply got a 3-week project mplete in 5 days. For me, the visuals were mundane.... But most nes I must specialize in taking mundane objects to a heroic level. d in a certain way this technology helps and his project was a markable proof. The merchandise never looked better...the color as saturated and beautiful, the client raved about the results... in this particular case digital capture was right on.

lso utilize the digital camera for copy work...for instance I can sily scan my own tear sheets. When I see an ad, I no longer en have to ask the client about obtaining proofs for my twelve rtfolios. I simply pin the ad up on the wall right out of the agazine, shoot it with the digital camera, adjust color, remove necessary copy or whatever in Photoshop and make full-size lor-correct prints on the Iris right in the studio.... It couldn't be npler.

nen it's appropriate, the digital camera also allows me to work personal projects from time to time later in the evening or early a Sunday morning without having to wait for lab processing in der to see the experimental results. So even internally, I actually e the camera for some interesting applications of my own, yond meeting a tight client deadline.

, what improvements are you expecting in digital cameras?

e Phase One is excellent but overall, there's got to be some provement with the digital cameras and like death and taxes, s day will come. What would I like to see? Well, number one, ey have to come down in price, have higher resolution and easier lor balance ability, so that everything comes out a thousand-rcent right with little effort. I'd like to see a 35 mm style camera at will generate an instant, electronically sharpened 40-megabyte with a great deal of accuracy in any lighting condition and ore 24 images on a removable card with optional RGB-CMYK nversion for under five thousand dollars. Many companies rchasing the current crop of digital cameras available are generally using them in-house for a specific task, the same thing day in and day out. I'm more of a general practitioner; I have a lot of different ideas and do a lot of different things visually so my next camera must be capable of a wider range.

Digital cameras are used a lot in the studio these days. What do you think about the future of the digital camera? What do you think about its ability to show us immediate results?

The answer to the first question lies more in where is the future of film. It is very clear to me that filmless imaging will take over the future just as the automobile took over from the horse and cart. It's a question of time and given all the competition among the various manufacturers to make the first buck in this area, I don't imagine we will have to wait for too long.

Personally, with art, I've always been the instant gratification type. It began with my dad's Polaroid camera at age 5 in 1960 and has evolved to what you see here today. Many times, I like things done immediately and usually work with three assistants to achieve this. If there's an out of place drop of water in the sink, I'm nervous, you know. I like things perfect, period. When I was going to art school, one design class involved the use of the first Polaroid SX-70 and each assignment delivered immediate results every week for the entire year. I passed through the course with simply an SX-70 and 365 images. The instructor loved it. I like to see things right away, see how an image looks, sometimes make experiments, know that the result is right, etc. Such instant feedback may not be right for everyone, but here digital technology is a perfect fit.

The black and white picture of the rippled vase is one of my favorites and was made with a digital camera. It was grand to see the vase on the table and have it "develop" in B&W immediately on the screen. For the final print, it was converted to a tri-tone and output with a two-pass Iris process on watercolor paper an hour after the exposure. The ability to see immediate results is fantastic and anyone who can think fast can adapt this technology and will improve their craft in the process. For me the results have been better than I expected and there is no longer the anxiety of will it work or will it not? It works for me.

Jody Dole

Since no chemicals are used in digital photography, it eliminates the problem of environmental pollution. Is this a concern of yours or not?

Obviously, this is a big concern for everybody and as a parent of young children, I am very concerned with the environment and digital photography will certainly decrease pollution. The only ones who are not concerned with this issue are the traditional photo labs because they are making huge profits from developing films in toxic chemicals, but the labs' high mark-up is not my affair.

What is my affair is that I do use Iris printing and have maintained the equipment right in my studio for several years. I have made thousands of prints without polluting the environment and I am very pleased with this fact. It does cost a fortune and I've made no profit from owning this equipment but it does come back to me in a positive way as my prints look a thousand-percent better than traditional C-prints and the Iris utilizes environmentally friendly vegetable-based inks so there is no pollution involved. It's a great advancement for everyone.

Could you tell us more about the quality of the Iris prints and their distinctive character?

I have tested every type of digital printing device while consulting for other corporations. I've made dye subs, dye transfers (which are no longer available), platinum prints, C-prints and everything in between. Although Evercolor is producing fantastic results, the Iris print when properly made is in a class of it's own. Basically, the Iris printer is a high-resolution inkjet device that sprays 4 million electrically charged droplets of cyan, yellow, black and magenta ink at a rotating drum with a sheet of paper attached. Each ink droplet is the size of a white blood cell and the tube that carries the ink to reach this point is approximately seven times thinner than a strand of human hair. Its ability to reproduce detail is a most exacting process. The Iris machine is physically printing at 300 DPI, but its perceived resolution is around 1800 DPI. It's just a fabulous invention.

The distinctive quality of a properly made Iris print is that it has much greater resolution than a conventional C-print and the color and saturation can be made tenfold that of traditional methods. has fidelity, it is a symphony. The color is much cleaner a because it is a CMYK printing process, one can see colors th are not obtainable with traditional photography! The shadow a highlight areas are crystal clear and show great detail. It's continuous-tone color and nothing else available comes ev close. Listen to the difference between vinyl records and digi CDs and you get the idea of the difference between a C-print a a properly scanned, correctly printed Iris print. It's the Pavaro opera of imaging.

These days, more and more images are being rendered computer data. What are the advantages and disadvantages this?

The only disadvantage as I see it, is possible loss of digital da That's why I back up my work in several formats. Each of r images is backed up on DAT tape, optical disk and CD-ROM dis each twice. Kodak claims that CD-ROM storage will last 50 to 1 years. Whether that's true or not only time will tell.

Whenever I address the digital issue involving photography, I fe like a horseless carriage salesman at a blacksmith conventio Clearly, the new technology offers many advantages to photographe For instance, when a client wants to see a picture, I can send it a CD-ROM disk and be assured that if the image gets reproduce at least my scan is correct from the start. My scans are high re accurate and reproduce beautifully. But, when we hand out transparency, I have to keep my fingers crossed because ma times, there's no telling what will happen to the reproduction. Lat though, given the state of the art, I've seen greatly improved resu from outside color houses that many of the large agencies ha affiliations with. Today's pre-press shops must deliver top quality their competition will have a feeding frenzy.

I try to draw the line between offering clients electronic pre-pre services and creative photography. There's nothing worse th doing a great job for a client photographically and then ha something become difficult with the scanning, etc. Many of r clients already have a set pattern of working with their pre-pre

3. Cross Pen

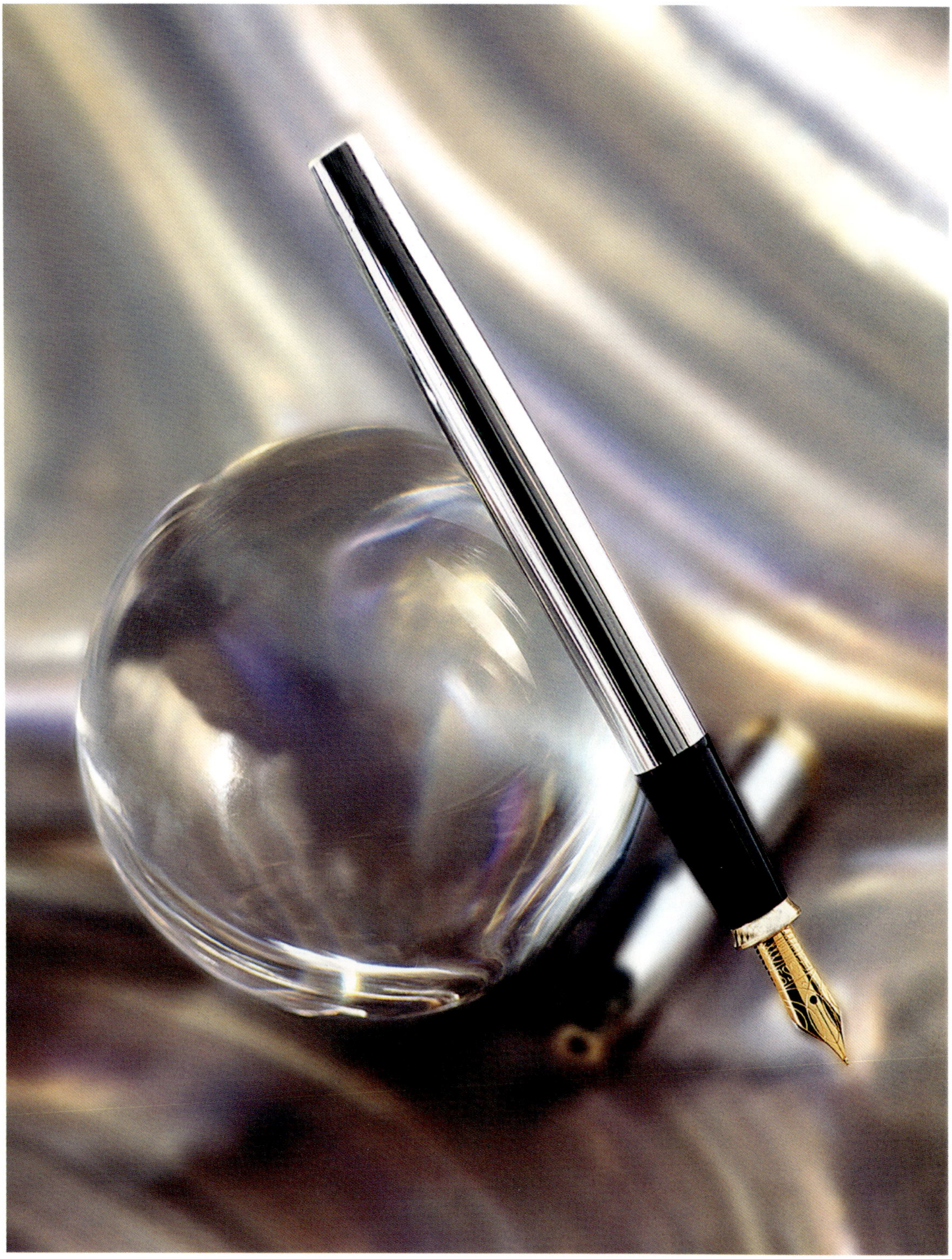

3.

Jody Dole

4. Bracelet Stack

people and in these cases, I've learned to leave well enough alone. I am first and foremost a respected photographer. I am also an experimenter on the frontier of high-resolution digital imaging. But being technically proficient in the printing process does not always make me a mind reader with the client's production department.

How do you see the future of commercial photography? For example, designers working in the photographers' area and vice versa, or the photographer encroaching more on the field of the printer.

Education and experience are two important issues to be considered in relation to this question. But first, I think that the future of high-end commercial photography is shrinking. Technology is allowing people who may not have much visual talent to create technically acceptable images that will reproduce. But this high technology is certainly not helping the content. So you end up with more people doing work that is not significant, but which has a certain degree of technique. There are lots of clients who can't tell the difference between excellent photography and mere technical proficiency. I have kids that come to work for me, want to work with my Iris printers, etc., and don't even know who Irving Penn is, but they sure know about Kai Krause!

As for designers working in the photographers' area...well, it all depends on the designer. There are some designers I love to work with and those designers are fabulous and helpful. Some know photography well, others don't care, some care a lot, some want to be photographers, some don't. The right combination becomes very important to a good working relationship.

I recently completed a project, two weeks, working every day, nine to six, with a wonderful art director. He knew great art, could draw like Michelangelo, was proficient on the Mac, had worked with all the top people and couldn't care less about being a photographer himself. He showed me things I didn't know in Quark and vice versa in Photoshop. We made some beautiful pictures together. In that case, there was a very successful collaboration. Point for the designer: simply being a master of Quark is a great start, but it will take much more than this to be great at photography as well.

That any untrained person, photographer or otherwise shou encroach on the field of the printer is a frightening thought. In m case, early on, I studied production at SVA in New York and lat at Pratt Institute in Brooklyn. I had taken a great deal of time examine the printing area as a student and later in my photograph career, electronic pre-press. I took time off to work with pre-pre shops and printers on dozens of projects. I learned about scannin retouching, four-color, duotone, hi-fi color, stochastic screenin PostScript, Iris proofing, separations, etc., from the best possib sources: successful printers and separation houses. I studied o timers and Mac mavens alike. Now, I understand what I can with a knowledge of pre-press and printing. But not eve photographer would want to get involved in that type of work.

Some inexperienced clients may become confused about issues quality and resolution; for instance, when a photographer tells the that he can deliver images scanned on disk. The first question to b asked is What type of scanner is the studio working with and w what RGB-CMYK conversion? I've heard stories of agency art buye accepting digital data from photographers only to find out at th proofing stage of a tight deadline that the scan was created with toy, not the two-hundred-thousand-dollar Crossfield that their pr press house normally uses. The untrained person discovered the ha way: the difference between low-end and high-resolution pre-press wo

This is why education is an important issue if the commercial wor is to have the photographer getting involved in the pre-press fiel As long as everyone is speaking the same language, opening communications and eliminating misunderstandings, everyor down the chain will be pleased with the results. I tend to ba away from pre-press when the client has a great deal of experti and knows how to achieve exact results. "Good color" is ve subjective. There's seldom any agreement between people abo this, but one thing I like to agree on is what makes a goo photograph.

What is your vision of the future? What projects are yo planning now?

My vision of the future is to have enough time to raise my fam

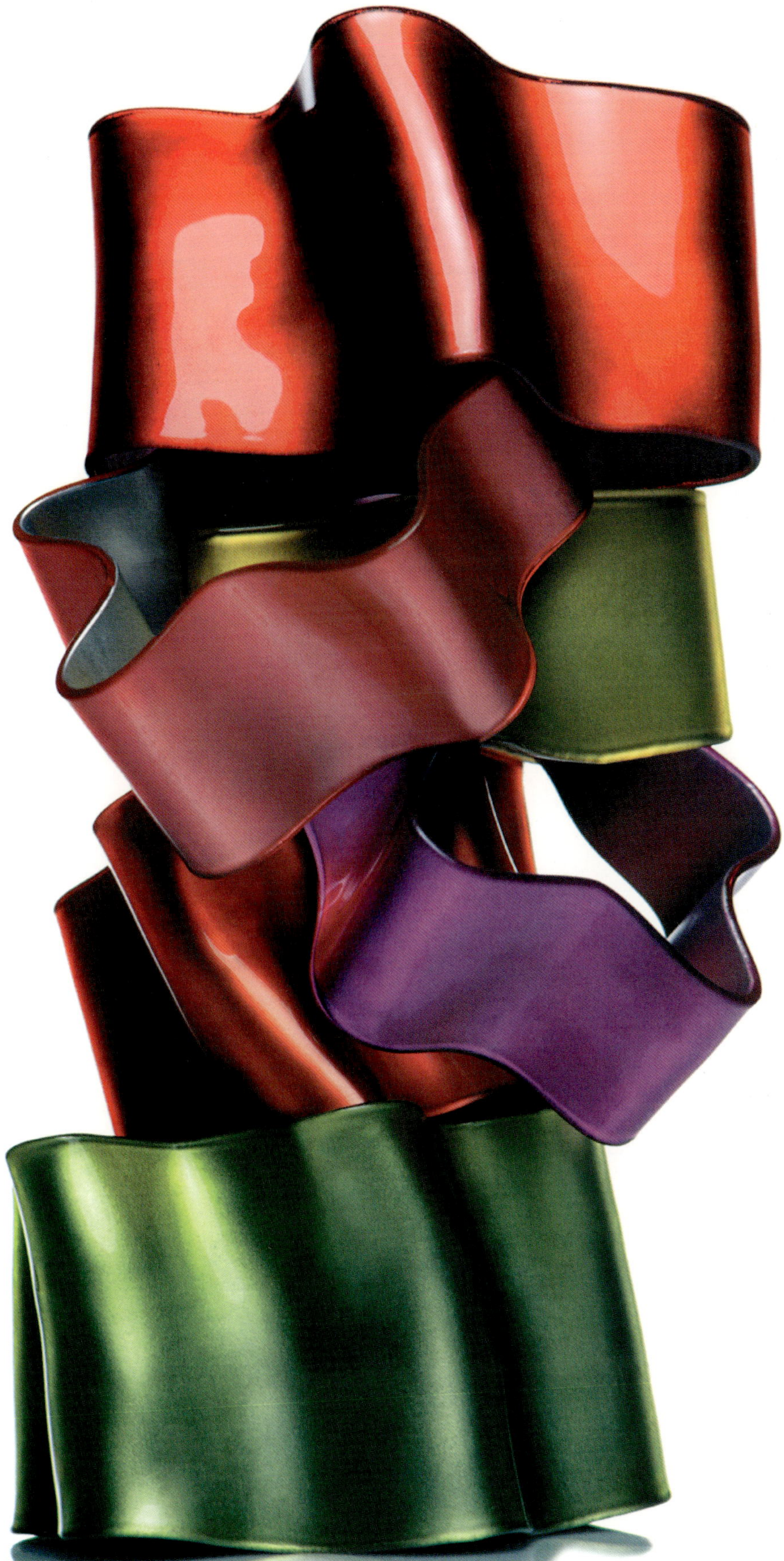

4.

Jody Dole

5. Grape Bowl
6. Opposite: Soap Vertical

by spending time with my wife, Abbe, and my children. But working with complex electronic equipment doesn't always allow for much free time. Lately, all the digital gear has been behaving and we've had few "breakdowns" if you could call them that. There are, however, disastrous moments when storage devices fail, and I loose important images. Usually, though, it's only temporary, but until we locate the backups I loose sleep. Small "bugs" are always turning up at every stage and I'm constantly testing and evaluating new digital equipment to replace the old. Many think that the wide-spread introduction of digital imaging to photography has made the process simpler and faster, but let me tell you that it has also opened up a whole new form of electronic aggravation.

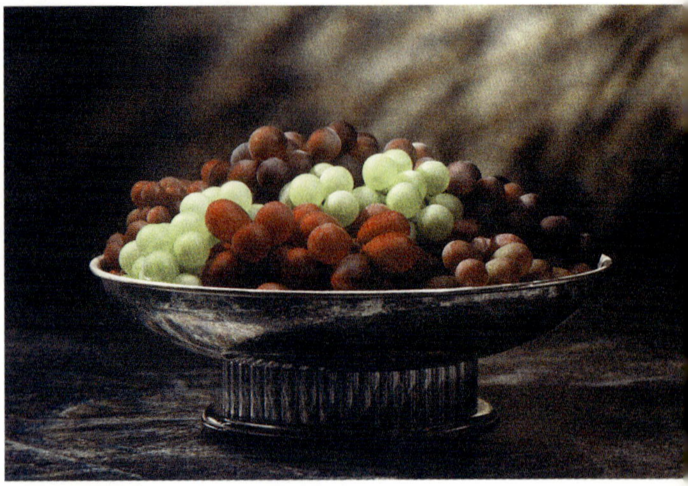

5.

My studio is currently putting the finishing touches on a CD-ROM portfolio of the latest photographic work and, when not prepping or shooting client assignments, I am working on the Iris, printing portfolios with archival ink sets or trying out new lighting techniques for photography, training new staff or consulting on a new series of educational CD-ROMs for kids. With few exceptions, I have worked on a photography-related project in one form or another every weekday since opening the door in 1988.

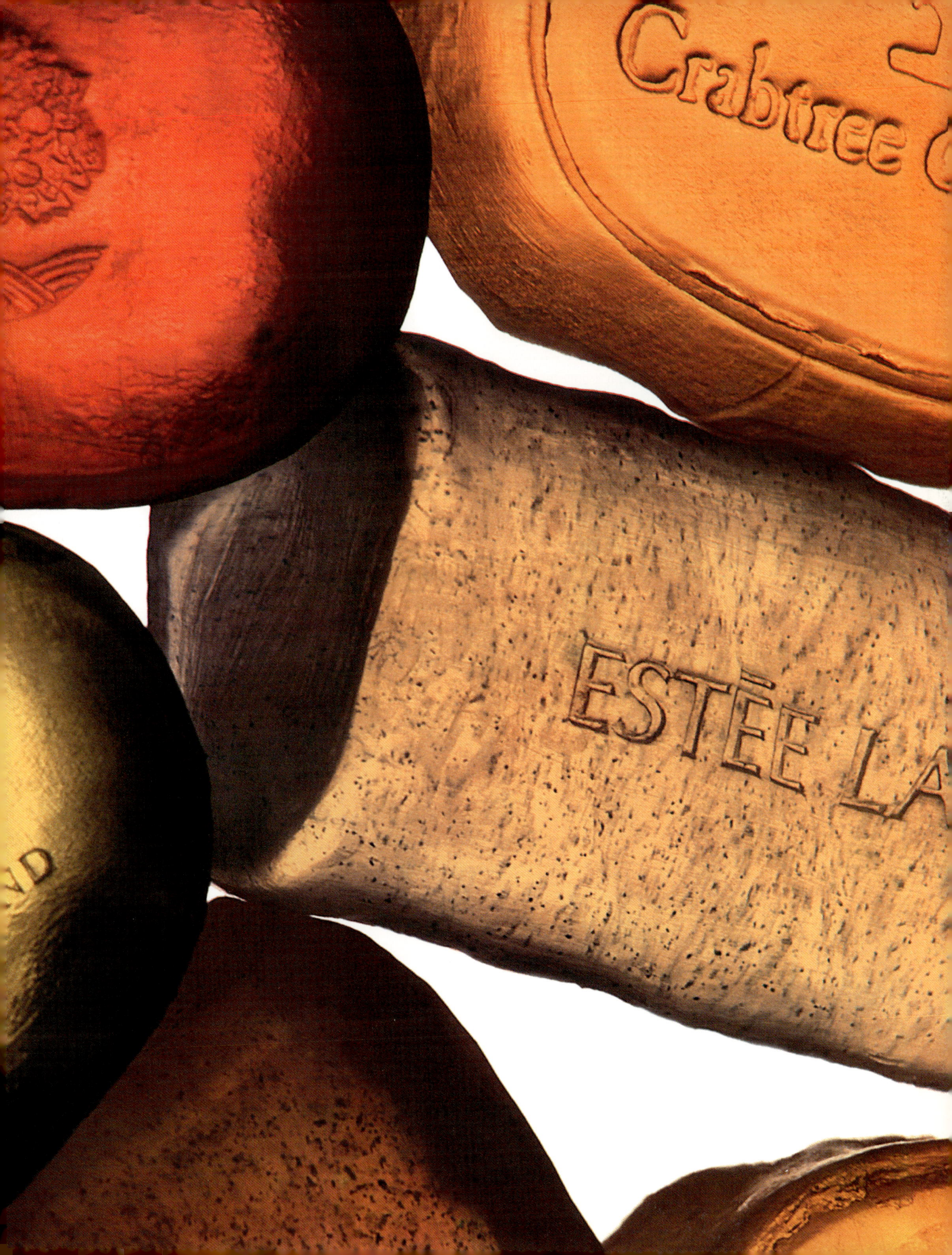
Crabtree
ESTĒE

Jody Dole

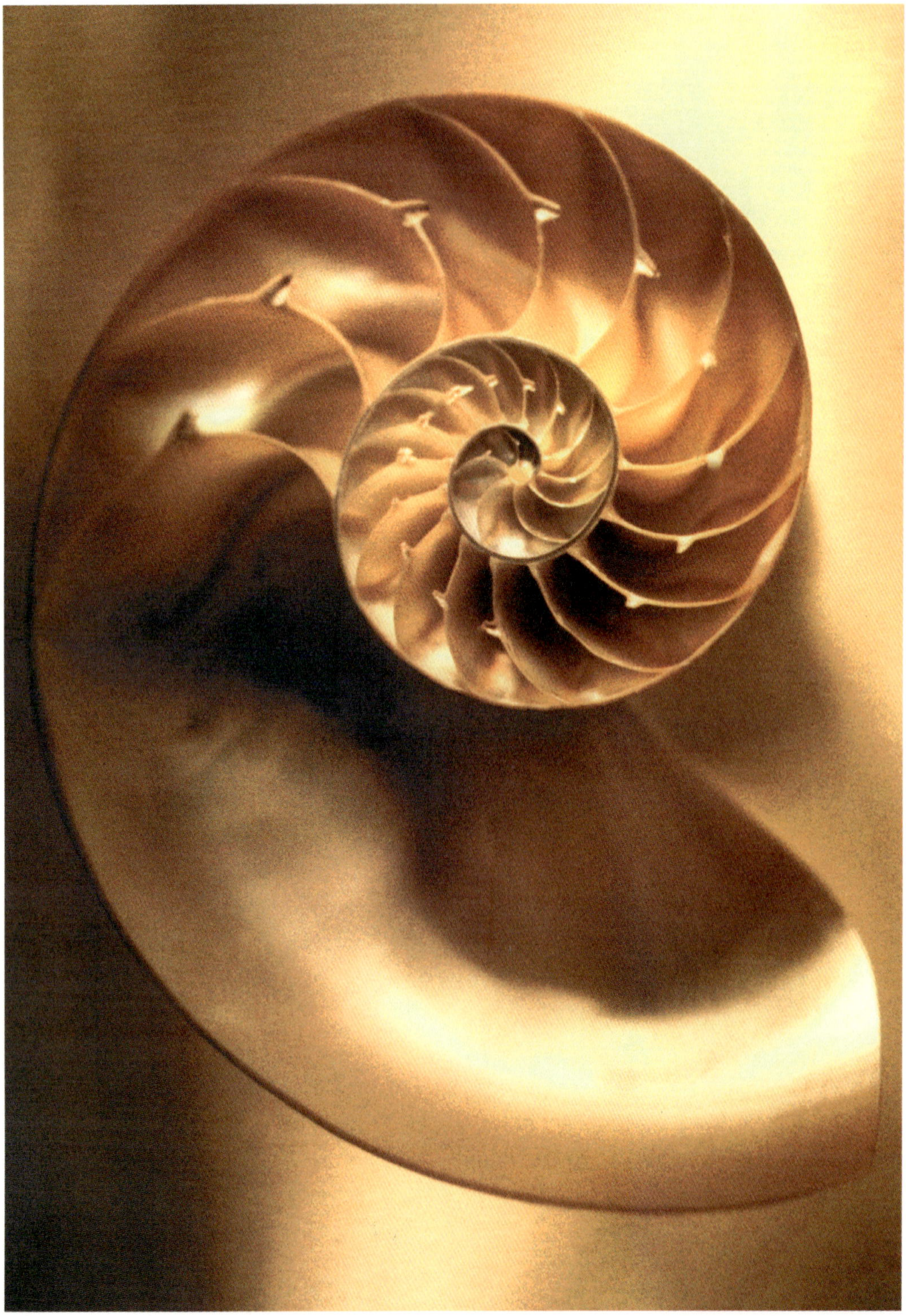

7.

7. Nautilus
8. Smirnoff So Superior

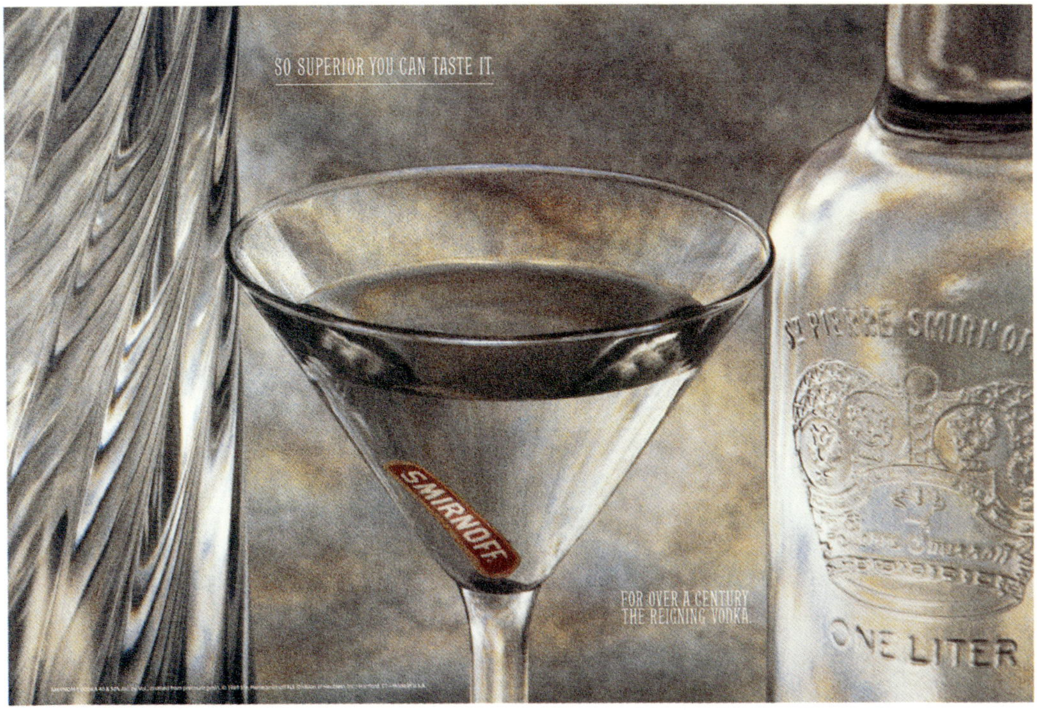

8.

Jody Dole

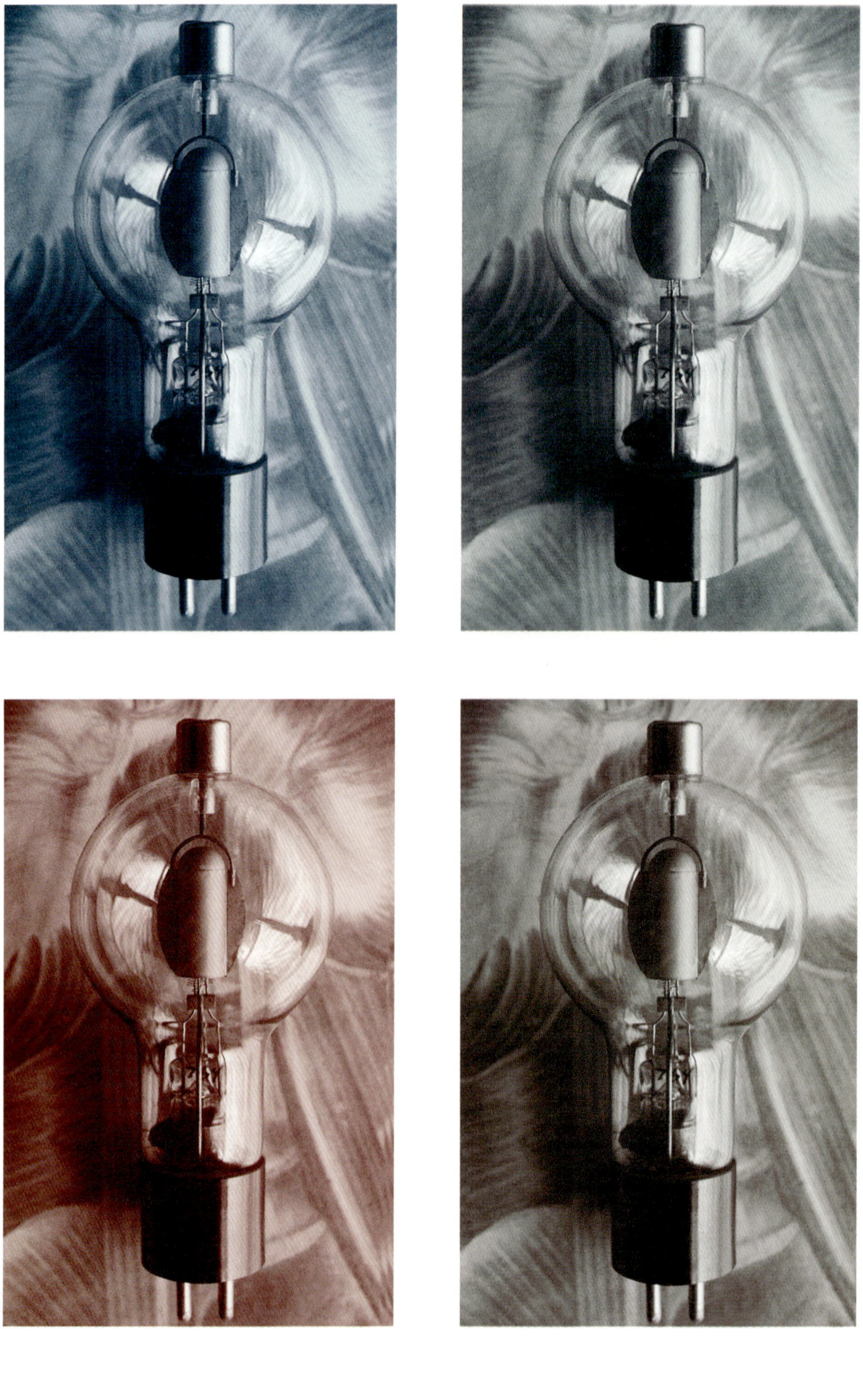

9.

9. Duotone Tubes
10. Green Bowl

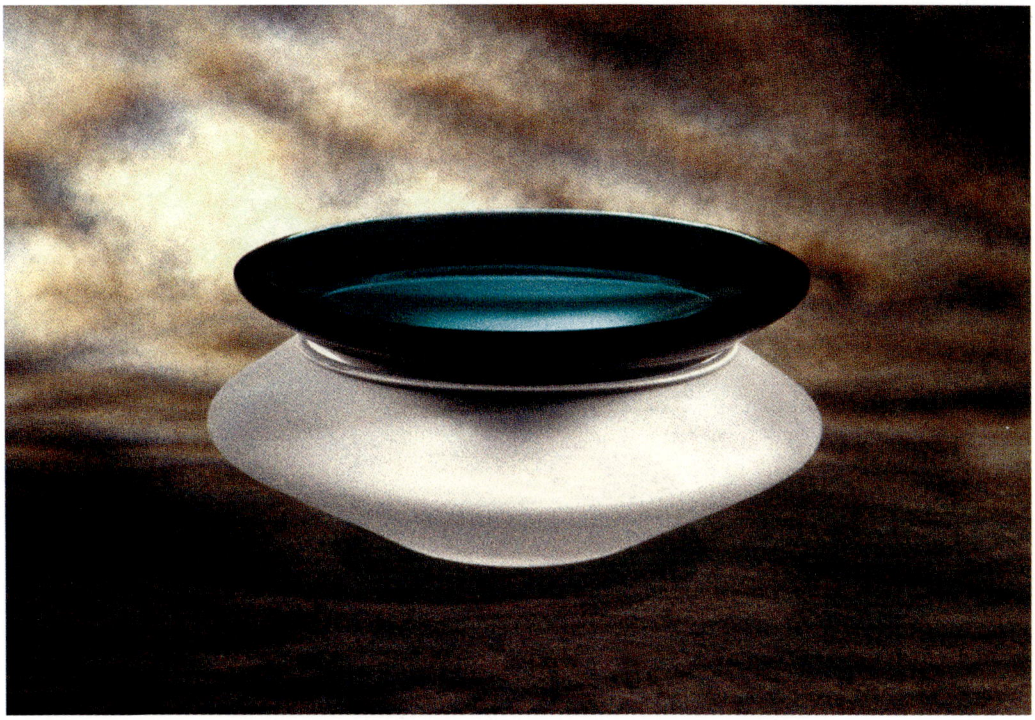

10.

Jody Dole

11. Green Urn with Orchid
12. Opposite: Prism

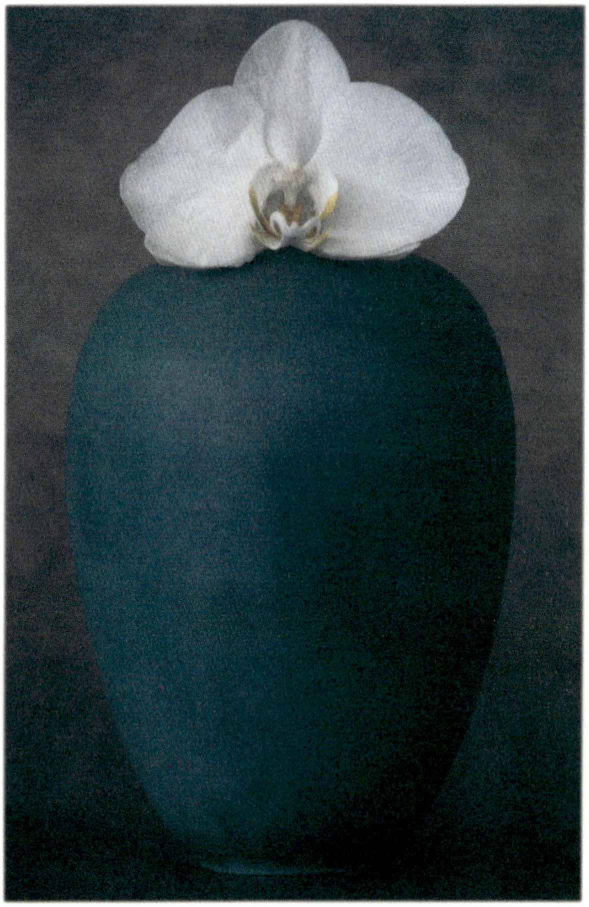

11.

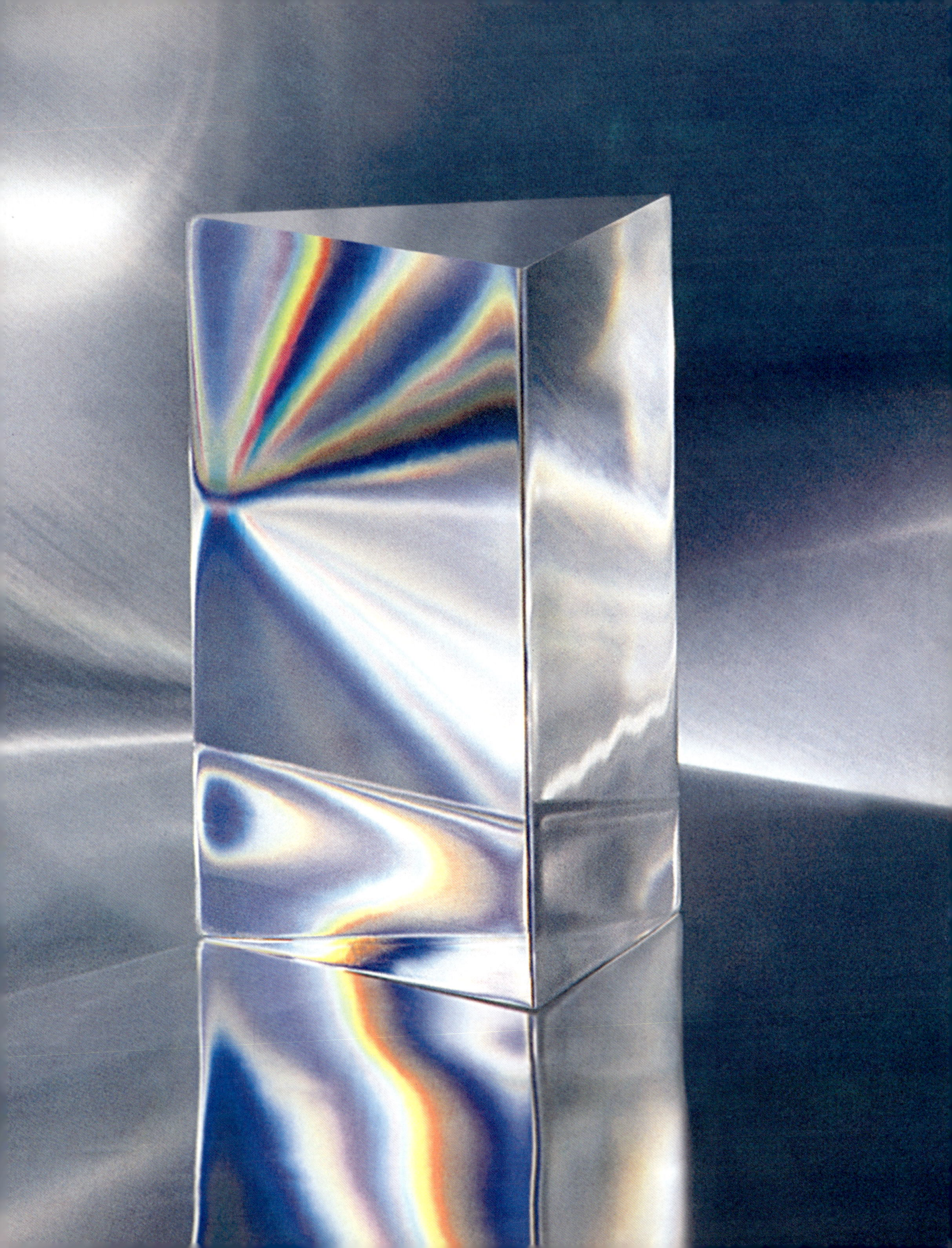

Jody Dole

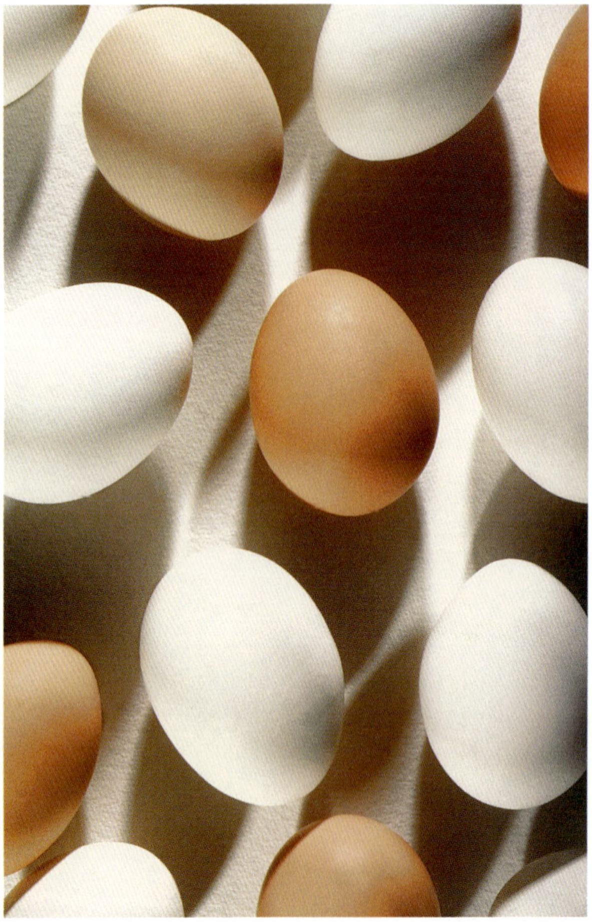

13.

13. Egg Assembly
14. CD-ROM

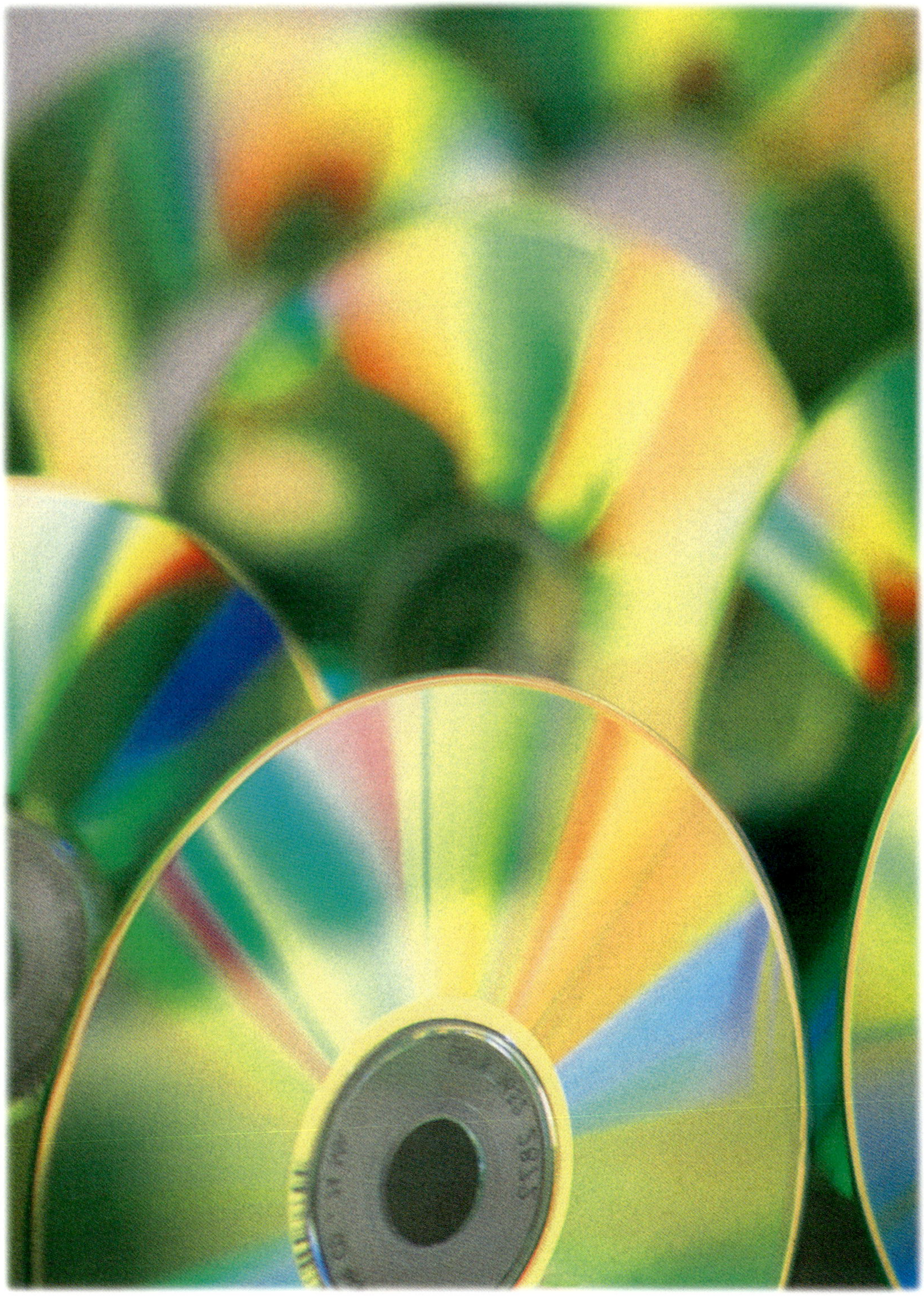

14.

Jody Dole

15. Horizontal Bracelets

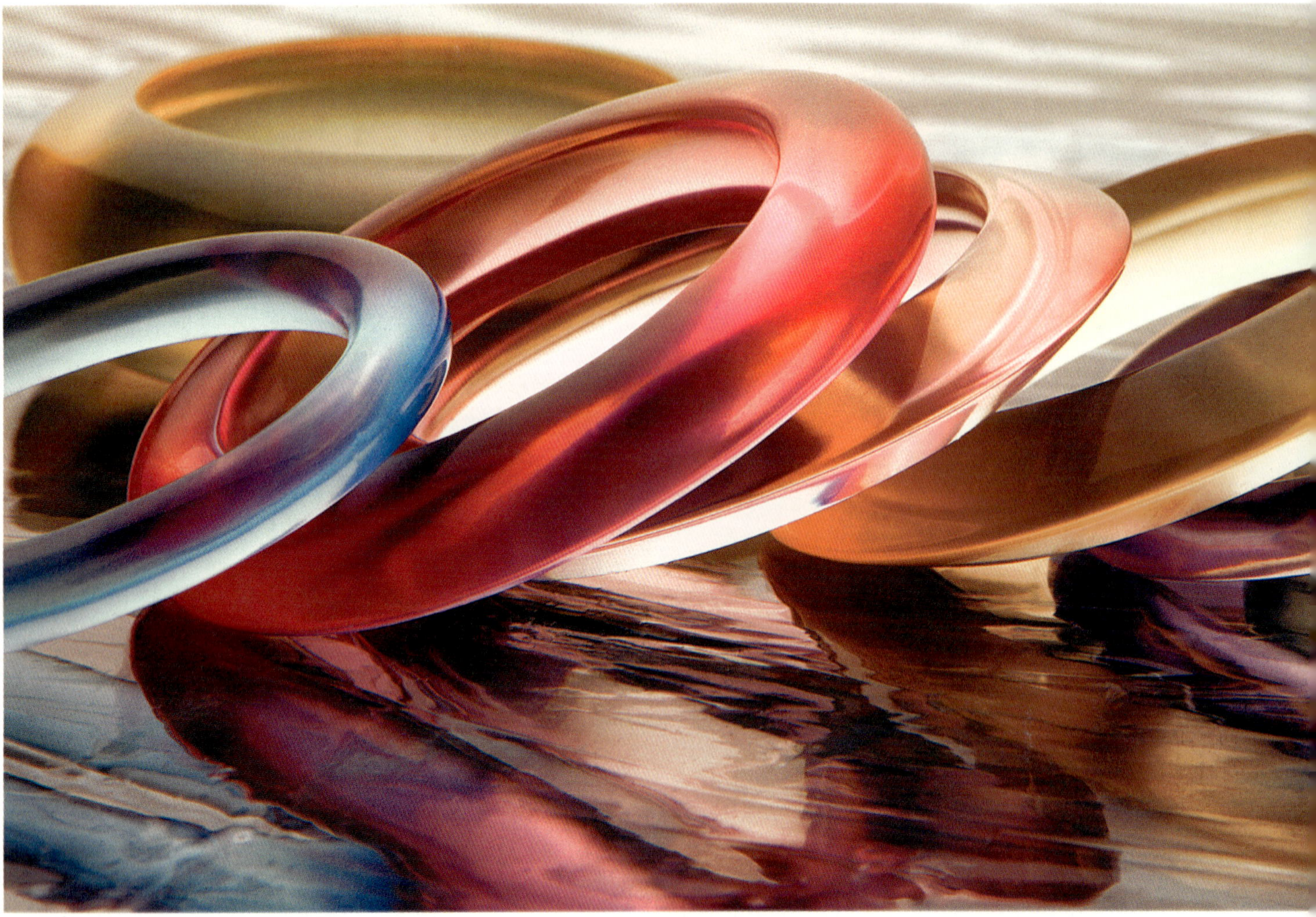

15.

Elle Schuster

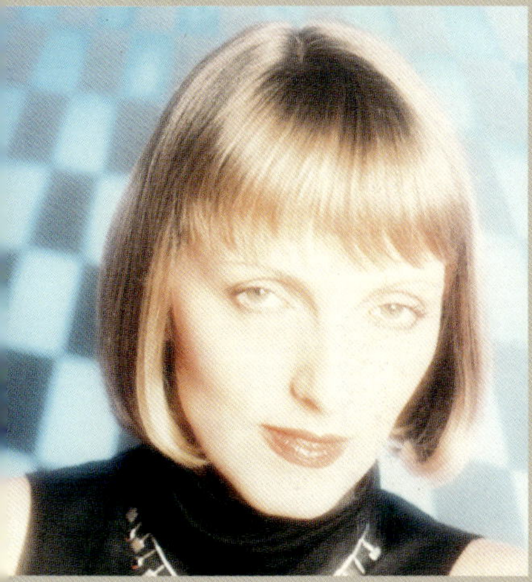

Elle Schuster was born in Pittsburgh during the postwar baby boom. She spent her childhood in Pennsylvania, Ohio, Australia and New York, finally settling in Texas in 1963. She married immediately after high school and had two children. For the next few years she worked at miscellaneous jobs, and was eventually exposed to photography when she became an advertising coordinator. Her career began in 1973. Within a year, Elle opened her first studio.

Her specialty is surreal and special-effects photography for commercial and editorial clients such as Texas Instruments, Neiman Marcus, Xerox, American Airlines, Budweiser and many more. Clients trust her judgment and allow Elle the creative freedom that has made her work so unique. Her photography is an eye-arresting blend of communications and symbolic artistry.

Elle has also been active as a lecturer at photo seminars and universities since 1983, has made many forays into the fine-art market and has numerous one-person shows to her credit.

Being self-taught, Elle is very circumspect about her techniques. How does Elle get her inspirations? She studies painters, architects, writers and musicians: their lives and philosophies. Her greatest influence has been the philosophy of Ayn Rand.

Elle Schuster

Could you tell us how you came to take up photography?

In the early 70s, I received a camera as a birthday present. I had always been interested in art, but my father wanted me to be an engineer. So at school I specialized in math and science. I left out the art classes. But when I got that camera, all of a sudden my artistic background came to the fore. I couldn't draw to my own satisfaction, but I could handle a camera.

Almost immediately after getting the camera, I started making money with it. So I quit my regular job, and decided to become a professional photographer. Then I opened my own studio. This all happened in less than a year. Although I didn't quite know what I would be up against, starting a studio, I had two children to support, so I was determined to make it a success.

There were many big studios in the industrial district of Dallas where I worked. They concentrated on catalog work. I decided I didn't want to do that. If I had had a big studio with a lot of employees, I would have ended up being more of an administrator than a photographer. So I decided I had to develop an individual style. Something unusual that I could charge good money for. So I started doing more personal photography to build up my portfolio.

How did you learn the technical aspects of photography once you had found your own style?

Well, I loved the surrealist painters...Salvador Dali, René Magritte and others. That was the kind of work I wanted to do. Coincidentally, I had a client who was an electronic equipment distributor, and the ad designer there liked "magic" or special effects. He would give me assignments where I'd have to take, say, a microchip and make it disappear in a puff of smoke. So, right from the start I had to learn how to do unusual, tricky effects and this jibed very well with my love for surrealist images. Also, there weren't that many people doing this kind of special-effects work, so I figured there wouldn't be so much competition. The work is difficult, and takes a lot of patience, so I thought I would be good at it.

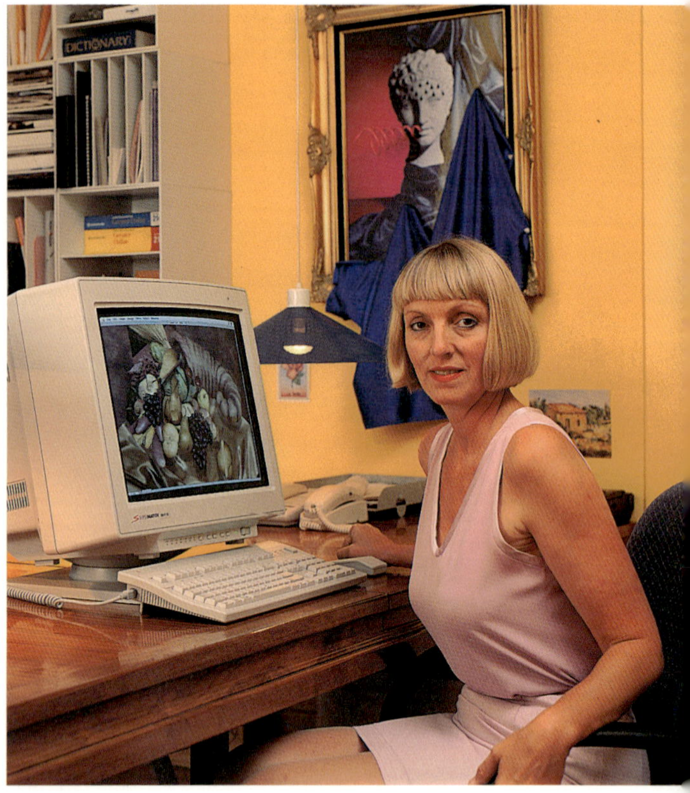

Elle at the Computer

a. Cubist Music Still life (pre-computer image)

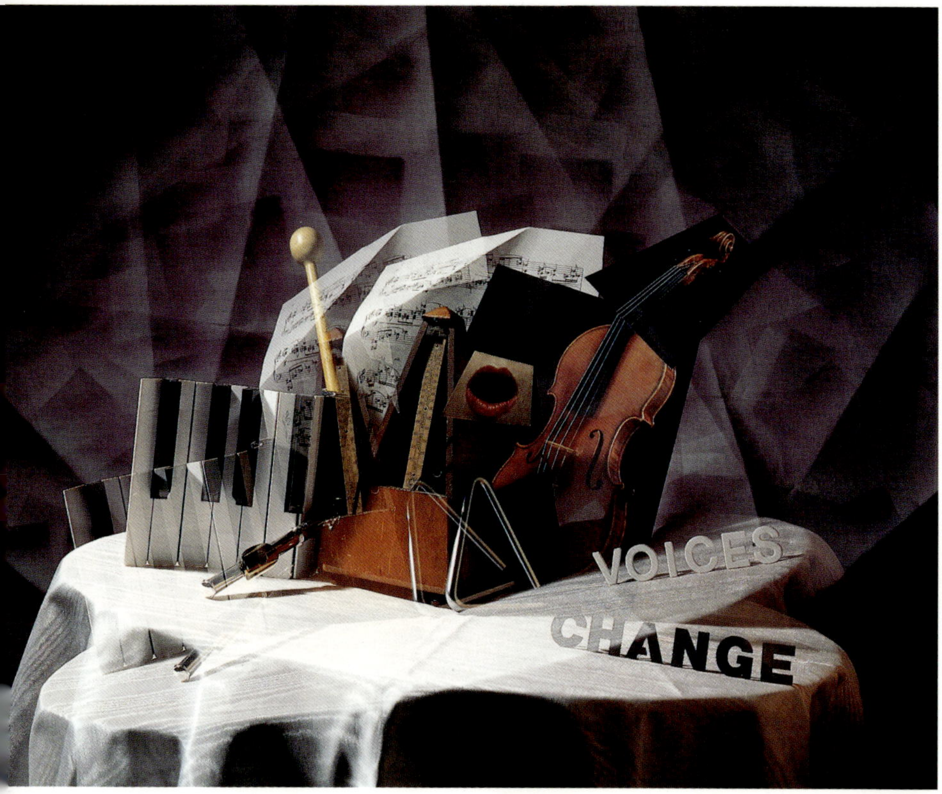

ᴾre-computer image "Cubist Music Still Life"

ade the background by folding seamless paper ich has been spray-painted in a "cubist" nner.

ssembled various props, including real items, eet music, a cut-up color print of the violin, a aroid of a mouth, plastic sign letters and a le top with cloth.

er everything was as I wanted it on the table , I took one shot with the "correct" exposure.

en tilted the set or camera (in this case, nera). I removed some of the objects and ered others with black paper. I then took a cond shot at about half the "correct" exposure. s gave a "ghostly," overlapping look to the age. Covering and removing some items vented the final image from looking jumbled or messy. If you double everything it gets to be too much.

Elle Schuster

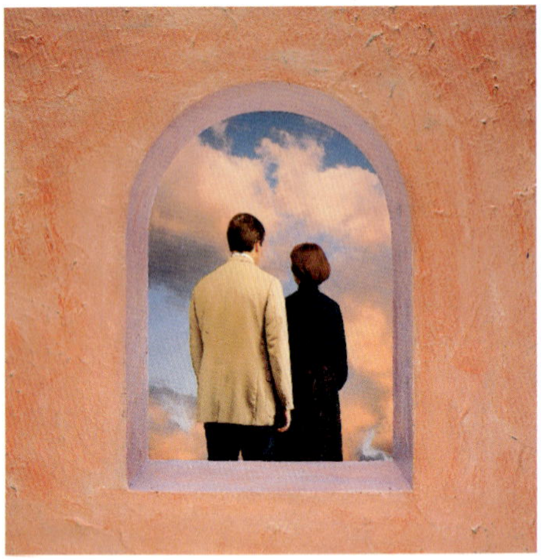

b.

c.

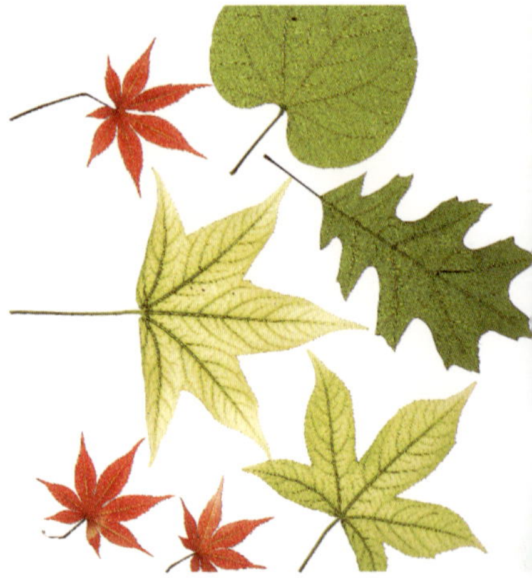

e.

b-g. Digital Image "Autumn"

b. I copied Photo b of the arched window (without the inside view of the people) and placed it in a new window which I corrected for size, sharpness and resolution for the final printed image. I changed the arch color to purple using Color Balance from the menu. I changed the inside edge surrounding the opening to purple with a yellow cast because the moon would throw a yellowish light on this area. I added the moon later.

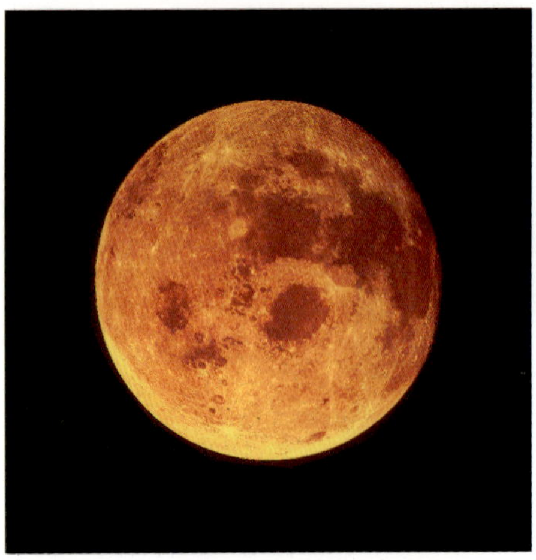

d.

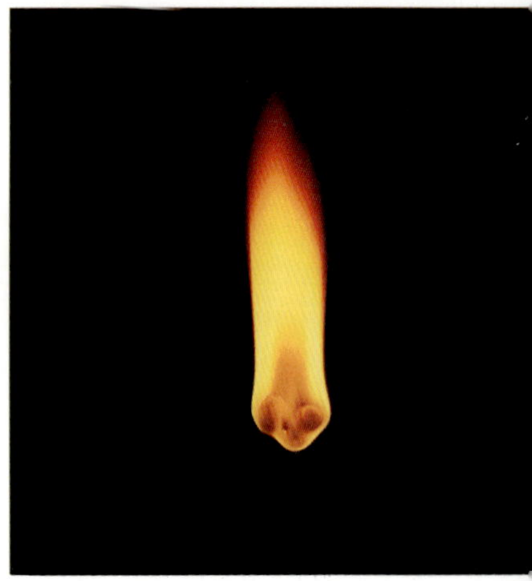

f.

c. I made the graded sky in Photo c in the studio, and copied and placed it in the center of the arched window using the Paste Into command. I sized it so that the yellow and peach colors at the bottom are hidden behind the window. Only the blue and pink are showing.

d. I outlined the moon and applied an approximately 15-pixel Feather. Then I copied the image into the window area. After positioning and sizing to my liking, I used Invert so that I could add a halo without damaging the moon. I chose a large airbrush tool to do the halo. I kept the yellow from the moon at a low percentage.

e. I outlined the leaves and altered their col
so that they looked like autumn leaves. (T
leaves were picked in spring.) I selected the ve
in the center leaf with the Magic Wand and ma
them red. I then copied the leaves one at a ti
positioned and resized them in the window
scaled some of the leaves so that they beca
distorted. This gave the effect of them flying at
angle instead of straight on as they w
photographed.

f. I copied the flame and pasted it on the edge
the foreground leaf. I then used the Clone a
Smear tools to add the flame around all the leav

b. Arch Window
c. Graded-Color Sky
d. Moon
e. Leaves
f. Flame
g. Final Work "Autumn"

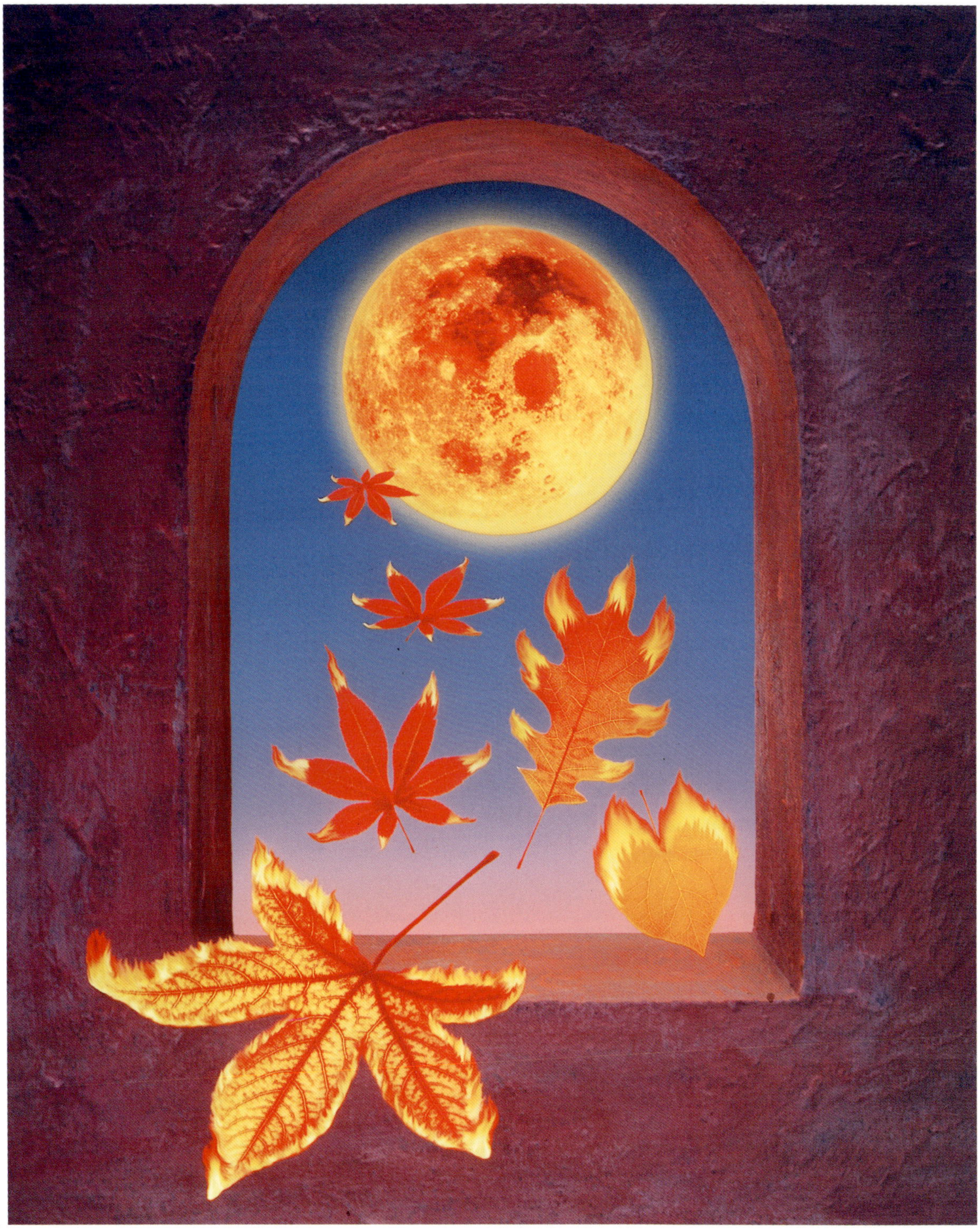

g.

Elle Schuster

Because I'd had no formal training, I had to figure out a lot of the tricks myself. For example, many times I would have an object that looked like it was floating in the sky. For this purpose I tried rear-screen projection. And I tried holding the object on a stick in front of a painted background. But none of the results looked real. I found that rear-screen projection didn't work because it was hard to match the light from the projector bulb with the light on the object. Then I hit on the idea of using a solid piece of plastic with a transparency on it. So I started using huge transparencies of the sky, which was a bit cumbersome, standing upright with all the supports involved. Then I decided to lay the transparency down on a table and illuminated it from below. I could lay the object on the transparency and shoot downwards. That was a lot easier. And the result looked just like the object was floating in the sky.

That was one technique that I came up with on my own. And I used that technique for many years to make objects look like they were floating. There are other examples, but basically it all boiled down to having a problem and thinking of new ways to solve it.

Many photographers like to composite in the darkroom — making masks and so on. I didn't like that way of working. So I would build sets where the perspective was distorted. If you shot it with a wide-angle lens, that would accentuate the distortion effect even more. I made props that were miniature or over-scaled so that the whole set would look just as I wanted it to look.

I used to do all the set constructions myself. Then I realized that my time and carpentry skills were limited, so I eventually hired a prop man. Everything was custom-built. Of course, now that computers have come along, all that has changed completely. Now, I can shoot real objects instead of building elaborate sets, and put those objects into the picture on the computer. I'm still basically doing the same thing, but now I'm using a different tool. And of course, the computer makes it possible to execute certain ideas that would have been forbiddingly expensive with traditional means.

What are your influences?

Well, I've looked at lots of photography over the years, but r influences are primarily painters. I've read the biographies of ma kinds of artistic people. For example, Frank Lloyd Wright, t architect. There was Laszlo Moholy-Nagy, a wonderful Bauha designer who founded the Chicago Institute of Design. He w also a photographer. I read so much about him, just so tha could understand how an artist lives.

I also listen to a lot of music. Ideas come to me when I'm listeni to music. I also read a lot of philosophy. I go to the opera and t theater and study the lighting. The way they create a mood w stage sets and lighting. That is also a big influence.

I read a lot of poetry. My work is very surreal, and I look at it visual poetry, where you are speaking in metaphors. You are n being totally realistic. I read novels also. These can expand yo mind to give you a better grasp of human nature.

So, there are many influences, and all of them come from the world.

How would you describe your work? Could you tell us abo the philosophy behind the work?

I think of the work as surrealism...but a better way to describe would be super-realism. One of the main philosophers who h influenced me is Ayn Rand. She wrote *The Fountainhead, Atl Shrugged* and other novels. She also wrote many books philosophy...*The Virtue of Selfishness* was one. Another bo about her philosophy of art was *The Romantic Manifesto.* O thing I had confirmed from reading Ayn Rand was that there w no such thing as the supernatural. Mysticism is a lie. There m be things in the world that we do not understand; things for whi the rules that govern them are not understood. But there nothing above nature. When we finally have all the knowledg we will realize that. We just don't know all the answers yet.

1. Shell / Butterfly / Sky

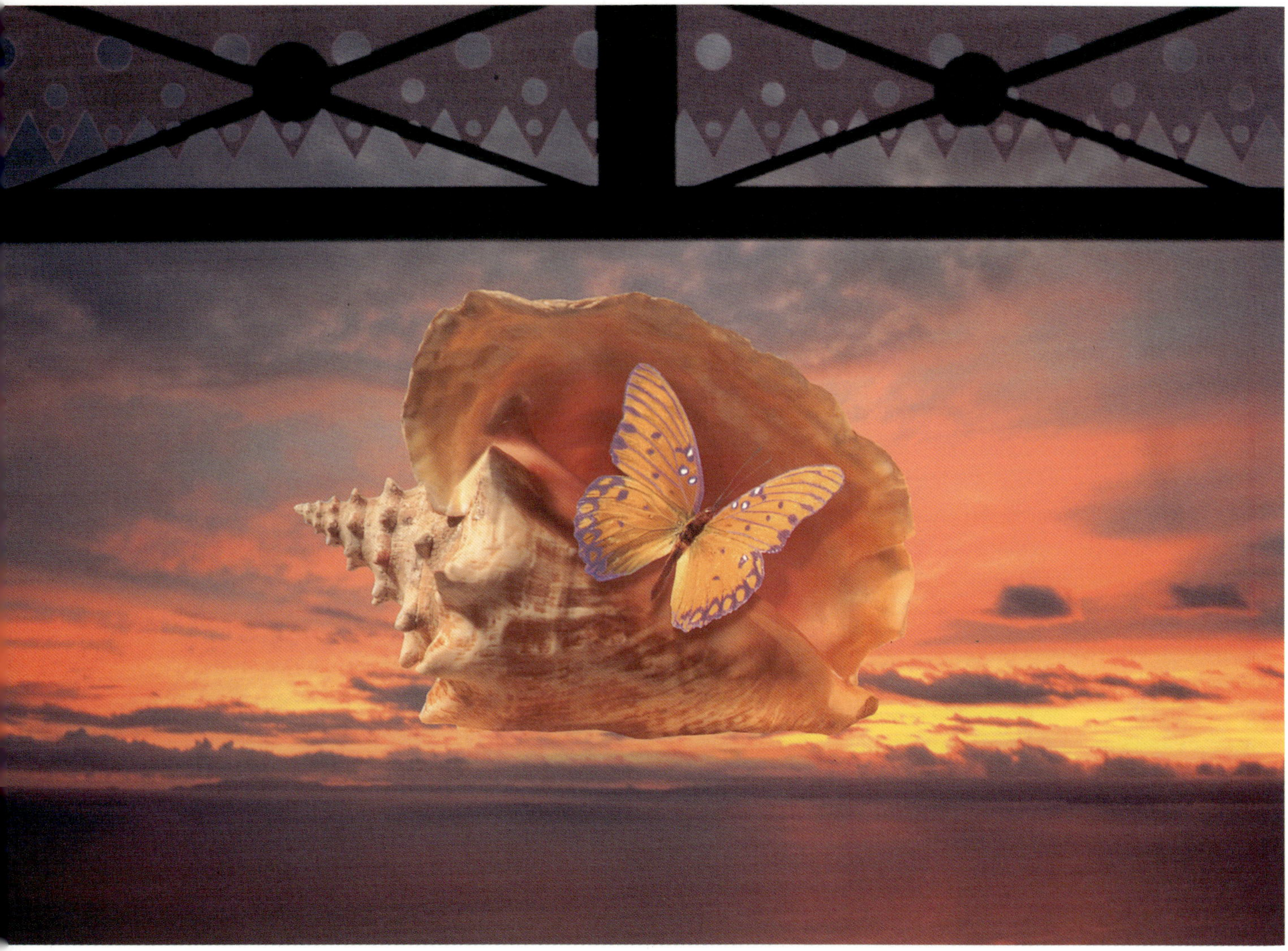

Elle Schuster

So that's the reason I look on my work, not as supernaturalism but super-realism. In other words, I am taking reality and magnifying it in a poetic way to make a statement. As Picasso said: "Art is a lie that reveals the truth." I didn't like that statement when I first heard it because I disagreed with the word "lie." What the artists are doing is exaggerating, but to such an extent that people know that you don't mean it literally. You are not lying, but exaggerating the point so that they will understand. That's why I see my work as super-reality. I'm using real skies, real trees and so on. I'm not making fantasy worlds like certain science fiction illustrators do.

Another important idea of Ayn Rand is that art is spiritual food. It should be sustenance for your soul. Something that helps you to keep going...because the world is not pretty, and there are a lot of unpleasant things around. Art should present things at their best...knowing, of course, that there is a lot of ugliness out there. But why make more ugliness? I try to keep a standard of beauty.

That idealism carries over into my work. For example, I was asked to do a cigarette ad campaign. Well, I used to smoke, but now I've quit. So I don't think it's right to encourage other people to smoke. I turned down tens of thousands of dollars because I would not feel right about using my art to promote cigarettes. What I'm saying is that if you have a talent, you should use it for the good and not the bad.

Also, while we are on the subject of commercial photography, a lot of my fine-art friends ask me how I could prostitute myself doing advertising. I don't think I'm prostituting myself at all. One other important thing I learned from Ayn Rand is that there are only three ways to deal with the world, either on an individual level or on a national level. You can trade, steal or beg. And trading or commerce is the only honorable way. Mutually agreed upon trade. People trade with advertising. There is absolutely nothing wrong with that. As long as you are not misleading people. So it doesn't bother me at all that I'm in this business. I am proud to be in advertising. In fact, I think the advertising work shown in magazines like *Graphis,* is far superior to much of the work you

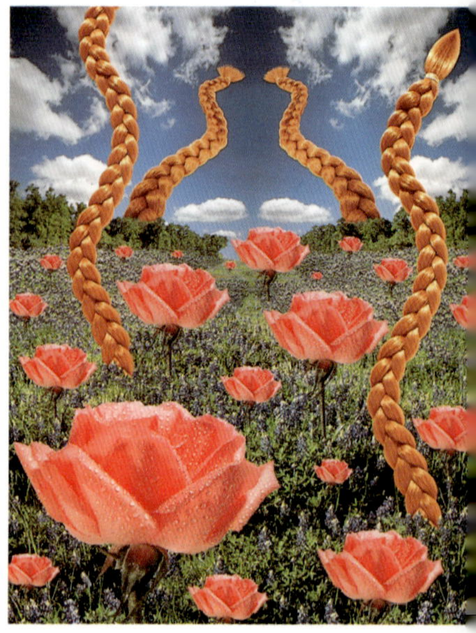

2.

2. Spring Too
3. Maitreya

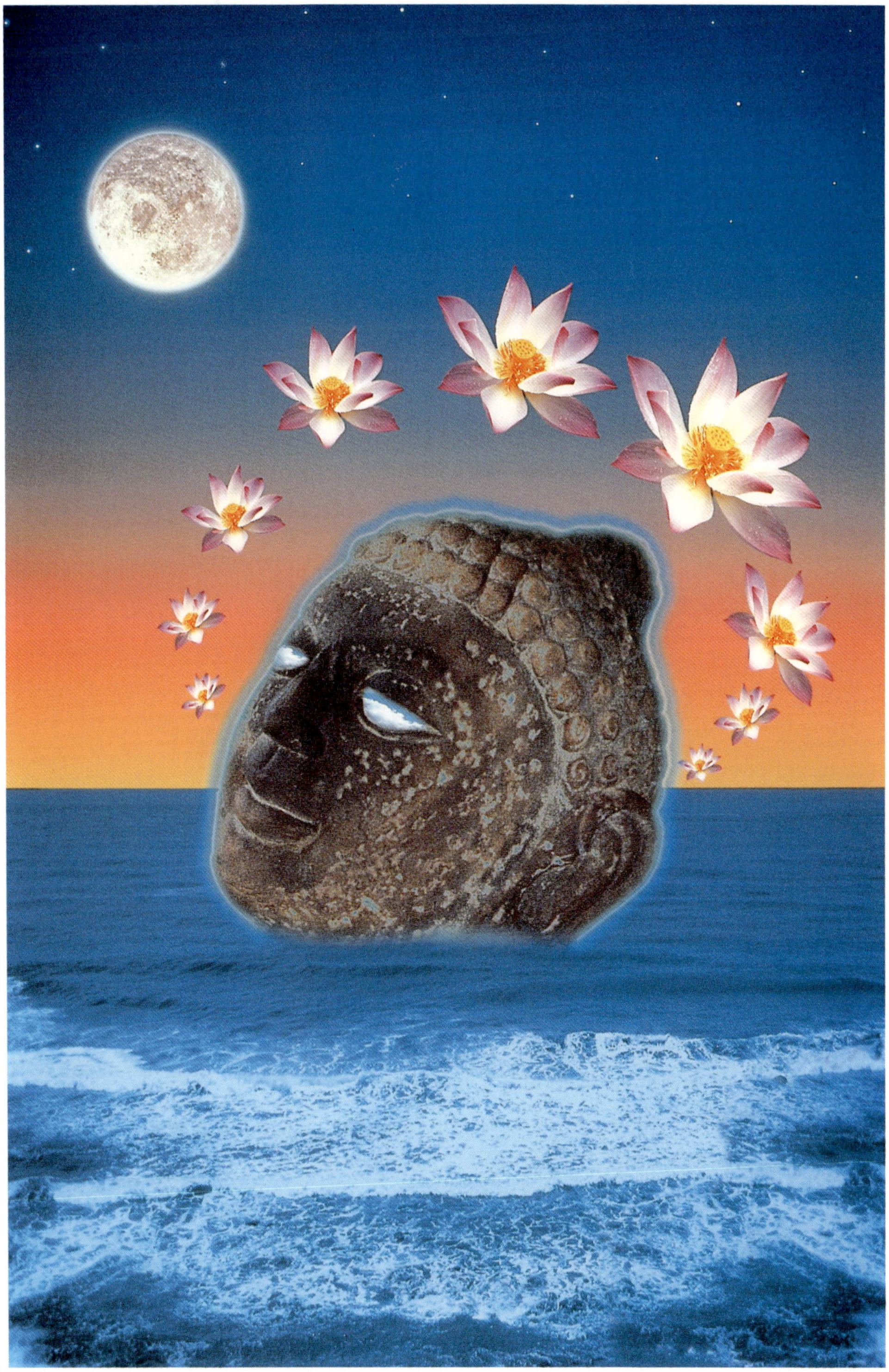

3.

find in fine art galleries. Much of the work that people take as serious art is depressing.

I get annoyed sometimes at people who come to speak at the art galleries who look down their noses at commercial artists when they are living on grants that I've paid taxes to provide.

What advice would you give to young photographers, especially women photographers?

When I started 22 years ago, there were only two women photographers in Dallas. Now, there are many of them. Women have an advantage in many areas. I chose special effects because it was so difficult, and it takes a lot of patience. I observed many of my male photographer friends, and saw that they didn't have the patience. So, being a female helped in that respect.

It also helped in dealing with other people. For example, I went to China with a group that was mainly men. They had trouble getting people to pose for them. That was mainly because the photographers were intimidating. Whereas I had no trouble at all with photographing women and children because I am not threatening. So I was able to get photos that they could not, simply because I was a woman.

But there are disadvantages to being a woman. It's hard to get a job as an assistant because of your physical limitations. You can't easily lug equipment around and so on...I never was an assistant, so that was no problem for me.

I would advise going to school. But on the other hand, there are advantages to discovering your own way of doing photography. I developed my own way of doing things, which was unusual. If I had gone to school I might never have done things in that way. So, I'd say the most important thing is to keep educating yourself in whatever takes your interest. And that never stops. You have to develop your own style, and that is hard to do. There's so much information coming in from friends, family and the media, that it is difficult to find your own style and what you believe in.

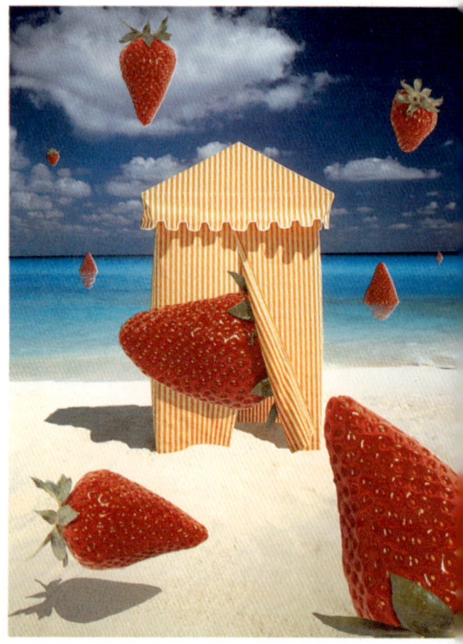

4.

4. Summer
5. Opposite: Winter

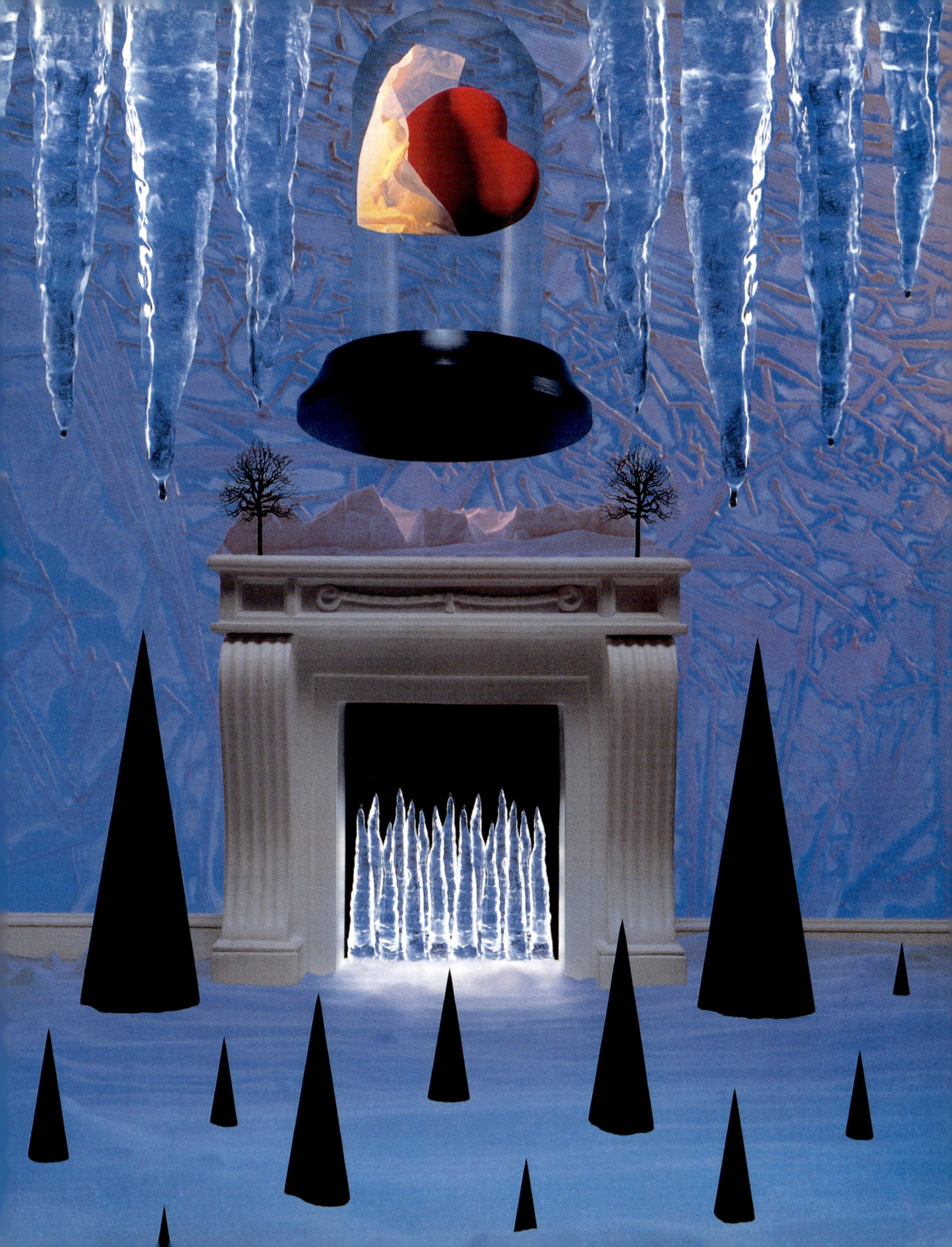

When I was studying the surrealists and other painters, I was also reading philosophy because I didn't know what I believed at that point. I wasn't really positive until I found some books that confirmed the truth for me. If you don't have a clear idea of what you believe, and what the rules are, you lack direction. Having a philosophy is probably the most important aspect. So I advise people to keep on reading until they find what they believe.

You also need perseverance. In the early days, every time I felt like giving up, I would remind myself that there weren't any jobs around that would pay you $500 a day, like photography did. Frankly, what first motivated me was the financial reward. Photography allowed me to become financially independent.

What is your future vision of business and creativity?

Well, the business will change even more rapidly in future because of computers. The type of work I'm doing now for brochures and magazines may not exist any more in five to ten years. Everything will come over that computer screen directly into your home. People will still need images, but they won't be on the printed page. You won't be able to control distribution and how many are printed.

So, I'm thinking that I may have to get into multimedia, because the younger generation today, growing up with TV, MTV and computers, are going to be bored by still images. Images will have to move, talk and have action, or you will lose the audience attention. I don't really want to get into that side of the business, but I will probably have to in order to survive.

I would love to do music videos, but they would have to be classical music videos, and there's no market for those. Also, in making videos, you have to deal with a whole team of people — lighting technicians, camera people and so on — and I don't like working that way. It doesn't suit my personality. I have avoided it, and shall continue to avoid it, but in the end I will probably be forced into doing some kind of multimedia.

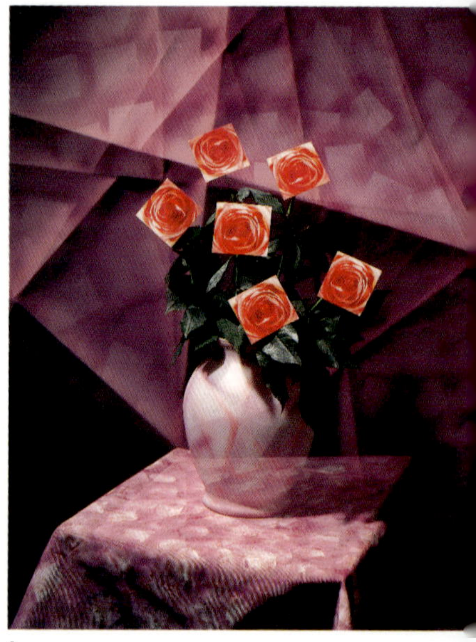

6.

6. Square Roses (pre-computer Image)
7. Cabaret

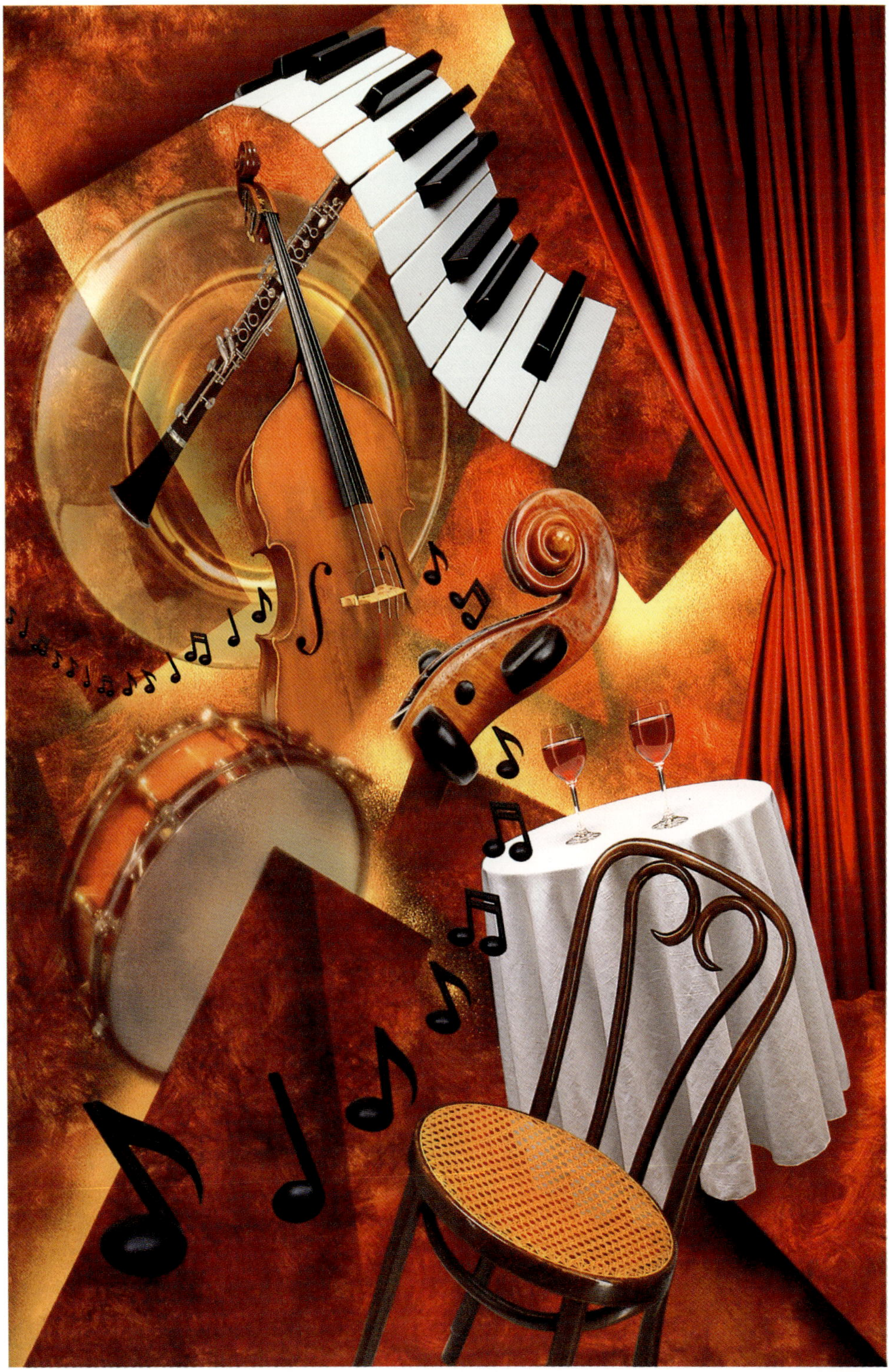

7.

Elle Schuster

As far as creativity is concerned...well, I wish I could see the answer to that. If you could see what the next style was going to be, and get ahead of the rest, you could be very successful. Right now, all we are doing is mixing and rehashing all the styles from the past. The whole postmodern look is a mixture of everything that has come before, but no one has come forward with a new look. What it is, I do not know. I like to think civilization is making progress, and that the future will be newer, cleaner and truer. But when you see movies about the future such as *Blade Runner,* it's all very dirty, overcrowded and a mish-mash of styles. Maybe that is our future. I hope not.

But as the world gets smaller because of computers, and as we are networking with computers all over the world, I think we will see more of a mixture of styles. When China opens up more, we will probably see more of the eastern styles. It's like what we have already in the United States. A mixture of cultures from all over the world. All the other countries might complain about becoming Americanized. But America is everything. It's Chinese, Japanese and Irish and everybody else mixed together. I think that's good because eventually I think there will be one world. With one world government. It may take another century or so, but eventually I think that is what will happen.

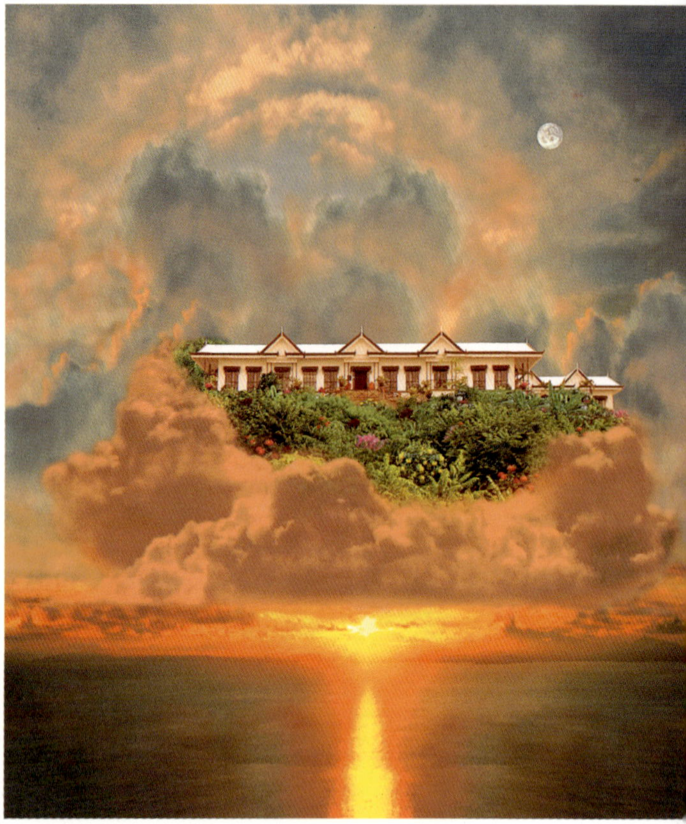

8.

8. Villa Caletas
9. Man / Table / Wine

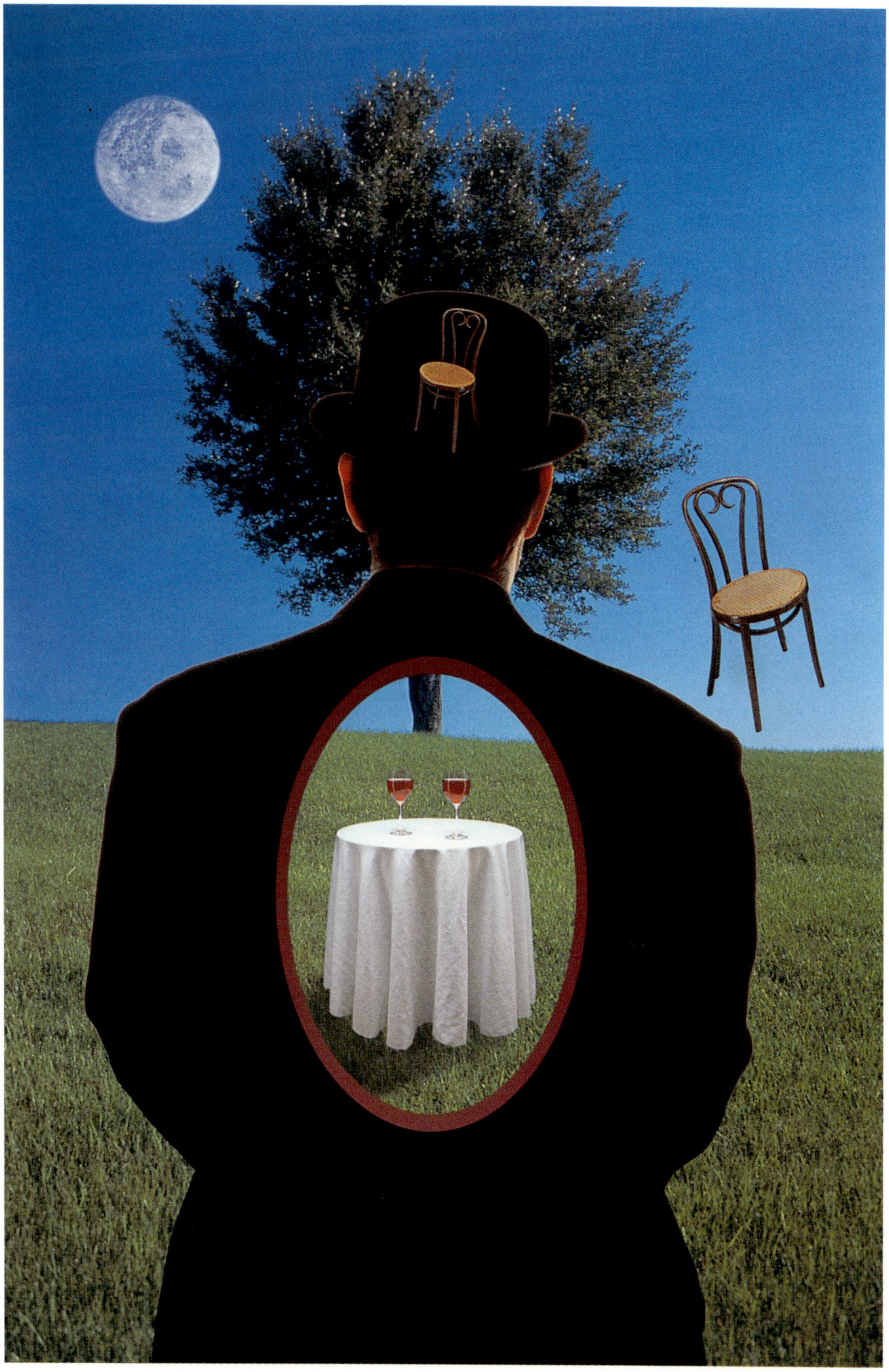

9.

Elle Schuster

10. Bridges over Chasms

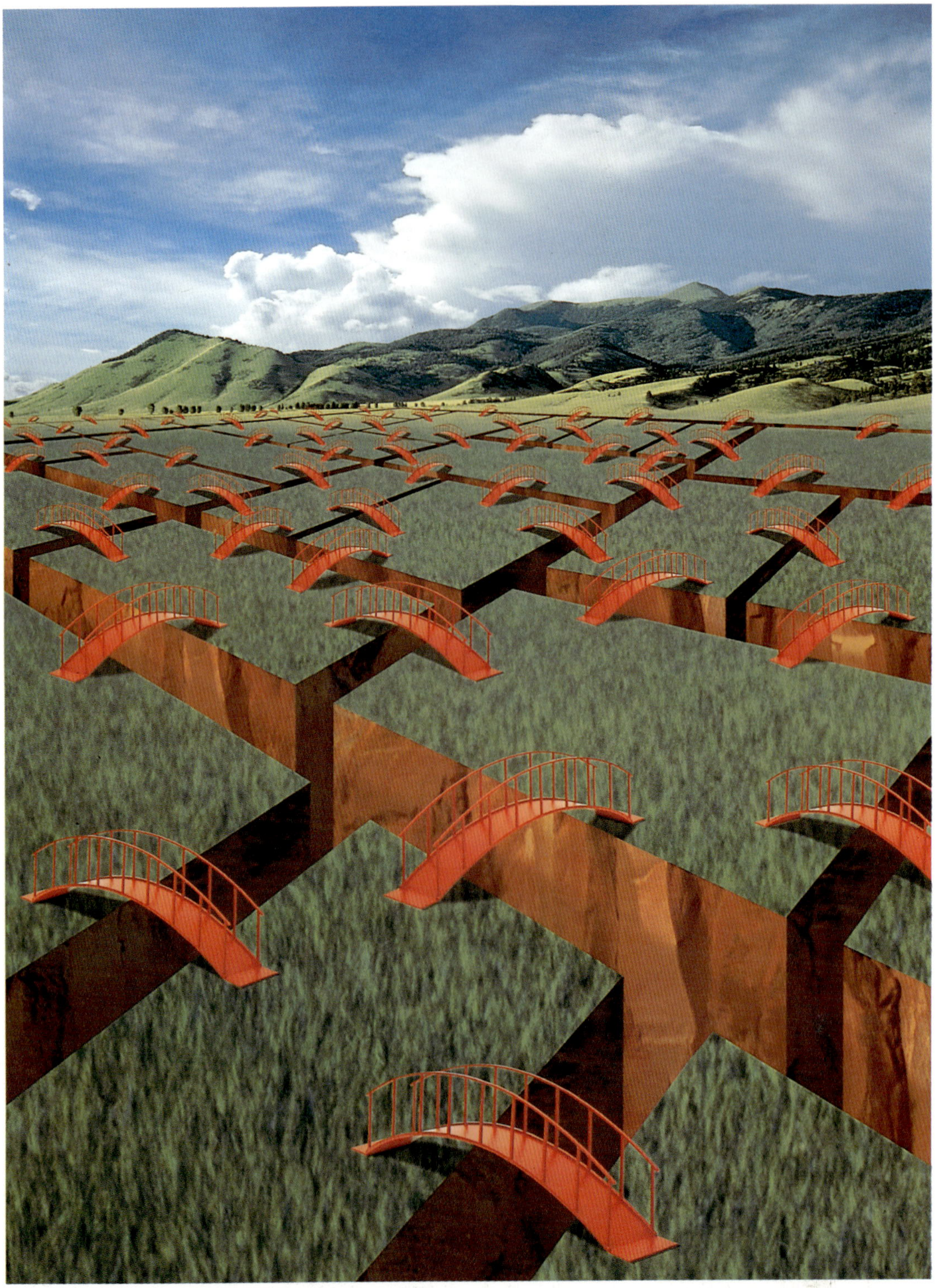

10.

Jim Carroll

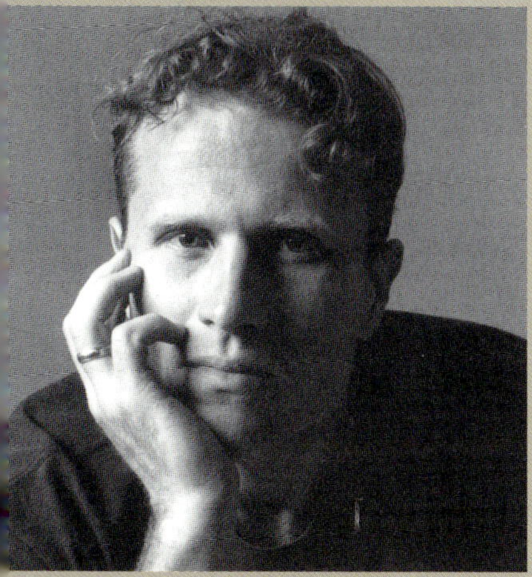

It has been said of Jim Carroll that "there is no other photographer or artist today who so successfully and beautifully blends the 'old world' of photography and painting with the new medium of digital imaging."

In the late 70s Jim studied with mural painter, Anton Refrigier. He went on to earn a Bachelor of Fine Arts degree from SUNY Purchase, studying photography, printmaking, painting and graphic design. Jim spent the next ten years in New York City. His move to the rural community of Old Chatham, NY, coincided with an influential meeting with computer impresario, Michael Martin. It was then that his gifts in photography, painting and design were meshed together with the new liquid digital technology. Continually exploring the vast and expansive potential for photo art on the computer, companies like Kodak, Warner Bros., RCA, Sony and Polaroid soon began pursuing Jim's photographic creations. As a result, his work has appeared on the cover of *ZOOM* magazine and been featured in such noted publications as *Photo District News* and *Communication Arts*. In addition, Carroll has created many award-winning images for corporations and individuals, art for CD and book jackets, posters and magazine covers.

Jim Carroll

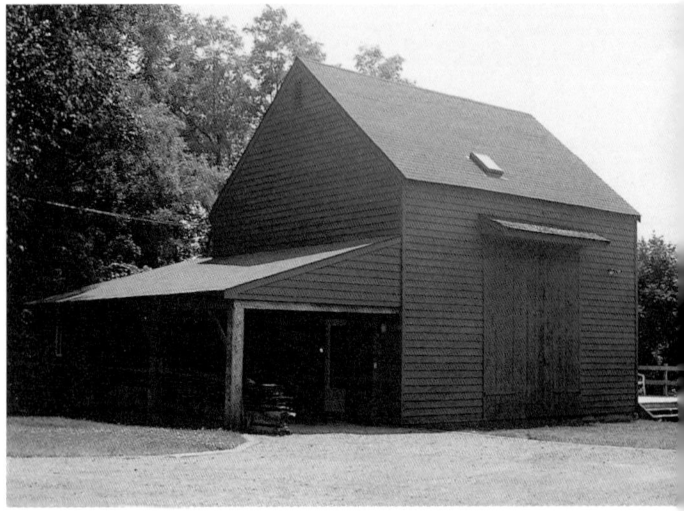
Studio

The place you live is about three hours from Manhattan. How does computer technology help you in your work?

The obvious and direct help is the ability to modem my work. I don't send finished art by this route because the resolution is so high that the files are too big to transmit by modem. But I can get a rough sample sent to an art director. Being able to exchange files electronically is a big help. I can send a file for approval, they can give me their comments on changes they want to have done, and this speeds up the work process.

Are you sending dye-sublimation prints to clients?

Yes, for the initial approval, just so that they have a hard copy to look at, and don't have to worry about viewing the image on-screen and having their interpretation be different from mine. There's always a possibility of a color shift, depending on the printer. But it gives you a good idea of the image.

But three hours isn't such a long time. I can go to New York and meet a client if I have to. Half of my clients are in New York. A quarter of them are local, and the other quarter are spread out over the country.

Is this environment conducive to creating your images?

Yes, I think the environment can have a lot to do with the kind of pictures you turn out. You are going to respond to whatever environment you are in, whether it's the desert or an urban city. One of the reasons I moved out here is that the surroundings are an excellent resource to pull my pictures from. I photograph the things around me, the mountains and sky...and the people.... Almost all of the models I use are people I know. All of these things influence my pictures.

I think it would be a lot more difficult for me to do this work in a big city because my work is based more on nature and spiritual values. There's a lot of great work being done by people in large cities. But in my case, I really need this kind of environment to work from.

a. Sketch
b. Infant Photo
c. Mom Figure Photo

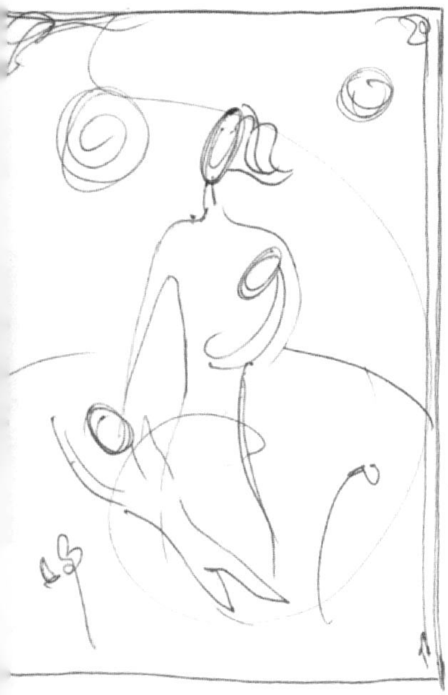

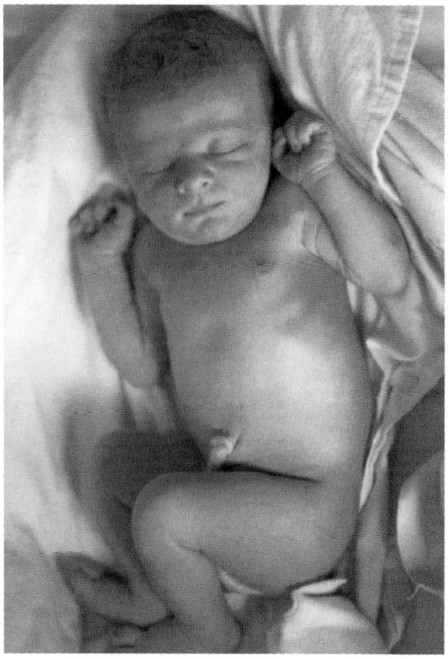

b.

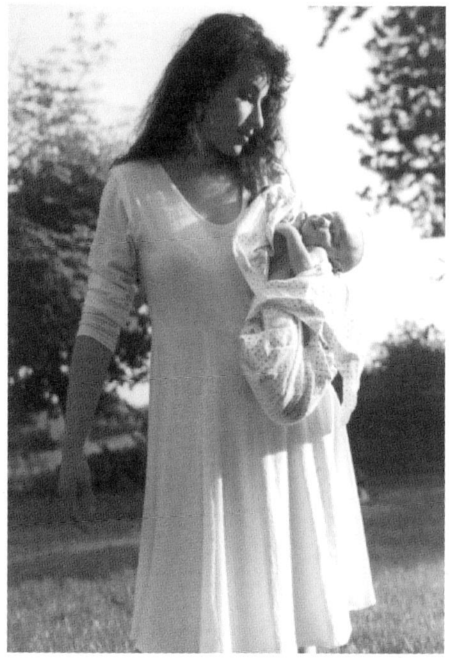

c.

inspiration for this picture was the birth of son, Marley. I wanted to create a portrait of family in the local environment with a playful, etic mood and a photographic, painterly lity.

rting with a very rough sketch and concept, I o out what I initially think the picture should tain and where it might be. I try to keep in d that this sketch is just a possibility, and I ve room for it to evolve and lead me.

The picture was created from five base photographs and two base pastel drawings that would make up the structure of the piece. These would later be scanned into my computer and manipulated with Adobe Photoshop software. (I usually work in CMYK color mode; this gives the truest screen presentation of a printed piece.)

The photographs of the mother and children were done with a 4 x 5 camera using high-resolution Polaroid, black and white film. The shot of the landscape was done with a 35-mm color film, then printed as a 4 x 6.

I like to shoot my models in black and white because it gives me the opportunity to color them in the computer (using the Paintbrush with the Color Only option chosen), and take away a certain typical "photographic" color presentation.

These pictures were shot outside and in a natural environment for the quality of light and spontaneity it allowed the models and myself. The figures would later need to be silhouetted from the background (using the Paintbrush with white paint selected). The silhouetting would have been easier if I had shot them outside and against a white seamless, though I probably would have lost some of the candid quality.

Jim Carroll

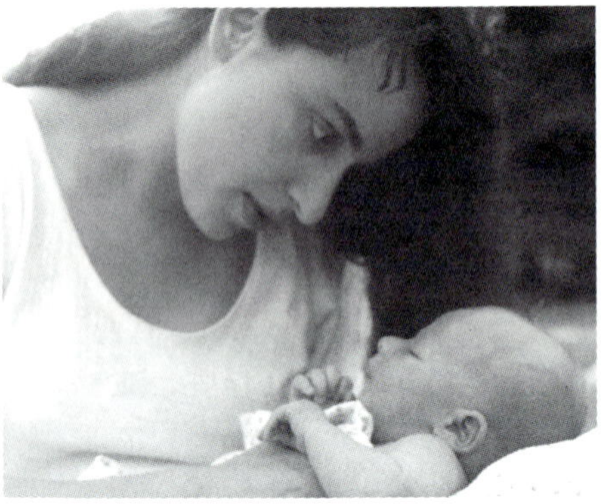

d.

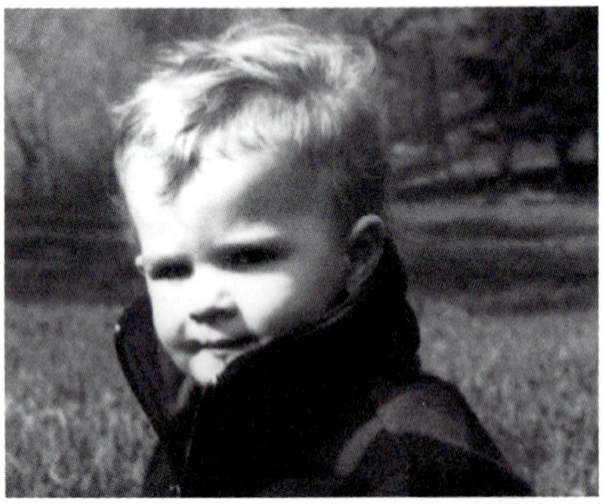

e.

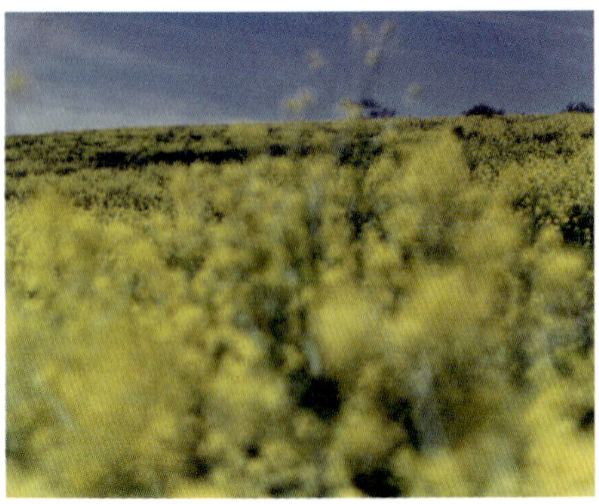

f.

The landscape was shot with color film and then enhanced in the computer using the color-balance controls.

These were all scanned into the computer at approximately 300 DPI.

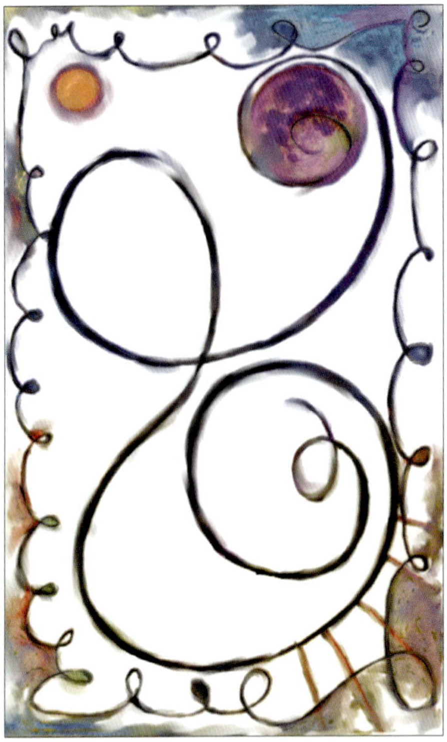

g.

The swirls were done as a traditional oil, pastel and ink drawing on board and then scanned.

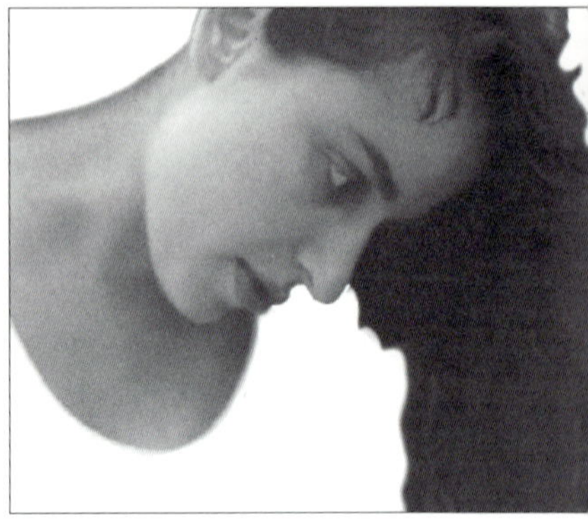

h.

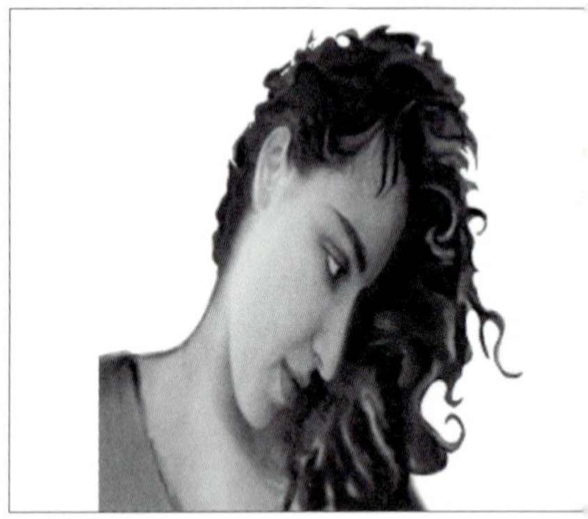

i.

Mom's head was silhouetted from background using the Paintbrush, the eyes mouth were enhanced using a variety of tc including the Paintbrush and the Dodge and B tools. The top of the ear and head w completed using the Paintbrush and Clone to

The face was distorted with the Scale and Dis options and later placed as the head on the figure shot. The white background would selected with the Magic Wand tool, then "invert to select the face, copied and then pasted c the figure. This technique would be us throughout.

d. Mom Head Photo
e. Toddler Photo
f. Field
g. Swirl Drawing
h. Mom Head
i. Mom Head Finish
j. Toddler Head
k. Outfit
l. Harlequin

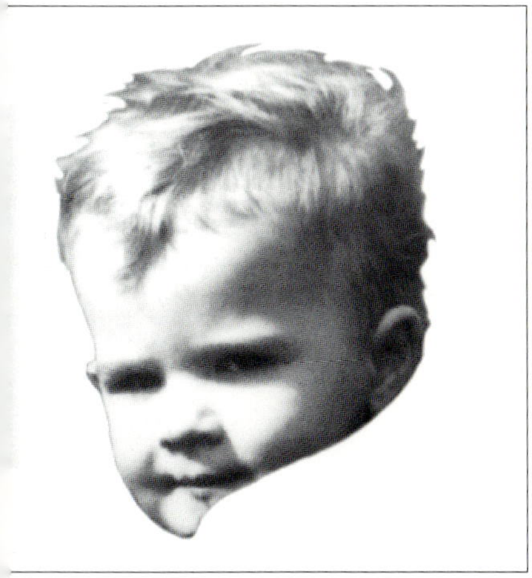

e same procedure was used for the toddler's ad.

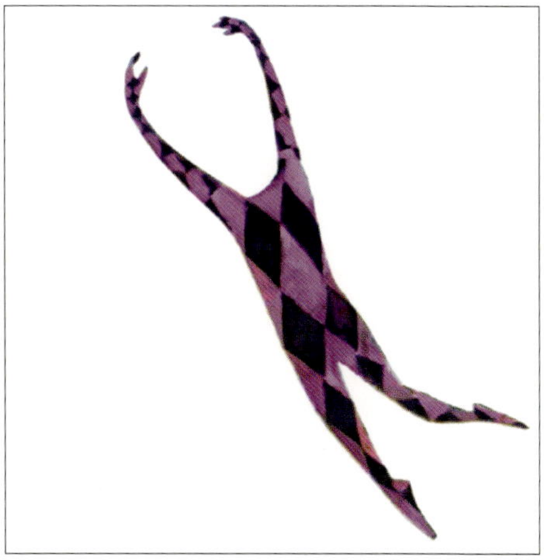

k.

A harlequin outfit was drawn traditionally using pen and ink, scanned and then colored with the Paintbrush. I would select each diamond with the Magic Wand, using the Hide Edges command to get rid of the marching ants marquis and paint within that area with the selected colors.

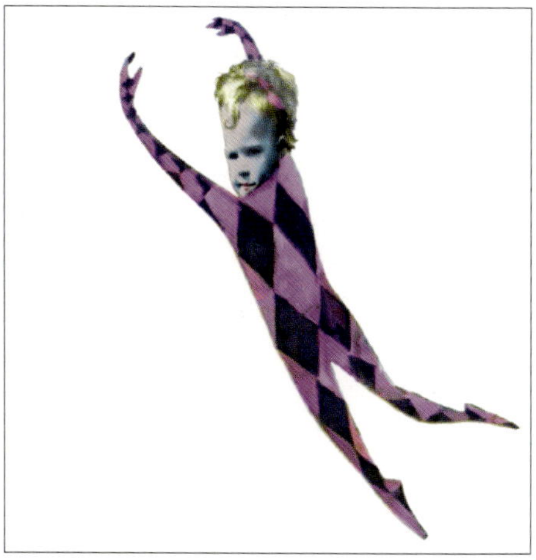

l.

The toddler's head was copied, then pasted onto the harlequin body. Exact sizing was done with the Scale option.

Jim Carroll

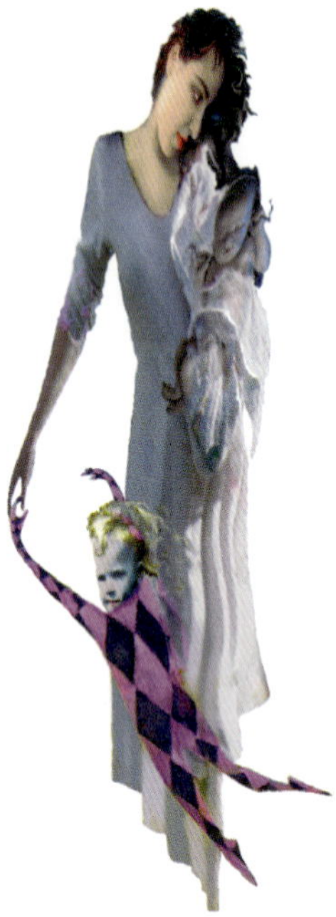

m.

After silhouetting the infant, each manipulated figure was selected and then combined together in a new file. The blending and translucency of the infant and the blanket were achieved using the Rubber Stamp tool with the option set to Revert to Saved. With a pressure-sensitive drawing tablet, I slowly brought back some of the underlying images of the mom and the blanket to work more interestingly with the baby.

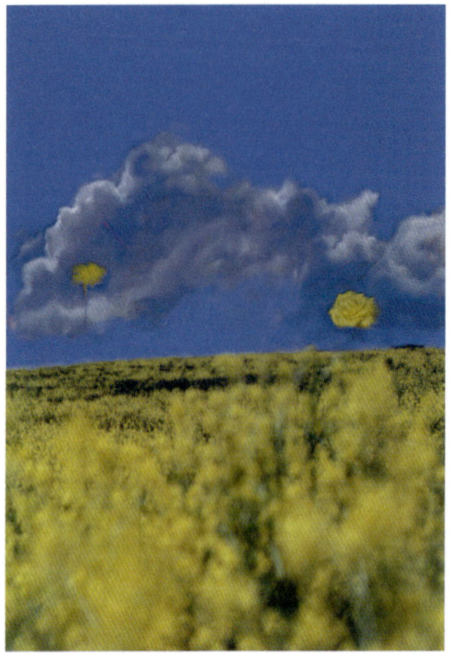

n.

The background of the image was created using the color enhanced shot of the landscape. I re-proportioned the picture using the Image Size option and then de-selected the Proportions and Size boxes and plugged in a new Height and Width.

The blue sky was extended by selecting the entire area above the field with the Lasso tool with the Feather variable at 5 to soften the blend. I then chose a blue from the Color Picker and with the Fill command, added this color to the top portion of the picture.

The clouds were added using a combination of painting in the computer and scans of photos I had in my archives.

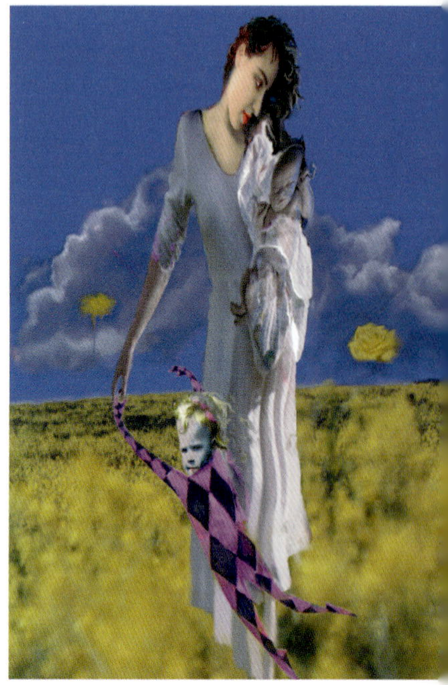

o.

I selected the figures from their white backgro and copied and pasted them into the exist landscape field. The edges of the figures w blended and softened to merge with background using a variety of tools including Rubber Stamp set to slowly erase the figures pull through some flowers; the Rubber Stamp time set to Clone to give a subtle ghosting of image; the Smudge and Blur tools to soften blend edges, and the Paintbrush to bring so colors from the background into the figures.

The final step was adding the swirls. Select the white part of the drawing with the Magic W tool, I inverted, copied and pasted this into base image.

All of these components were worked o pushed and pulled, using whatever tool method came to mind to finally bring the wh picture to its finished state.

m. Combined Figures
n. Field
o. Field / Figure
p. Young Family

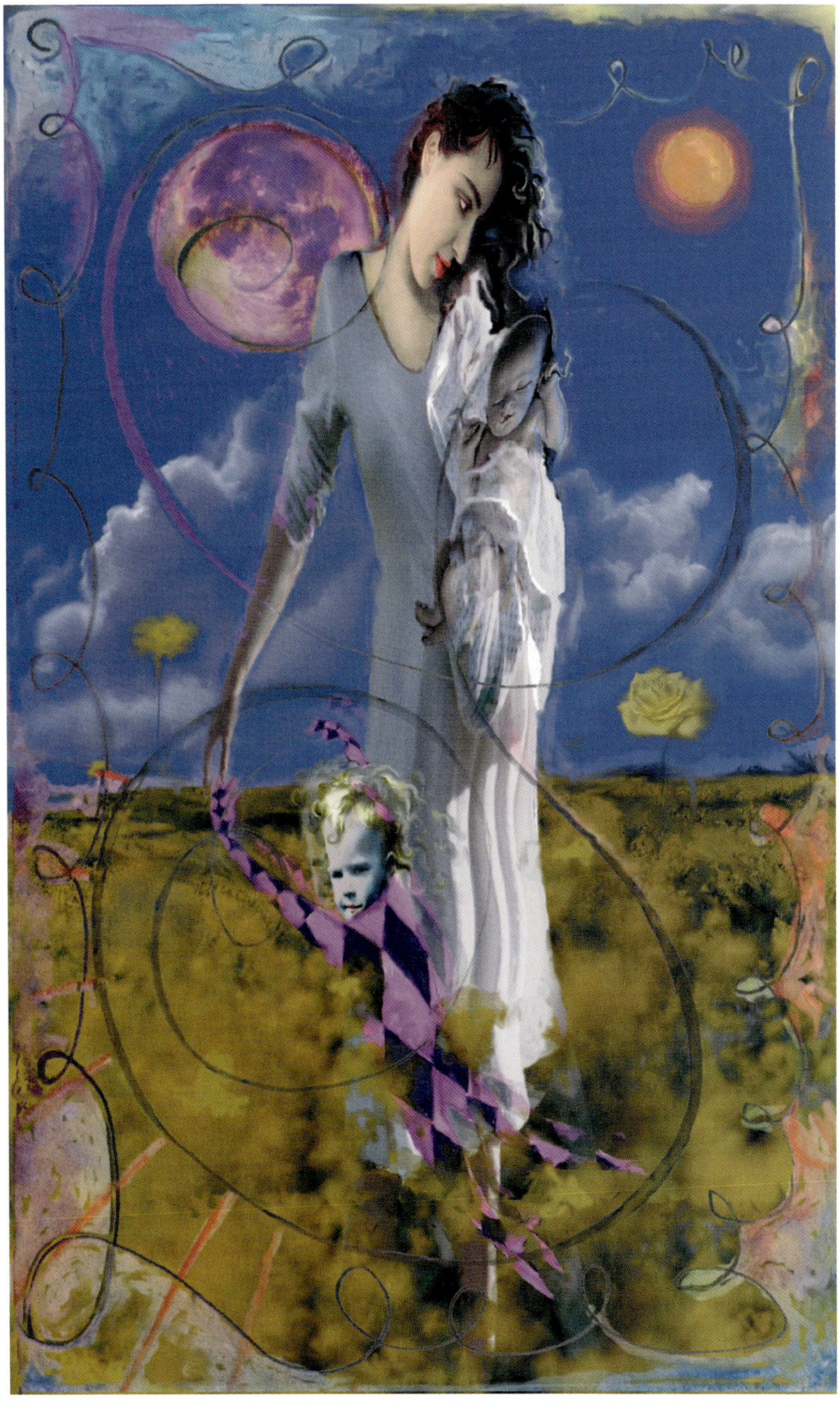

p.

Jim Carroll

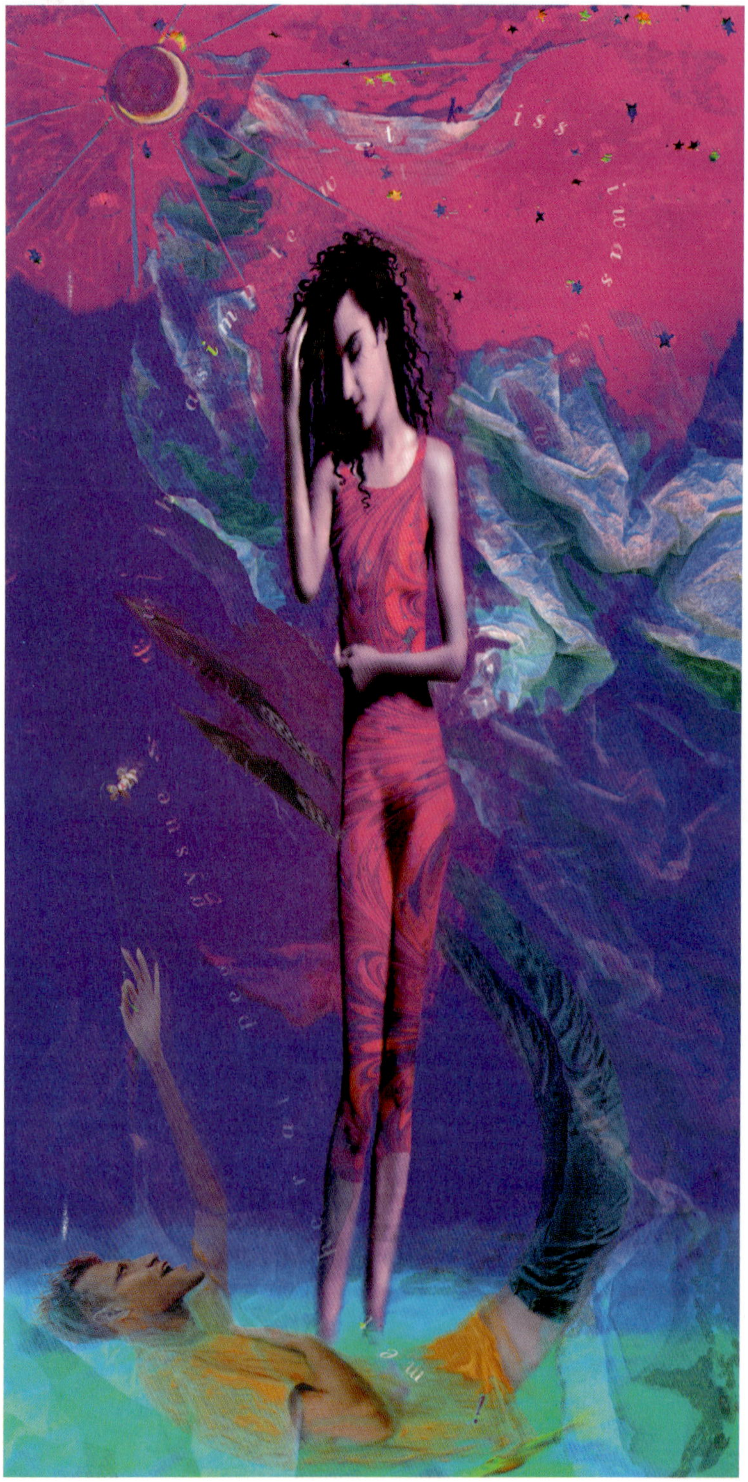

1.

1. Mountain
2. Gaudi Girl

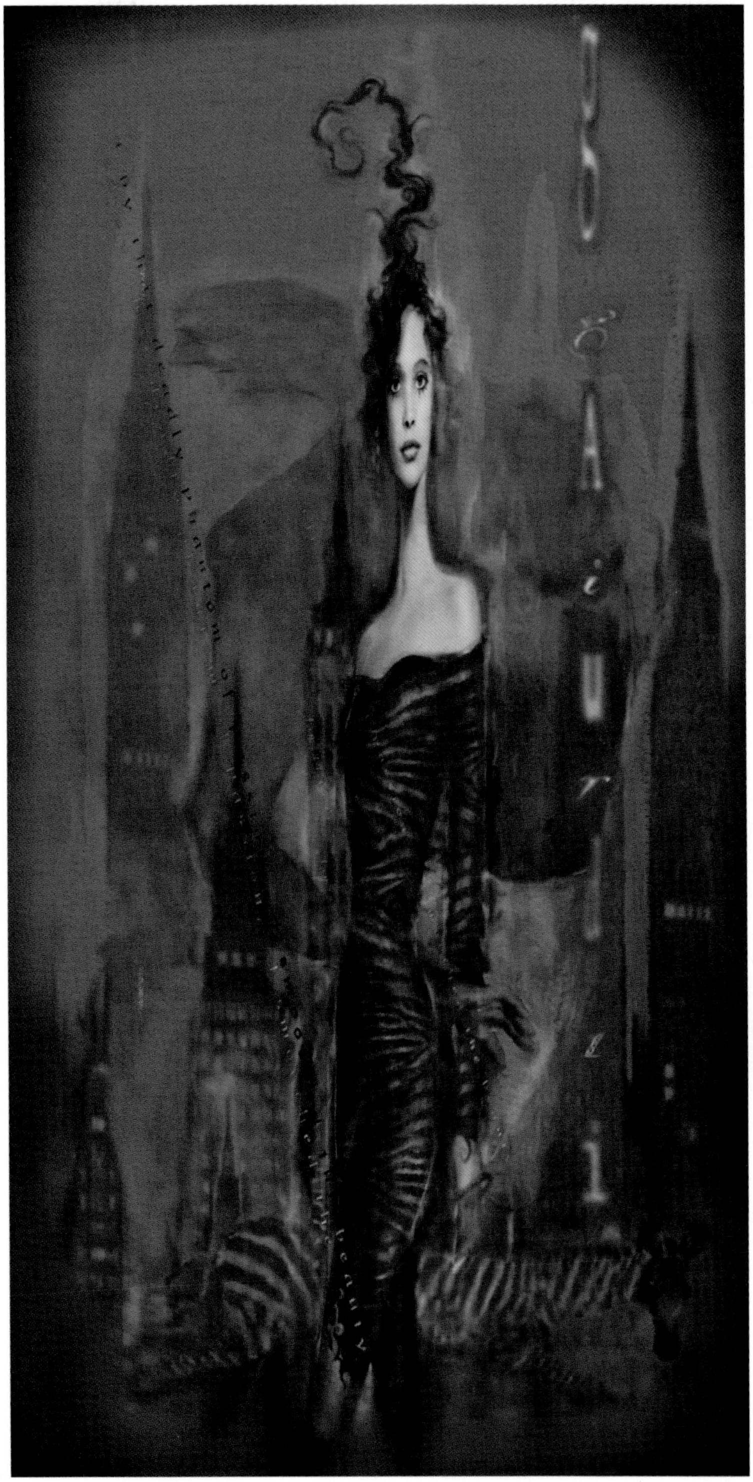

2.

Jim Carroll

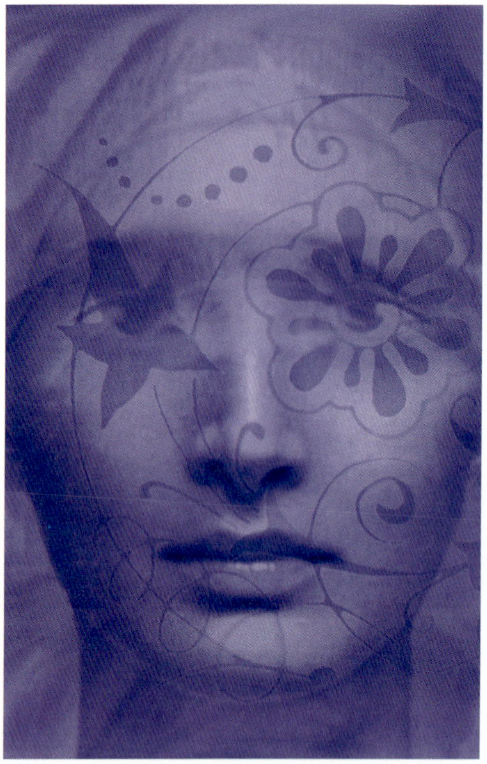

3.

3. Gentle Face
4. Somalia

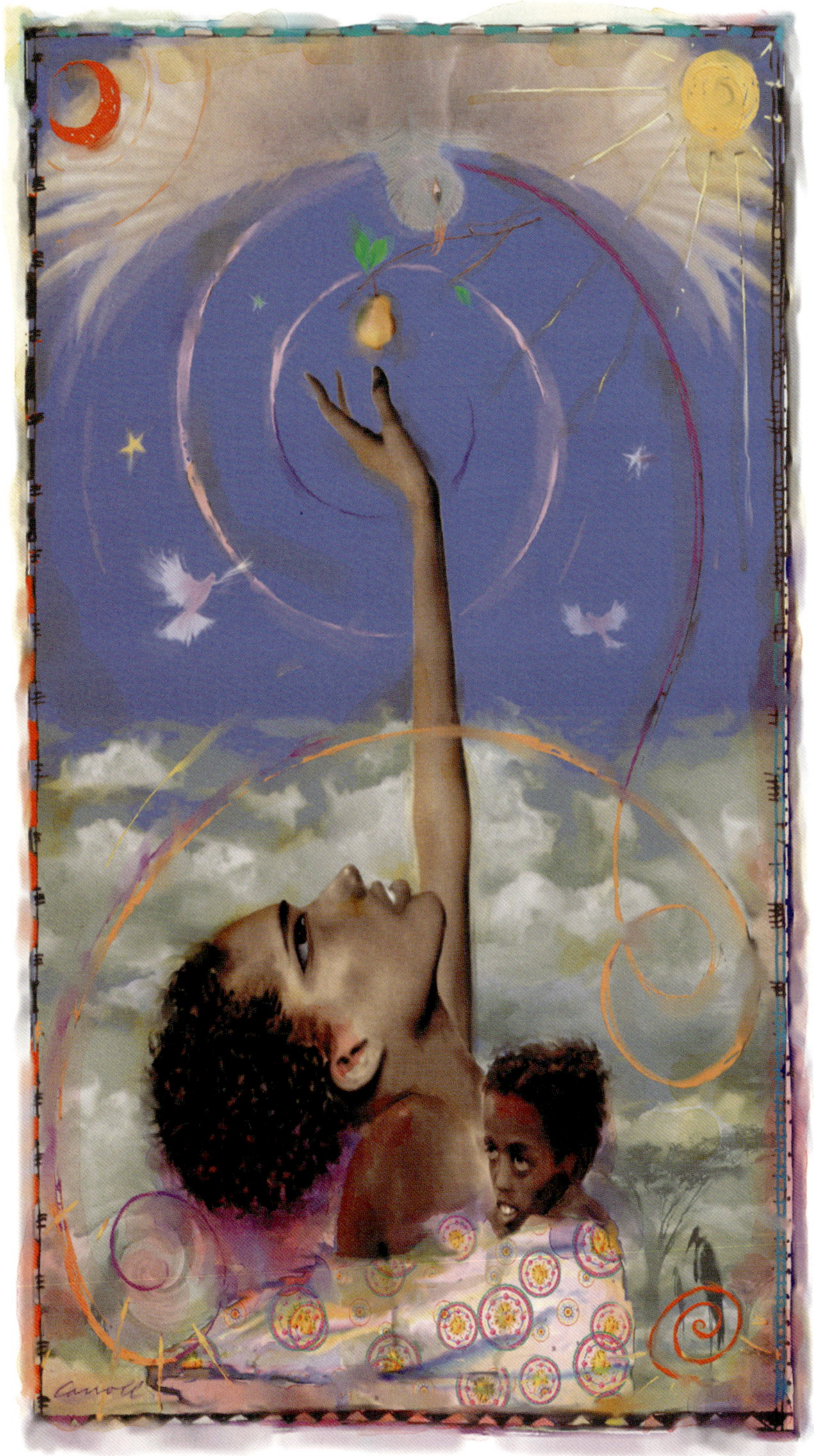

4.

Jim Carroll

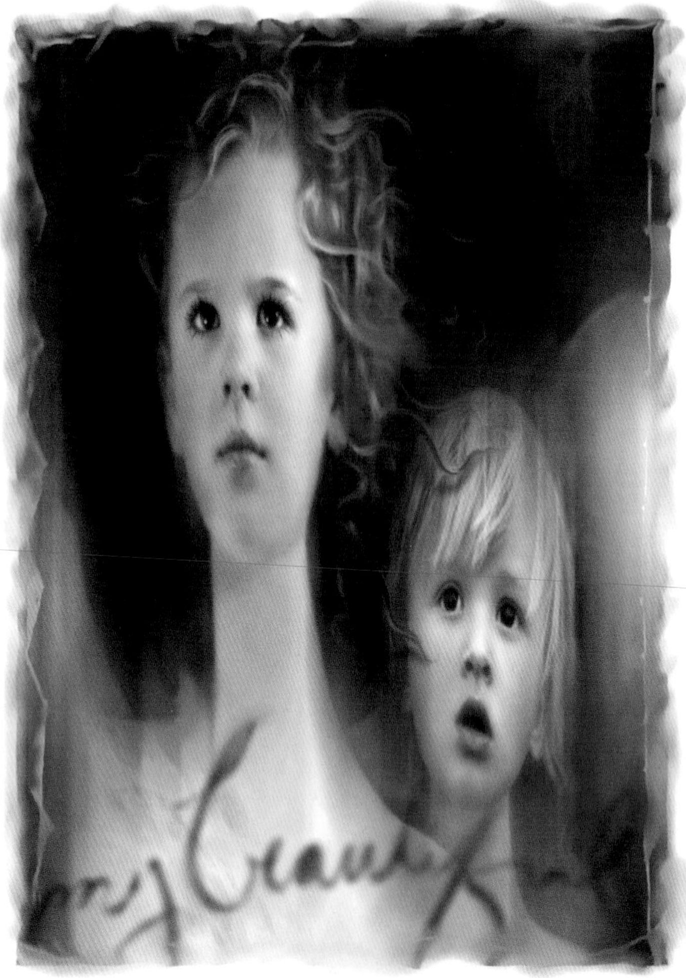

5.

5. Angels
6. Opposite: Fresco

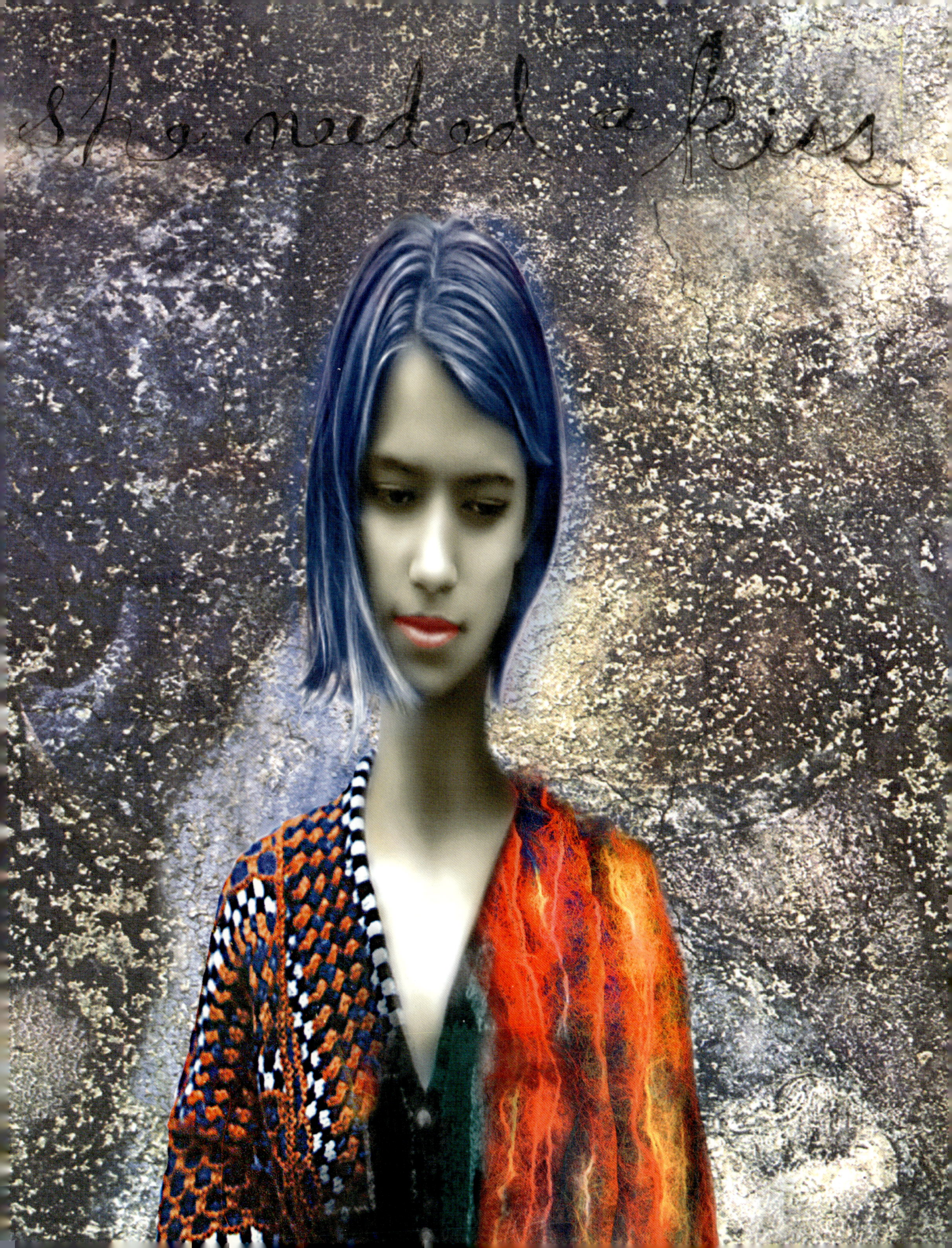
she needed a kiss

Jim Carroll

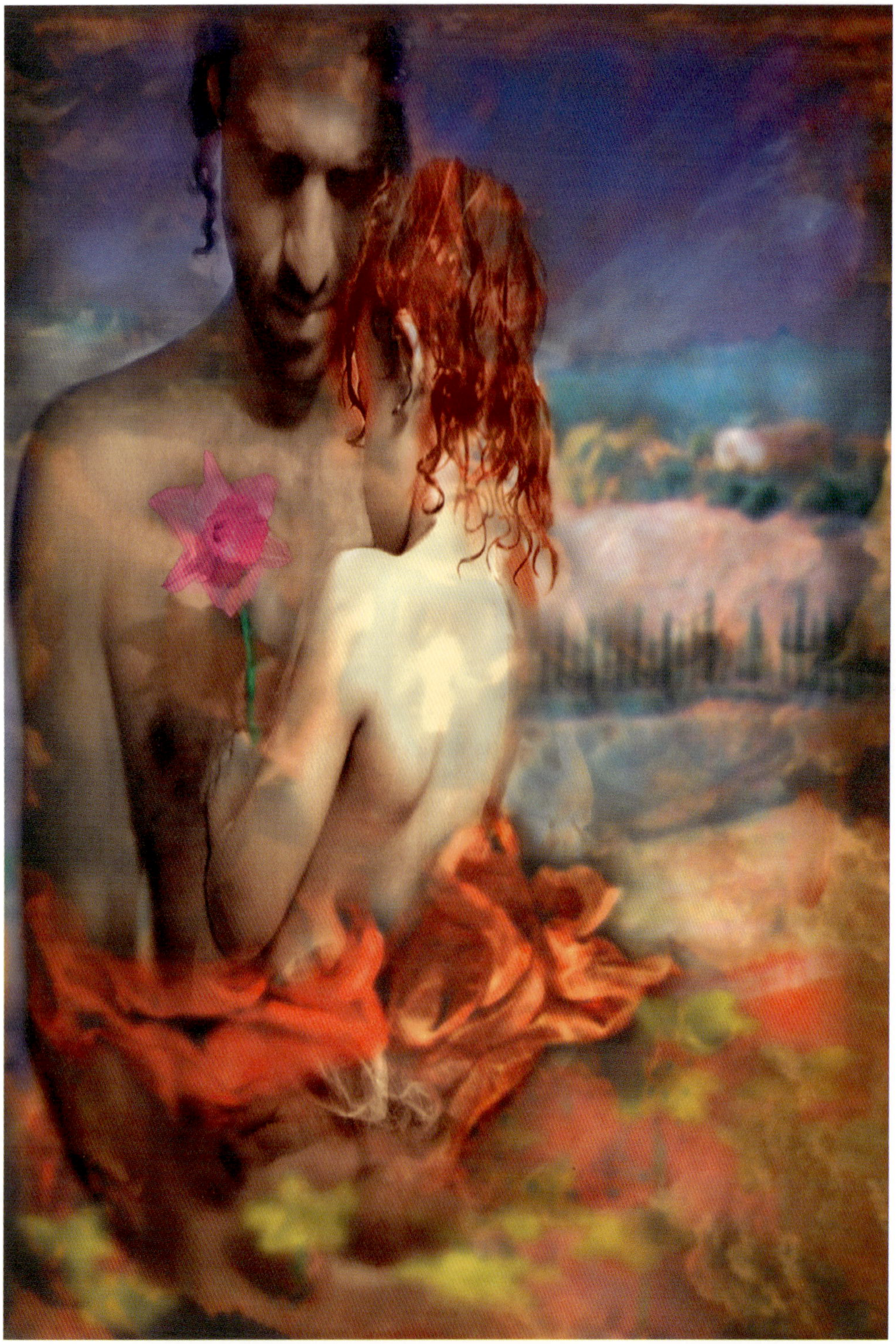

7.

7. Elana and Papa
8. Girl and Ghouls

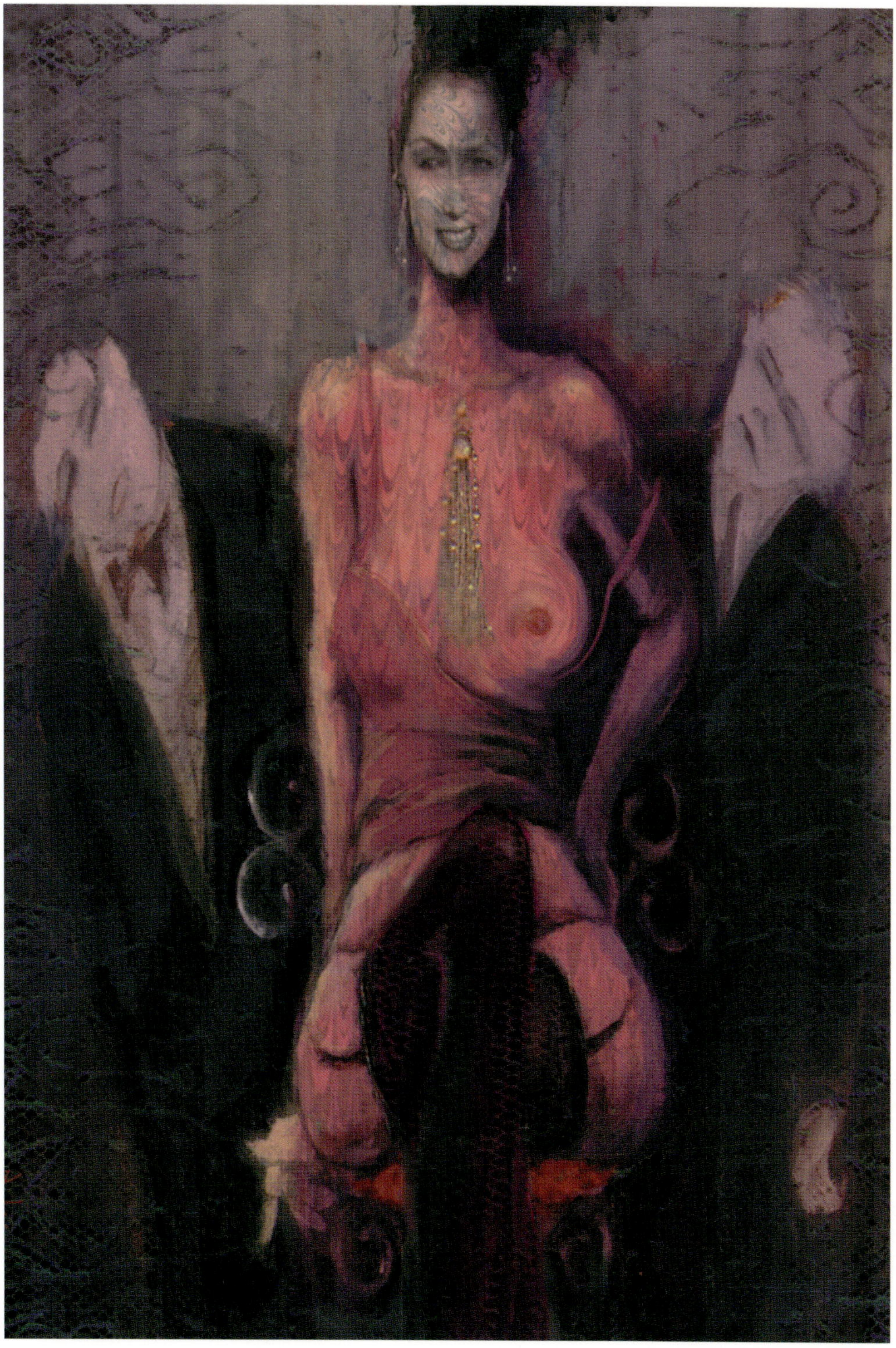
8.

Jim Carroll

9. Beach

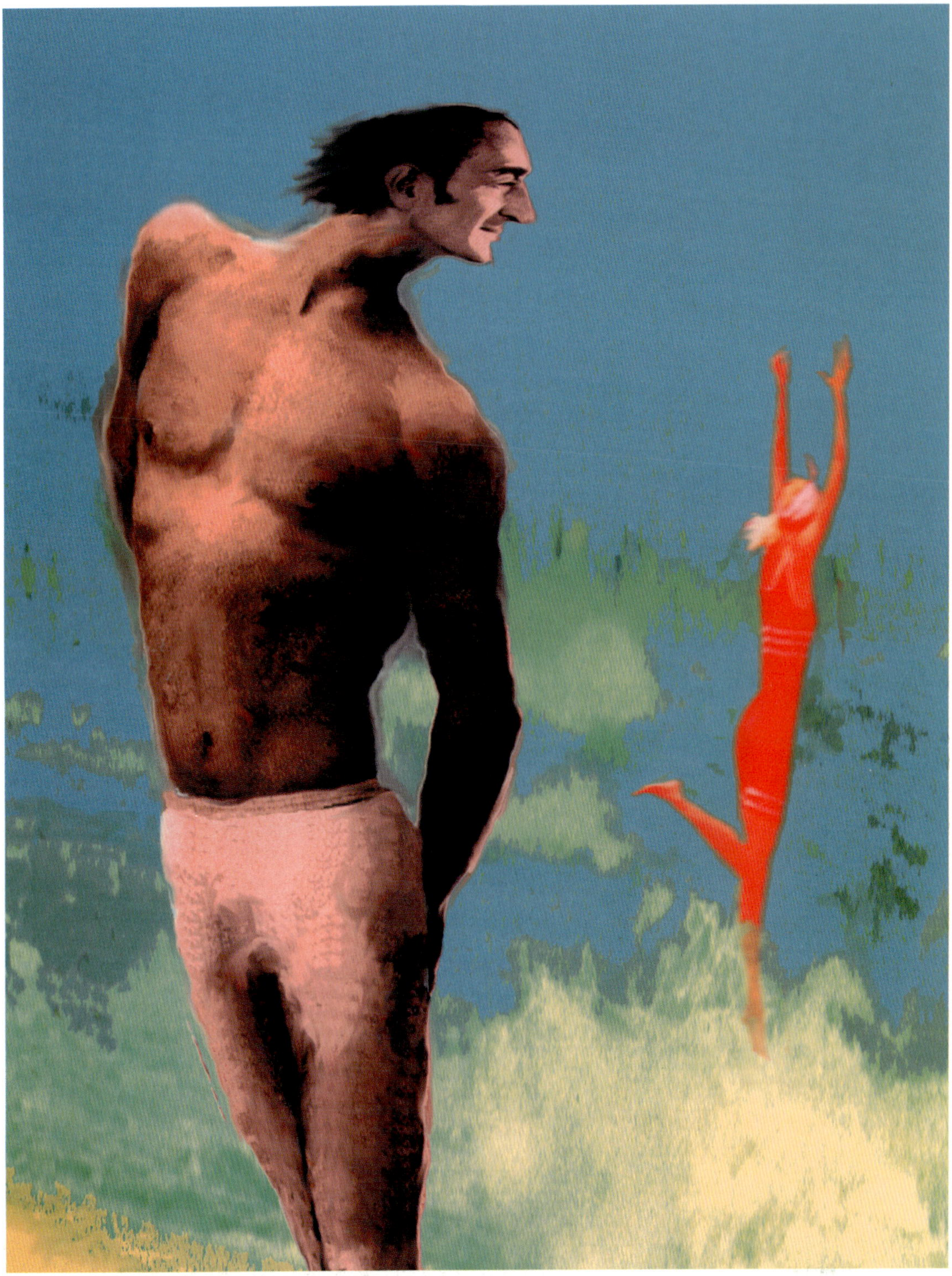

9.

Robert Bowen

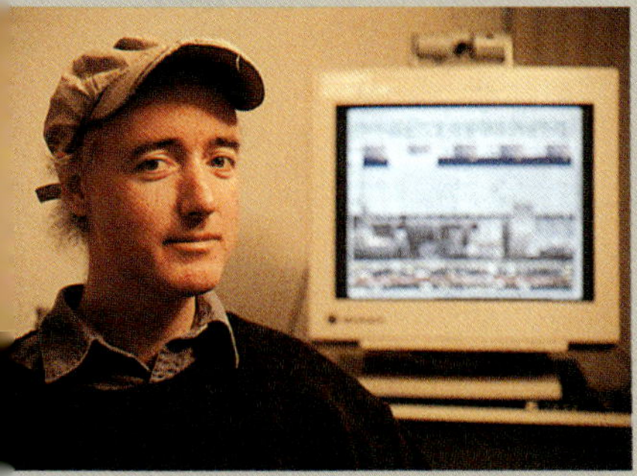

Robert Bowen is a visual-effects artist for print media. Like many of today's photographers, Bowen has left the darkroom behind to pursue the unlimited freedom in imaging that he gets from computer technology. His amazing images make the majority of us wonder just how he managed to produce them. But then, he is something of a magician — only one who uses the computer to create his illusions.

Bowen works directly with advertising agencies and in close collaboration with many premiere photographers who know how to shoot for effects. In his work with Ryszard Horowitz, for instance, Bowen has broken new ground in the blending of film with digitally generated art work.

Judging from his extensive list of clients, Bowen's images are in great demand. Unisys, ITT, Lockheed and Kodak all seek the expertise of Robert Bowen Studio. He even does advertising work for SGI. But that's not surprising when you consider that the majority of his visual effects wizardry is done on that machine.

(Portrait of Robert Bowen by Mark Leet ©1994)

Robert Bowen

What are the activities of the Robert Bowen Studio?

I work in computer visual effects, photo-design, stock photography and retouching, for both print advertising and editorial projects. But I'm also involved in the production of fine art work along with general image research. I also conduct imaging seminars and teach graduate level photography and computer art at School of Visual Arts here in New York.

I usually think of my work as a collaboration with art directors from advertising agencies and photographers. I am often brought in at the concept stage, or at least before the images begin.

Typically, the way this works is that I get faxes from photographers or directly from advertising agencies, containing preliminary sketches for ads. By this time the agency has already spent a long time developing concepts. And now they have some interesting and wacky ideas that they want to have happen. This is when they contact me.

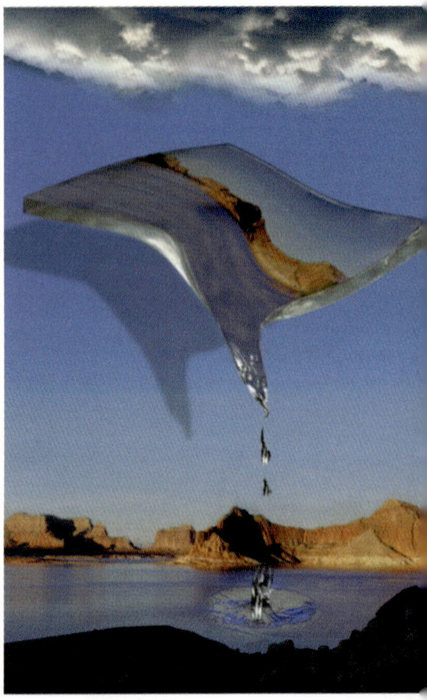

a.

The project begins in earnest by trying to understand exactly what the art director is looking for. Then I respond with an estimate and wait for approval. If the job goes forward I go to some meetings, and begin the process of working directly with the photographer and the art director. I sometimes think of myself as a hired gun for the advertising trade. An agency can hire me to solve their problems in a unique and elegant fashion. I can really do anything, given the appropriate time-frame and budget.

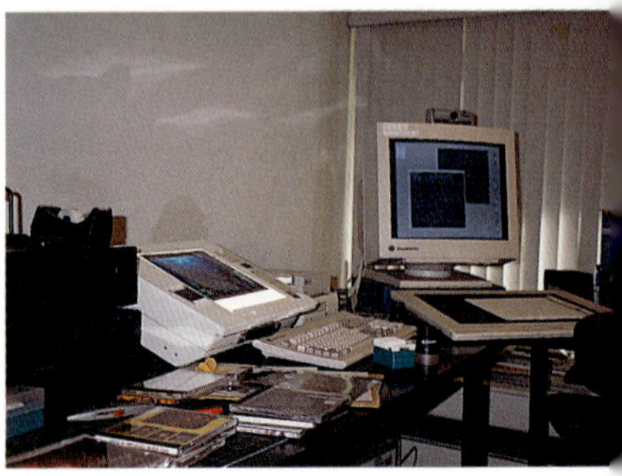

Robert Bowen's Studio

One of my specialties is combining 3-D computer graphics effects with 2-D photography.

Please tell us about the photographers you work with in the studio.

I usually work closely with a small group of photographers who are regular clients, but the way things go, I might end up working with anyone. I often work with such photographers as Ryszard Horowitz, Eric Meola, Steve Bronstein, Howard Berman and Grant

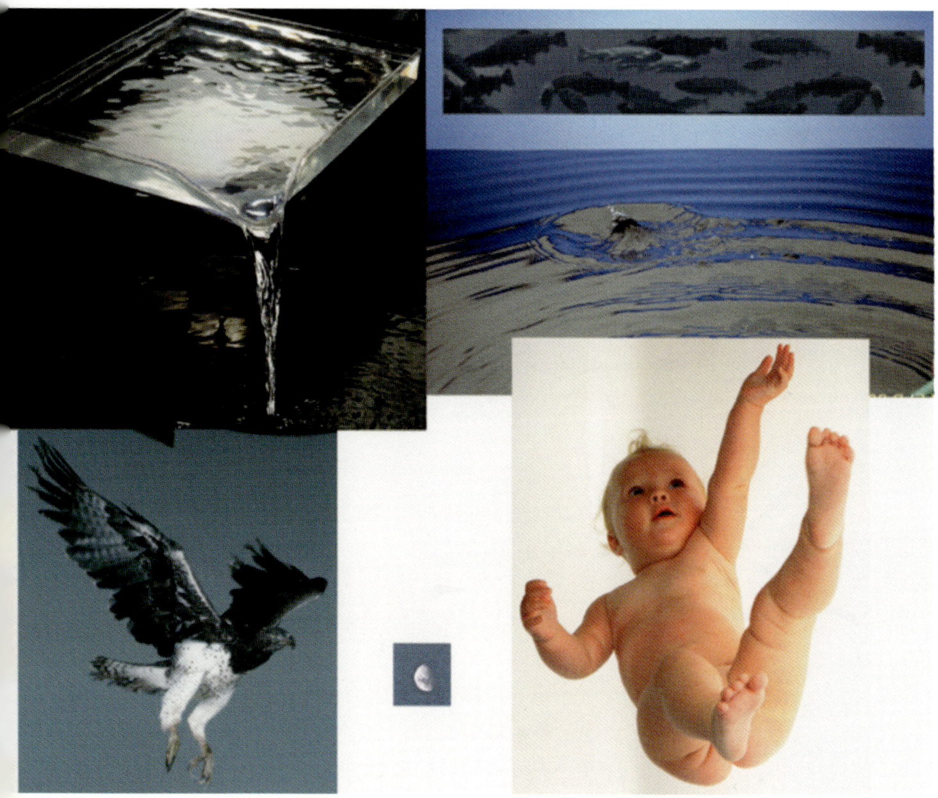

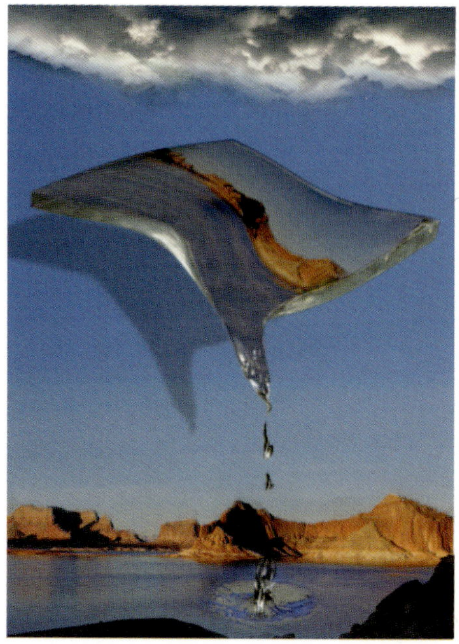

c.

ɔw did we do that?

'egory II was created in collaboration with ˈszard Horowitz as a promotional image to ghlight the work we've been doing together. as Power Animator and Adobe Photoshop for 'icon Graphics were used in the production of e image. Ryszard sketched the preliminary idea paper and I worked out a sequence of riations as low-res, digital, conceptual etches. A few of these variations appear here these pages (b-d). Of particular interest is the ird Tray" image because it was this picture that ggested to us the inclusion of an actual eagle the final image.

r a promotional image to be successful it needs have some of the qualities of Cecil B. DeMille. this I mean it has to be a dynamic and ematic tour de force. At the same time it is portant to tell a meaningful story. In constructing the narrative the original photographic elements become signs and symbols within the story. Included here are some of the source photographs we used in the image: baby, fish, eagle, landscape, splash, etc. Everything depends on subtle arrangements of position, scale and value. For example, the addition of the fish in the foreground created a wonderfully engaging perspective that subtly corrects the scale of the image. Even though I photographed the fish straight on in an aquarium, it is a completely believable illusion in the picture that we are looking down on the fish. I sometimes think of theater design and staging while working on such images.

This type of computer imaging has much in common not only with set design, but also with special-effects films. The goal of special effects is the mastery of nature through tricking the eye. In order to aid in the suspension of disbelief, the viewer is in collusion with the effects artist in the sense that both parties really want the illusion to work. The principal requirement needed to allow this process to succeed is photorealism. Trompe l'oeil pictures work because of the intellectual co-perception of two divergent forms of surface information: illusory space and the medium's own actual two-dimensionality (the pixels, monitor, paint, canvas, grain or noise).

Robert Bowen

d. Allegory II
Photographer: Ryszard Horowitz
Note: There are several support files (both source images and conceptual sketches) for this on

1. Opposite: Digital Noise

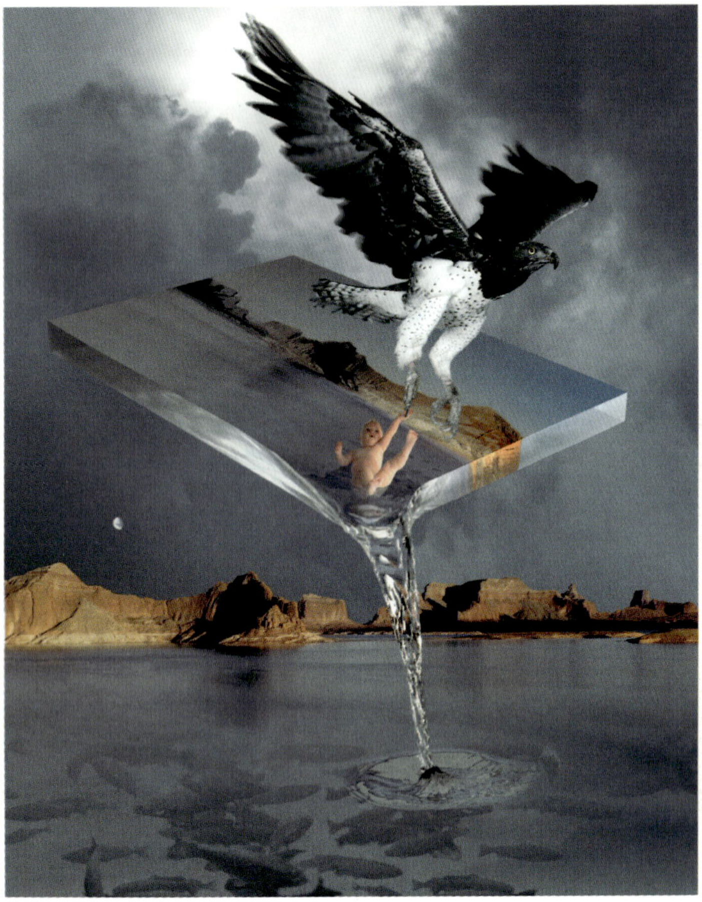

d.

Peterson. Many collaborations with these photographers a featured in this book.

I've done numerous projects with each of these photographer They are all based in New York. There is excellent chemistry the working process. These artists are all accomplished and th each understand photography in a very universal way, and th includes how to photograph in order to achieve certain effect It's a very exciting collaboration. No one is bored with the wor Some projects are more exciting than others but there's sustained level of energy throughout all of the images we creat

I heard that you use the Macintosh and Silicon Graphics Inc (SGI). Could you describe the character of each machine, ar say something about their compatibility?

Well, I wouldn't be able to have this business and take on th jobs that I do without both of these machines. They each have unique character. The Silicon Graphics machine has a 150 MH high-speed processor. I do all the 3-D graphics on that machin I've been running Alias Power Animator for 3-D and I've al started working with ElectroGig 3D-GO. There is really r equivalent on the Macintosh for 3-D imaging. There are 3- programs on the Mac, but they are toylike in comparison wi the programs that are available for SGI.

Also, another SGI-based program that I'm working with is call Barco Creator. This is a very powerful 2-D image processing progra for doing photo-retouching and certain effects. In particular it h an extremely powerful mesh-warping tool that I constantly ta advantage of. I can do single frame 2-D morphing with this tool real time and in high resolution. There is nothing to compare with on the Macintosh. There are warpers on the Mac...like Flo, Elas Reality and Morph...and Photoshop has many great filters. Li Picture has an excellent distort brush tool. All those things are gre but the Barco mesh warper is the best thing I've found so far f doing many of the warping operations that I most often need.

I am also a beta site for Photoshop on the Silicon Graphi machine. Just recently they came out with version 3.0.

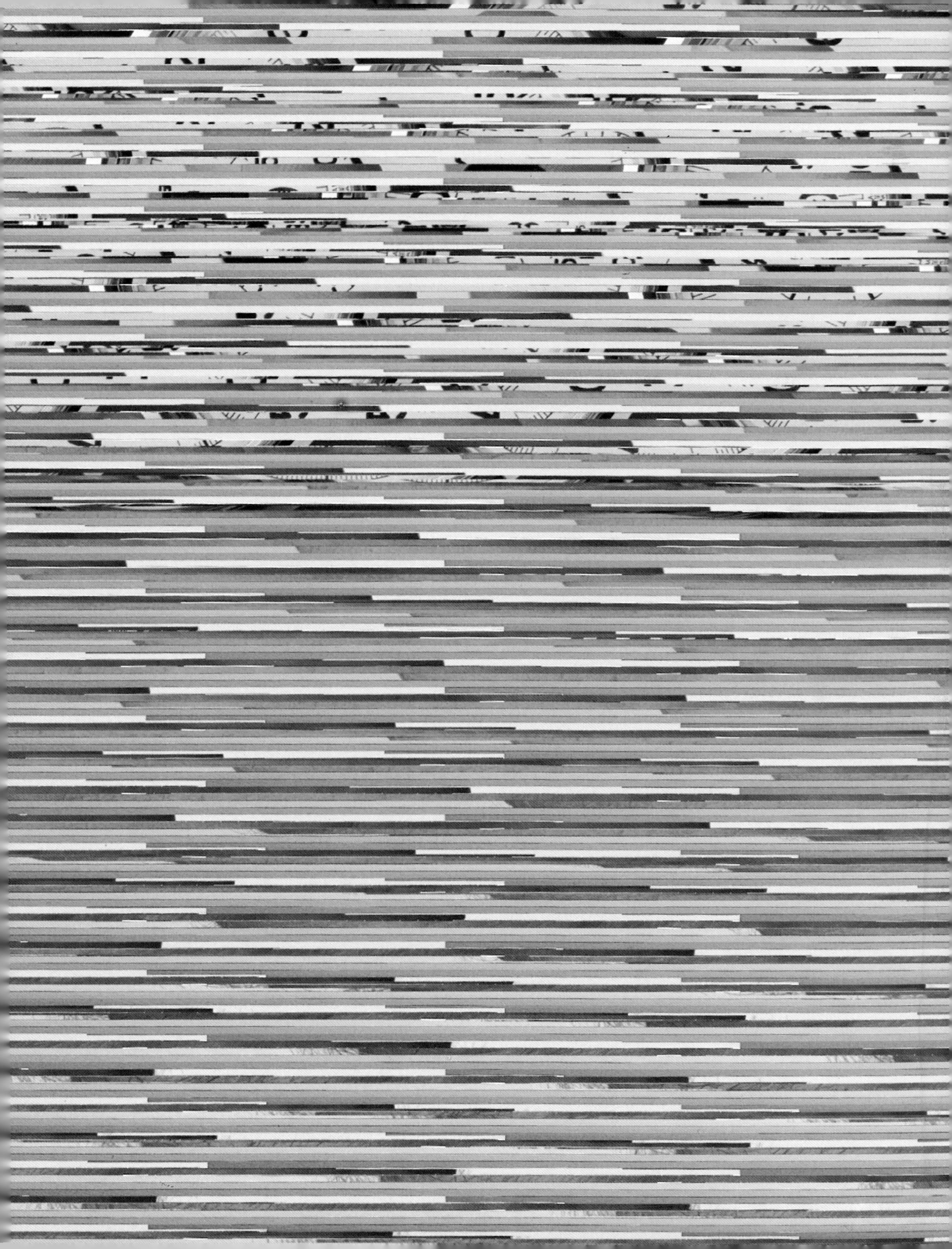

Robert Bowen

I'm connecting the SGI to the Mac with a product called Xinet. This is a high-speed Ethernet, and it works extraordinarily well. So, for a little more than the amount of time that it takes to load a file from a local hard disk, you can move a file from the SGI to the Mac. It's fast.

I bring in all of my scanned data through the Silicon Graphics machine using a UNIX utility called TAR. I use DAT as my principal storage medium and for moving the data in and out to the service bureau.

I work very closely with a service bureau called Graphic Systems Group. They do all of my scanning and transparency outputs. I don't do these operations in-house because I just don't want to. 8x10 transparency output devices and similar quality scanners are very expensive. To justify owning one you really have to be pushing work through it all day long. And then you would become a service bureau. I have never wanted to do that. I want to concentrate on the creative work.

Anyway, on the Macintosh we run Photoshop and Live Picture. Then there's the various PostScript programs like Quark Express, Adobe Illustrator, and others...as well as word processing software. I also do bookkeeping on the Macintosh.

But the Silicon Graphics machine really empowers me with the ability to create anything that I can imagine. The Macintosh is a sort of support for that. I use the two together, and they are both absolutely necessary.

Could you tell us about other tools that you use such as scanners, printers, etc.?

The in-house scanner is a Nikon ScanTouch, which is a good flat-bed scanner. I use that for scanning in all kinds of reflective and transparent art. It's an enabling device that allows me to get layouts or anything else imaginable scanned into my computer. The quality is perfect for comping, but for final art I need higher quality.

And for printers...at the moment I have a 600 DPI black and whi laser printer. Soon I may purchase a dye-sublimation printer or good color laser printer. Currently I'm using the service burea for proof prints. What's interesting is that more and more I' sending in-progress work out for approval over the Internet. Mo agencies now have an Internet account.

I also have a Syquest and a CD-ROM reader. We are getting CD-ROM writer. That's about it for equipment.

What other upcoming tools do you need, and what kind improvements do you want for the existing tools?

I've been working with computer graphics for almost a decad When I first started, it was impossible to buy quality, off-th shelf graphics software. You had to write your own. I made simple wire frame modeller on a VAX computer with which I cou do some transforms of basic primitives: scale, rotate an translate. I had the idea that I'd like to combine this work wi photography. It was something I could see happening down th road. Of course that's the kind of work I am doing now, but decade ago there wasn't any way to do it.

Software is getting easier to use all the time. The graphical us interface for these tools has become increasingly intuitive. Som of the 3-D tools are still quite challenging. But they will als become more transparent. Also, of course, hardware performanc is getting better. The next Macintosh computer I buy will probab be a 10-times speed-up over the one I currently use. And if yo can close the speed gap along with making the interfaces mo intuitive then the creative process will be less constrained.

However I don't really feel limited by my current tools. What I' doing is amusing, and part of the amusement is that it's changin It used to be that if you were an artist, for instance a painte you'd work in a studio for many years under the master in ord to learn technique, and if you had good taste you might go on become a master yourself. Now, with all of these convenie tools at your disposal, technique has gotten easier to achiev You don't have to spend all those years working towards th

2. Digital Man
Photographer: Ryszard Horowitz
Art Director: Diane Lazarus
Agency: Bozell
Client: Unisys

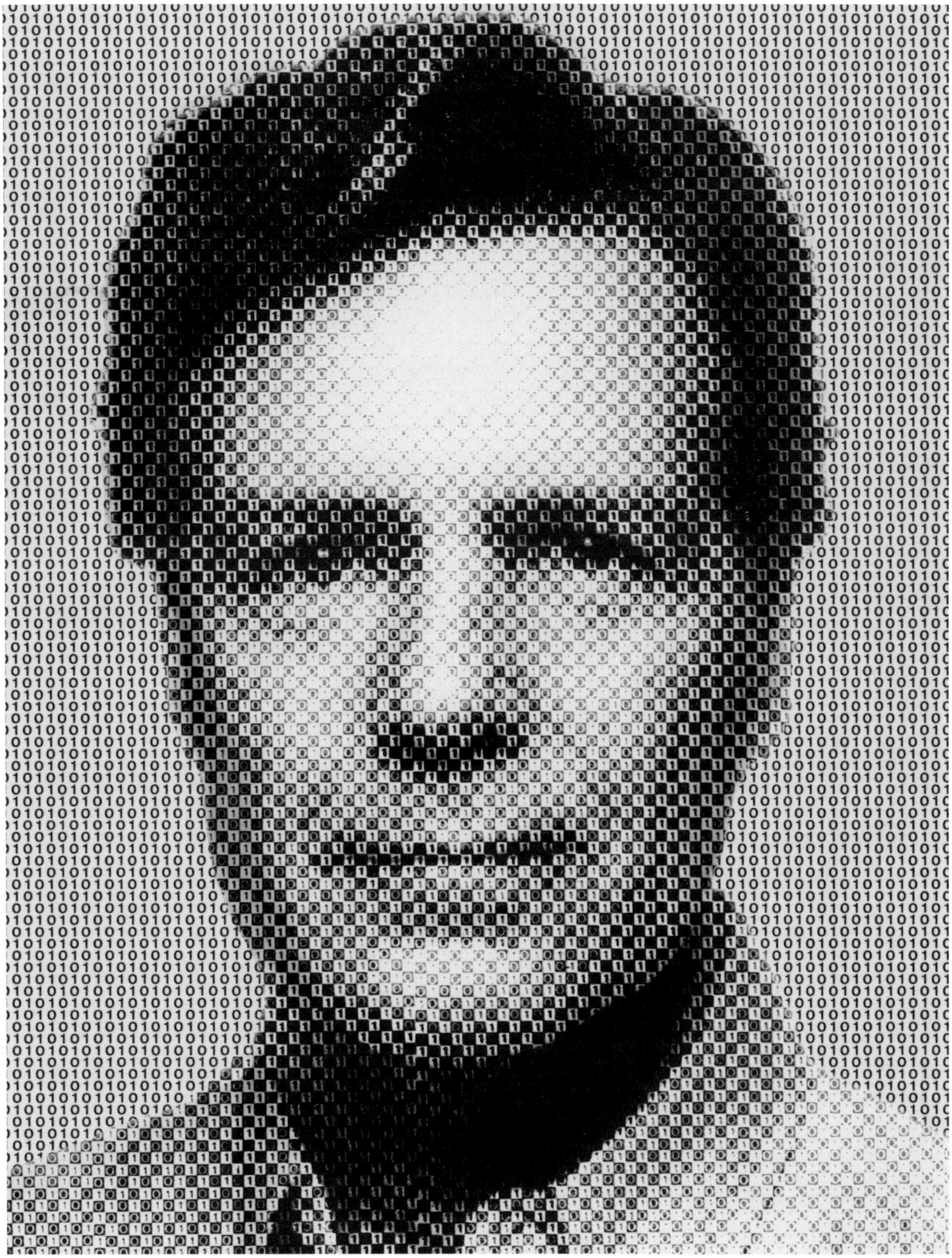

2.

Robert Bowen

3. Bass Player
Photographer: Eric Meola
Art Director: Bronson Smith
Agency: Avrett Free & Ginsburg
Client: Johnnie Walker Black Label

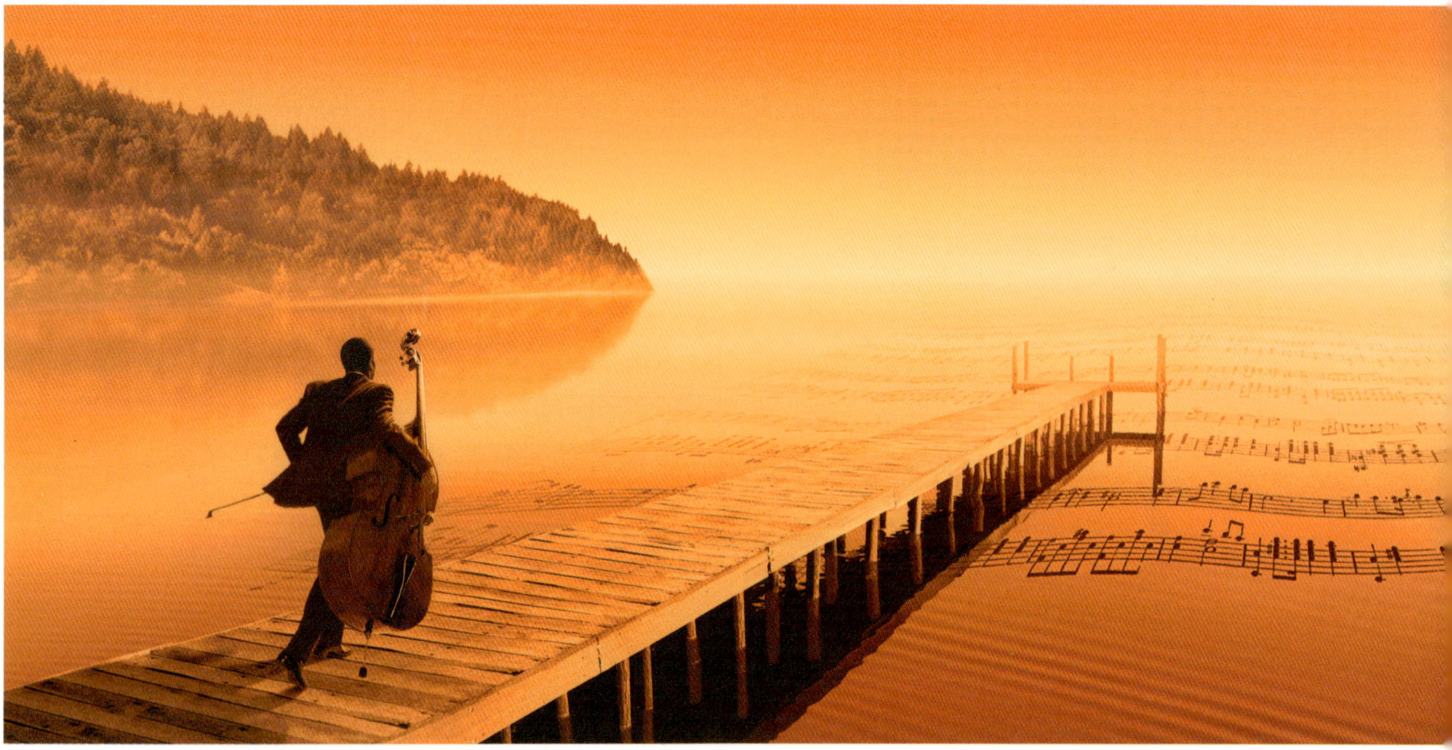

3.

articular goal. But you still need to have good ideas and good ste. These attributes will always be rare. This is one of the ways at the art-making process has changed. The flip side is that a omputer artist must continuously adjust to an ever-changing ray of tools. You have to read journals and be prepared to gularly change the way you do things. Otherwise, you will agnate. Before this technology appeared an artist's craft was r more stable.

hat is your opinion of the relation between video and still hotography? What meaning does each have for you?

hat we've been observing over the last five years is that image chnologies for film, video and print are being processed more nd more with the exact same equipment, sometimes referred as "white box" technology. The difference between a white ox and a black box is that the latter is a dedicated machine hich does only one thing. Whereas with a white box, for example Silicon Graphics machine or a Macintosh, you can do many ings. You can write your novel, make a movie, do photo-ompositing for advertising, whatever you like. It's just a question what software to choose along with the most important thing, hich is having the knowledge you need to do the job.

hough the work may be done with the same hardware and with oftware tools that look and feel similar, it remains an easily verlooked fact that all these disciplines are different. Even ough anyone with a computer may have access to sophisticated pographic design tools, this doesn't mean that all of these eople are type designers.

R. Greenburg Associates I had the experience of working on ature films, large-scale TV commercials and also print dvertising. It was very enriching to work with such a large group extremely talented people on such a variety of projects. And ow throughout the industry there's a lot of action in interactive edia, and in particular the current excitement over the branch the Internet known as the World Wide Web. But for the moment, all of this, I have chosen to specialize in digital photography.

The digital camera has revolutionized DTP. What do you think about this?

I think that, as digital camera technology improves, it is inevitable that for most applications film will become obsolete. More that 90% of all film sales are in the consumer area anyway and that portion of the industry is just waiting for a real cheap digital camera. I don't have any idea how many years it will take to replace the conventional film camera, but it's already making inroads in photojournalism and catalog photography. It will be some time yet before it conquers high-end advertising because it's slower and more cumbersome, and the resolution of most of these cameras isn't high enough. There are some digital backs which do have a high resolution. I, myself, along with other photographers whom I work with, are extremely interested in this technology. I'm always testing new things. Some of the work that I do has many small objects flying around. Although digital cameras might not be good for creating location backgrounds, for imaging small objects in the studio, I think it could be perfect.

I think it's just a matter of time before almost all photography will be grainless.

These days, images are being increasingly rendered as digital data. What are the advantages and disadvantages of this?

Remember that at the moment we are only a few years into this technology, and film is for now a convenient middleman process. In the advertising world I often deliver 8 x 10 transparencies. They are easy to see, and from them you may engrave for many usages. They also give you a point of reference, something to compare to. It's crazy, though, the way it works...it starts off as photography, which is analog. The photography is scanned in, and then it's digital. Then it's manipulated on the computer after which it's often output to another transparency. So then it's analog again. Then it's scanned back in on Scitex for separation. So once again it's digital. Then it's printed, where it's analog again. So it's always going back and forth between analog and digital the whole time. That's crazy. And yet it seems to work for the things that I've been doing.

Robert Bowen

And in the next few years we will close the loop between color spaces across different devices...these will improve significantly from the scanning process all the way through final engraving. There are a lot of color calibration systems which are getting better. What you'd like to have to happen is that, what you see on the screen is exactly what you get in the final magazine or the book. A lot of people are working on this. It's a big business. So its inevitable that it will evolve to the point where what you see is what you get. But we'll have to wait a little longer.

How do you see commercial photography changing in the future due to digital imaging?

I think what's going to happen is that a lot of photography will become even more of an assembly-line process. And the difference between creative photography and other types of photography will become greater.

Obviously, in my work I can do practically anything with photographs. But there's something that the real photograph carries with it, a kind of essence. The real photography in the picture is the soul of the picture. It's something slightly unexpected that would be impossible to create in other ways. It's a kind of magical moment, if you will. Great photographers know how to achieve this more often. Those photographers will always be in demand. The fact is that with the exception of the product shot it is possible now to build an advertising campaign out of stock images. But unless you have a unified photographic eye that runs throughout all the elements then the work just doesn't come together with the same kind of dynamism.

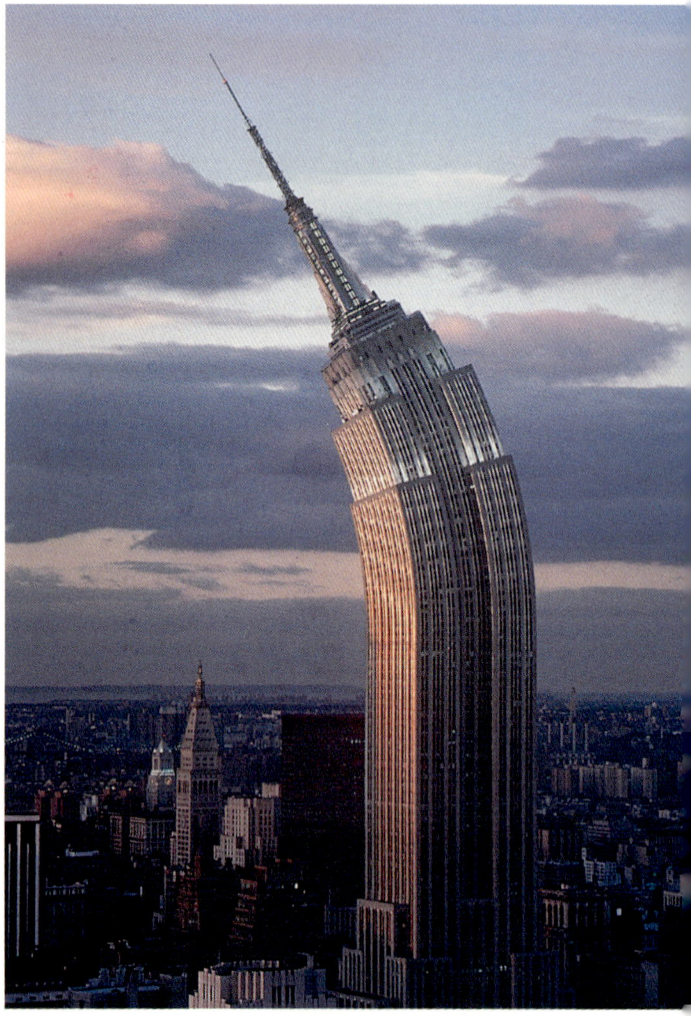

4.

What is your vision of the future?

I think that visual effects imagery is, in a cultural sense, the most distilled form of our digital technology. Visual effects entertainment is directly connected to technological progress. The first special-effects photography was ghost photography. We look at early ghost photography today and for the most part it all looks fake. Of course most of it was deliberately faked, but to us we see in these pictures a lot of cheap darkroom tricks. As

4. Empire Bend
©R/Greenberg Assoc. 1991
created with Jaques Stroweis
at R/Greenberg Assoc.
Client: Kodak

5. Instinet
Photographer: Ryszard Horowitz
Art Director: Mark VonUlrich
Agency: Capital Vectors
Client: Instinet Corp.

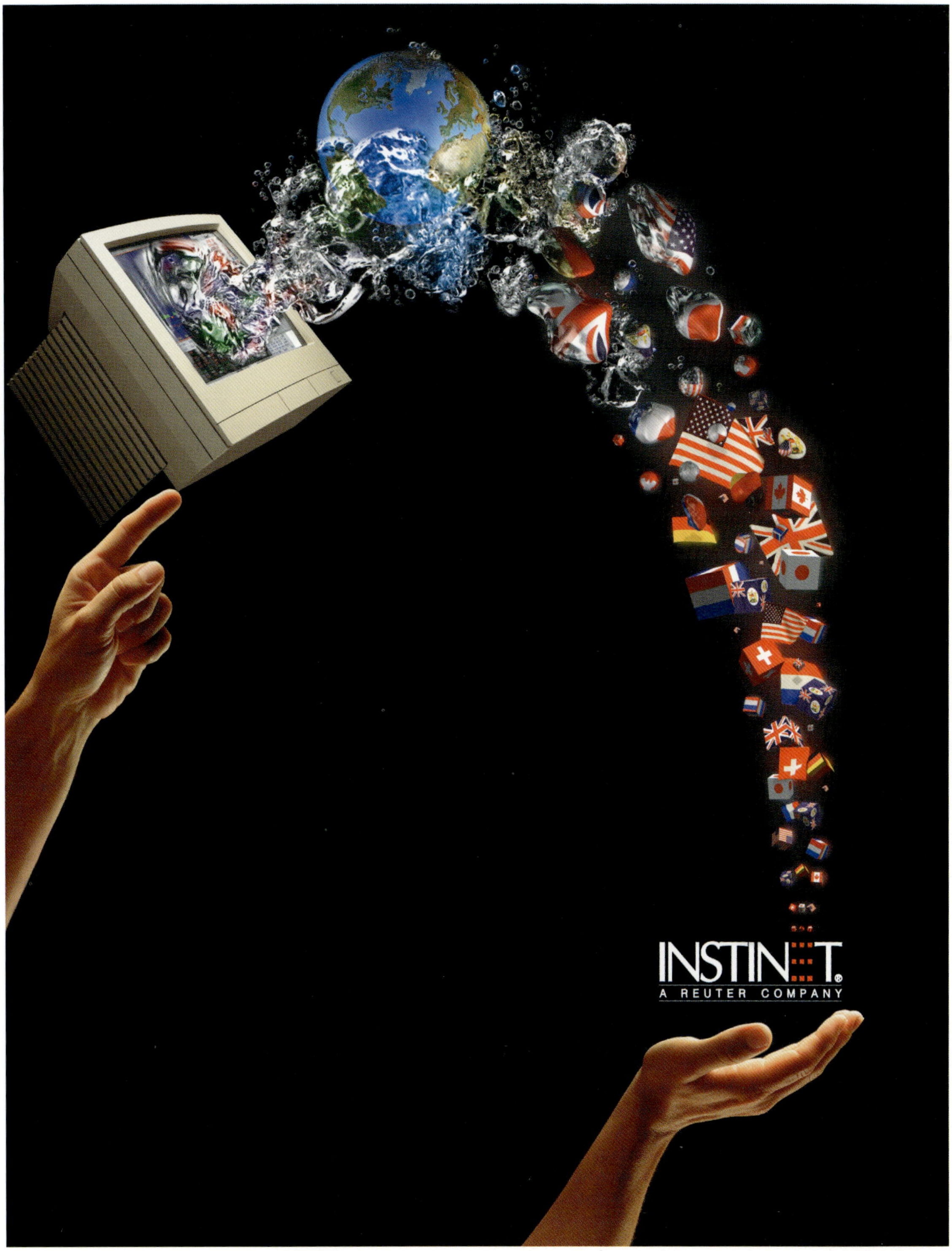

5.

a society, we are far more visually literate when it comes to effects, we can easily see that in the Victorian period they did a poor job with most of these images.

So the ante for visual effects entertainment and advertising imagery has been upped significantly over the years. What we desire is photo-realism. When we go to see a big specia-effects movie like *Jurassic Park,* we want the experience to succeed so that we can be entertained. And nobody today is ever suggesting that these dinosaurs are actually real. But if the film is done photorealistically, it will succeed in establishing an illusion. The historical analog to this is trompe-l'oeil painting, which in French means "trick of the eye." A trompe-l'oeil painter learned to paint a little jewel or an insect, in such a way that it looked convincingly real. In experiencing the visual effects imagery you apprehend the real surface of the picture, whether it's the canvas, screen or the pixels, and at the same time you apprehend the illusionistic space. The illusionistic space is what's portrayed within the picture. It's the objects in the overall perspective. So, for an effect to work, you apprehend both the grain of the film as it is projected on the screen and the illusion.

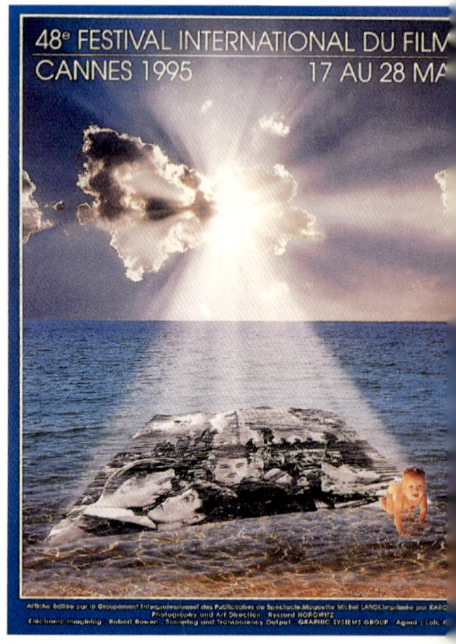

6.

Technology is enabling us to make a synthetic image which is more and more photorealistic. And at the same time, to make things not easily distinguishable from reality. In the future those lines will blur even more. Right now, virtual reality is a low-resolution experience, but it will seem more real as the resolution increases. So there are perhaps some potential difficulties in blurring our imagination with reality. The next generation will have to deal with that. But really, all we can do about this for the moment is sit back and enjoy ourselves.

What projects are you planning next?

I have been collecting and synthesizing images containing digital noise patterns. Two of these images are in this book (p. 69, p. 81). I have the idea that information is a form of noise. As we live our everyday lives, we read books and magazines, and we see advertisements everywhere...We go to school, come to know people, do business. We do all of these things. And all kinds of noisy information is filtered through us.

6. 1995 Cannes Film Festival Poster
   Photographer: Ryszard Horowitz
7. Anamorph
   This is an anamorphic picture and is meant to be viewed with a mirrored cylinder.

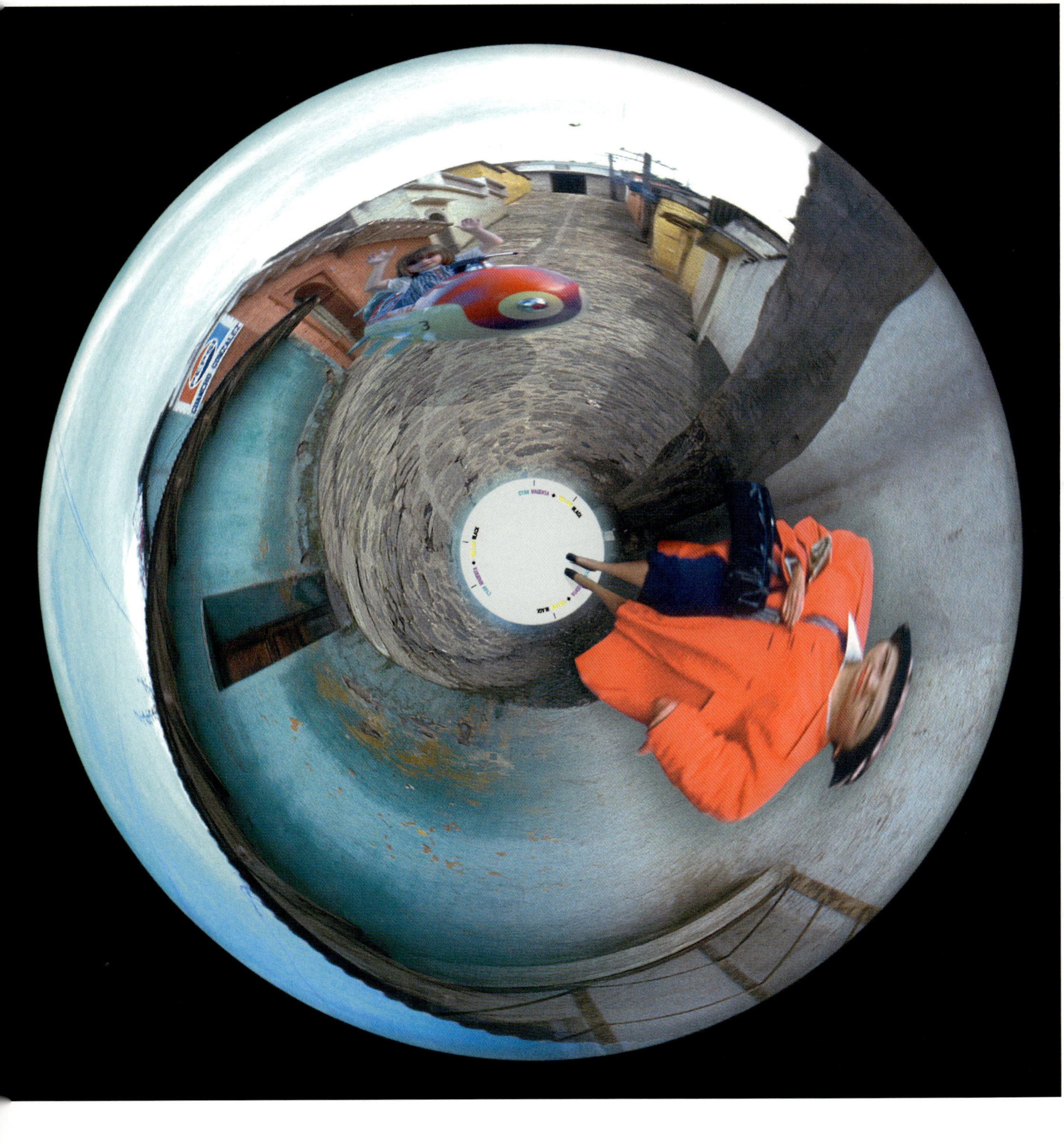

Robert Bowen

And so I've come to look on this information as fields of noise. I'm interested in the way our own ideas and images emerge in response to this information. So I see these images as mind maps.

Those images represent one project. I have also been collecting images for a project that's been ongoing which is a history of handbills. Handbills are the most primitive form of advertising. They are items just handed out or sometimes left in the streets. Early handbills were woodblock prints. But what we've seen in the last decade is that the technology for creating these has gone from analog to digital. So I've been collecting hand bills through this transition period. It is very interesting to see the strategies of distribution for these images, and the kinds of information which are distributed in this way. And I'd like to put all of this into a book. This distills my interest in advertising. Of course, handbills are a completely different form of advertising from the kind that I do. It is a microcosmic mirror of our culture. And a lot of interesting images emerge out of this primitive communication form.

In general the strength of much of my work comes from an involvement with perspective and often perspective correction. For example, one of the images in this book is the bass player for Johnny Walker Black Label (p. 72). We wanted a dock going out into the water in forced perspective. Because of seasonal and geographical constraints it could not be photographed on location. So we had a model maker make a miniature. The miniature would have taken far longer to build if it had been built in this extreme perspective. So instead he made a regular model and the photographer tried to push this perspective as far as possible. Then I had to do some 3-D perspective correction with texture mapping to get the final effect.

And one of the historical sources for this kind of work is stage design. Last week I went to a used book sale, and was terribly excited to find several books on the history of stage design.

In my fine-art work there are some very unusual perspectives, for example, anamorphoses. Some of this work is represented here.

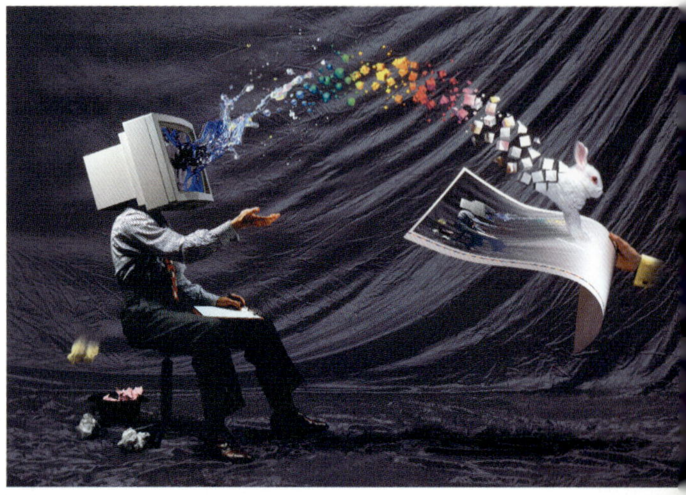

8.

8. Rabbit
Photographer: Ryszard Horowitz
Art Director: Mark VonUlrich
Client: Washburn Graphics
created with Joe Francis and Karen Sideman at R/Greenberg Assoc.
©Ryszard Horowitz and R/GA Print

9. Opposite: Fabric Woman
Photographer: Grant Peterson
Art Director: Dickan Donelian
Client: Shalimar

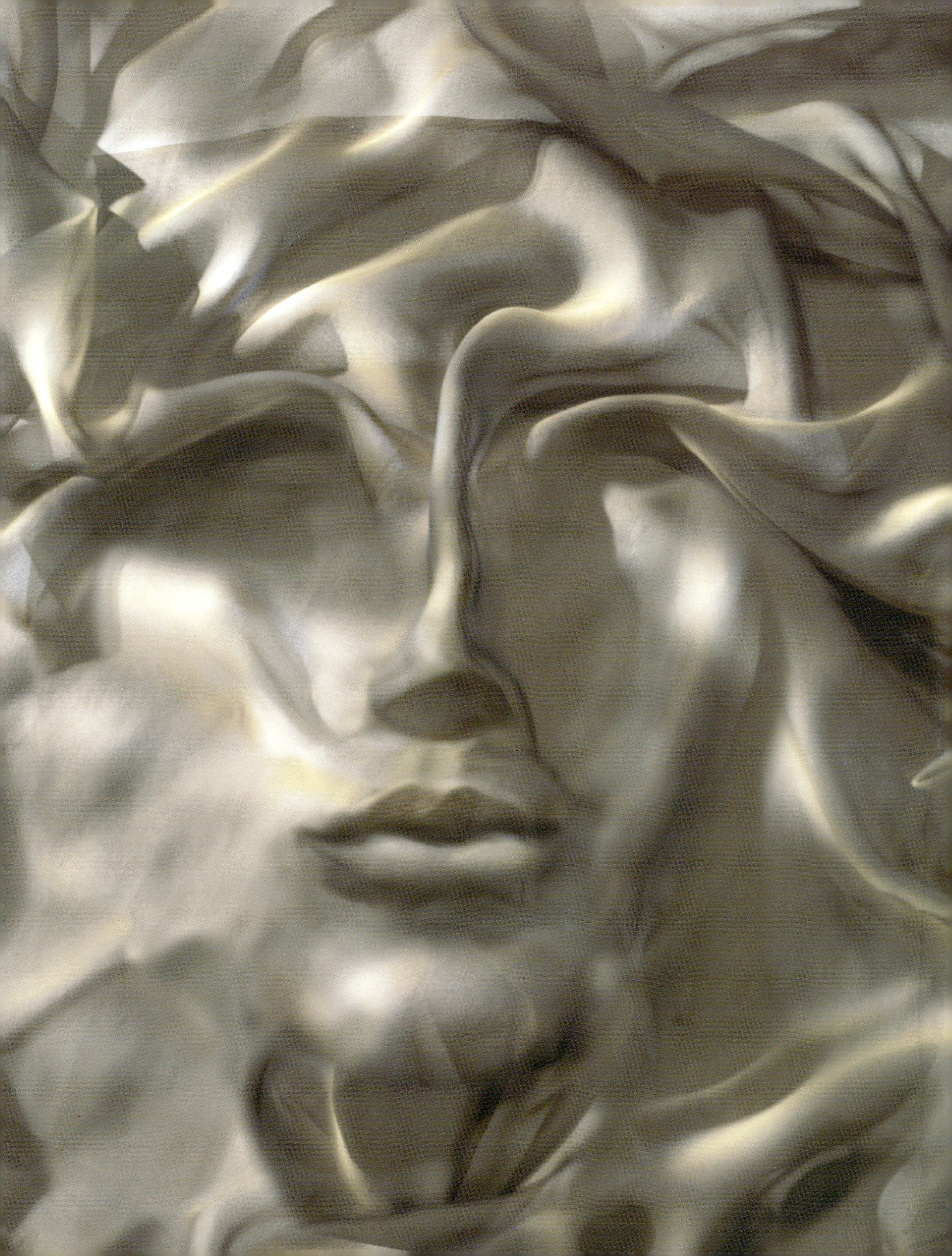

Robert Bowen

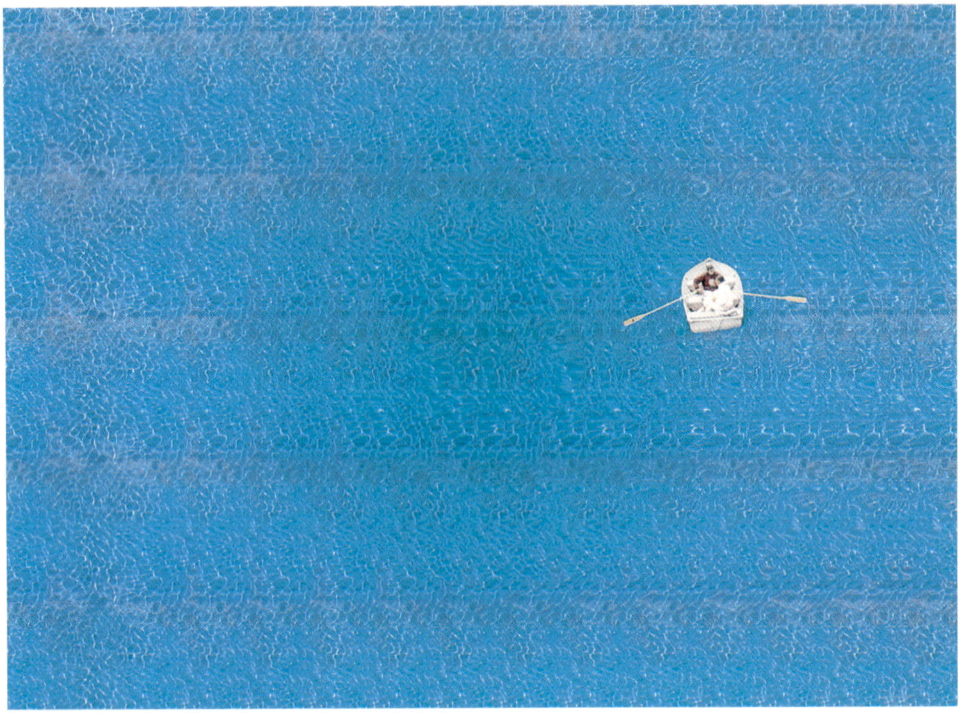

10.

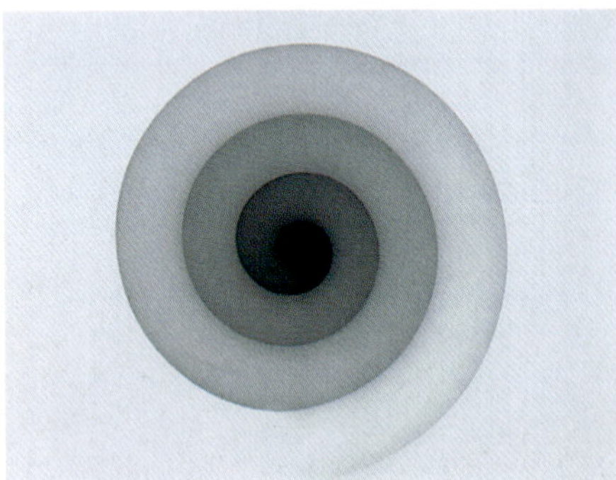

11.

10-11. Whirlpool
© R/Greenberg Assoc.1993
Created at R/Greenberg Assoc.
Note: This is a 3D random-dot stereogram
12. Circular Math

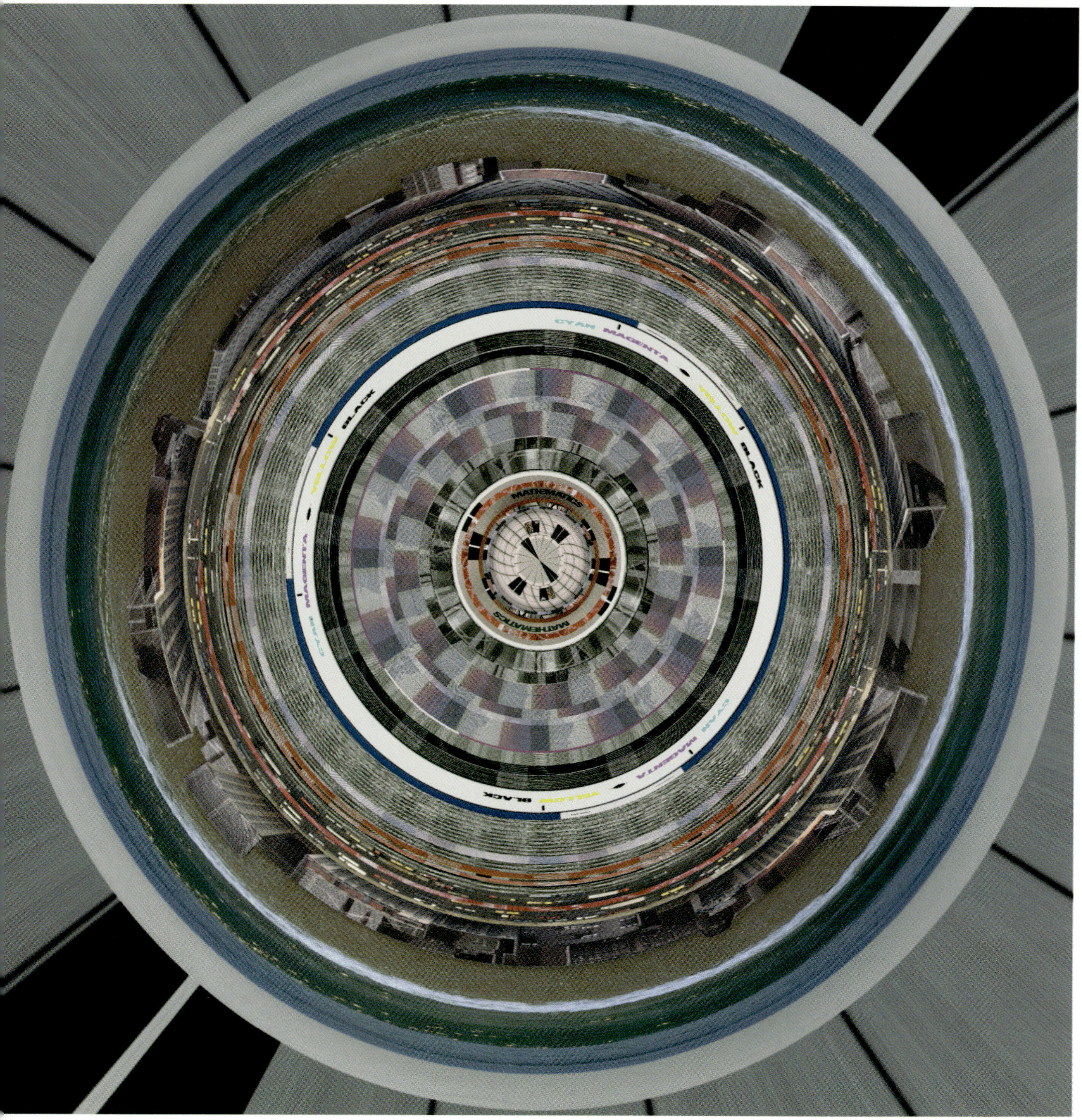

Robert Bowen

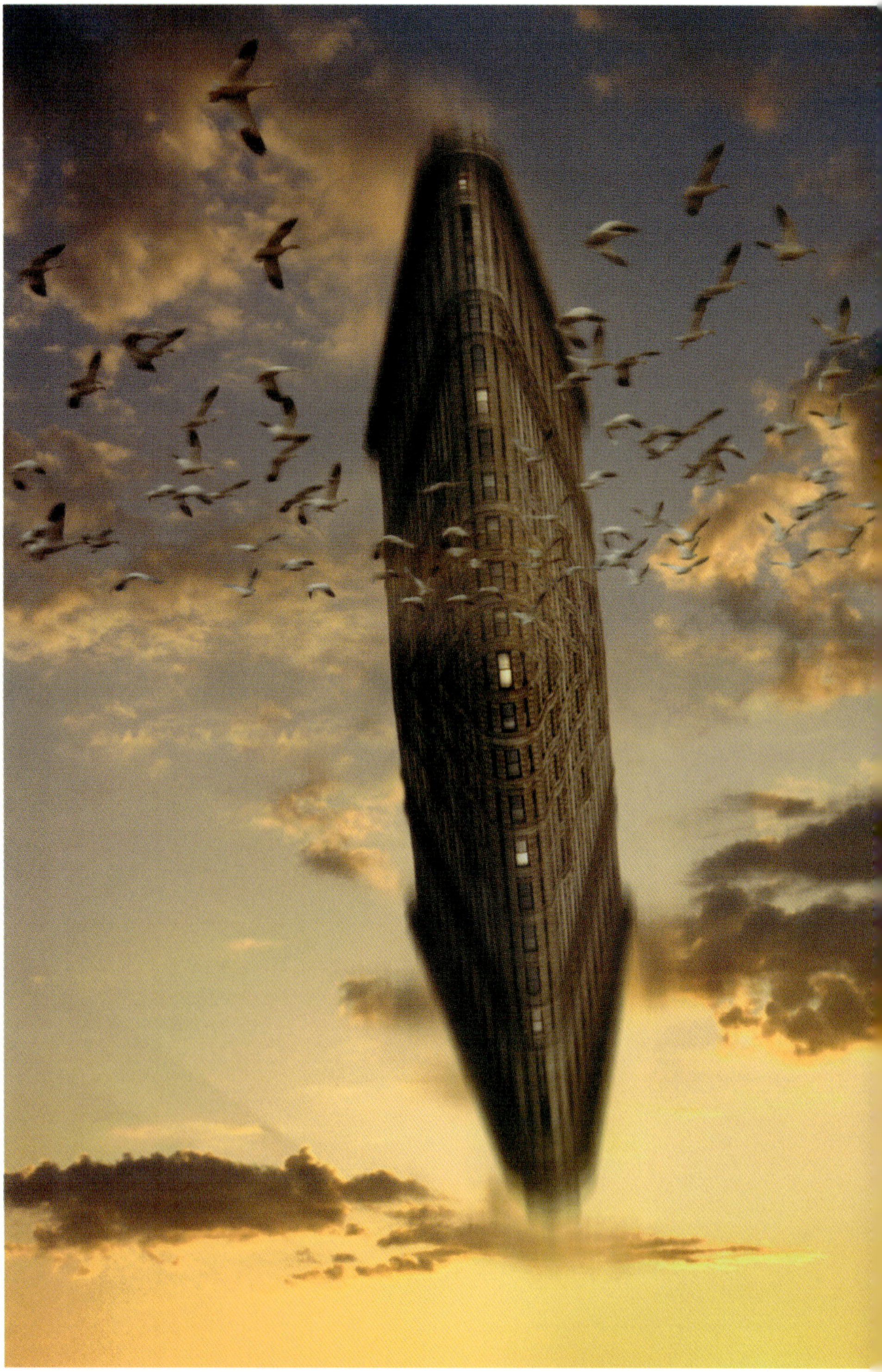

13.

13. Flatirony II
14. Portrait of Jerzy Kosinski
Photographer: Ryszard Horowitz

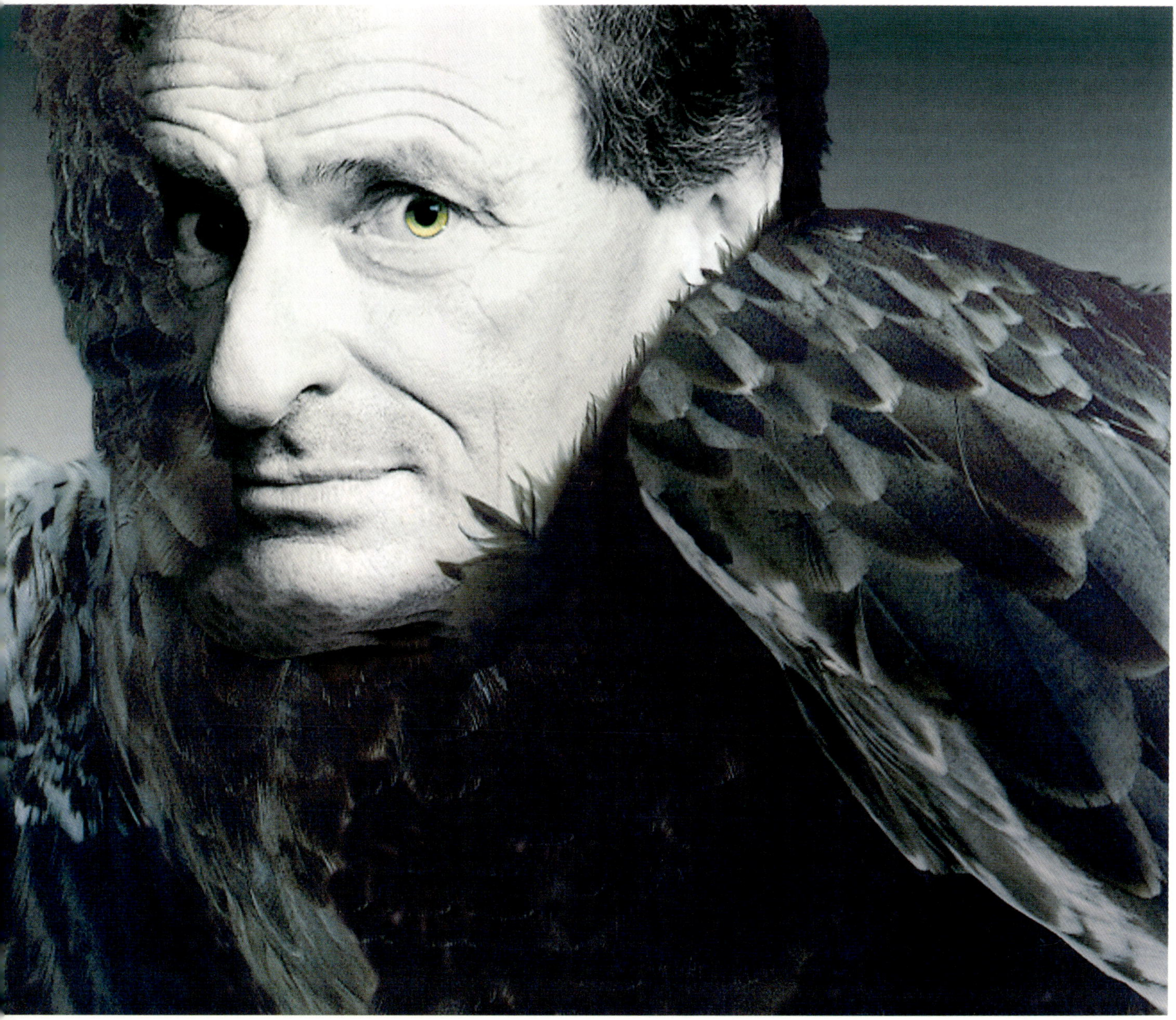

Robert Bowen

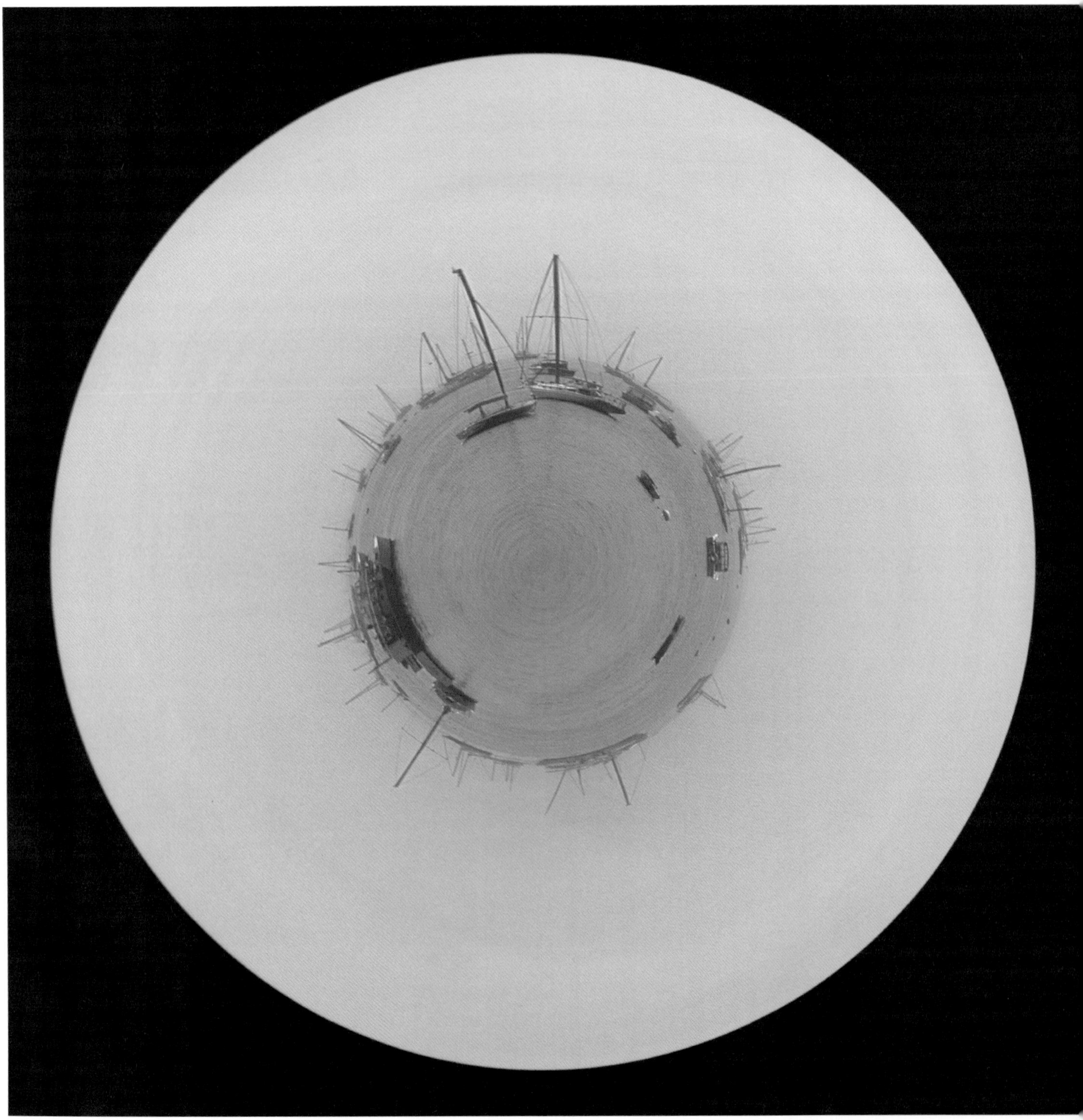

15.

15. Macrobe
16. Altec
Photographer: Ryszard Horowitz
Art Director: Chuck Taylor
Agency: Barenter Greenhouse and Webster
Client: Altec Lansing

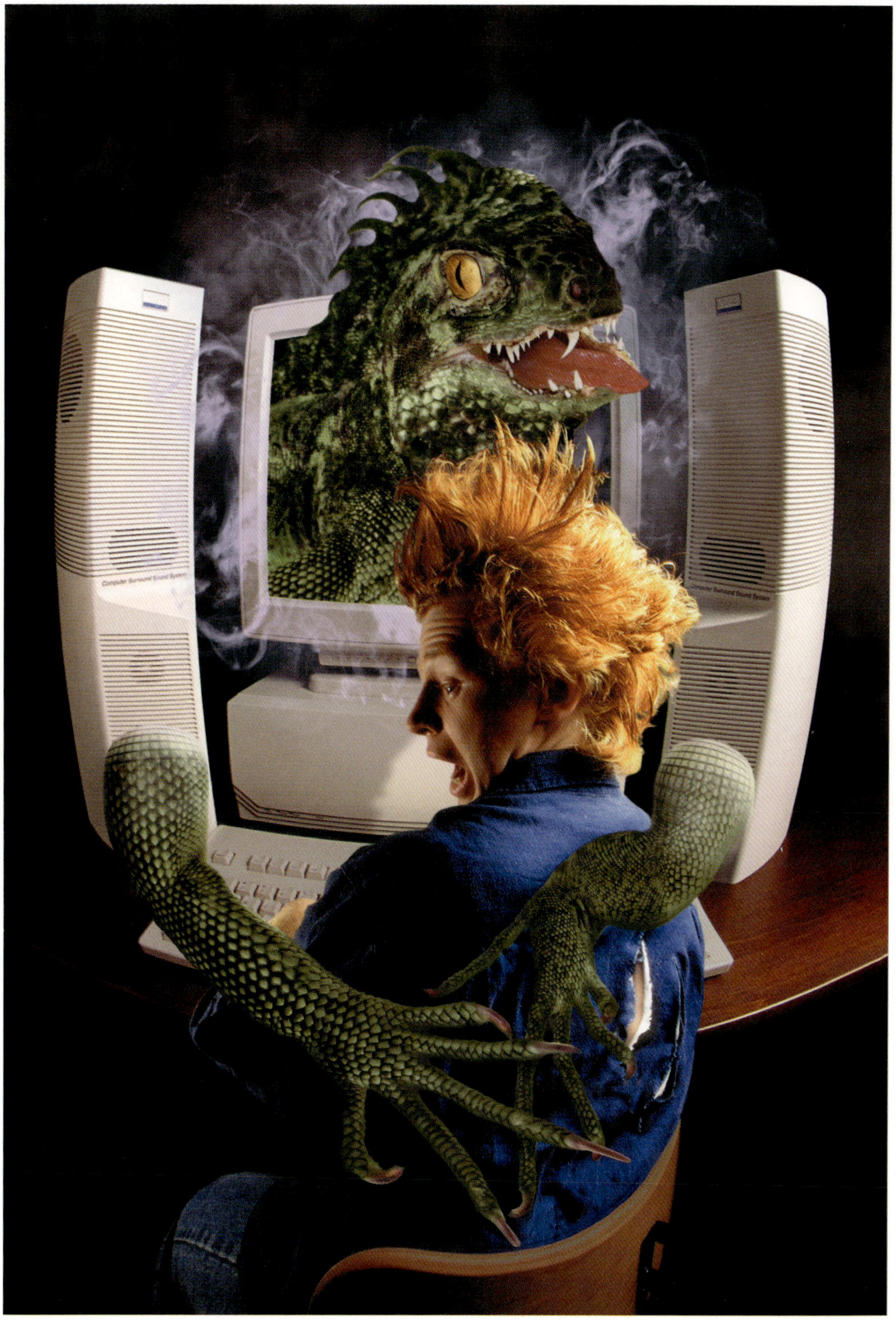

16.

Robert Bowen

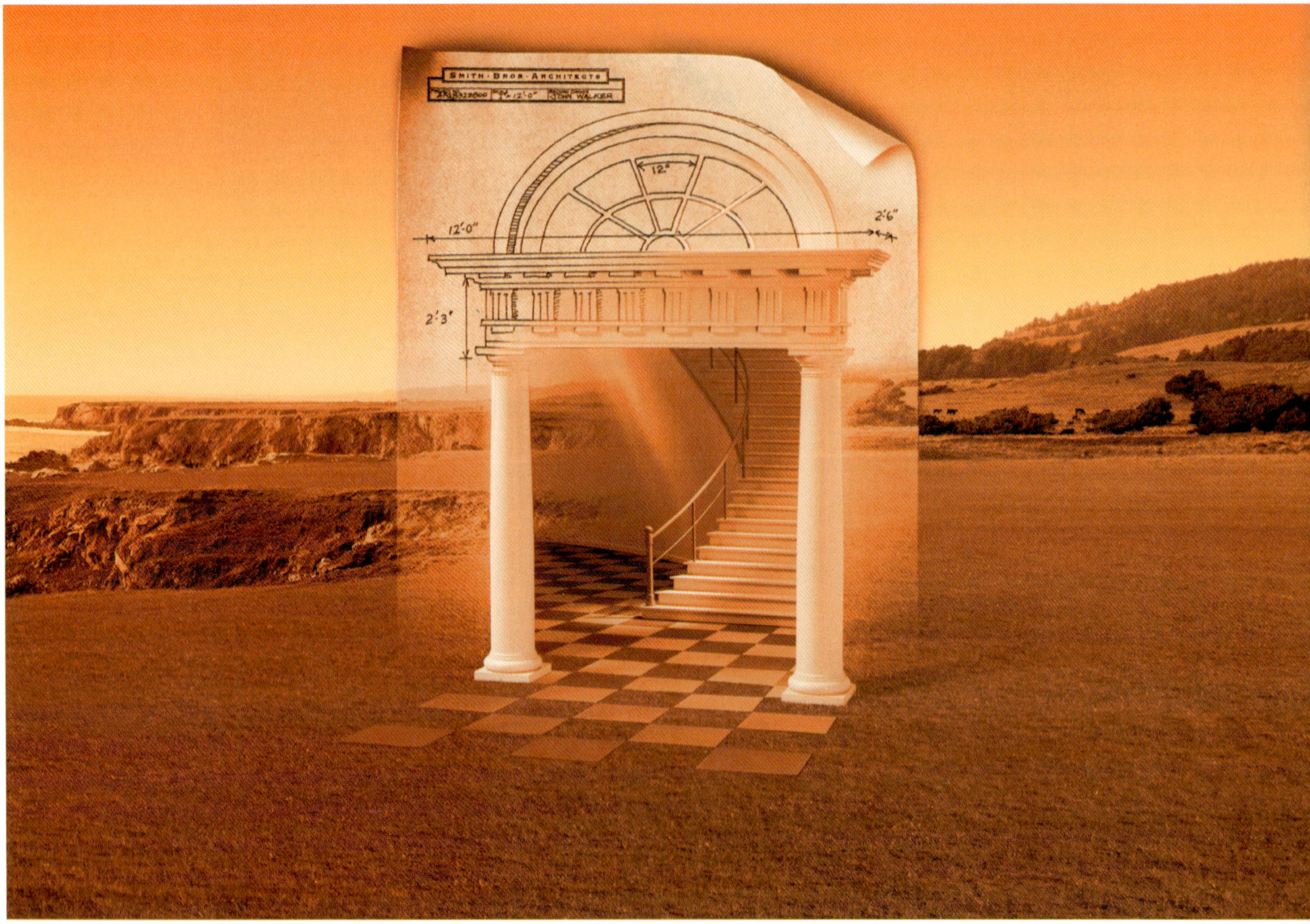

17.

17. Architect (detail)
    Photographer: Eric Meola
    Art Director: Bronson Smith
    Agency: Avrett Free & Ginsburg
    Client: Johnnie Walker Black Label
18. Musical Car
    Photographer: Steve Bronstein
    Agency: MARS
    Client: Harman Kardon

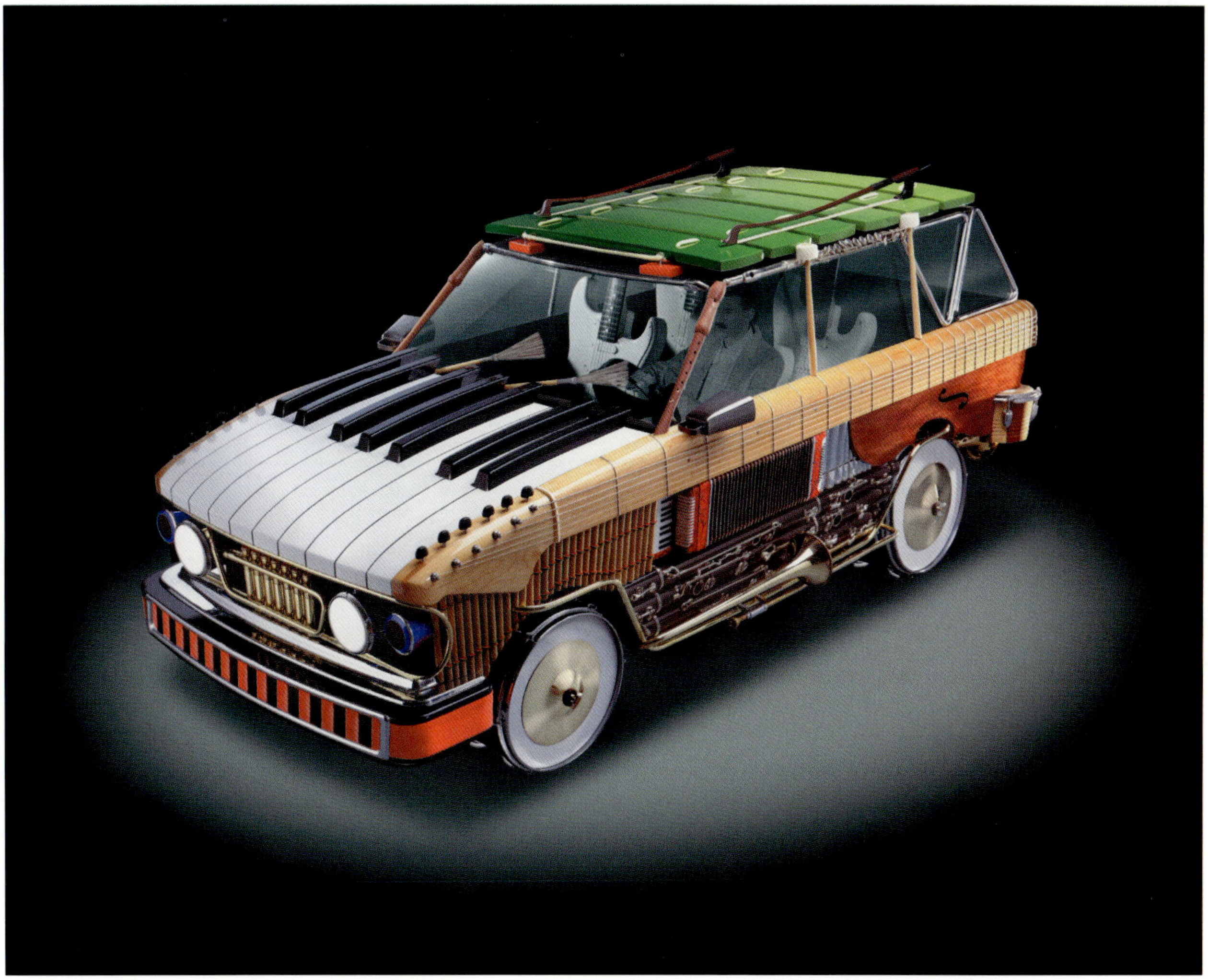

18.

Robert Bowen

19. Balancing Act © Howard Berman
Photographer: Howard Berman
Client: Computer Associates
created with Frank Lantz at R/Greenberg Assoc.

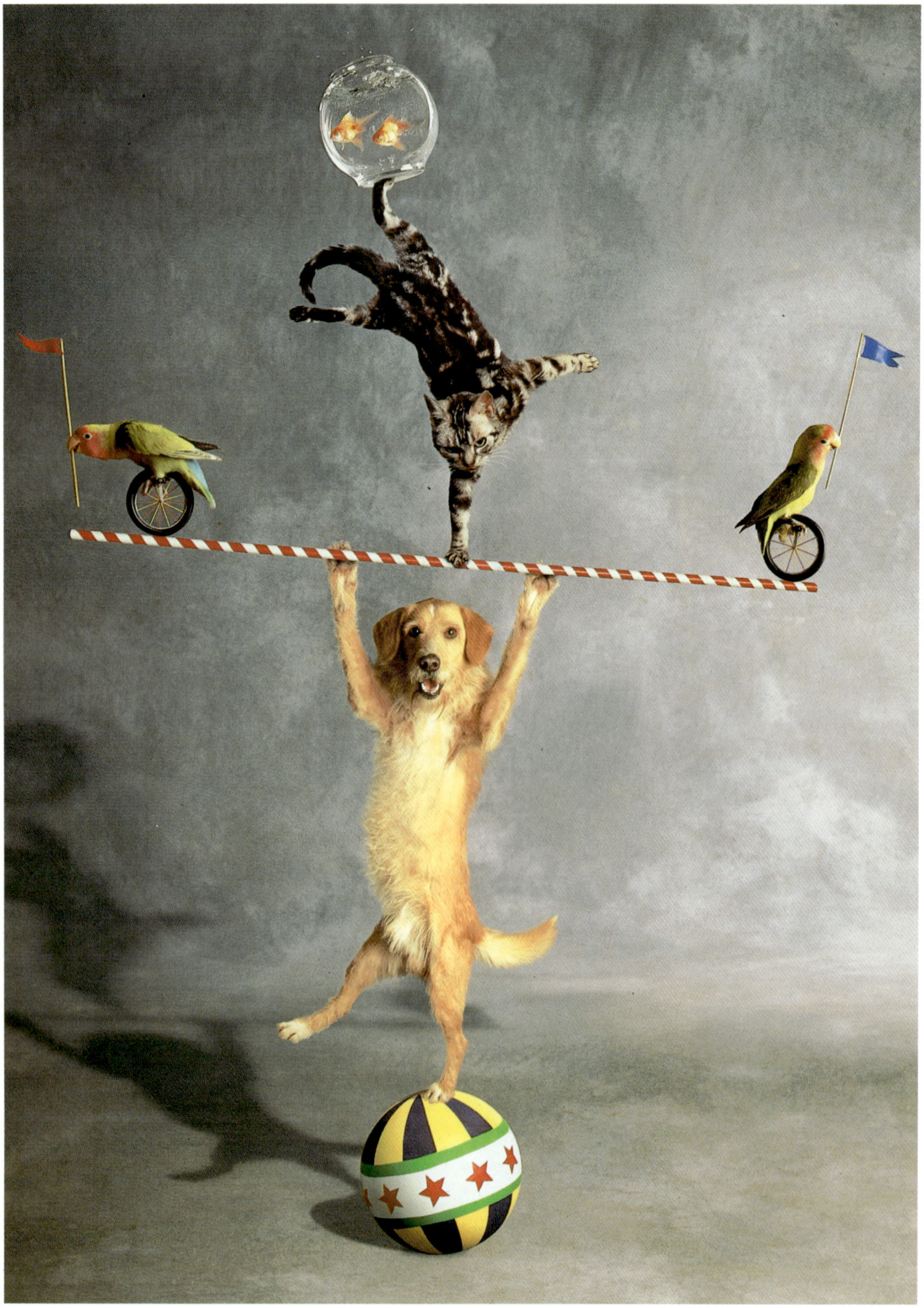

19.

Michel Tcherevkoff

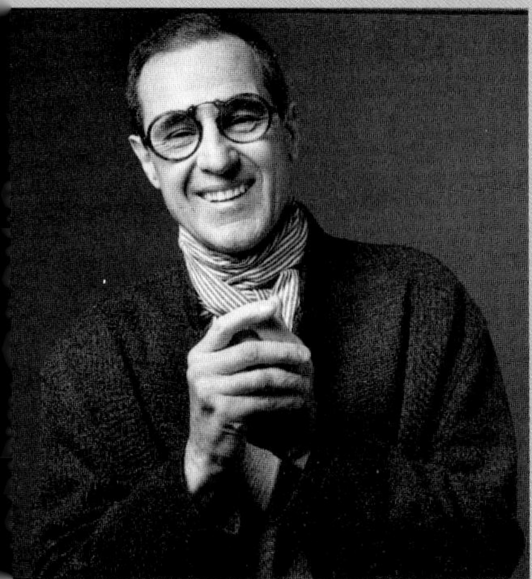

Michel Tcherevkoff is recognized as one of the world's pre-eminent conceptual photographers and is internationally known for his unique ability to create "visual metaphors" for clients such as Panasonic, Canon, Eastman Kodak, Estée Lauder, Federal Express, etc.

Years before the advent of computer technology, Michel was creating intricate images in-camera and in the darkroom. "I always thought of photographs that were more illustrative in nature — that told a strong story with a completely different approach."

Michel Tcherevkoff was born in Paris of Russian parents. After graduating from law school, Michel came to New York where a series of unrelated circumstances took him into photography. He is the vice president of the Advertising Photographers of New York, chairman of APNY's imaging technology committee, Creative Consultant on the Advisory Board to American Showcase Publishing and has been a guest speaker on Digital Technology Worldwide. He has received numerous awards for creative advertising and editorial imagery, and has had exhibitions of his work all over the world.

Michel Tcherevkoff

How did you get started in professional photography?

I was visiting my sister in New York after I finished law school in France. My sister was a model, and was living with a photographer. I fell in love with what I perceived to be the glamorous lifestyle of fashion photography, beautiful models, traveling and so on. I decided I wanted to be involved in all that. But I quickly realized that it was the *photography* and not the lifestyle that interested me.

I got a job as an assistant with a photographer who opened my mind, and encouraged me to explore and discover what he saw as my talent for visualization. Because I had no formal training in this medium, I could bring to my work a point of view that was, at the time "radical" and completely fresh.

I continued assisting for four years with different photographers, learning as much as I could about technique. Then I started on my own on the strength of one job a month for one client. It was for a cosmetics account. Meanwhile I continued to work for magazines like *Glamour, House Beautiful, Forbes, Fortune, Discover* and many others. The editorial work built my portfolio.

But to really "make it" in the business, I would have to get involved in advertising photography. I searched for an agent, and found one that I liked, and who liked me. The agent was very good and very established and I immediately got to work on top-notch accounts. After a couple of years, I was able to get some of the best work in New York.

Before the emergence of computer technology, you were creating intricate images in-camera and in the darkroom. Could you tell us about the differences between the traditional methods of photography and working on the computer?

The techniques are basically very different. When I was working in traditional photography I wanted to push the limits of what was technically feasible. I was constantly inventing techniques to achieve the effects I wanted. Even now I am always looking for ways of doing effects that enhance the photography, or give

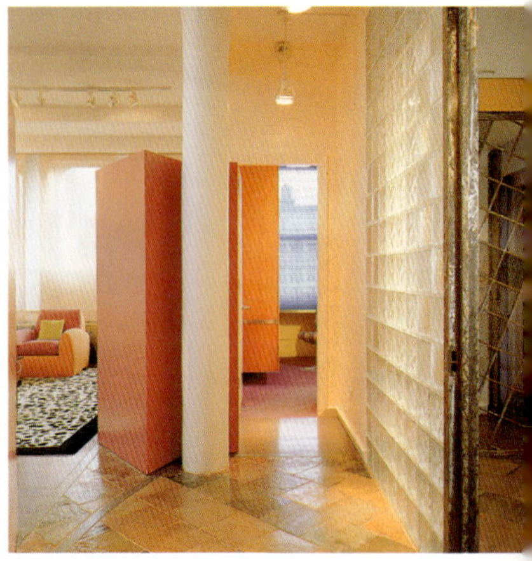

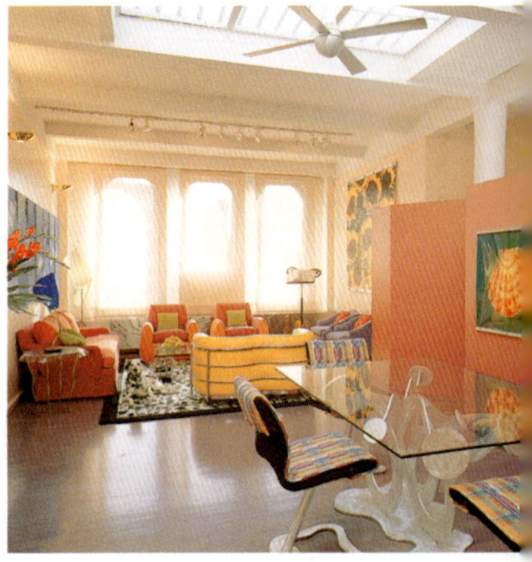

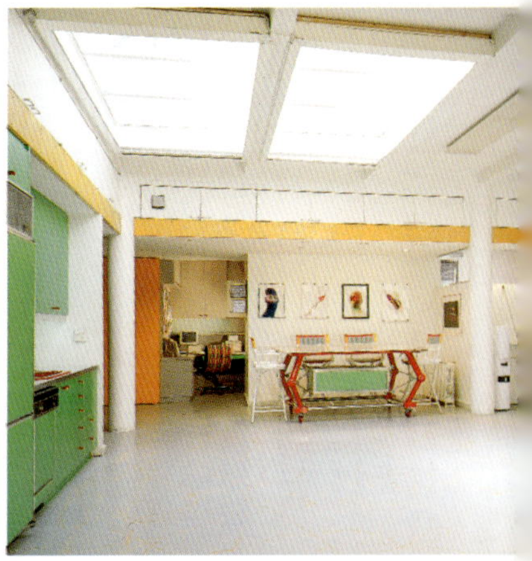

Michel Tcherevkoff's Studio

a-h. Work Steps: Flying Basketball

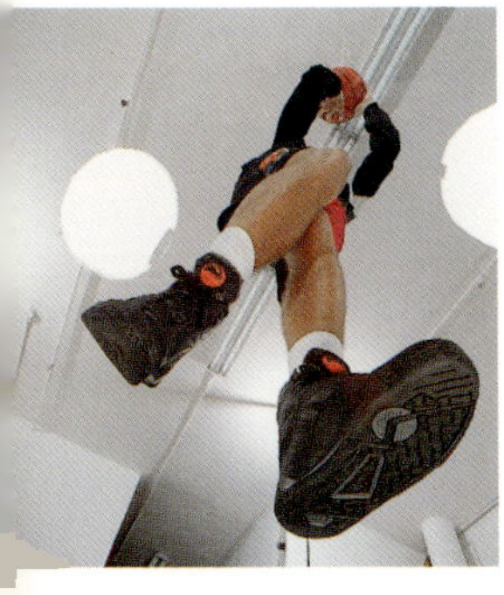

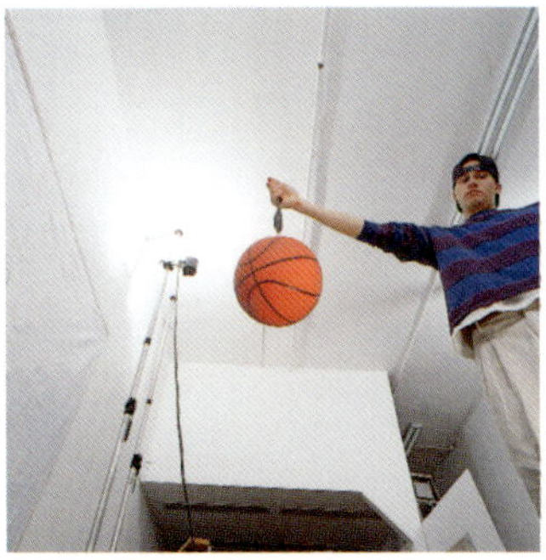

c.

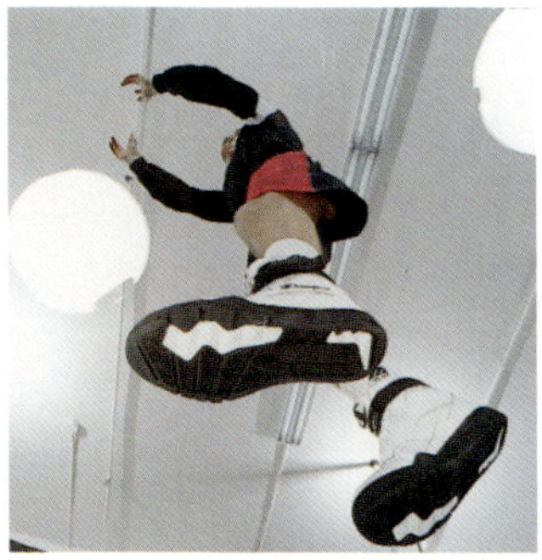

e.

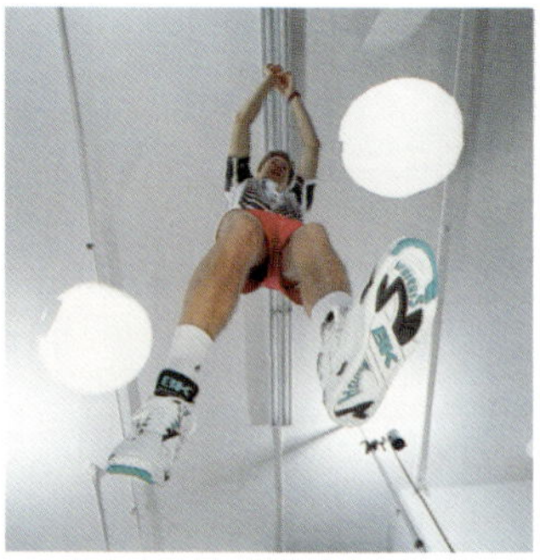

g.

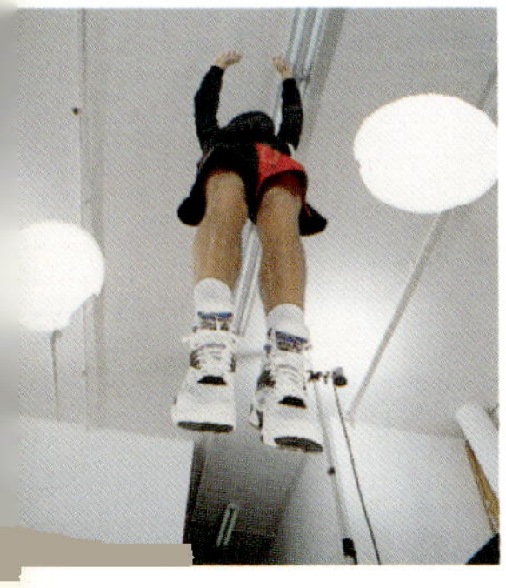

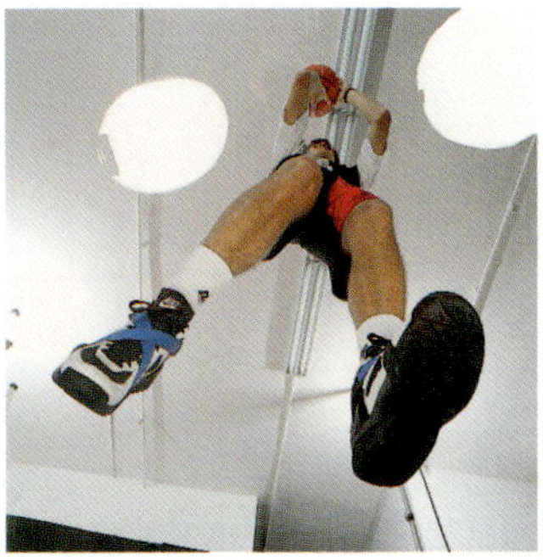

d.

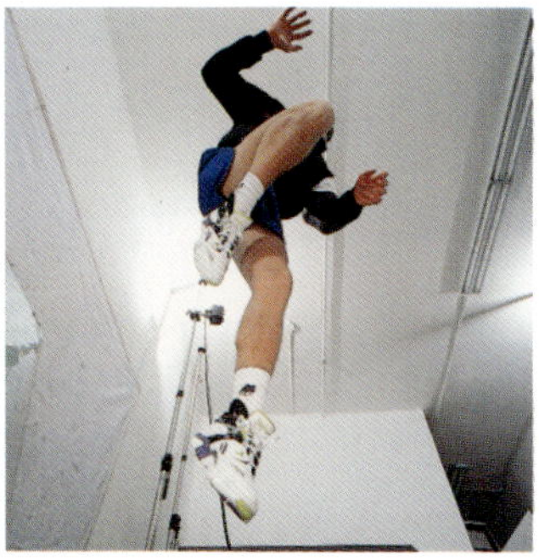

f.

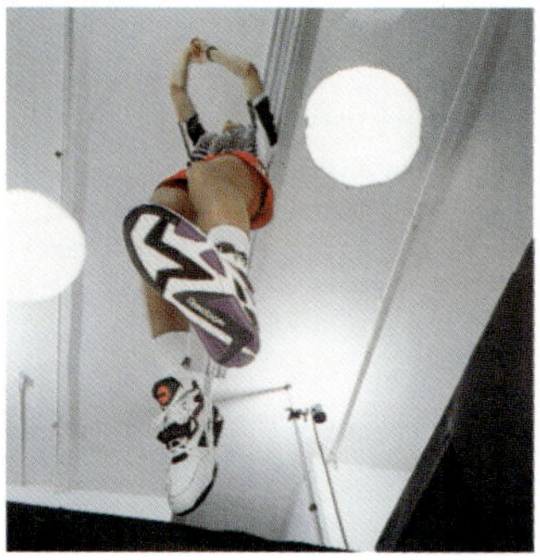

h.

'or the concept, I was thinking how much fun ould be if basketball were played without a r, without a ceiling — and with the players just ıg in the air. Our art director was asking me to trate a story on sneakers. He said, "Just make dance sneakers look good. I have X amount ollars and I need the image in two weeks."

ɜw it was a tough challenge. I wanted the bodies ɜally fly — to look absolutely weightless. The t thing about the editorial work is the great ortunity it gives photographers to experiment new ideas. Although the budget is generally the creative reward more than makes up for it.

t I used a digital camera and imported the ges at low res into the computer. Then I made rough layout on screen. Then I reshot all of images on film. I was able to scan, assemble retouch all of them right in the system. The visual was output and delivered to the client ın 8 x 10, on time and within the budget.

Michel Tcherevkoff

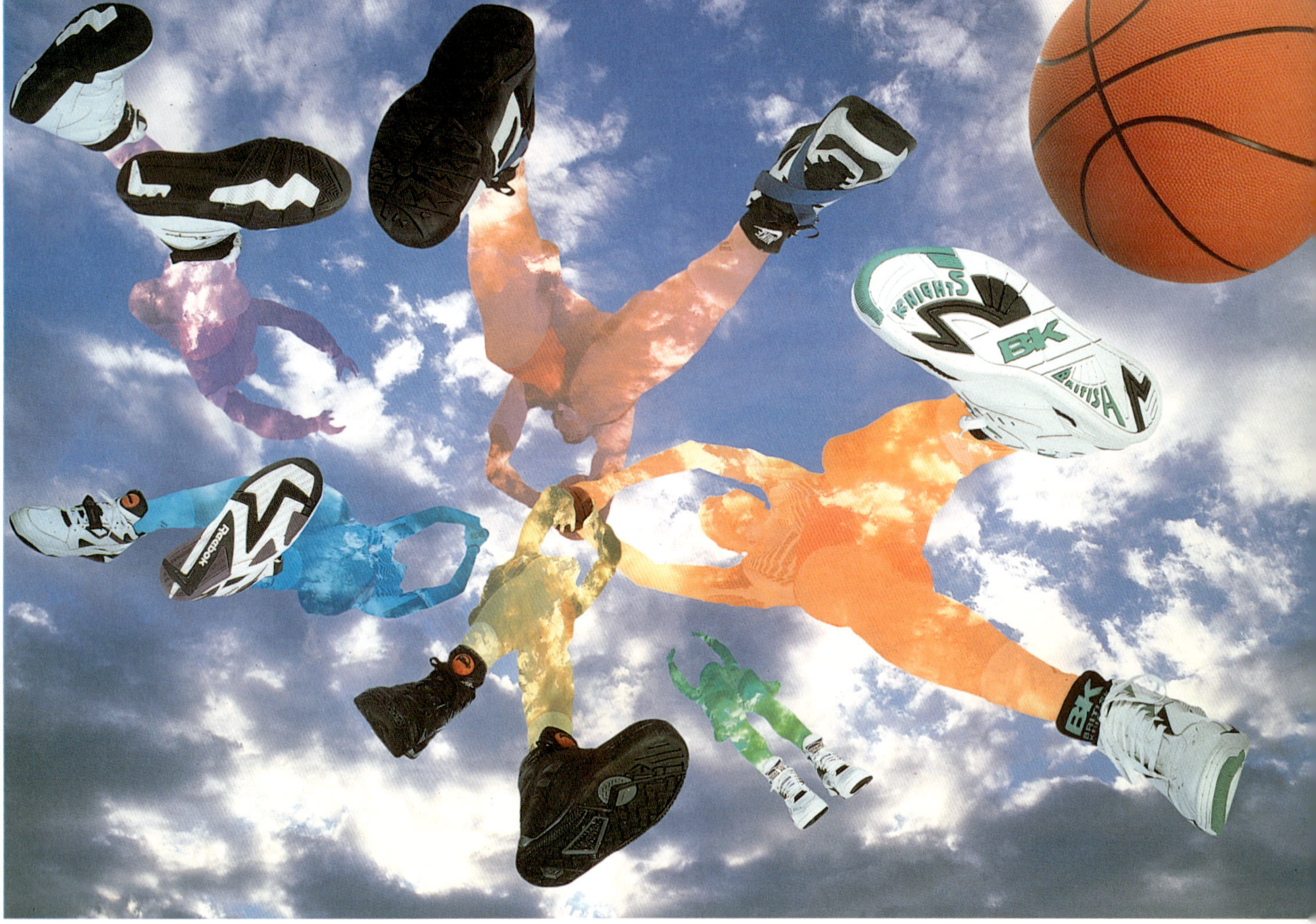

i.

i. Flying Basketball

tronger expression to the story I want to tell in the picture.

developed a unique style working in camera and in the darkroom. ow, because you can employ those techniques fairly easily on ne computer, many people can imitate the kind of work I used o do. My role now is to try to do with the computer what I did ith photography ten years ago; that is, to invent new visuals. I se techniques on the computer in a way that's out of the ordinary. can achieve a lot more with the computer than I ever could with aditional means. But the thinking behind the work is still the ame. I am using a new tool to create the kind of images I have ways dreamed about.

ow I spend more time on the computer, and less on tricky echniques on the set, like hanging objects from the ceiling, oating spheres and so on. But I have noticed one major ifference in these two ways of working. When you do certain ffects directly on film, there is something more organic about e image than if you do the same thing on the computer, because e computer is really a very different device from film emulsion, nd I still do a lot of the work in-camera before I take it to the omputer. There is a different feel to the image. The way the mulsion reacts to light...to mixing, to double-exposing. You just on't get the same effect with the computer.

may decide to do more of the work on the computer in the ture. If my work becomes more illustrative, I might choose to se the computer more like an artist's palette. But for now, I still ve the photographic feel of the image.

ike to work on high-end systems so that I can use larger files. o when I enlarge the pictures, they still look like photographs, nd not like computerized images.

o you use both a traditional camera and a digital camera? hat kinds of works are suitable for the digital camera? What e the advantages of the digital camera?

ney are both basically tools, each with its own purpose. But, as said before, I still like the feel of film so that's why I use the traditional camera. However, as the technology advances, the digital camera will change, and will eventually allow us to produce images of similar quality to a traditional camera. Not the same, but similar. The technology isn't advanced enough at the moment for the kind of work I do. I haven't seen a digital camera that offers the flexibility, or the feel that I'm looking for.

However, as the technology progresses, the camera — be it a traditional film camera or digital camera — is still only a tool. Without a good idea, good lighting, good composition and other criteria, it doesn't matter what kind of camera you use. It's just a way of recording your visions. If I knew how to paint, I probably wouldn't take photographs at all, but express my vision through that medium instead, it's more flexible.

Could you describe the characteristics of the Macintosh and the SGI?

Well, first of all there are the technical differences in the operating systems of these two machines. The SGI operating system allows you to work on "Real time" with no limitation on file size and it's also multi-tasking. Productivity is critical in a busy studio. It's really a high-end system.

Now, we are just considering hardware here. But it's not just a question of Macintosh versus SGI. For me, it's software versus software. I have Photoshop on SGI, but mostly I use Barco Creator for 2D applications and for 3D work I use Alias, also Wave-front Soft Image, Side effects, etc., SGI has a clear advantage.

How do you see commercial photography changing in the future due to digital imaging?

It's not only digital imaging that is changing this business, but digital technology in general. For example, the facsimile machine is a digital device. It lets me get a layout from anywhere around the world as fast as a telephone call. I can also send a file to a client by modem, and he can approve it instantly. All this communications technology is changing the

1. Opposite: The New Lipstick

industry. The pace of change is accelerating simply on the strength of this technology.

Right now we are living in the "global village." I can communicate daily with Japan the same way as I do with people here in New York.

As for digital imaging...it allows you to work a lot faster and cheaper than before. It also lets people do the kind of work they were unable to do before with traditional methods. So in one way it ups the competition because more people are able to get into this field. But then the clients will be able to discriminate good digital imaging from bad. There's a lot of digital artwork out there, but much of it is mediocre.

Commercial photography is a business. You take pictures for love and money. What counts is a good idea, good lighting, and good composition. You have to deliver the work on time and on budget. Before digital technology came along, it took longer to produce the work and maybe the budget was a little bigger and better. Now you are expected to get the work out quicker and cheaper, you just have to adapt to the changing technology, just as people in the old days adapted to the automobile after the horse-and-cart era.

How would you describe the work you do? Could you tell us about the basic philosophy behind your work?

How would I describe my work?

Cognitive, visual metaphors that tell the story. I have come up with three criteria for why I do this work. First is the pleasure I get from the work. That is very important to me. Second, I consider the particular client. Third I consider the fee.

The first — "whether the work is fun to do" — is the most important. I always think of these three criteria whenever I am offered an assignment. Decision making according to these criteria is mostly subconscious by now. Maybe fifty percent of the decision rests with the fun part. Then twenty-five percent would be prestige, public relations considerations and whether am going to get a good tear sheet out of the work, and so o Another twenty-five percent is about the rest.

I love to do work that solves a problem with an idea. The clie gives me a tag line and I illustrate that line with a visual. The fu is creating the image to go with that line. Coming up with a illustration for an idea — a metaphor — that's the fun part.

So to sum up my philosophy: I want to deliver to the client good product, well done, on time and on budget. And most have a lot of fun in the process.

You produced your CD "I SIGHT" in 1994. Could you tell u about the concept behind this work and the process c producing a CD-ROM?

The main reason for doing that CD-ROM was that I was give the opportunity. The idea was to produce an interactive CD-RO for photographers. I agreed to do the job for several reason First, I knew it was going to be a challenge. It fitted nicely wit my work philosophy. It was going to be fun and creative. Secon because of my involvement in digital imaging, I wanted to d something that was very technically up-to-date. Obviousl CD-I is a very current technology. And third was the busines angle. I wanted to show my current and potential clients a ne visual edge. Many people know of my traditional photograph and untraditional thinking, but I wanted to show them my ne approach with digital imaging.

The concept and the process of producing the CD were quite simpl but at the same time technically demanding. First of all, I'd had n experience with CD-I. I had to learn the work really quickly. It wa an interesting challenge. I designed the CD with my producers ju as I would for a production shoot or a TV commercial. I started b asking the same two key questions I always ask my clients whe start a project. These are: 1) "What do you want to say?" and, 2) "T whom are you saying it?" The same holds true for the CD-ROM.

I wanted the CD to say something about my work philosoph

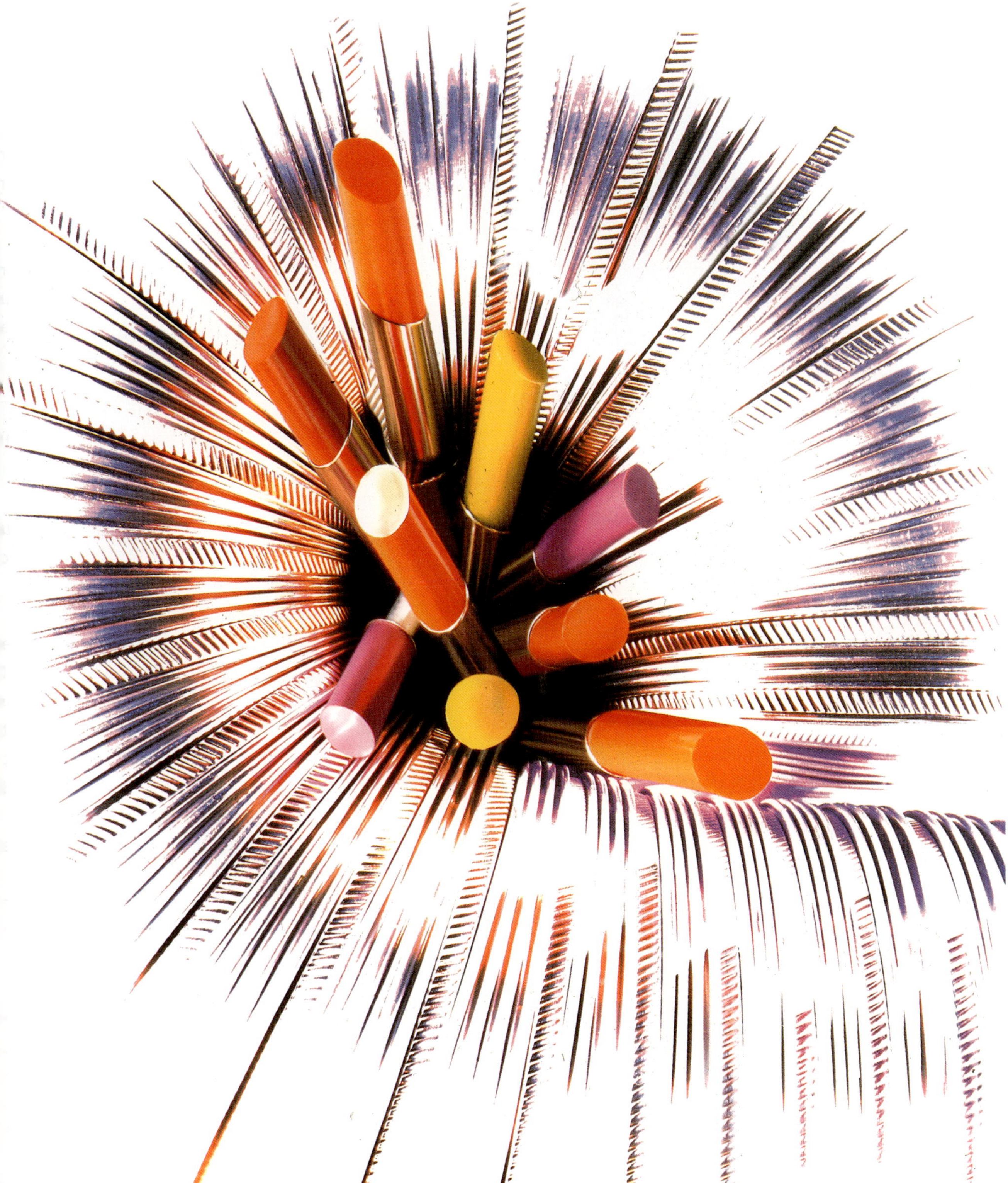

Michel Tcherevkoff

How do I work? Why do I work? I wanted to give more information about these things. So I created a gallery of my images, and I described the background to each of the images and how I achieved them.

What projects are you planning next? What is your vision for the future?

I think it would be interesting to do a series of CDs for other photographers. I have two books in the works. One of them is tentatively entitled, *Head Shots.* This is a collection of portraits, unusual portraits because they are not of people. The other book may be entitled *Digital Dreams.* That book will contain simple images that have been treated digitally and show the evolution of my work.

What is my vision of the future? Since I have started in the business I have tried to set goals for myself every ten years. This helps me plan my future. So, if I look forward to the next ten years, what kind of things would I like to achieve? First of all, I want to finish the two books I've just mentioned. Do more CDs. The studio may become completely digital. I will be working on personal projects. I want to travel more. Maybe I will do less special effects than in the past.

I am going to try to plan and implement every decision I make — from now to ten years hence — to attain the goal I have set. The more decisions I accumulate, the more chances I have of attaining my goal. If, however, something completely unexpected happens in this ten-year period — something I never thought of, something more interesting than the goal I have set — then I will change the goal. But having the goal in mind helps me focus, and keeps me from working in a kind of random fashion that might not amount to anything. At the same time I am looking around to see if anything else is interesting. Just looking...always looking.

I certainly don't plan to retire. The body will retire but the images will stay on forever.

Assignments help me to focus myself. Clients come to me with

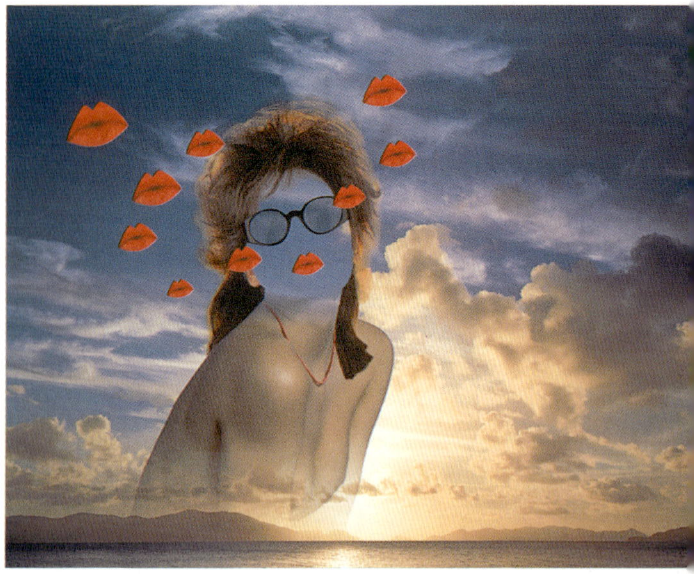

2.

2. Red Lips
3. Green Head

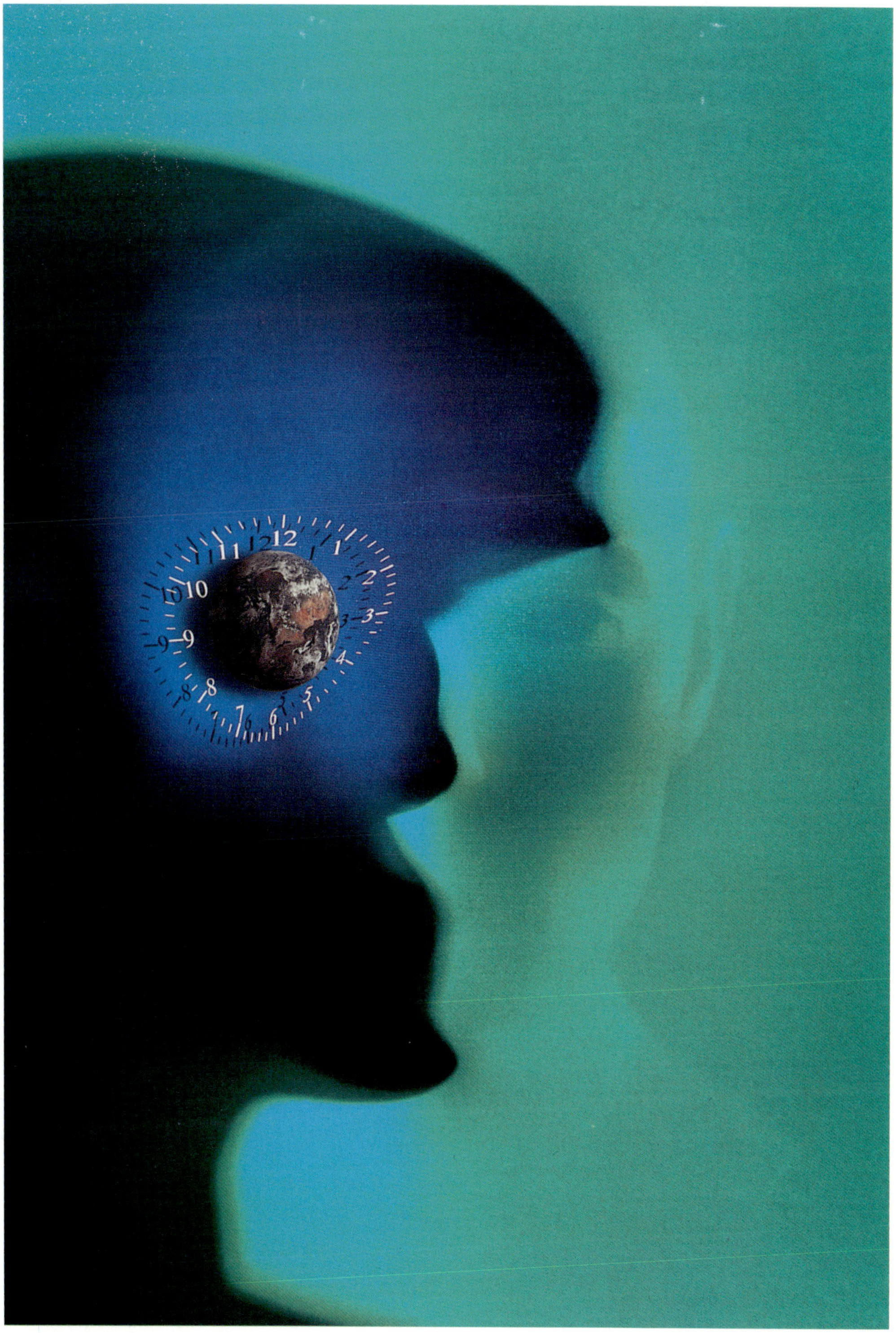

3.

Michel Tcherevkoff

specific ideas they want to have expressed visually. One of the most difficult things is to be given carte blanche — to be told you can do anything you want. "Anything I want," leaves the field wide open. What I want to know is what the client has to say. I like to solve specific problems. I have to mix art and commerce. Thank goodness.

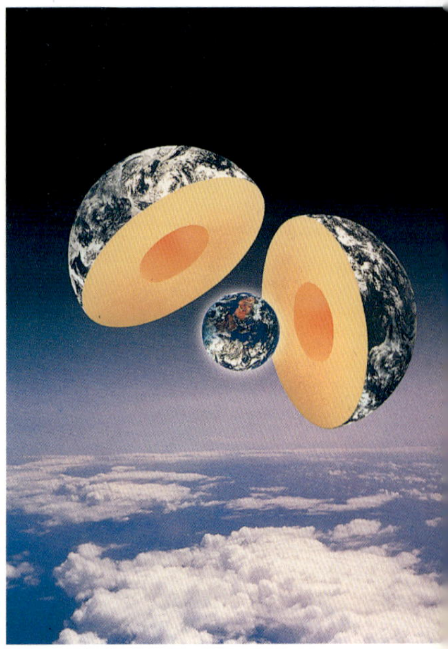

4.

4. New World
5. Opposite: Calyx Leaf

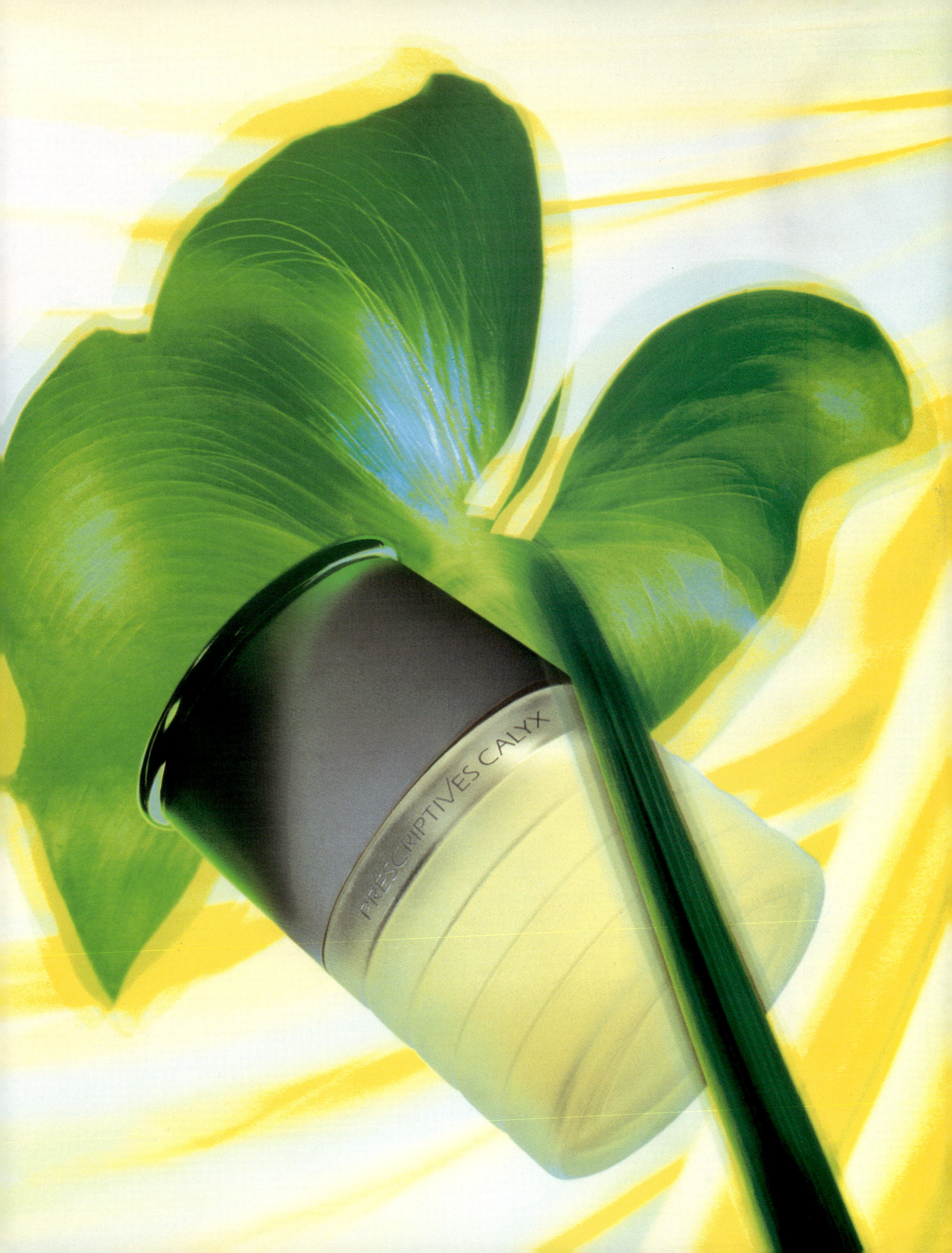
PRESCRIPTIVES CALYX

Michel Tcherevkoff

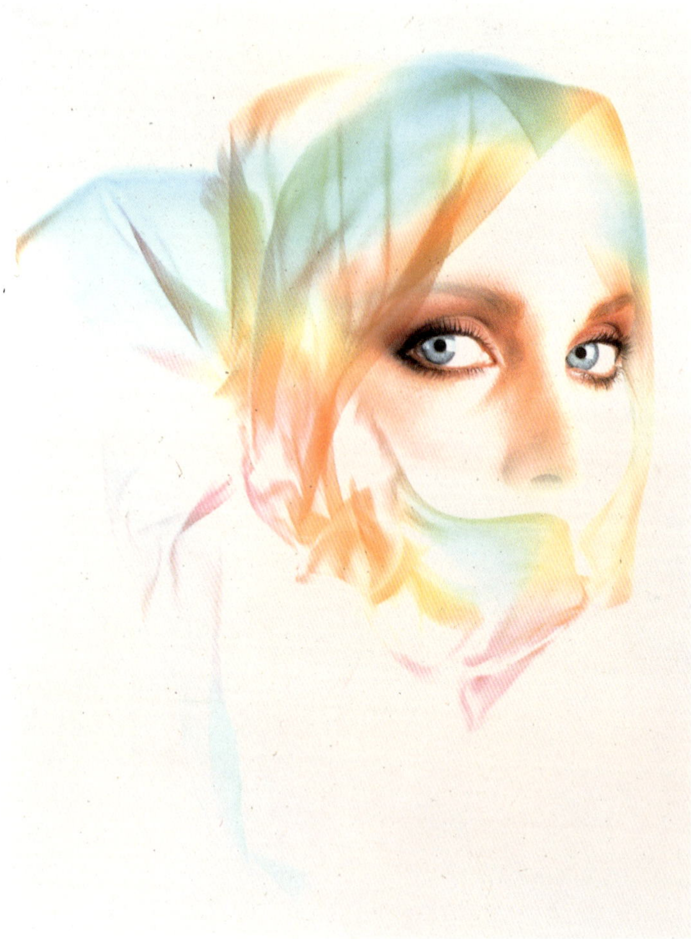

6.

6. New Women
7. Virtual Reality Head

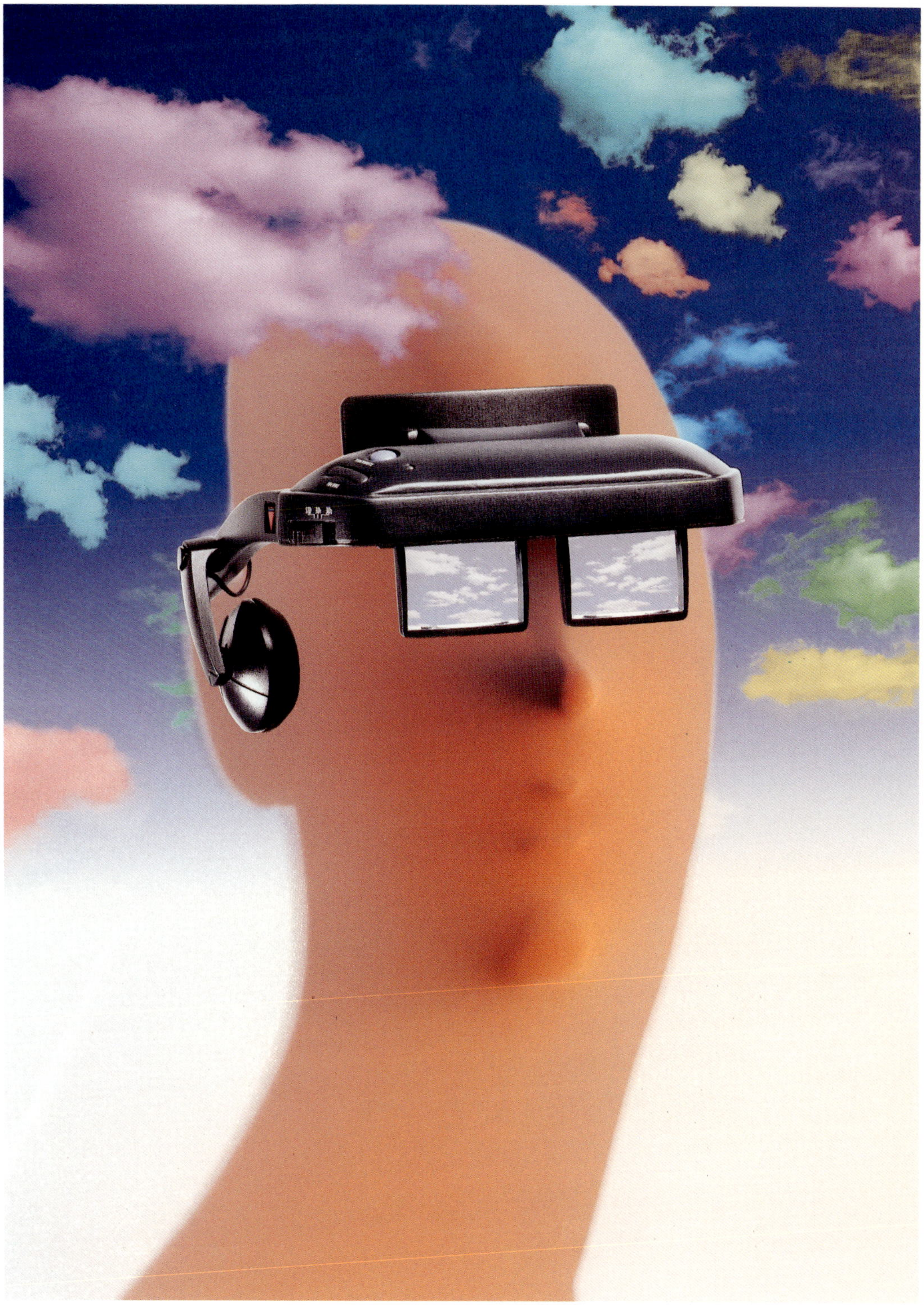

7.

Michel Tcherevkoff

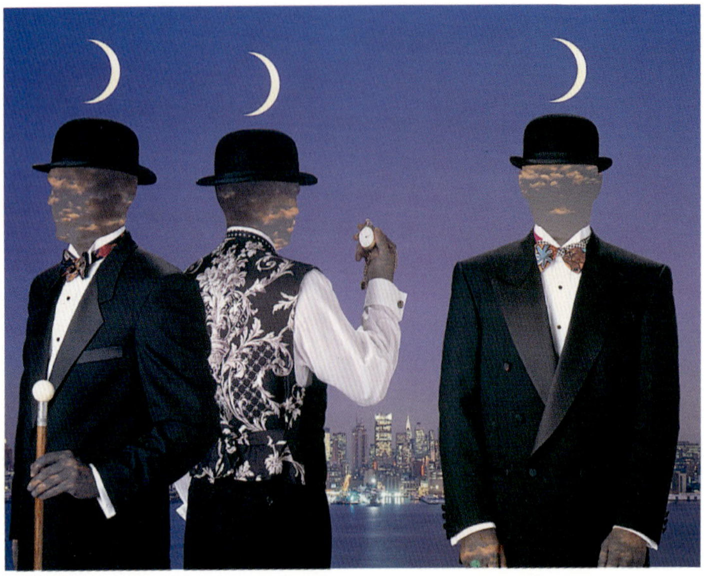

8.

8. Tuxedo Men
9. Button Head

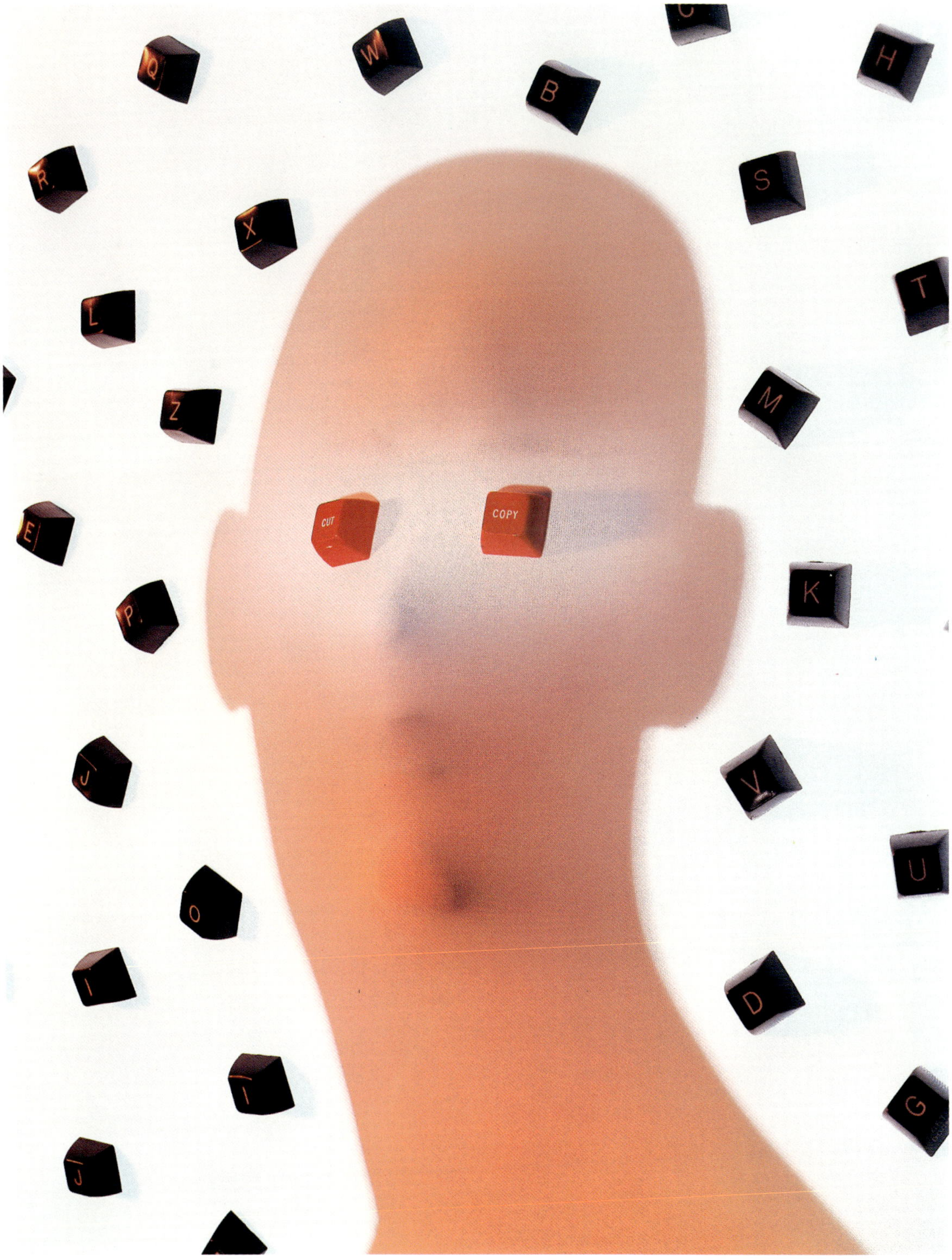

9.

Michel Tcherevkoff

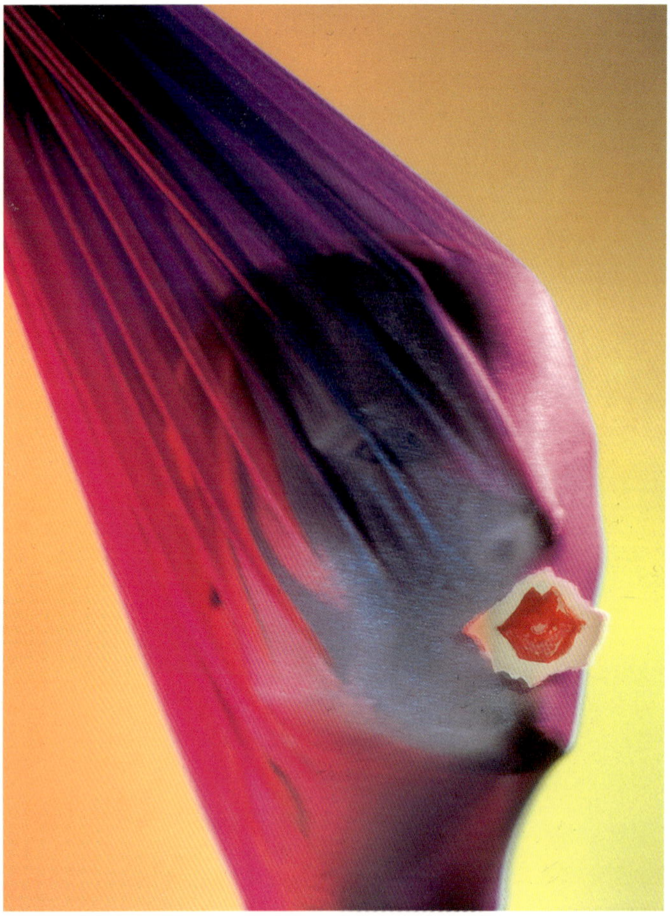

10.

10. La Femme Lumiere
11. Brilliant Earth

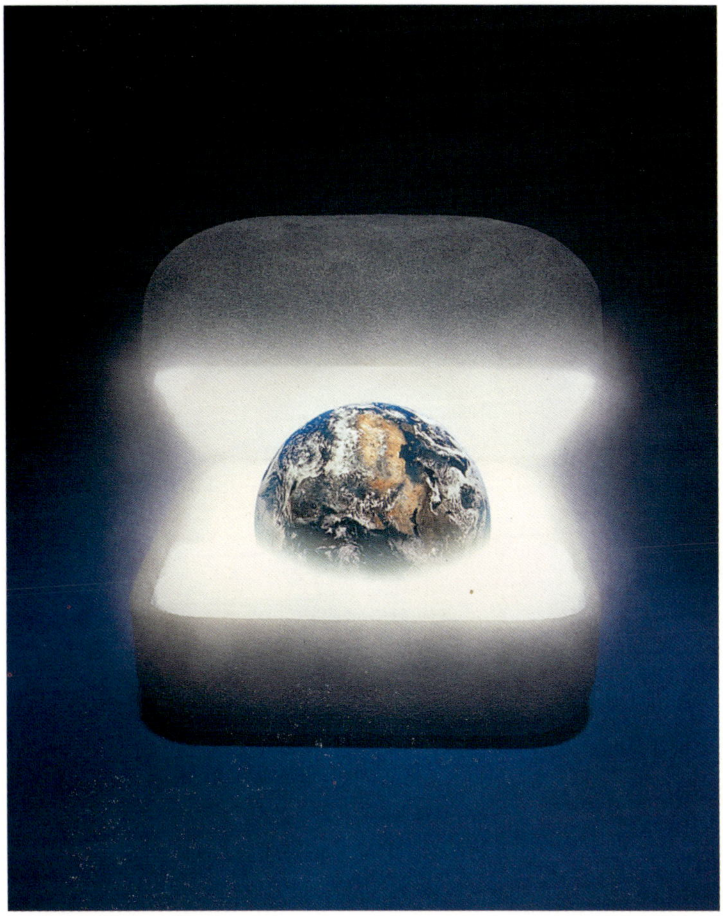

11.

Michel Tcherevkoff

12. Watch Man
13. Opposite: Blue Vodka

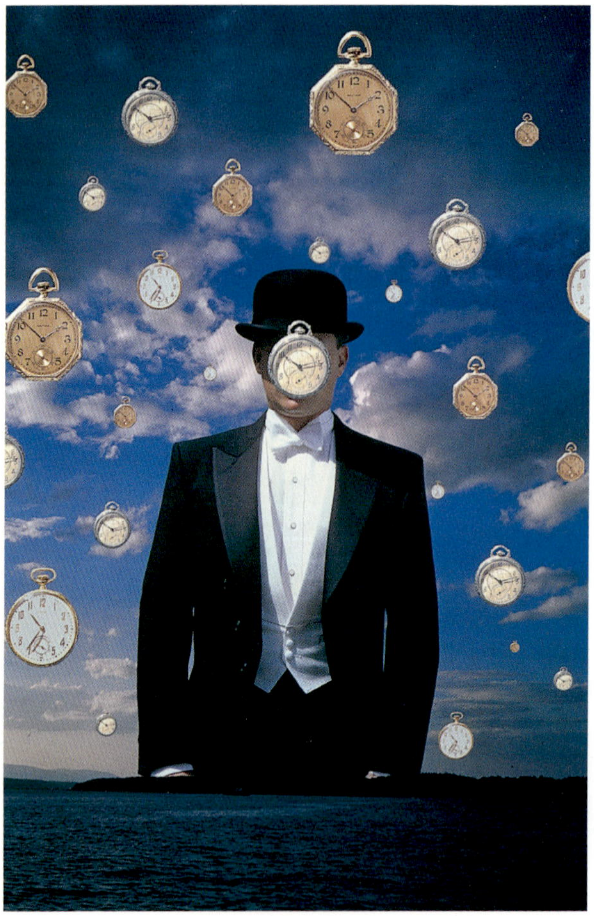

12.

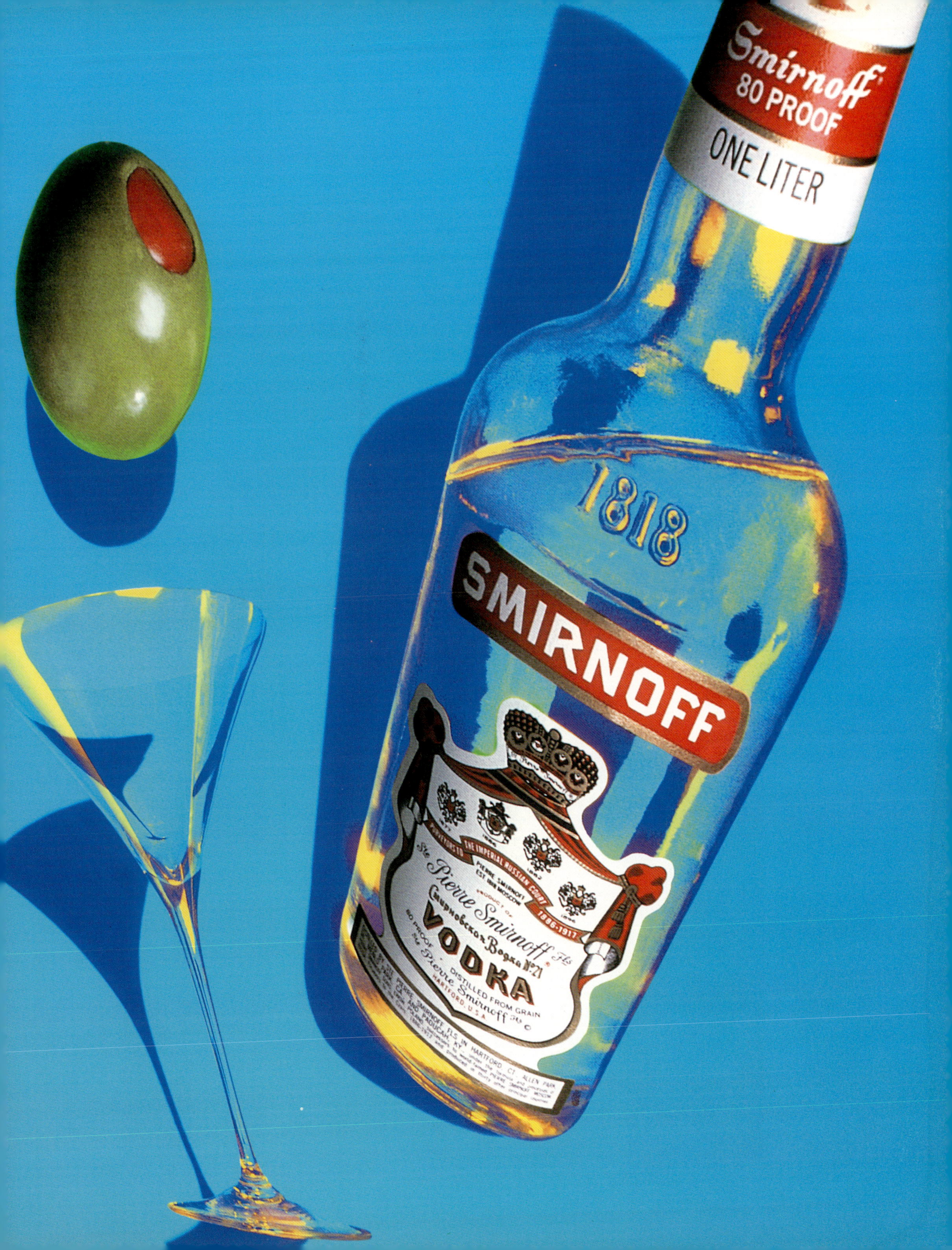
Smirnoff
80 PROOF
ONE LITER
1818
SMIRNOFF
PURVEYORS TO THE IMPERIAL RUSSIAN COURT
1886-1917
Ste Pierre Smirnoff Fls
VODKA
DISTILLED FROM GRAIN

Michel Tcherevkoff

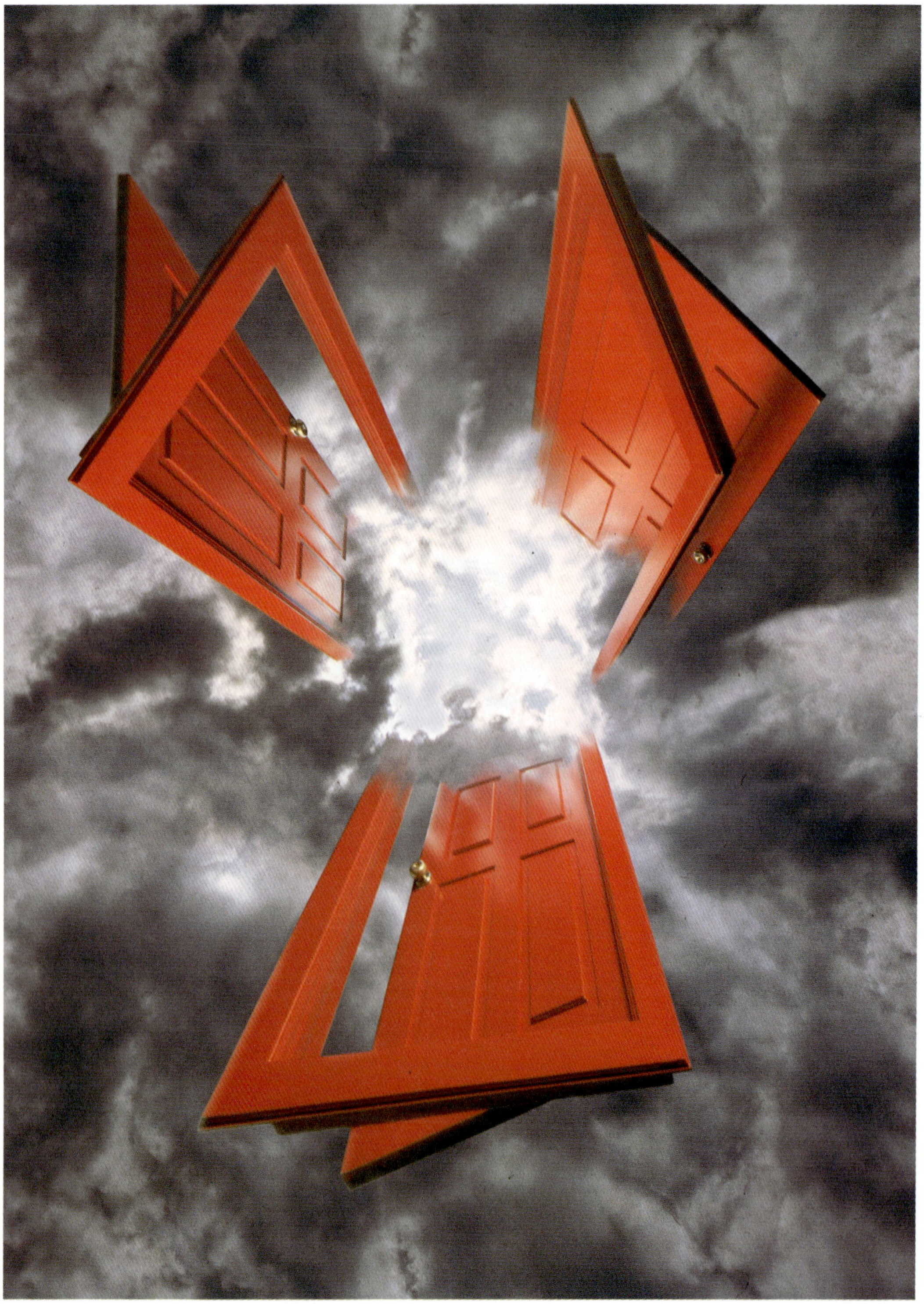

14.

14. Red Doors
15. Migraine

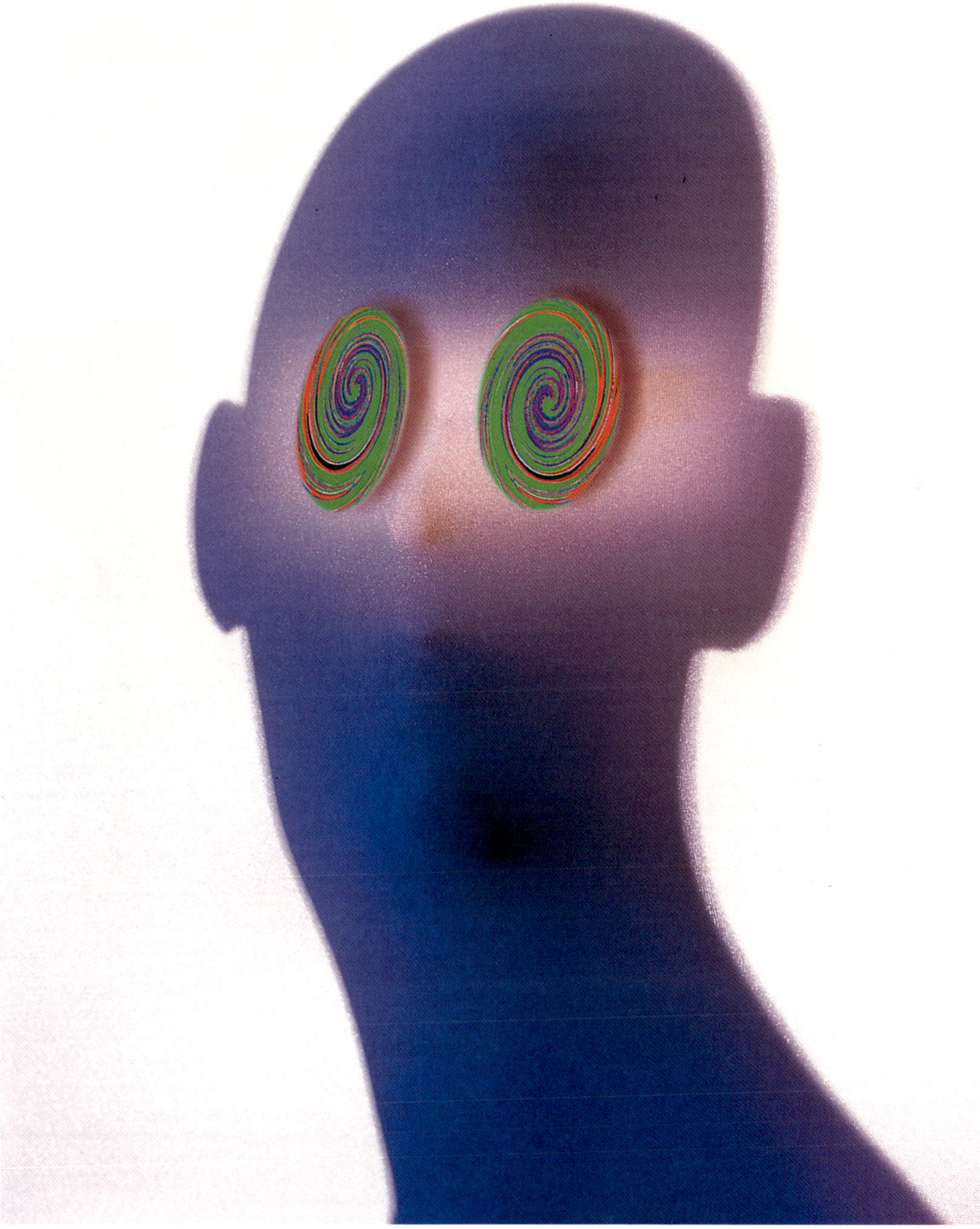

15.

Michel Tcherevkoff

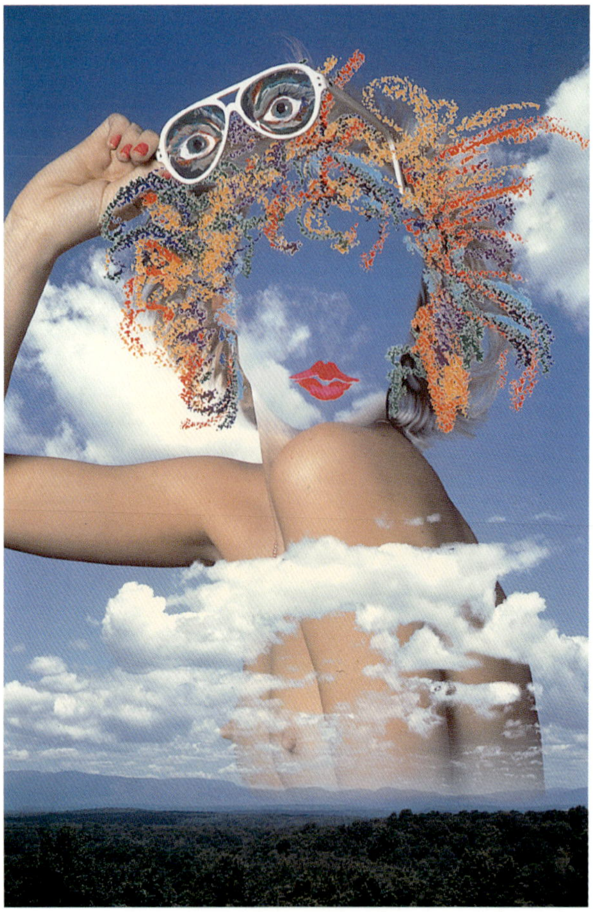

16.

16. Hair Head
17. Night Vision

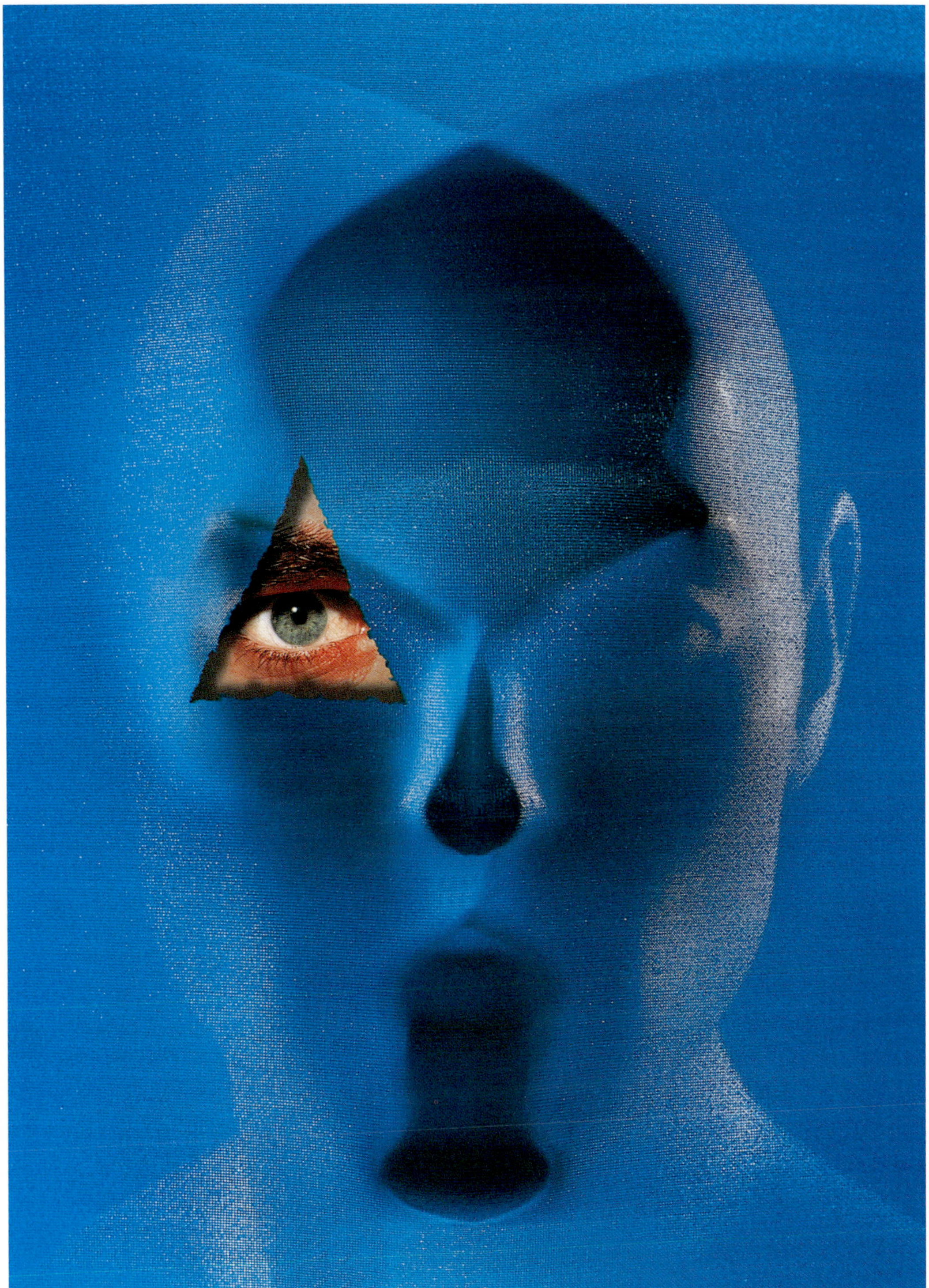

17.

Michel Tcherevkoff

18. Red Head

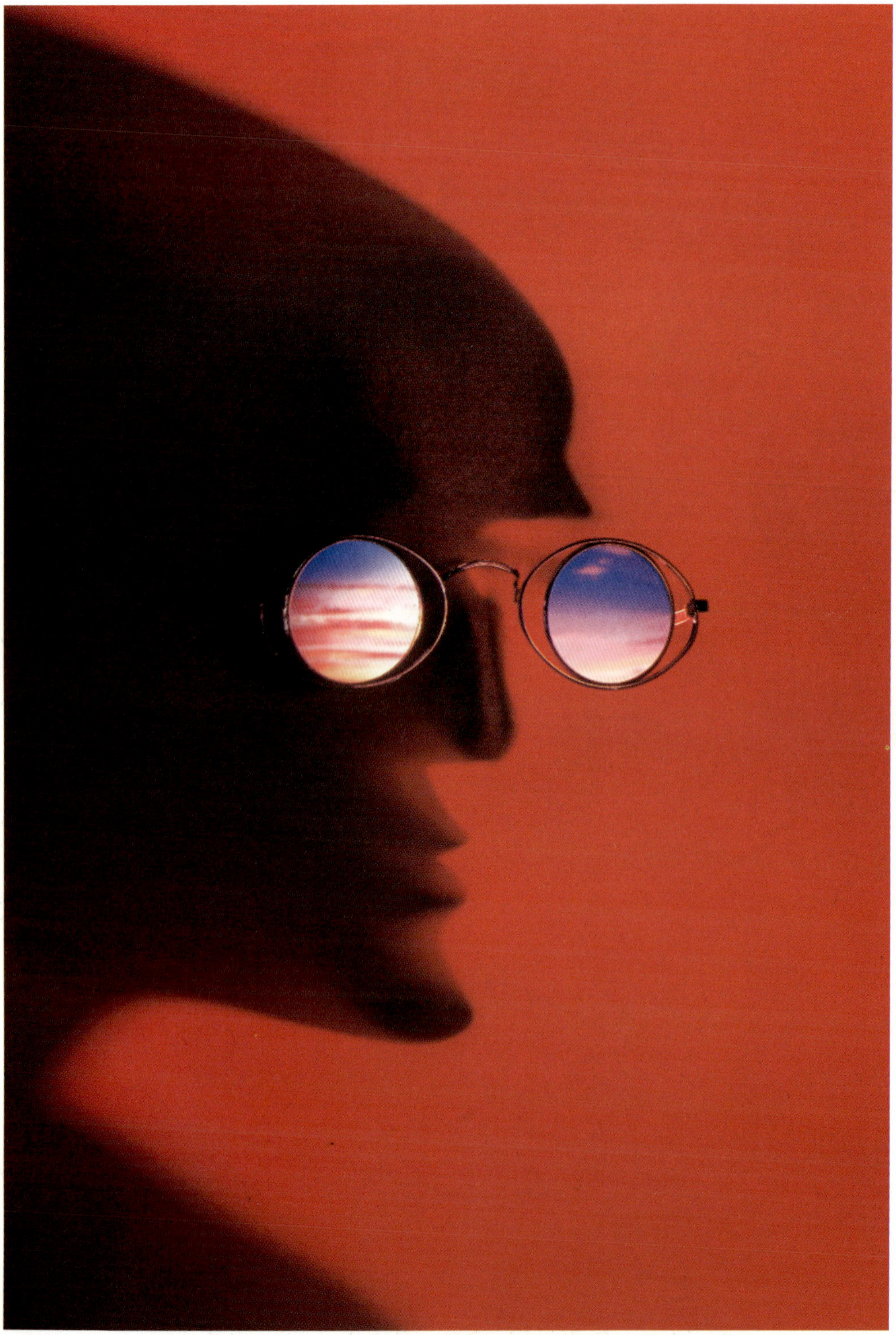

18.

Nash Editions

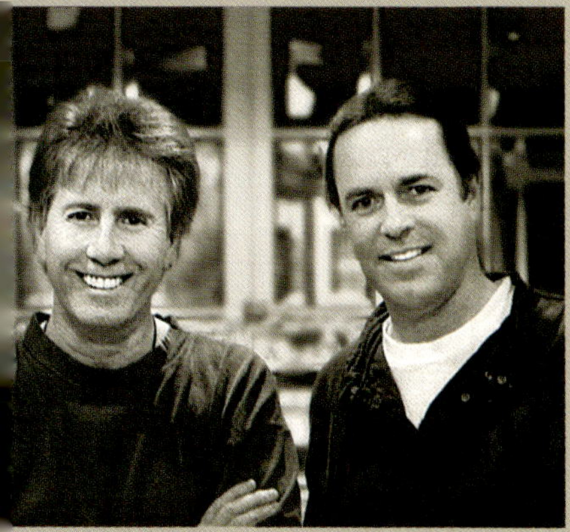

In the world of fine-art digital printmaking, the reputation of Nash Editions is second to none. Formed in 1991 by Graham Nash and his partner, Mac Holbert, Nash Editions has revolutionized the fine-art printing field using its own custom-built scanner, Macintosh-based computer system and Iris printers.

Though the technical expertise of Nash Editions is undeniable, Mac Holbert is quick to point out that the real strength of the company lies in the artistic sensibilities of its staff. Everyone at Nash Editions is closely involved in the creative process of expressing the vision of each of its artist-clients on paper.

While Holbert devotes all of his time to the artistic and technical work of Nash Editions, Graham Nash continues to investigate the artistic possibilities of new media. One of his current projects is an interactive CD entitled *Life Sighs*. This will chronicle major events that have occurred during his life and career. Whether devoting himself to music, digital imaging or social and environmental issues, Graham Nash is continually searching for new and exciting ways to express his vision.

(Left: Graham Nash, Right: Mac Holbert)

Nash Editions

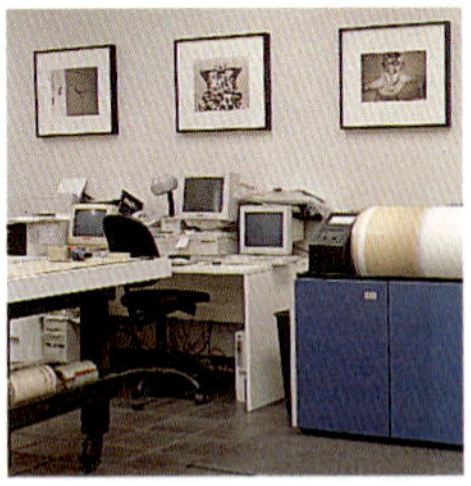
Studio

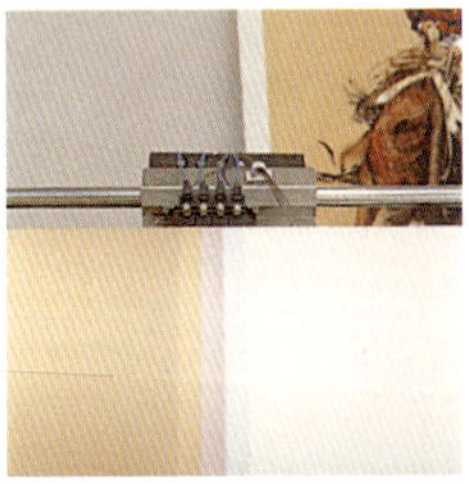
Iris Printer

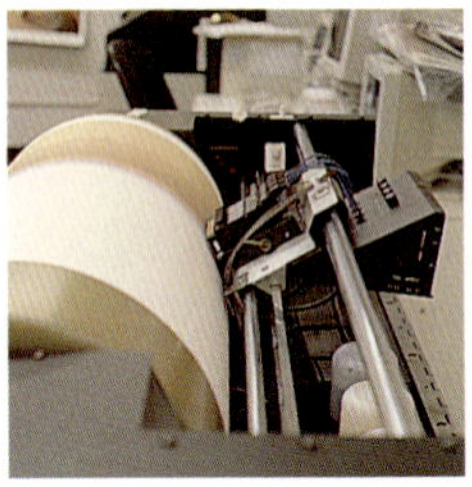
Iris Printer

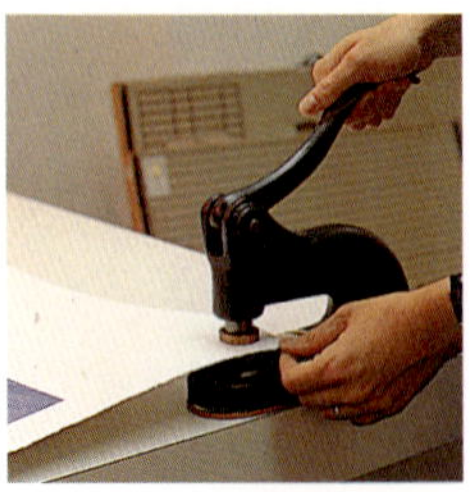
Applying the Chop

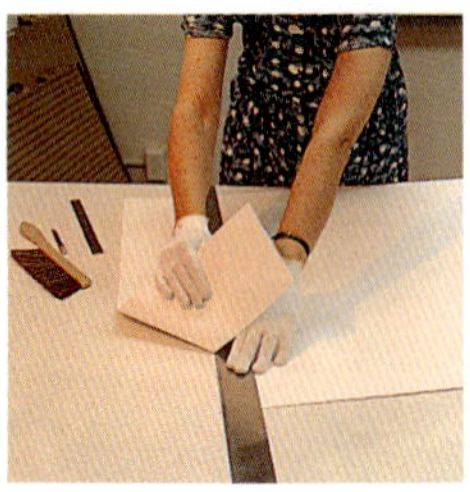
Hand Deckling

Mac Holbert, we know that you have worked with Graham Na for a long time, and that Graham is better known for his wo as a musician with the group Crosby, Stills and Nash. Wh and why did he start to be interested in photography?

Well, Graham actually became interested in photography pri to his involvement with music. When he was about eight yea old, his father had begun developing film at home. There w very little space in the house, and Graham would help his fath set up a makeshift darkroom in his bedroom by putting blank over the windows. And the two of them would do this magic process of photography together.

This early influence encouraged Graham to start taking his o pictures. In fact one of the exhibits for his show in Japan at t Parco Gallery was a photograph he had taken of his mother w back in 1954.

How did you and Graham Nash come to establish Na Editions?

I was the tour manager for Crosby, Stills and Nash from ea 1970 until 1991. During that 21-year involvement, Graham an formed a firm friendship, and one of our areas of common intere was art. When we were on the road, we spent much time goi to art galleries, photography galleries, and just looking at image

With the help of his wife, Susan, and several other people, Graha put together one of the world's largest collections covering t history of photography. That collection was sold about five or years ago, at a very famous auction at Sotheby's. There we images dating back to the 1840s — Henry Fox Talbot images and leading up to the present.

Graham was a photographer himself, and was looking for n ways to print his images. One of the things he was missing we the printing papers that were being phased out. Many of t papers that Graham really loved just weren't available any mo So, around 1989, I got Graham involved in digital imaging. bought him one of the first Macintosh computers and a scann used software such as Digital Darkroom and early versions of otoshop to manipulate the images.

started investigating various ways of getting digital hard copy tput. Nothing that we saw was satisfactory. There was solutely no aesthetic quality to the kind of output that was ailable in those days. We tried dye-sublimation and wax thermal nts. We tried photographing the screen. We tried film recorders d making 35-mm slides from the digital images. But all these thods left a lot to be desired.

en, we heard about the Iris printer through JETGRAPHIX. We mediately went to see one of the machines in action at George ce & Sons, a color house in Los Angeles. And we were solutely bowled over by the quality. The output looked so otographic. We couldn't even believe we were looking at an jet print when we saw those first images.

ortly afterwards, Graham bought his first Iris printer. He was ntent to print his own work on the Iris for a while. Then one y, while we were out on the road in Australia, I suggested that ving such an expensive piece of equipment lying unused while were out touring was really a waste. He should really be nking about using it to set up a business. After all, everybody emed to be responding well to the quality of our prints. And I d been looking for a way to get out of managing rock-and-roll rs and spending more time with my wife and daughter. So we reed at that point, in early 1990, to start Nash Editions. We set date for the establishment of Nash Editions for July, 1991. I my last tour as a rock-and-roll manager in June of that year, ved my family here to Manhattan Beach, and haven't looked ck since.

uld you tell us about the activities of Nash Editions?

sh Editions is a fine art digital printmaking studio. We have ed from the very inception of the company to place the phasis on the art as opposed to the technology. We provide sts and photographers who are working in this digital realm, h a way to express their vision on paper. We handle their work on a level that they would not get in a traditional service bureau. Normally, you would need millions of dollars worth of equipment to do a lot of the work we do. With a regular service bureau, you hand in your work to a technician as an image, a transparency or a digital file. The work is scanned and the technician is solely responsible for printing the image on paper.

Now that kind of operation will not work for artists who are interested in getting a very specific vision on paper. It takes the interaction with someone who is steeped in traditional fine art printing and who has a fine art sensibility. We decided early on that we would only hire artists who had an understanding of the technology as opposed to technologists with only a minor understanding of art. It is difficult to inculcate an artistic temperament in a technologist. Whereas it is very easy to teach an artist how to use a particular piece of equipment.

At the moment, there is a lot of opposition to this technology. And strangely enough, a lot of the antagonism is coming from photographers. This is unusual since photographers come from a very technical tradition, and one which has had to fight the stigma attached by the world of fine art. But some of our staunchest critics are from the world of photography.

But I think that once people understand that Nash Editions is here just as another way of producing an image, they will come around to our way of thinking. We are not trying to replace traditional photography. A well-rendered silver print is one of the most beautiful objects of art anyone could hope to have. I am not trying to match that. I am just trying to become another color on the palette. There are certain images that would not look right as Iris prints. Some images are only successful as Cibachrome. However, certain Cibachromes would look much better as Iris prints.

Nash Editions

Could you tell us something about the look of Iris prints compared with traditional prints?

The look of the Iris print has everything to do with surface. The Iris lets you print on many different types of substrates. The transparent inks are absorbed deep into the paper. So you are not viewing an image that's sitting on the surface, but something that has actually become an integral part of the paper. This gives you a depth, an authenticity and a veracity that you very rarely see with other methods of printing.

Nash Editions has an excellent reputation for its artistic quality. How is your company different from a typical Iris printing operation? What kind of things do you pay special attention to?

What sets us apart from just about everybody is that we have a master printmaker working for us. Furthermore, every single person who works at Nash Editions has an artistic background. Our staff has master's degrees in photography or fine art. I was a university art student.

Service bureaus can only do so much, and for artists it is just not enough. When we are dealing with artists, in person or on the phone, we have to discuss just how we are going to get their particular image onto paper. Having a staff that is committed to realizing our clients' dreams on paper is a crucial part of the operation. It's not just equipment. Anybody can use the equipment. But just like the camera...I would rather see a picture from a camera that was in the hands of Ansel Adams than one that came from a camera in my own hands.

What kind of substrates do you use most? What other materials are available for printing on with the Iris?

About 85% of the work was done on Arches cold-press watercolor paper. That paper has a lot of texture and weight to it. It's a really beautiful paper. However, about six months ago we were made aware of a new paper made by an English company called Somerset. Now, this paper has one attribute that a lot of photographers like, and that is its brilliant whiteness. The Arches is creamy by comparison. And since we are using transpar dyes, we can't print white. We have to rely on the color of paper to create the white for us. So, the whiter the substrate more sense of color you get. The colors have more punch.

One of the characteristics of Iris prints done by service burea is that they tend to be a little flat. Here, I am talking in artis terms. The colors may be correct, scientifically speaking, but the eye and to the emotions, they don't have that punch to the The Somerset papers, however, really add to the impact of image. The papers were also designed with the Iris in mind, a have an available size that is the largest you can use with the printer.

What is the largest print size you can make?

The largest we can make is 34 x 46 inches. That can be done a piece of 35 x 47 inch paper.

Could you tell us about the inks you are working with?

Well, the inks have changed a little bit since we first start Initially, we were using inks that were developed by Iris. But th were very fugitive...meaning that they faded quite quickly wh exposed to all sorts of light — from UV light to incandescent a fluorescent. So the images only had a lifetime of three to f years.

We decided early on that we had to find the kind of inks t were going to hold the image a bit longer. We are still not th yet, but we are making a lot of progress. One of the things are doing is printing on watercolor paper, so we are capable producing three to four times more saturation. There's a hig density of ink to fade, and that in itself extends the image We also cover the final image with a UV coating. This doe pretty good job of screening out UV, although it doesn't blo incandescent or fluorescent light. But the most effective th we do is educate our clients about the care of fine art on pap We send out a guideline which we developed in collaborat with the Metropolitan Museum in New York. This covers

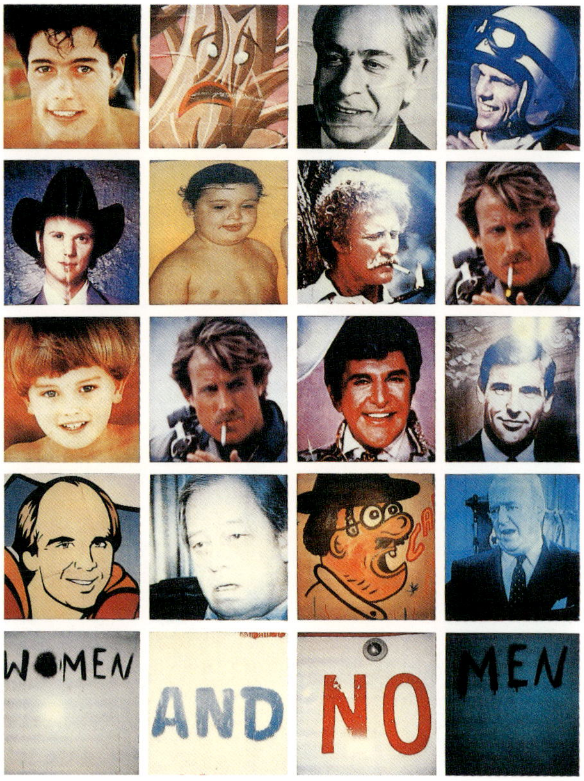

1.

1. David Byrne: Women & No Men
22.65" x 29.29"

handling and care of all fine art paper prints — not specifically Iris prints. Any art done on paper is fugitive. We recommend that the client follow the guideline, which includes being aware of the intensity and kind of light you use for illuminating the image. We also recommend UF3 Plexi, a kind of Plexiglas with an ultraviolet absorber, to protect the print. We give advice on rotating your collection. We don't recommend you to keep a piece up on the wall for many years but to keep it there for a just few months and rotate the art collection.

If clients follow the guideline, we are confident that these prints will last about twenty years under museum conditions.

We have also been working on the microdispersion pigment. This is a suspension of pigment with an extremely small particle size — fine enough to pass through the inkjet nozzles we currently use. These pigments are much more stable than dyes. We had a Nobel Prize winning chemist helping us with this work, but unfortunately his other commitments got in the way. But just a couple of weeks ago, the Toyo Ink Company sent some of their microdispersion pigments to Iris. Iris will be testing those in the next month or so.

At least Iris is now paying attention to this technology. Initially, nothing was driving Scitex or Iris to develop a permanent ink set. As far as they were concerned, the Iris printer was solely a proofing device. But now that digital photography is really starting to make an impact, people can see a mass market down the road. There will be mass market digital cameras, as well as a mass market demand for digital printmaking. I think that Iris and Scitex want to be on the cutting edge of that market. So they are giving very serious consideration, manpower and dollars to solve the image permanency problem.

Now, if we can get a microdispersion pigment that will work within the current technology, we will definitely be using it. At the moment we are restricted in the range of inks we can use. The usable inks are limited by their electrical conductivity, fluidity and other parameters.

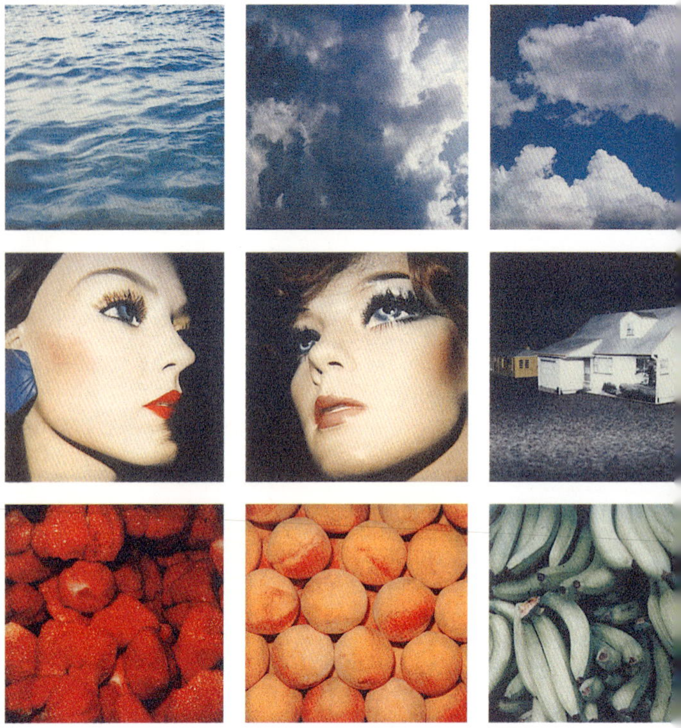

2.

2. David Byrne: Clouds / Mannequin / Fruit
24" x 24"
3. David Byrne: E.A.R.
22.50" x 30.95"

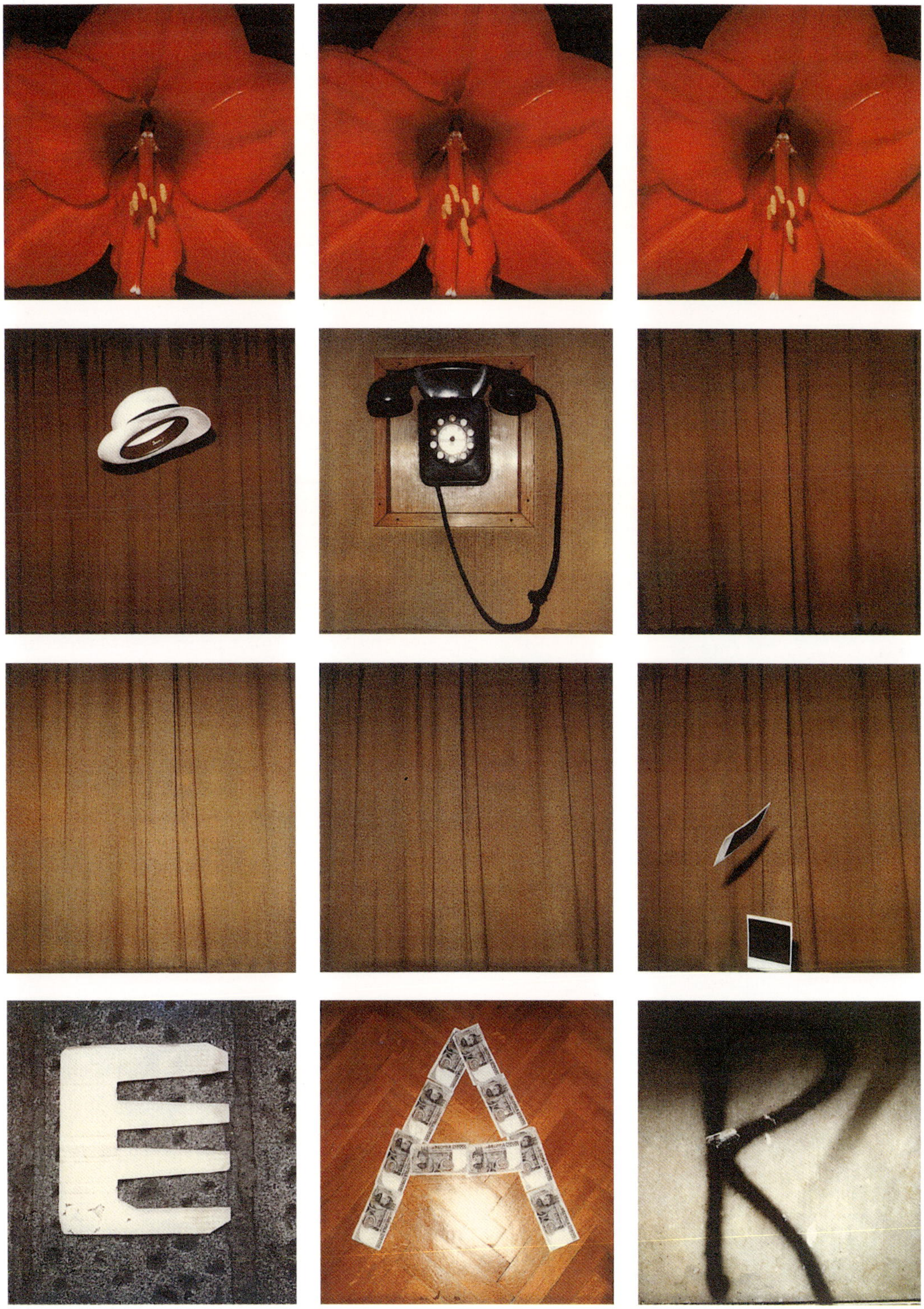

3.

Nash Editions / David Byrne

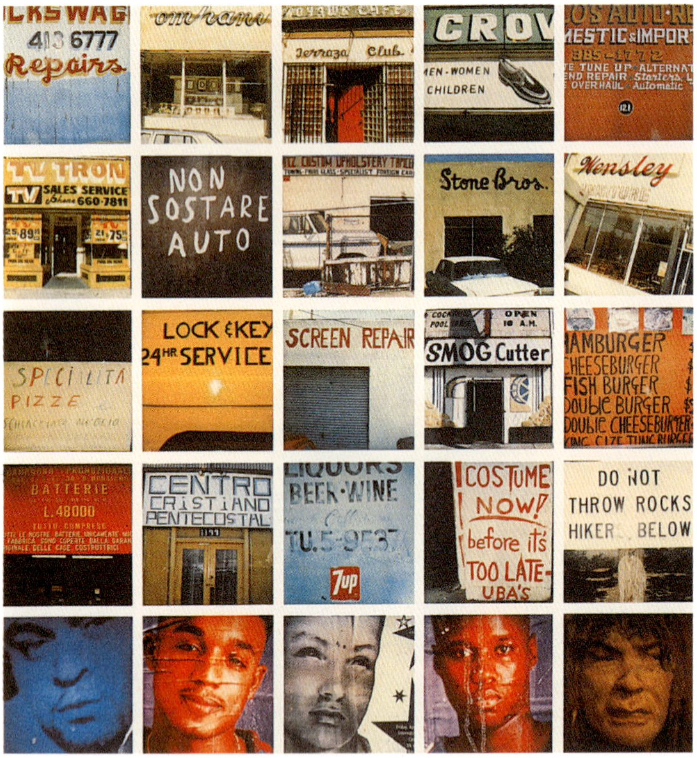

4.

What kind of image format do artists usually send you — digit data or transparencies?

Absolutely everything. We built the world's largest flat-be scanner so that we could scan original art images up to 36 x 4 inches. We also get many transparencies — everything fro 8 x 10 down to 35 mm. We get digital files, Photoshop files, Cor Draw files, Macintosh-based, PC-based and SGI-based files.

What kind of scanner do you use?

We built our own scanner from the ground up. It was a liqui cooled CCD manufactured by Photometrics for scientific us We adapted that to a Nikkormat lens, just like a camera. We mo the camera over the artwork using a German-made machinir bed that we adapted for scanning purposes. We modified th gears and stepper motors so we could get much finer resolutio The artwork is placed flat on the table, and the camera mov over the image taking hundreds of tiny pictures of it. Then w use the software to seamlessly stitch together all those tir images. The result is a single piece — a very high resolution imag of the original work of art.

How much do you charge for making one Iris print? (How muc does it cost to make one print?)

We have separate charges for scanning, imaging, proofing ar printing. But, to give you a basic idea of pricing...Nash Editior will take your digital file, and we will proof it. You get two proo for $75. We send you one proof, and you can annotate it with th changes you may want to make. We will then do everything w can to implement those changes at the printer end. We can adju density, contrast and so on. Then, when the final print is ready be made, we charge between $125 and $350 for that prir depending on the size. The minimum size we charge you for is 20 x 24 inch image. We can print smaller, but we have to charg you for the minimum cost. That is $125. We base that on 27 cen per square inch. So a full-size Iris print of 34 x 46 inches shou cost in the region of $400 to $500, but we only charge $350.

4. David Byrne: Signs / Faces
23.07" x 24"
5. David Byrne: Hands / Turn Light Off!
24" x 31"

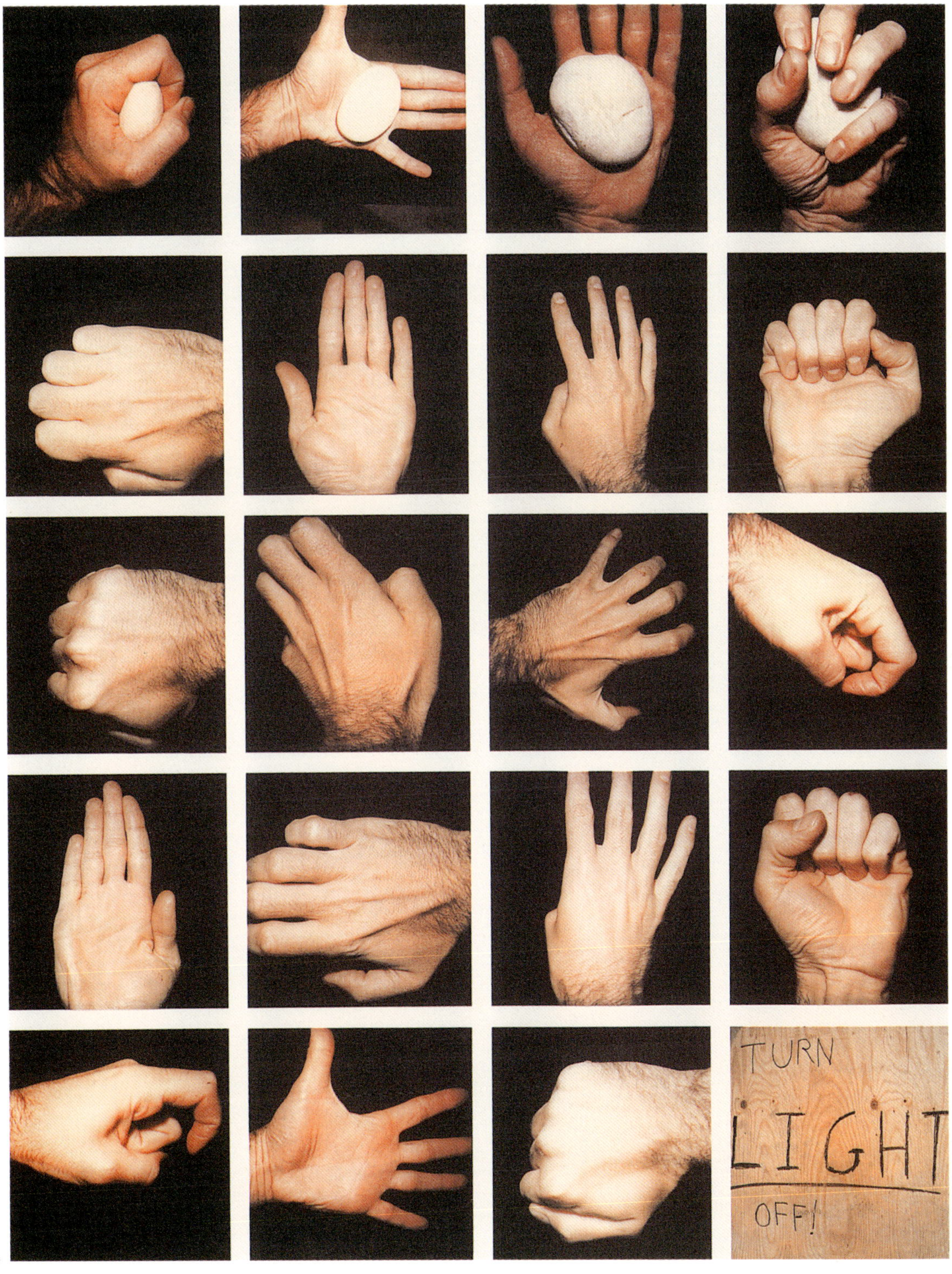

5.

Nash Editions / Eileen Cowin

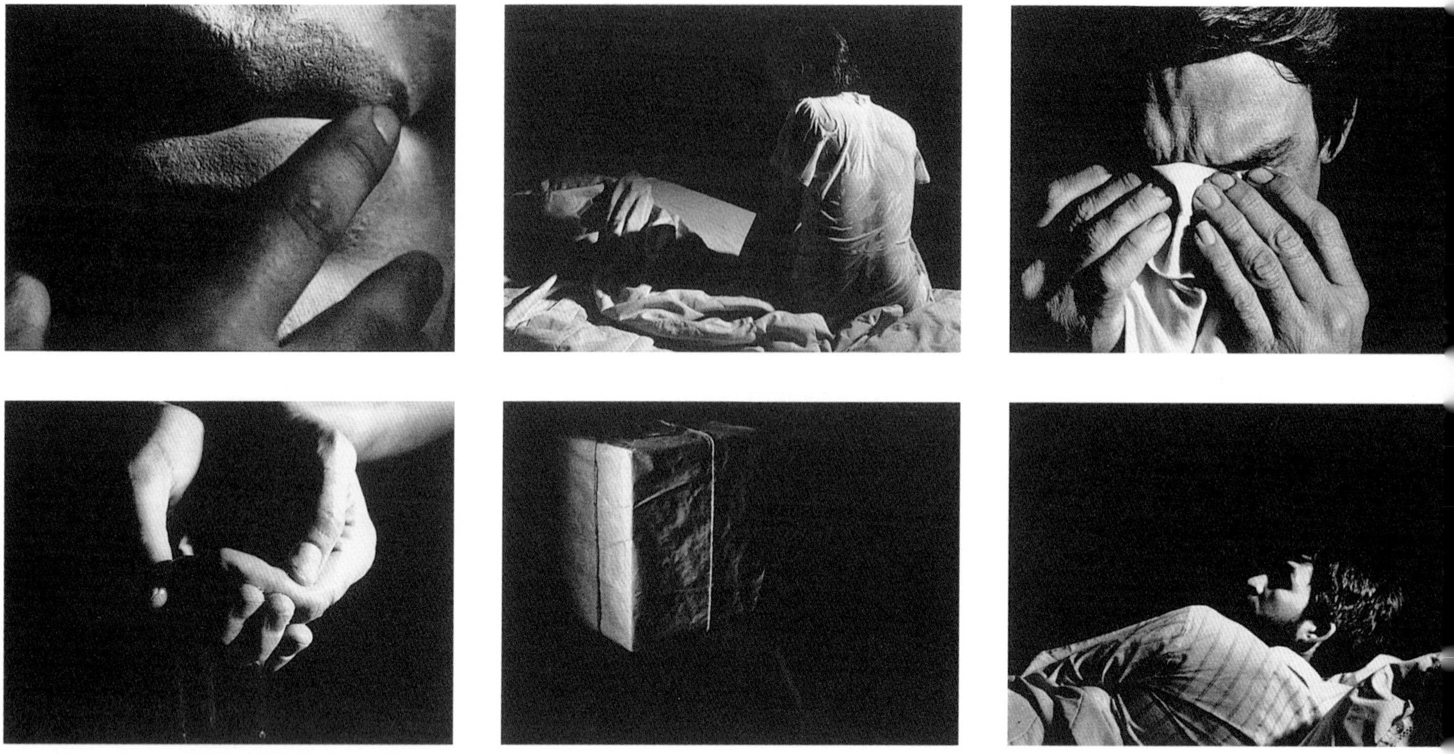

6.

6. Eileen Cowin: Based On A True Story
   7.94" x 16.06"
7. Eileen Cowin: Landmines
   6.38" x 15.97"

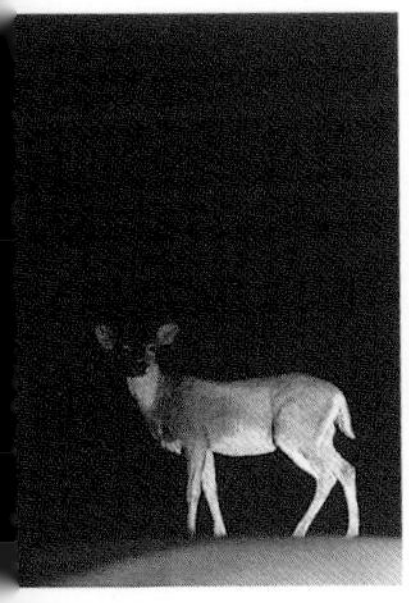
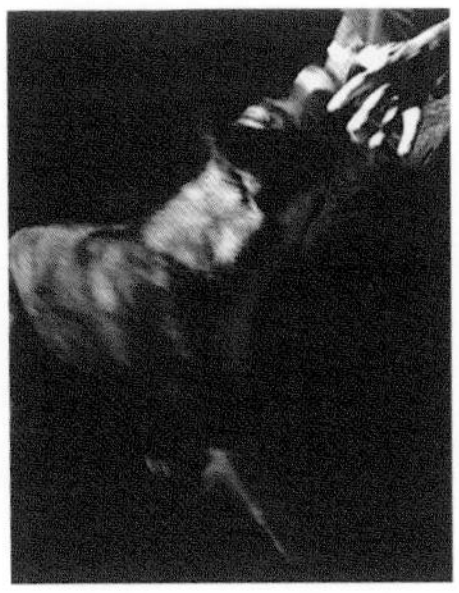
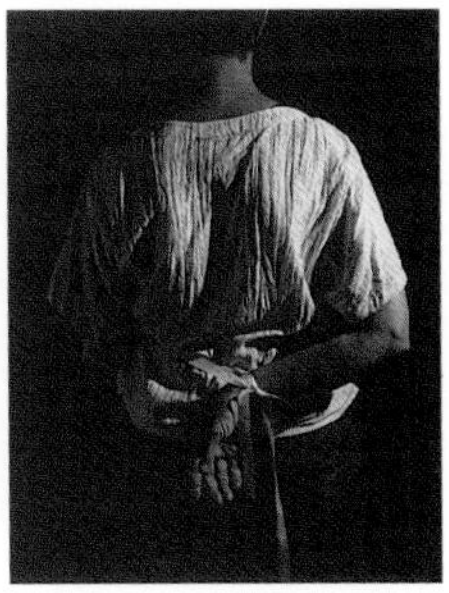

Could you tell us something about the philosophy of Nash Editions?

We are first and foremost a fine art printmaker. We really want this firm to be perceived as an endeavor that began with, and will continue to give, priority to the artistic quality of the work and not the technology.

Could you tell us about the artists who come to Nash Editions for Iris prints?

One of the first people we worked with was Pedro Meyer. He is a Mexican photographer who has exhibitions all over the world. We've done an extensive amount of work with Douglas Kirkland. David Hockney was also one of our first clients. Just yesterday we received four more images to do for David. I talked this morning with Jamie Wyeth, the son of Andrew Wyeth. He will be sending us one of his pieces next week. We did some digital work with Sally Mann, and also Elliot Erwit. They are only interested in silver prints, but we were able to do some digital work with them. Other clients include George Krause, Olivia Parker, Robert Heinecken and Joyce Neimanas. We also work with many other artists who are not as well known, but who are doing fabulous work.

Could you tell us a little about Graham Nash's interest in collecting photographs?

Graham has always been involved in collecting photographs. He has pieces that he picked up in a junk store for 50 cents, alongside pieces that cost him $150,000. He's more interested in the image itself rather than its collectability.

What is the future vision of Nash Editions?

Sometime in the next year we are going to try to split off a graphics division of Nash Editions. This division would allow us to do more art reproduction as opposed to limited edition printing. Hopefully, that will be successful enough to allow us to continue with our work at Nash Editions. Because Nash Editions is not a money-

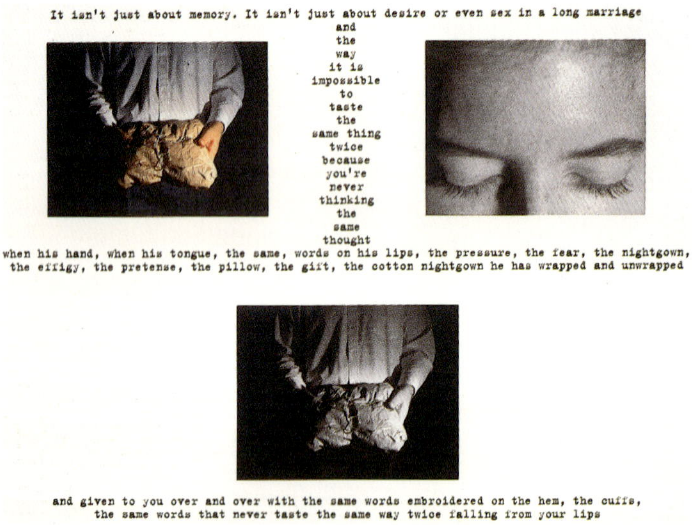

8.

making operation, the graphics wing will lend some much neede support.

I don't want people to perceive Nash Editions as a place whe you go to get art "reproduced." We look at our work as creatir new originals in multiple form. This may seem to be a trick semantics, but to our way of thinking, there's a real differenc We participate with artists in the creation of new works of art.

We will also be expanding our locations, while we try to mainta quality control. With the advent of affordable high-speed da lines and new software, it would be possible to open new faciliti in other parts of the U.S. and other countries, and maintain quali by being able to exchange information at very high speed.

Again, we are not a profit-oriented company, but the one thir we have gained is a worldwide reputation for artistic quality. Fro the very beginning we have only been interested in putting quali out there. There's enough bad art around already, and we dor want to add to that.

8. Eileen Cowin: Nightgown (in collaboration with Louise Erdrich)
   8.15" x 11.32"
9. Darryl Curran: I'm Gone! I'm Here
   16" x 23.50"

9.

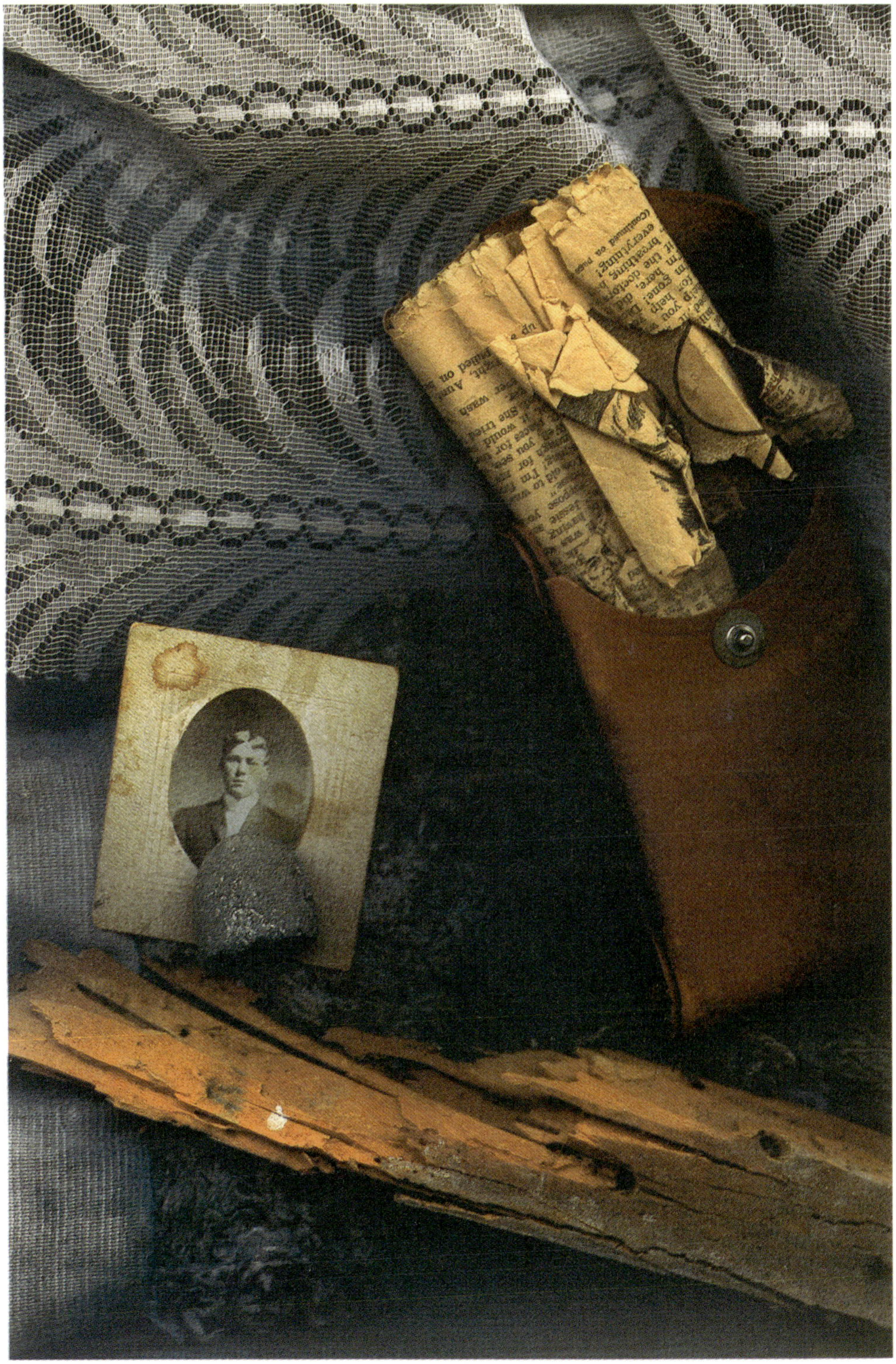

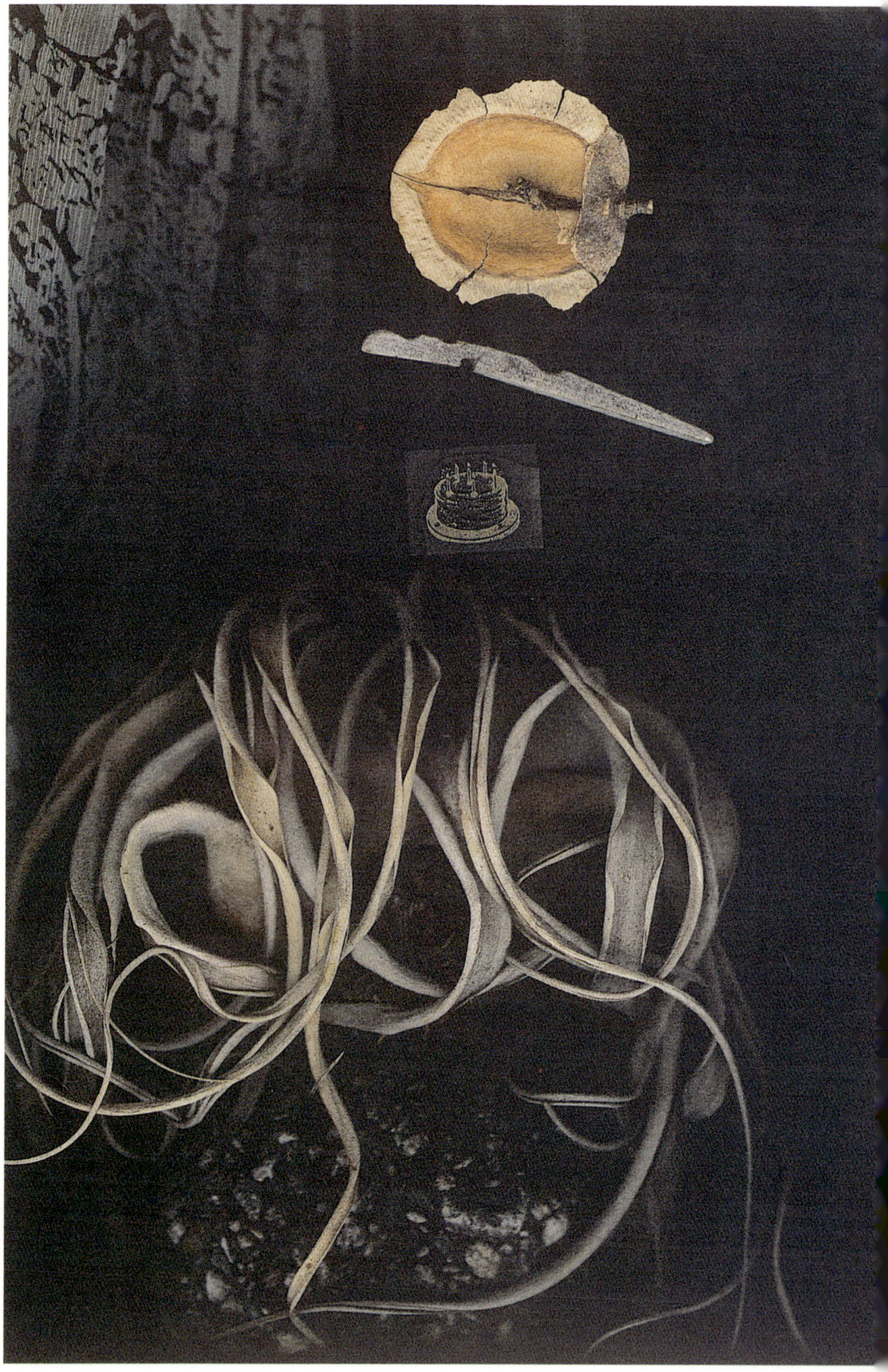

10.

10. Darryl Curran: Fugue
16" x 23.50"
11. Darryl Curran: Feathers & Friends
16" x 23.50"

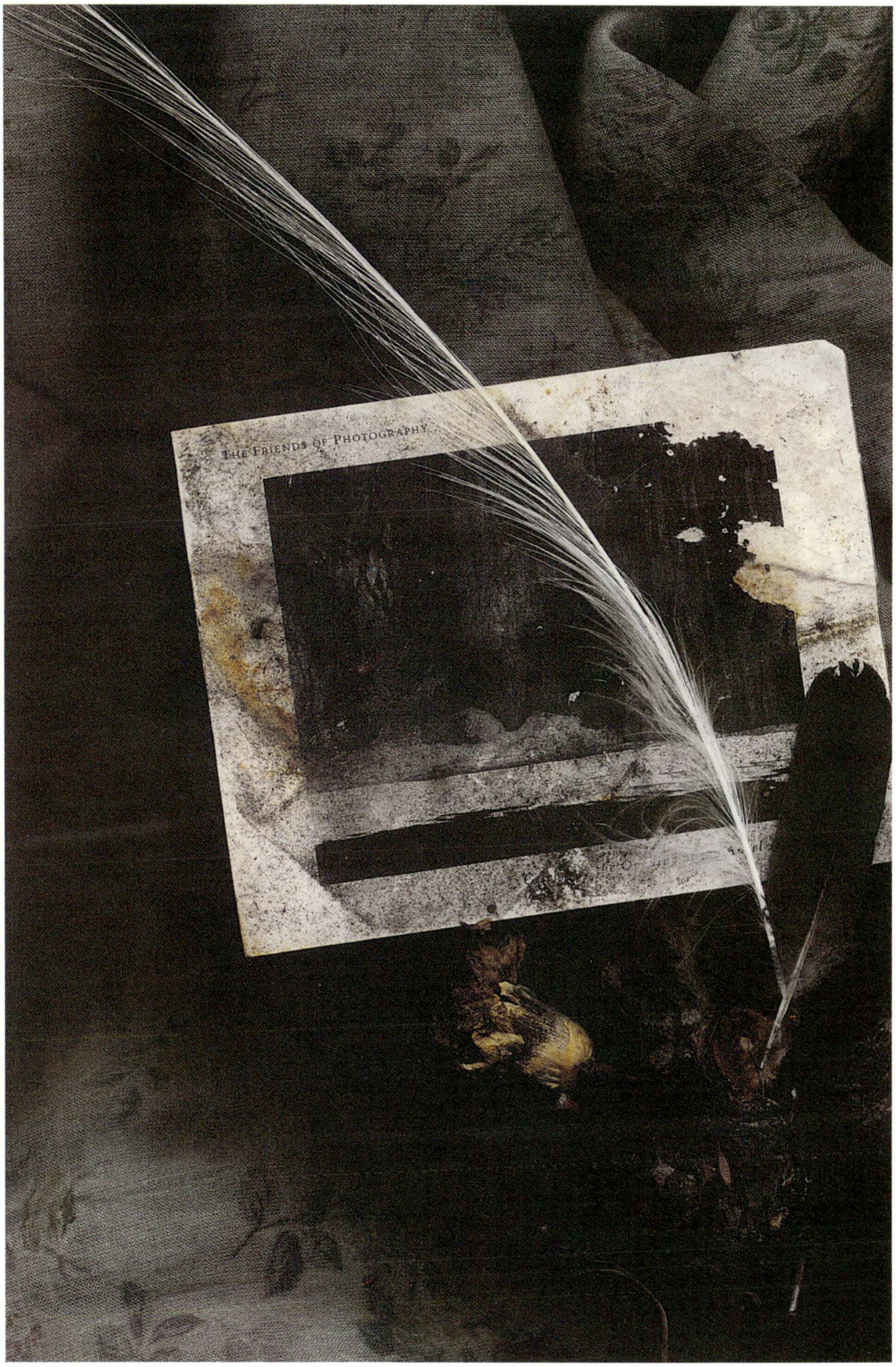

11.

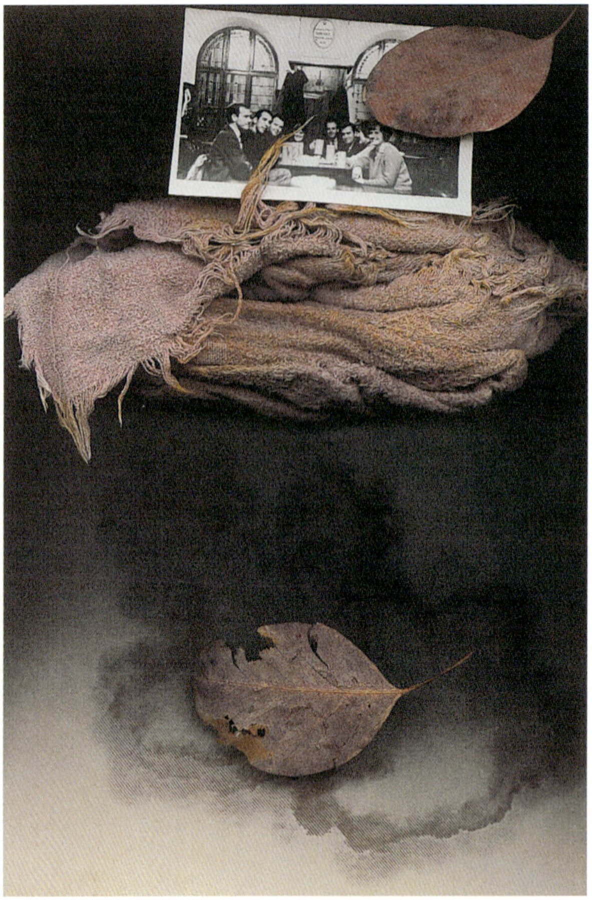

12.

12. Darryl Curran: Cloud Crowd
    16" x 23.50"
13. Carol Flax: My Mother's Eyes
    29" x 38.38"

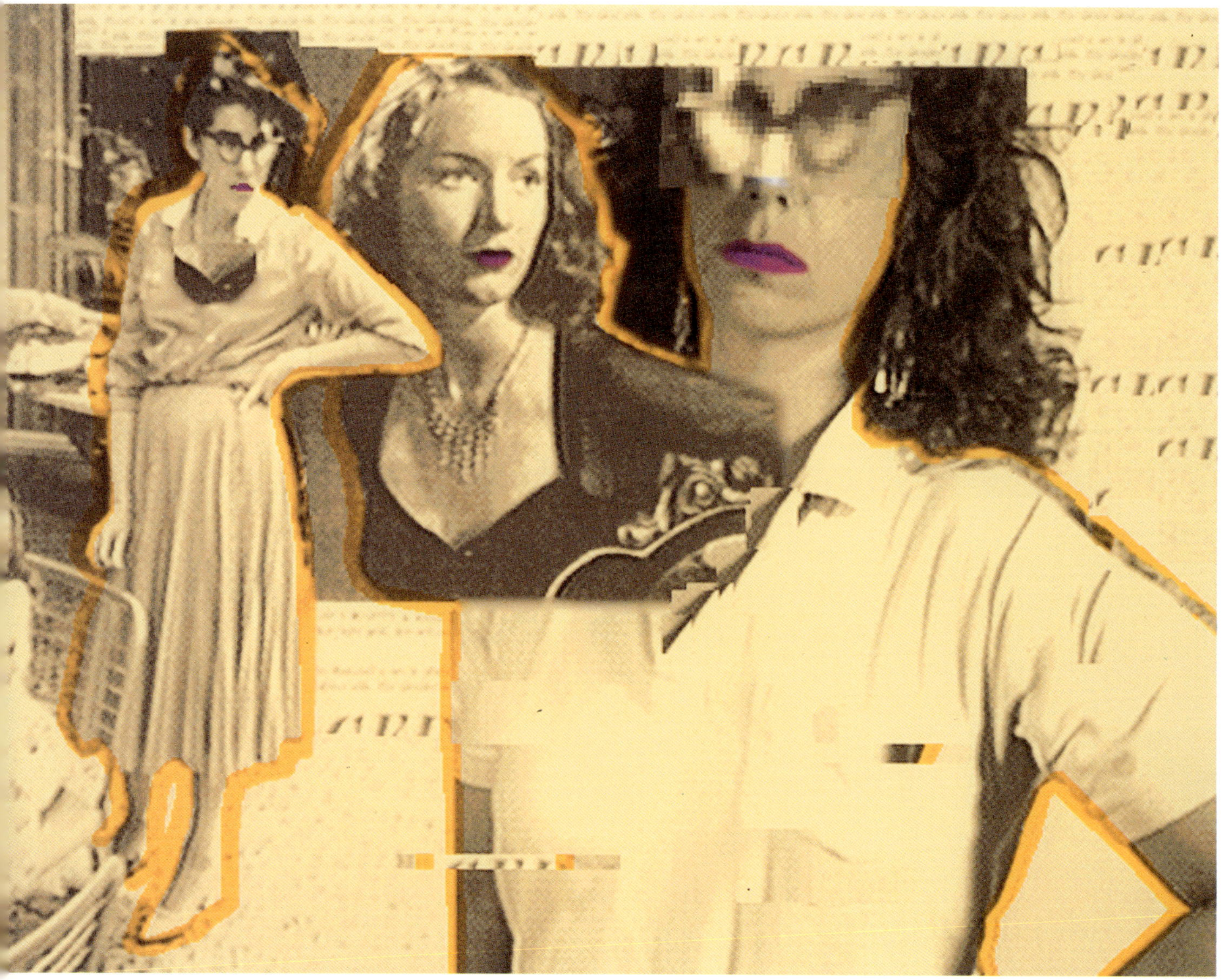

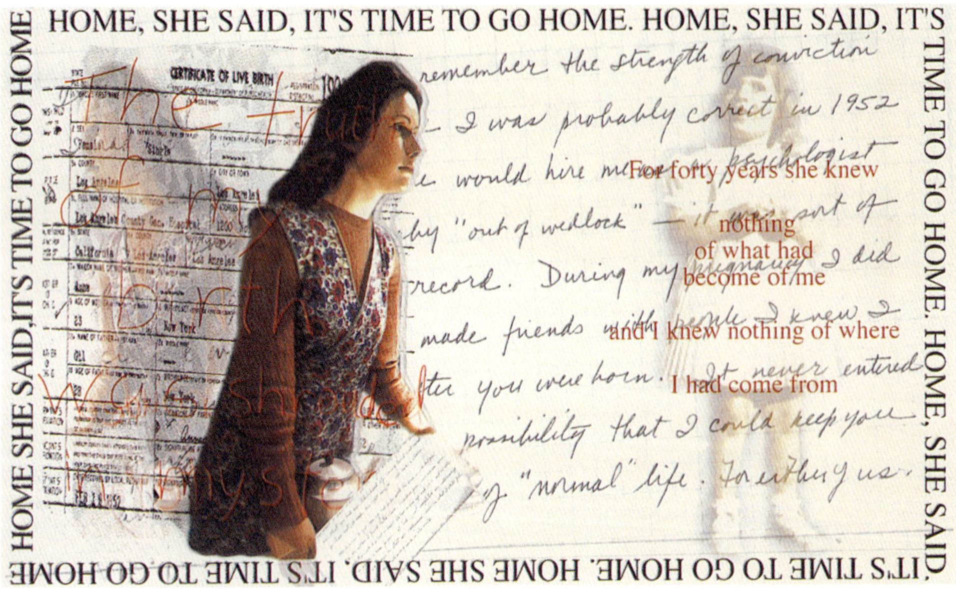

14.

14. Carol Flax: Some (M)Other Stories: A Parent(hetic)al Tale, page 2, 11.91" x 20"

15. Carol Flax: Some (M)Other Stories: A Parent(hetic)al Tale, page 3, 14.55" x 21"

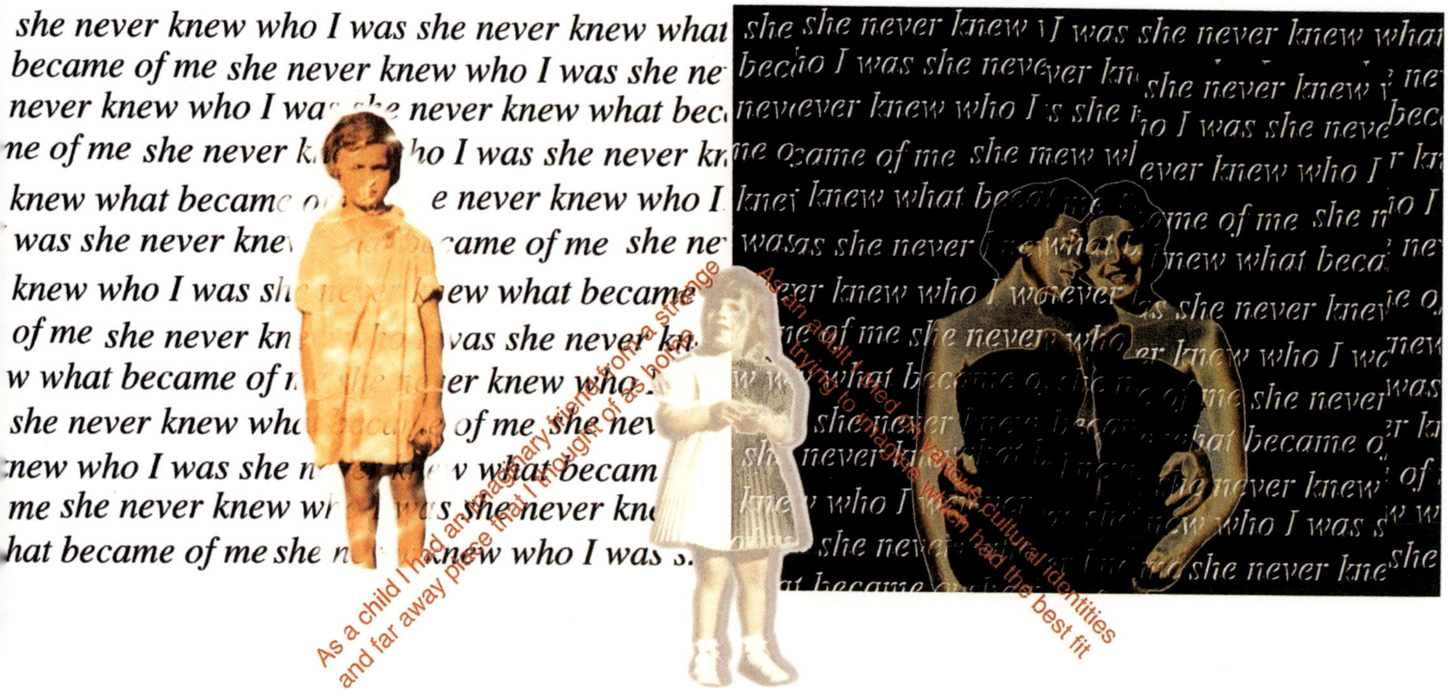
she never knew who I was she never knew what became of me
As a child I had an imaginary friend from a strange and far away place that I thought of as home
As an adult I tried on various cultural identities trying to imagine which had the best fit

16. Robert Heinecken: Shiva and Parvati Embracing, and Their Son, Ganesha
54" x 92"
17. Olivia Parker: Action Toy
20" x 24.17"

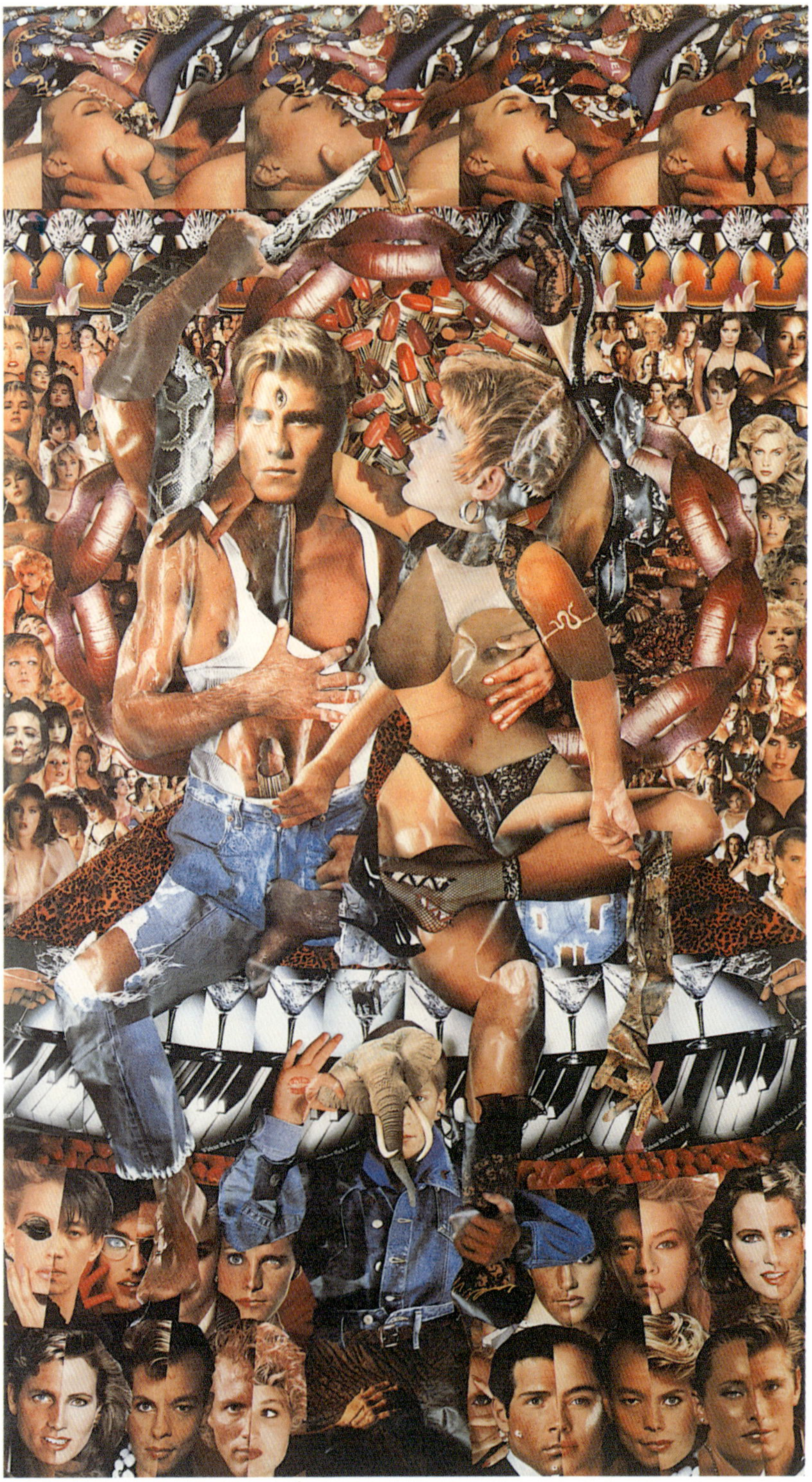

16.

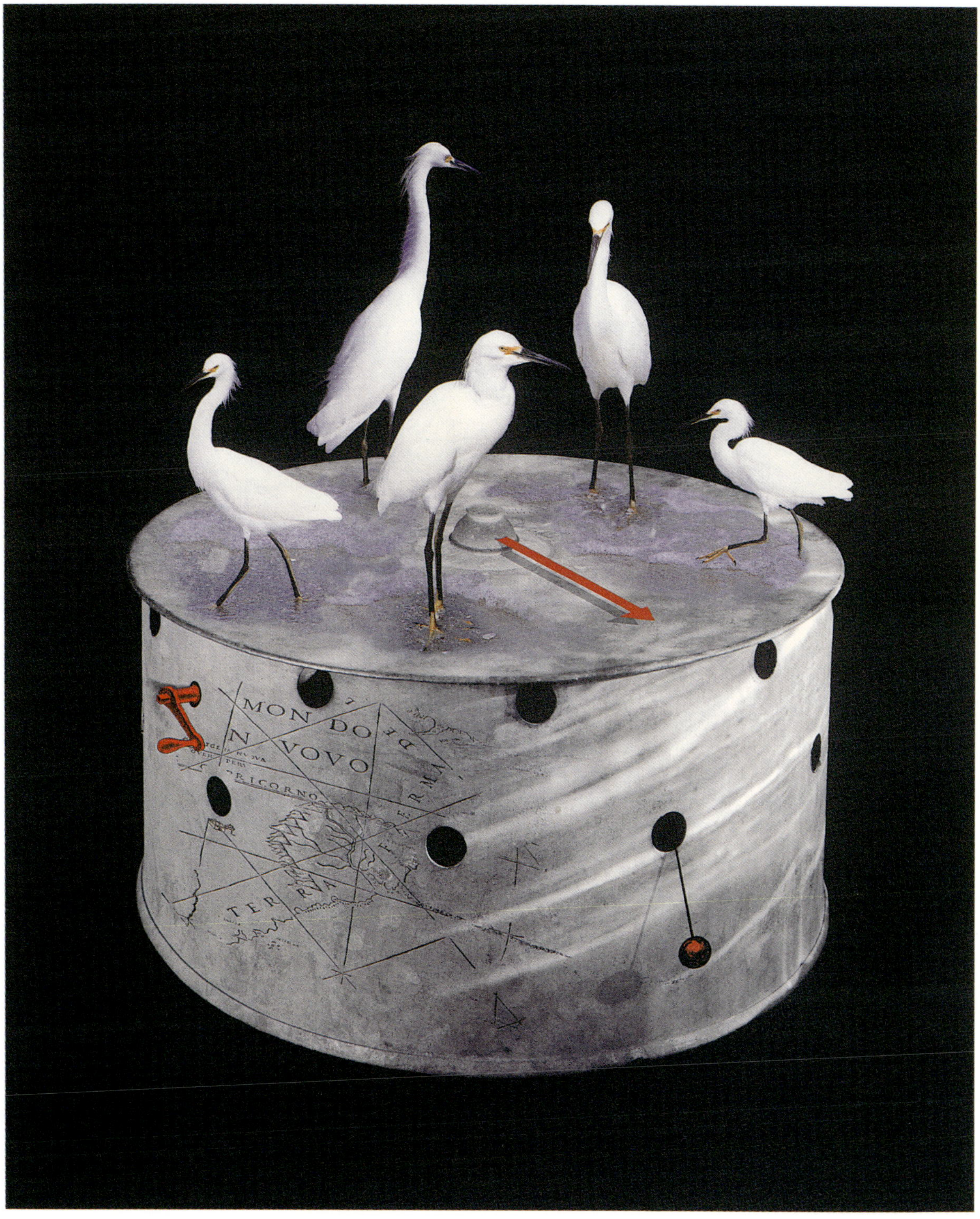

17.

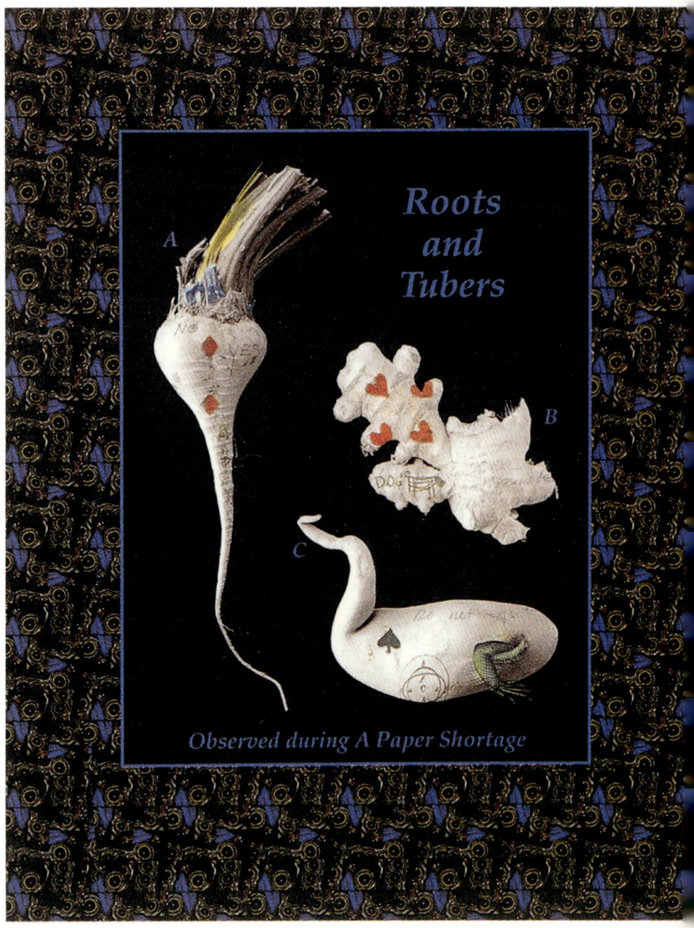

18.

18. Olivia Parker: Roots & Tubers
    16" x 20.17"
19. Opposite: Olivia Parker : Missing Piece - Ibis
    8.79" x 10.25"

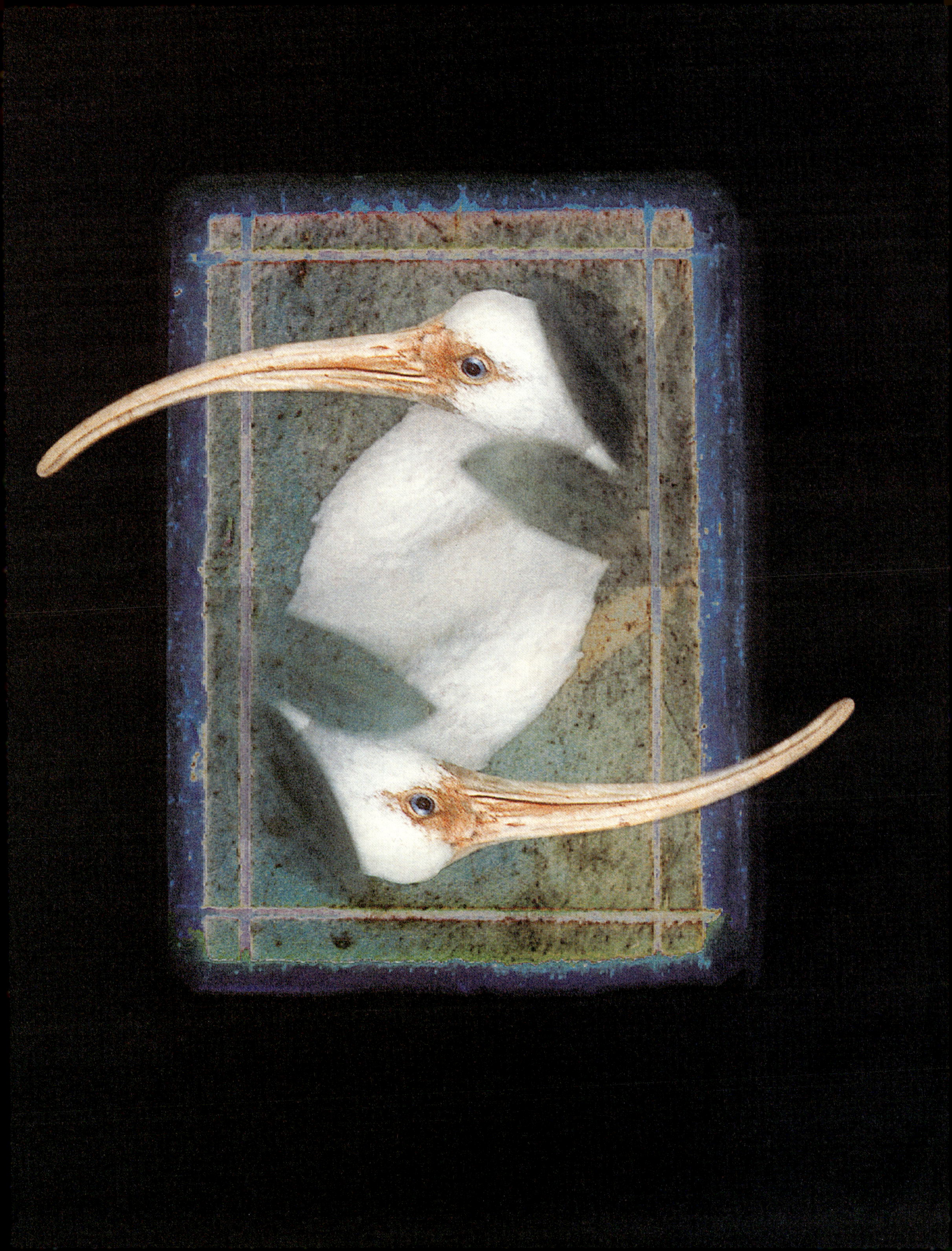

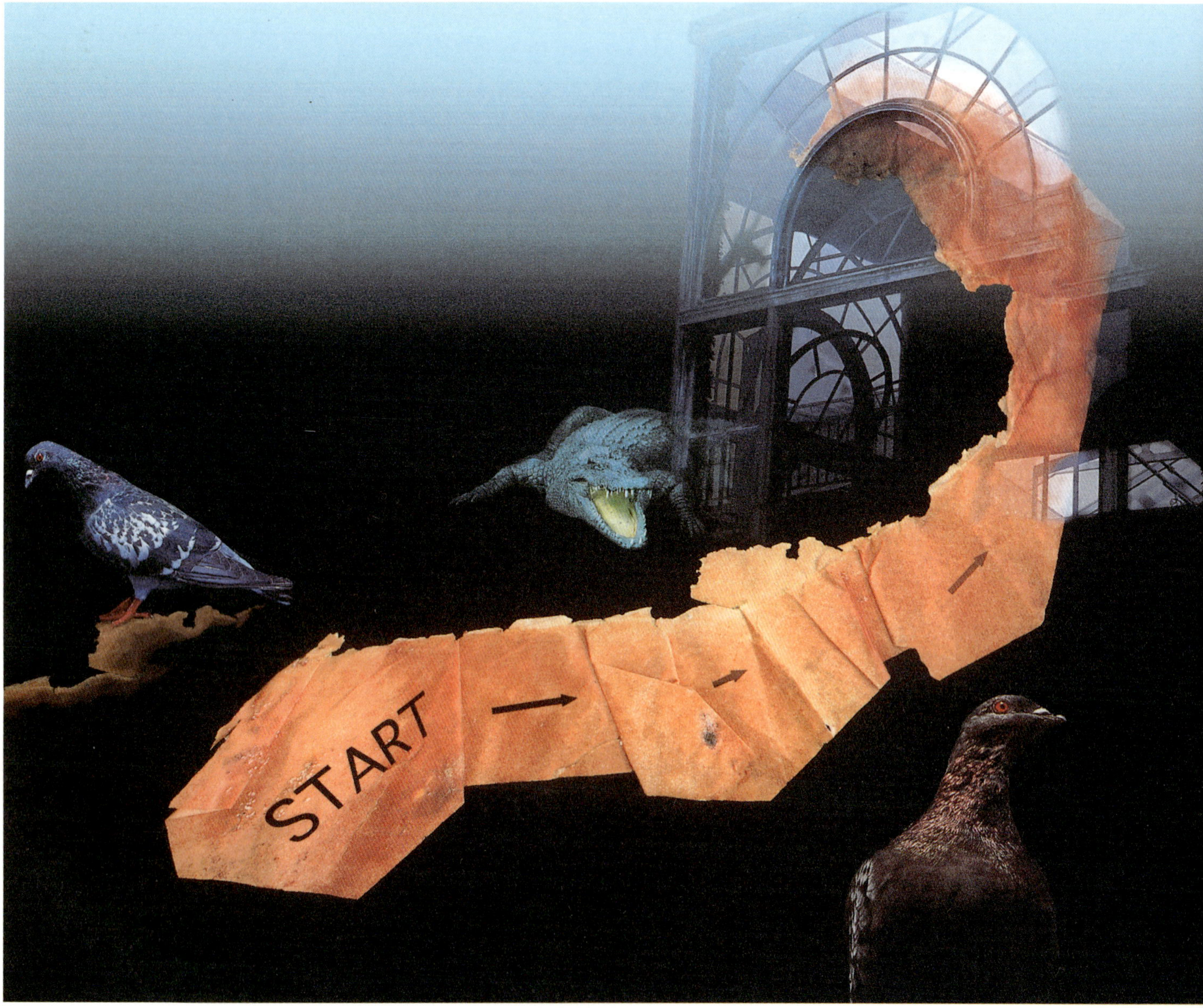

20.

20. Olivia Parker: Path
24.01" x 29.94"
21. Olivia Parker: Horseplay
20" x 25.11"

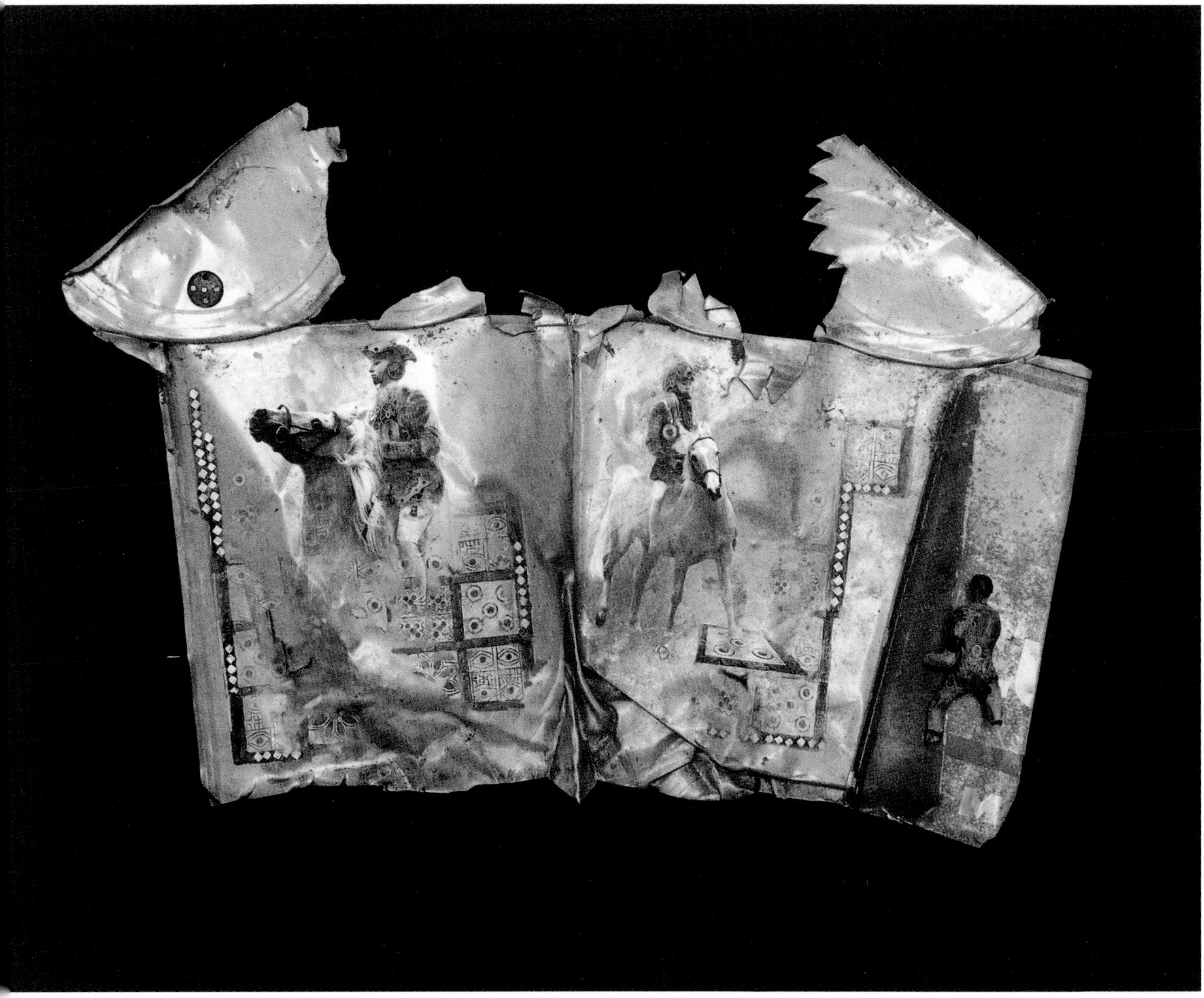

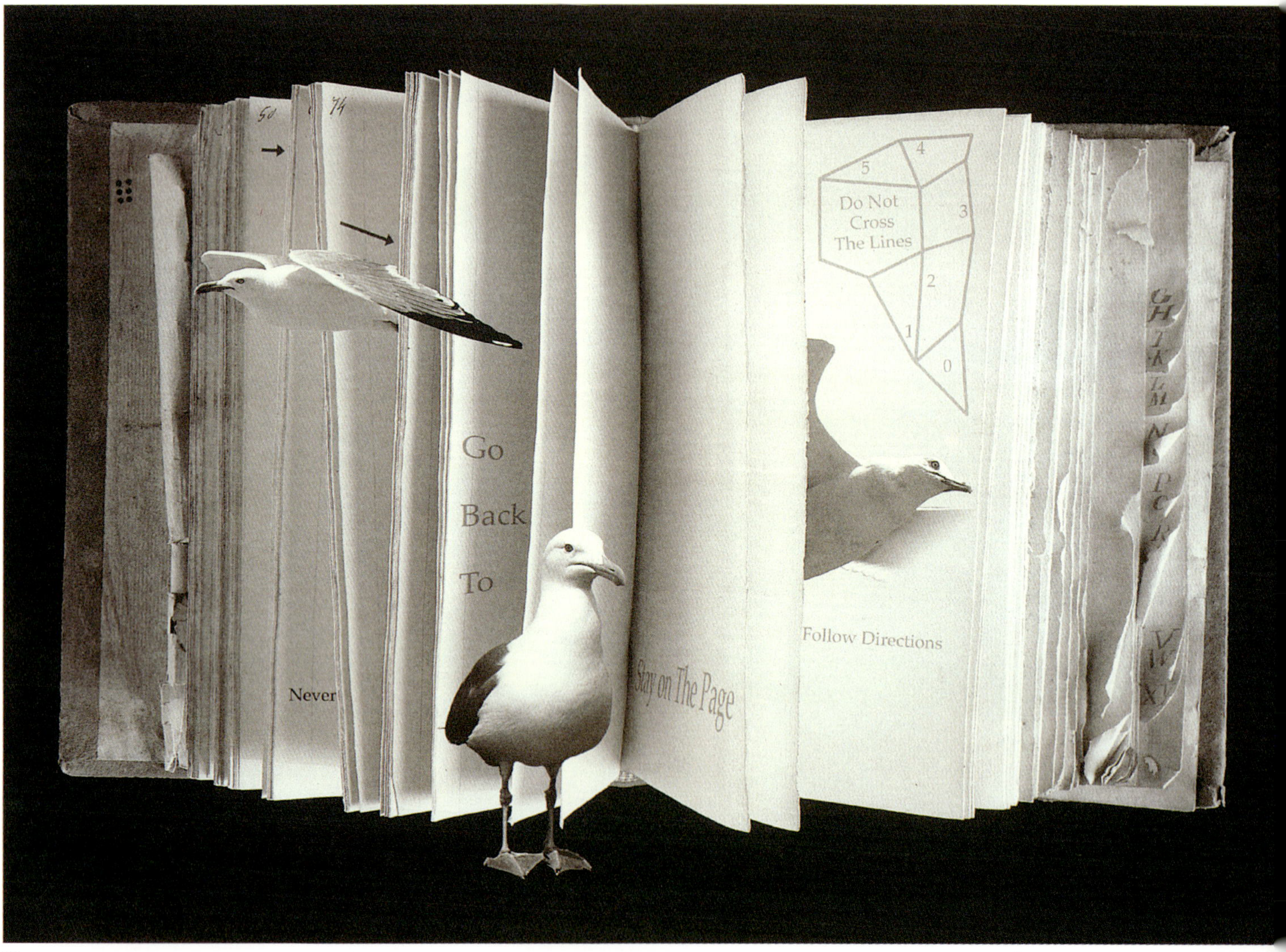
50
74
Go
Back
To
Never
Stay on The Page
Do Not
Cross
The Lines
5
4
3
2
1
0
Follow Directions

22.

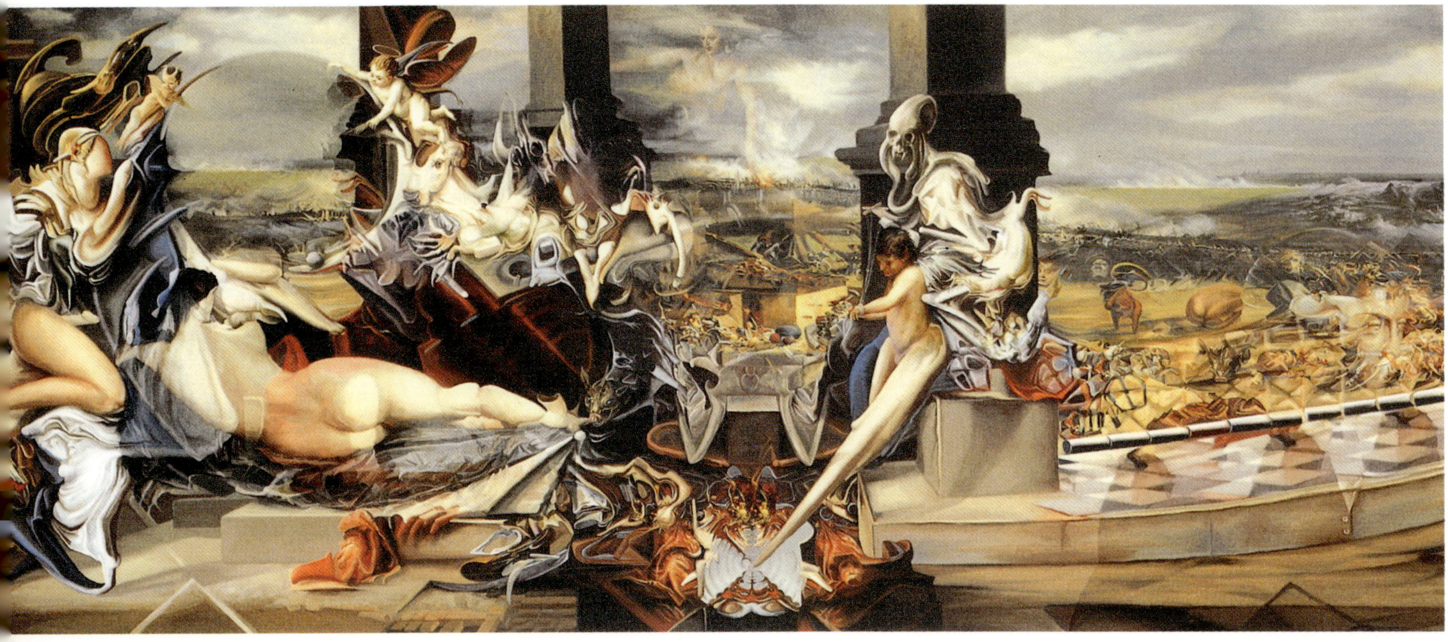

Olivia Parker: Book of Broken Rules
19.52" x 27.36"
Allen Toney: Neo Paranoic Opera of Hallucinogenic Inter-Relationalism
11.59" x 28"

Nash Editions / Allen Toney

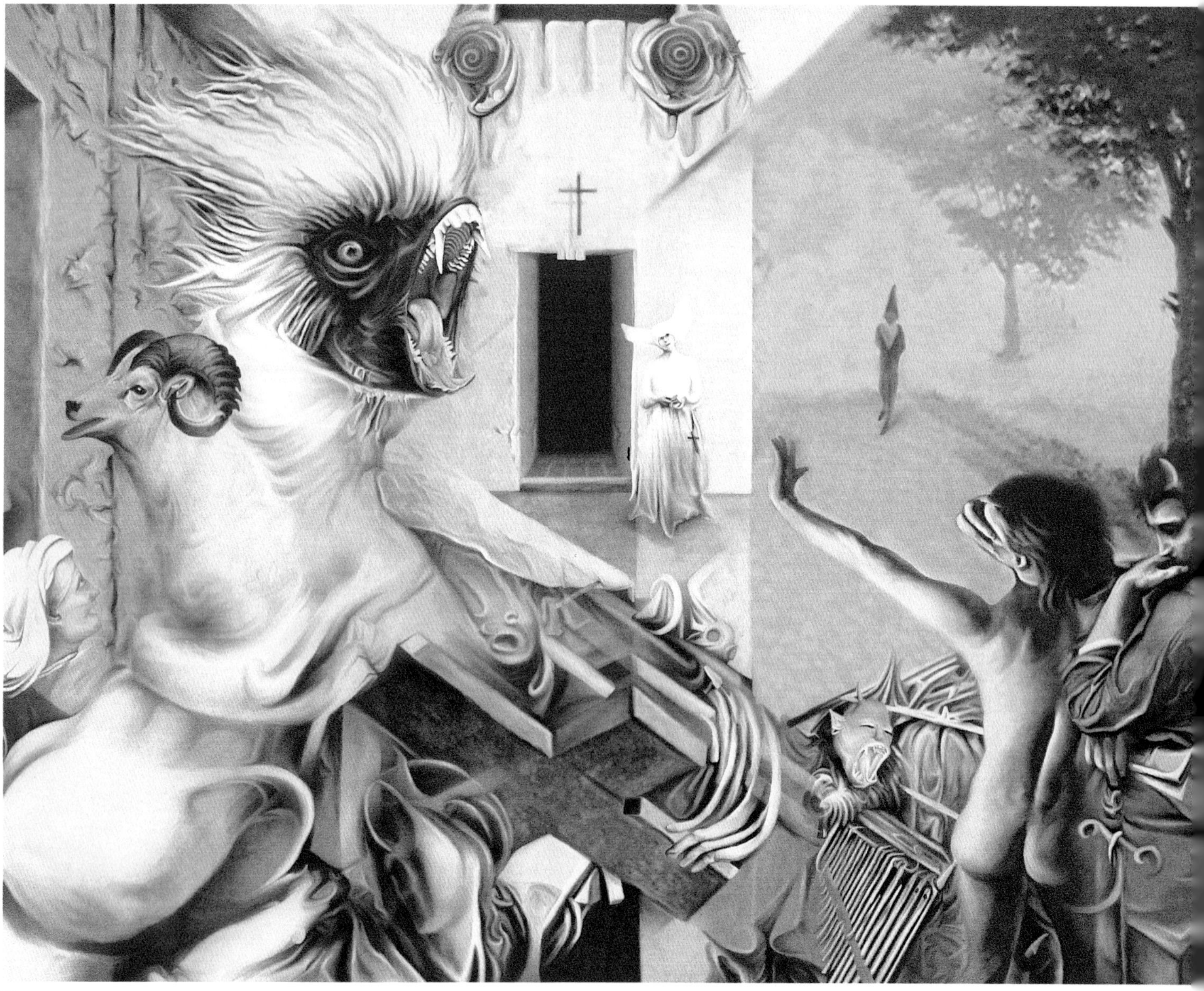

24.

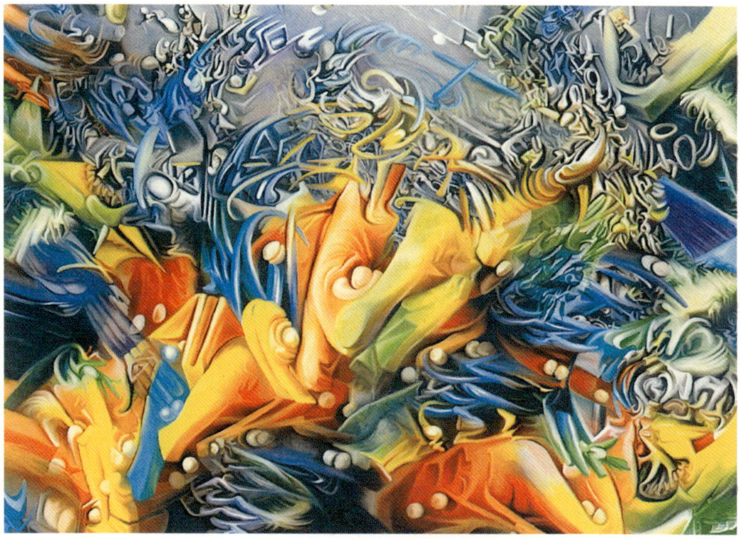

25.

llen Toney: Mystical Enigmatic Synthesis of Paranoia, Mathematical Chaos,
nd Hyper-Anxious Religiosity 18.05" x 23"
llen Toney: Shadow of God
9.69" x 28"

26. Allen Toney: Meta Ta-Ta Apocalyptoid
24" x 24"

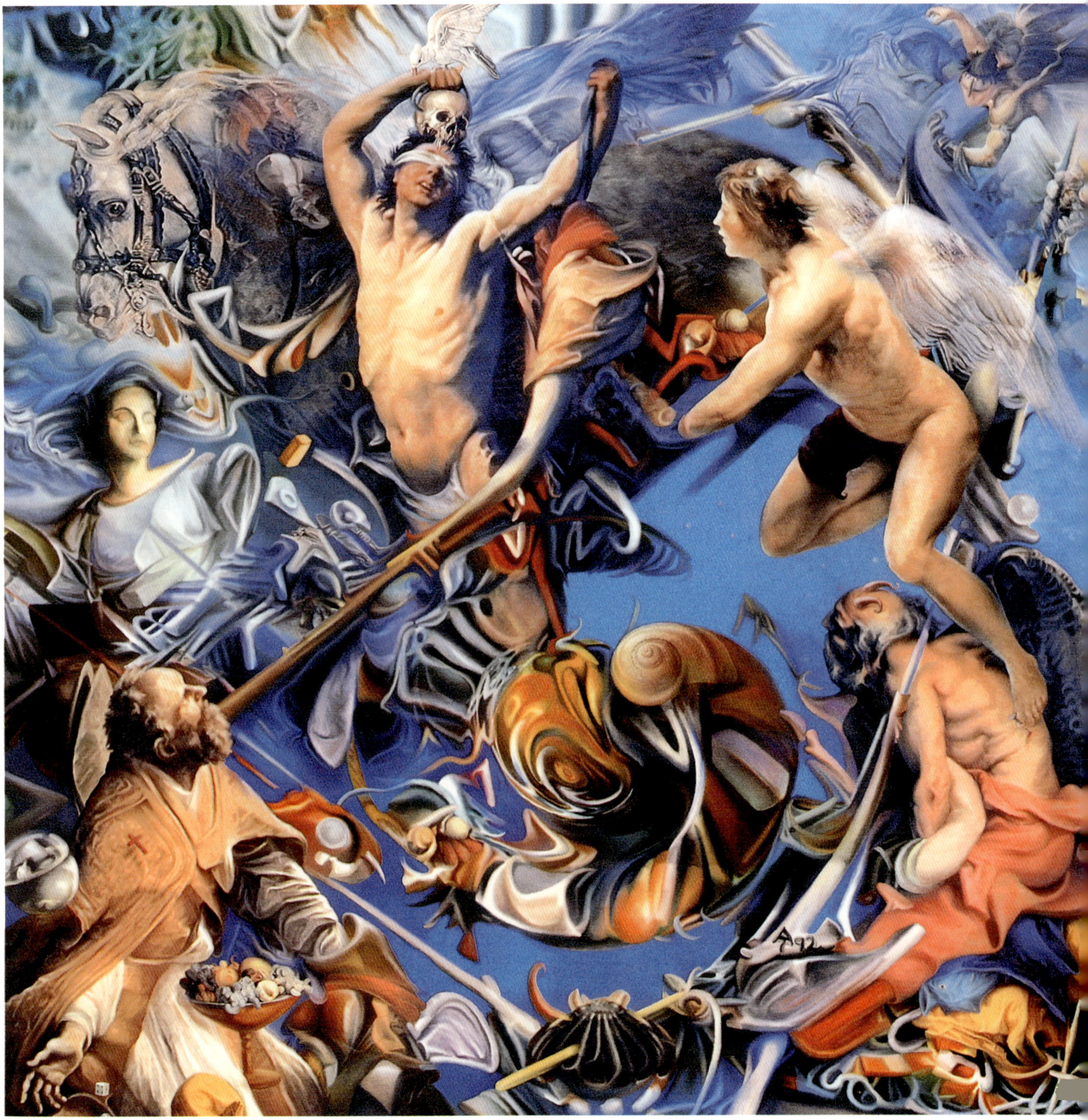

26.

vid Byrne

en something makes us feel strange it often kes us feel good,too. The two sensations are nehow linked. Strange = Good. David Byrne

vid Byrne has been taking photographs since art school days, rich and subtle color otographs ranging in subject from household ects to religious monuments to decaying sters of pop icons. He has said of his otography, "My picture taking began as a ndless activity. It's been going on for a long e. It was not preconceived of as 'Art.' There s no end in sight as there was no end in my nd. It is an ongoing activity, as if I am in an notic state, letting the camera guide my hand d eye."

happy destination of this hypnotic path is a ection of images which work on two distinct els. The subjects, whether a light fixture in a tel lobby or a window display of kitschy gious icons, are chosen because they already rk as art, exist as what Byrne calls ntemporary art exhibitions that only lack cumentation." But in the photographing, nething more than mere documentation occurs; camera works as a "pleasure tool," adding ue with its gaze, investing the mundane with sacred, and the ridiculous with the sublime.

vid Byrne has exhibited in Europe, Asia, Latin erica and the USA. Recent solo exhibitions ve been held at Tokyo's Parco Gallery (*Sacred ects,* 1995), at Centro Cultural Recoleta in enos Aires (*David Byrne - En La Pared,* 1994), d in New York City at Christinerose Gallery *vid Byrne Photographs,* 1995).

photographs have also been published in nerous art magazines, including *Blind Spot, erture, Parkett*, and *ArtForum*. His first book photography, *Strange Ritual,* was published year by Chronicle Books, San Francisco.

Eileen Cowin

Eileen Cowin is currently a Professor of Art at California State University, Fullerton, where she has taught since 1975.

Her work has been exhibited internationally and has been included in numerous museum collections in the United States and Europe, including the Museum of Modern Art in New York, the Los Angeles County Museum of Art, the Seattle Art Museum, the Whitney Museum of American Art, and the Museum Moderner Kunst, Vienna.

Selected publications of her work include *New American Photography* by Kathleen Gauss, and *The Privileged Eye: Through the Narrative Portal,* by Max Kozloff and Eileen Cowin, published by the Min Gallery, Tokyo, Japan.

Her work has been represented by the Light Gallery, the Witkin Gallery, OK HARRIS Gallery, the Jayne H. Baum Gallery, the G. Ray Hawkins Gallery, the Roy Boyd Gallery, the Ezell Gallery, as well as in domestic settings.

Eileen Cowin received a National Endowment for the Arts Workshop Grant in 1973 and National Endowment for the Arts Individual Fellowship Grants in 1979, 1982 and 1990. In 1990, she was commissioned by the Public Art Fund to do an installation at Penn Station in New York.

Darryl J. Curran

Darryl Curran has been active in the fine art photography field since 1965. His various roles in the field have included exhibitor, curator, juror and board member of several arts organizations. He joined the faculty at California State University, Fullerton in 1967, where he initiated the Creative Photography BA and MA programs.

Curran's creative work is housed in major public collections and has been included in numerous important group shows such as *Photography into Sculpture,* and *Mirrors and Windows* at the Museum of Modern Art in New York, *Vision and Expression* at the International Museum of Photography/George Eastman House, *Photography into Art* at the British Arts Council, and *Light and Substance* at the University of New Mexico. In 1995 he was invited to Madrid as the U.S. artist representative for the opening of *Empowered Images: A Cultural Presentation of the United States of America,* a traveling exhibition of contemporary photography.

As former president of the Los Angeles Center for Photographic Studies (LACPS), Curran led the effort to produce *10 Photographers/Olympic Images,* a project sponsored by the Olympic Arts Festival and exhibited at the Museum of Contemporary Art. Darryl Curran is currently chairman of the Department of Art at California State University, Fullerton.

Carol Flax

Carol Flax recieved her MFA from California Institute of the Arts. She currently teaches Electronic Media at the University of California, Santa Barbara.

In her work Flax uses new digital technologies to focus on issues about identity and access to information in both the private and the public realms. Her most recent project, *Some (M)Other Stories: A Parent(hectic)al Tale,* addresses issues of her own adoption along with the larger societal implications of how women are viewed in culture.

Flax has completed a number of public art projects in recent years, including a 1993 installation in the Scottish Highlands. Her six week residency there resulted in eighteen digitally produced, double-sided banners installed at the Inverness train station as part of Fotofeis, the Scottish International Festival of Photography. Recent exhibitions include a one-person show at the San Francisco Camerawork, as well as inclusion in *Digital Photography,* at the Centre

National de la Photographie in Paris, *P.L.A.N.: Photography Los Angeles Now* at the Los Angeles County Museum of Art, and *Iterations: The New Image* at the International Center for Photography in New York.

Her work has also been represented at the Seattle Art Museum, the Southeast Museum of Photography, the Bank of America Art Collection, as well as numerous private art collections.

Robert Heinecken

Robert Heinecken received his Master of Arts degree from UCLA in 1960, and began teaching photography and related media at the UCLA Department of Art the same year. He was appointed Professor of Art at UCLA in 1975, becoming Professor Emeritus in 1991.

Besides teaching at UCLA, Heinecken has also been extremely active over the years participating and acting in workshops as a juror. He has lectured extensively in the U.S., as well as in Europe and Asia.

Since 1964, Heinecken has had a total of 60 one-person exhibitions in numerous galleries, academic institutions and museums throughout the U.S., Europe and Japan, including the Museum of Modern Art, New York, the Chicago Center for Contemporary Photography, the Pasadena Art Museum, the University of Kassell, Germany, and the Min Gallery, Tokyo. Heinecken has also participated in 330 group exhibitions, including the Los Angeles County Museum of Art, the Barbican Center, London, the Goethe Institute, Munich, the Kyoto Museum of Art, Japan, and the Tokyo Metropolitan Museum of Photography.

Heinecken's published works and portfolios include *Mansmag,* 1969, *Just Good Eats...,* 1971, *He/She,* 1980, *Docudrama,* 1986 and *Recto/Verso,* 1988.

Olivia Parker

Olivia Parker graduated from Wellesley College in 1963 with a degree in Art History. She began her career as a painter, and became involved in photography in 1970. In 1992, Parker began to work with digital imaging using photographs shot in her studio as source materials. At present she is working on three groups of photographs and digital images: *Object of Comfort and Despair* (concerning the nature of still life), *Toys and Games,* and *A History of the Real* (concerning the visual history of science).

Parker has had more than 100 one-person exhibitions in the United States and abroad. Her work is also represented in major private, corporate and museum collections, including the Art Institute of Chicago and the Museum of Modern Art in New York. Portfolios of her work have been published in *Art News, American Photographer, Camera, Camera Arts, Photo Japan* and many more magazines in the United States, Europe and Japan.

There have been three monographs of Parker's work: *Signs of Life* (Godine, 1978), *Under the Looking Glass* (New York Graphic Society, 1983) and *Weighing The Planets* (New York Graphic Society, 1987).

Allen Toney

Allen Toney began his art career in 1989 wh still a student at Marshall University Huntington, West Virginia. There he focused traditional oil painting, printmaking a photography. Since 1990 he has work exclusively with "electronic painting," using graphics computer and electronic drawing tab to produce his images.

Toney's digital work combines liquid, sensu neoclassical forms with mystical, mathemati and surreal sensibilities. In so doing he forms new hybrid visionary style unique to t computer medium.

Since 1992, Toney has been in five one-pers shows as well as over 45 group and juri exhibitions throughout the United States, Euro and Japan. His work has been published both numerous traditional print publications such *Leonardo Journal, Photo Electronic Imaging,* a *Wired*. Many new media publications such interactive multimedia CDs, Internet, World W Web galleries and electronic magazines ha featured his work as well.

Charly Franklin

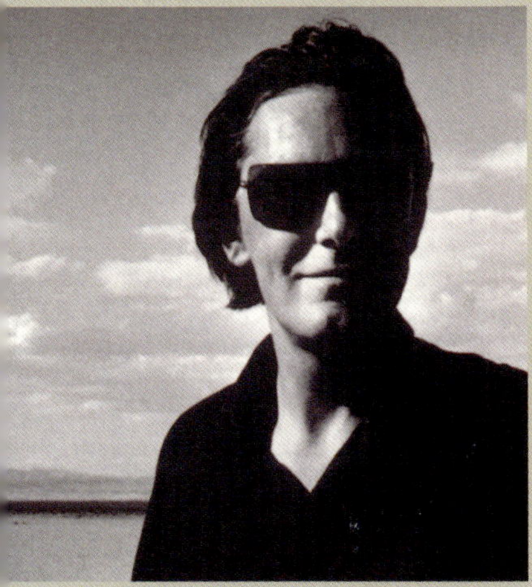

Charly Franklin has specialized in a surrealistic style of photography since the late seventies. Back then, his images of levitated objects set against strange, barren landscapes demanded long hours of hard work and considerable technical ingenuity. Most of the work had to be done on the location shoot, with some tricky techniques later in the darkroom. Now, the computer has eliminated much of the toil and guesswork, and enabled Charly to work on ideas that would be impossible to realize by any other means.

The 45-year-old English photographer based in San Francisco believes that the future of commercial photography clearly lies in digital imaging. Although he still sets up elaborate location shots, he does all the subsequent work in Adobe Photoshop on his Macintosh Quadra 950. Every image he has produced since 1991 has been digitally manipulated.

Franklin's often bizarre images are the result of active participation in rendering the concepts his clients need to illustrate. His work is in big demand by various corporate clients and his photographs have appeared in such publications as *Communication Arts, Print, Photo Metro* and on the cover of *Graphis Design Annual*.
(Photo of Charly Franklin by Erich Muller)

Charly Franklin

What was it that got you started using the computer? Could you describe your first digital images?

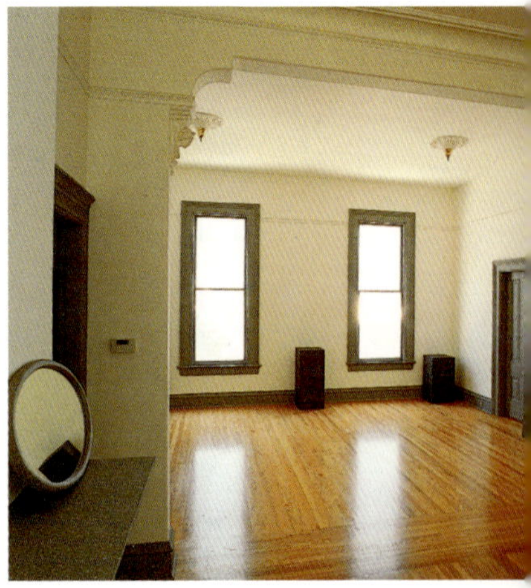

Charly Franklin's Studio Shot

I had used Scitex machines for various jobs. The main problem with using Scitex was coordinating what I wanted with what was possible to do, and also the cost factor which was very hard to estimate and usually considerable.

Well, I'd been following what was going on with computers...and I'd been hearing that there were photo programs available, but the things I saw were black and white with pretty low resolution. Then Photoshop came out, and enabled you to work in higher resolution and color. So things got to be more interesting. The possibility of having a mini-version of a Scitex in my studio was very exciting to me.

I went to a Photoshop workshop that Henry Brimmer of *Photo Metro* organized. At that time I'd never seriously used a computer, and I couldn't really understand what was going on. I could see that some of the things the instructor was able to do with the machine had a lot of potential. It wasn't really spectacular stuff — not by today's standards. But when I saw him using the outlining tool and transferring parts of the images...making parts darker or lighter and so on...it reminded me very much of watching the Scitex operators work on my images.

Then I just knew I had to get one of those computers. So I bought a Macintosh IIci, with 20 MB of RAM and a 250 MB hard-disk drive. That would be around April 1991.

At that particular moment, I was working on a project for Kit Hinrichs at Pentagram Design here in San Francisco. It was to be a black and white photo for a swatch book cover for the Simpson Paper Company. I had proposed the idea of a mobius strip floating over a beach with the ocean (p. 150). I thought we could suspend the strip with fishline and retouch that out later. I was all set to go shoot it when Kit asked if we could do it in color instead. I thought, "Oh my God. In color? How are we going to hide the fishline?" My computer arrived that very same day so I decided to have a go.

a. Background Scan
b. Background in Progress
c. Bronze Award
d. Man in Progress

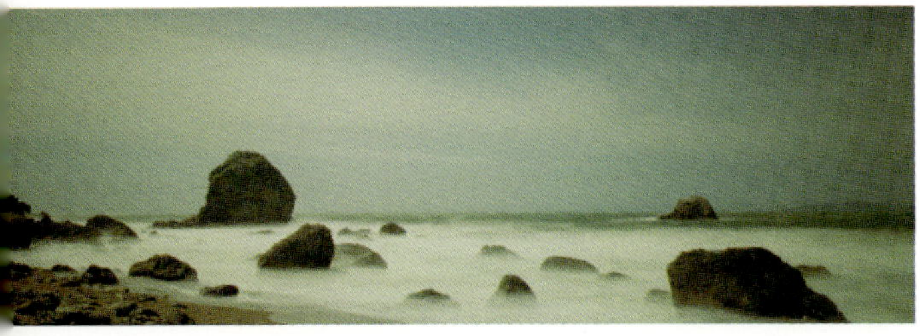

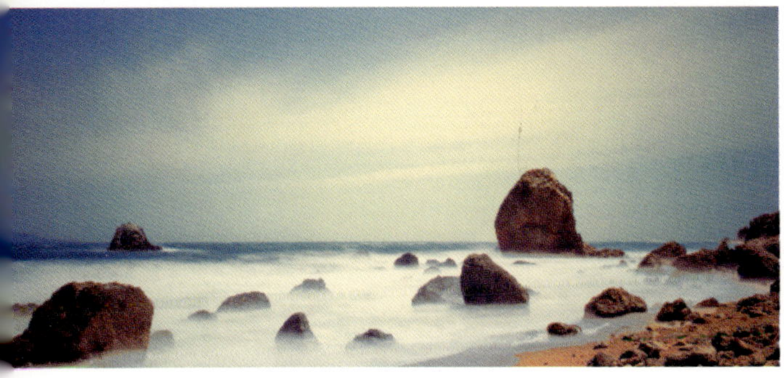

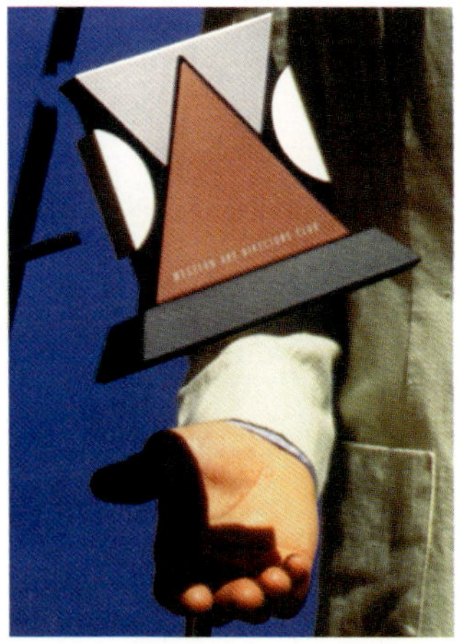

c.

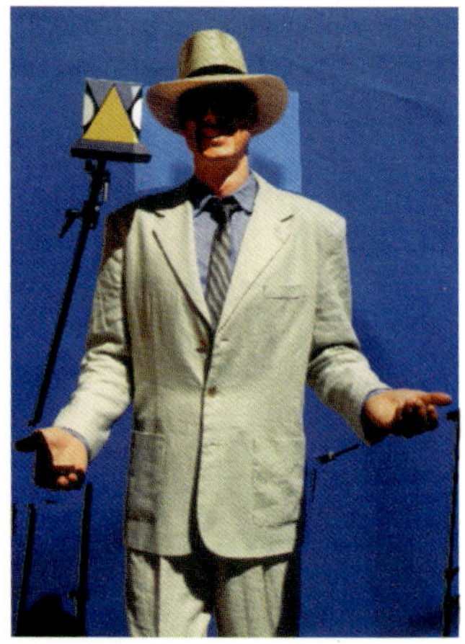

d.

e Process

ˌas approached by the Western Art Director's ub to create an image for their 30th annual ˌards competition call for entries. The image is to be 11 x $25^{1}/_{2}$ inches. They wanted a ckground that would have a western United ates feel to it. I thought of a man in a white suit a rocky Northern Californian beach, juggling gold, silver and bronze awards with sharks imming above the water in the background.

Background Scan
hotographed the background image at a beach ar San Francisco, using a panoramic camera th a neutral density filter during the day to crease the exposure to about 30 seconds.

Background in Progress
sed Photoshop to remove the green cast used by the long exposure, to enhance the lors, and to squeeze the image to fit the format the poster.

c. Bronze Award
I photographed each of the awards in front of the model in approximately the correct relationship.

d. Man In Progress
I then photographed the model, positioning one of the awards to cast a shadow on his shoulder. I didn't photograph the model with the awards in front of him, because then I would not be able to move them around later.
I then substituted the model's right hand for one with the shadow of the bronze award. I lightened the shadowed part of his face.

Charly Franklin

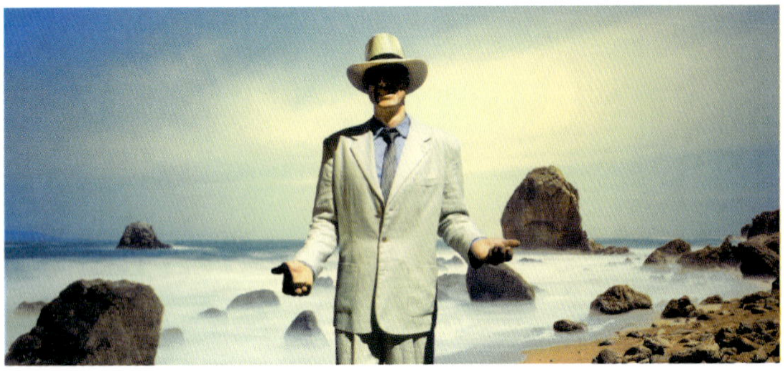

e.

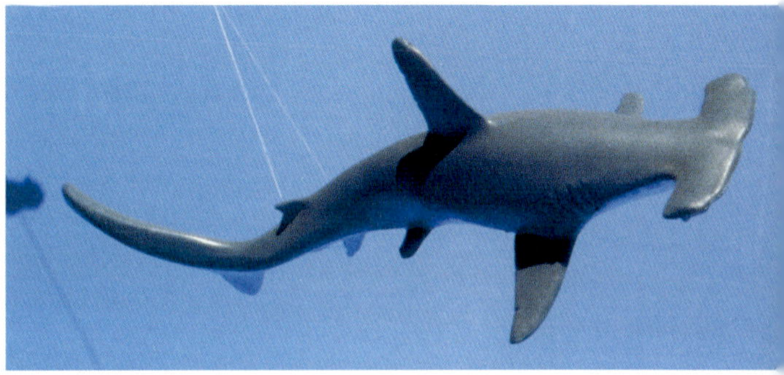

f.

e. Background with Man
I then composited the model into the background.

f. Shark Example
I photographed model sharks in several different positions.

g. Final Image
I then composited the awards and the sharks create the final image.

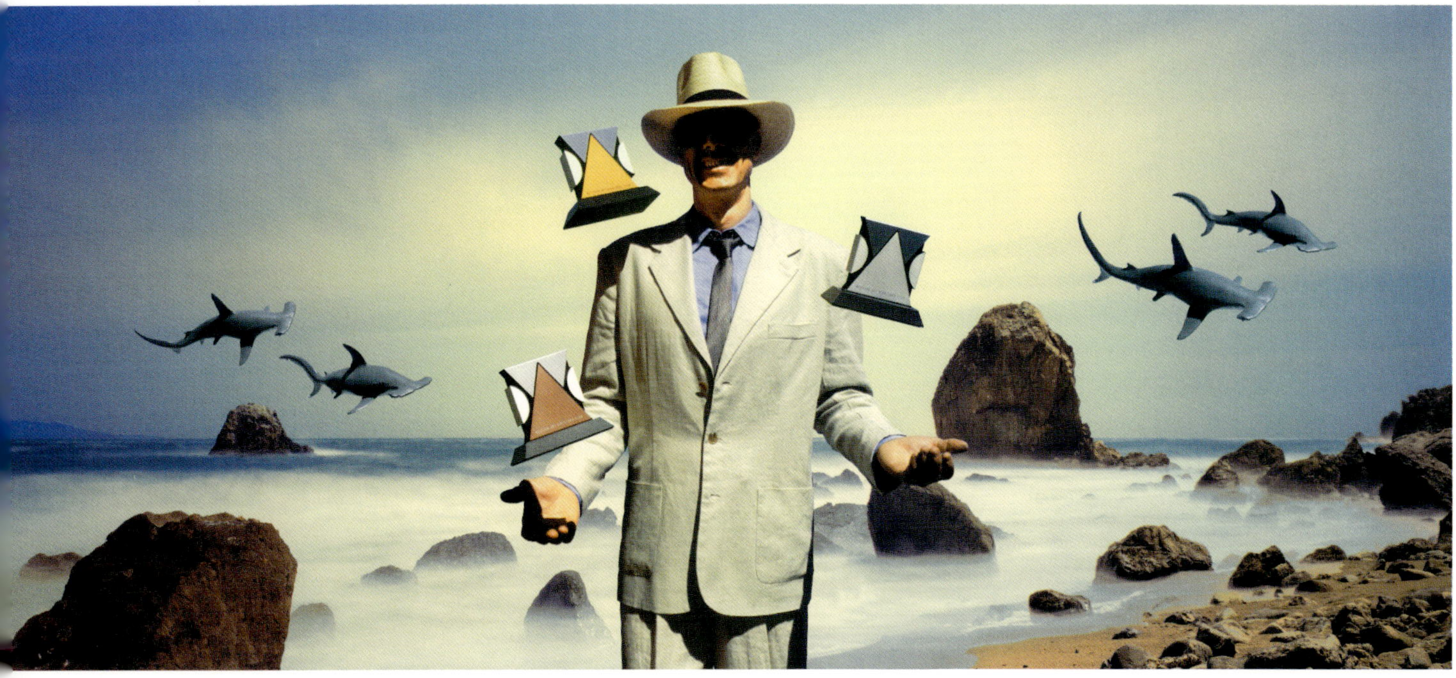

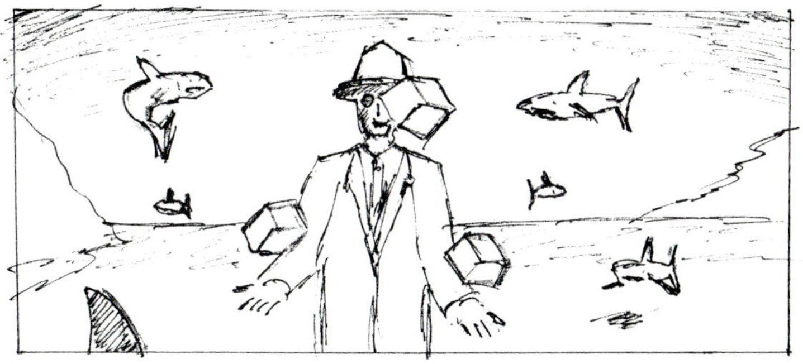

h.

Background with Man
Shark Example
Final Image
Sketch

Charly Franklin

I shot the seashore with a neutral density filter. I gave it a long exposure to get the misty effect from the moving water. And I shot the mobius strip — a strip of aluminum from a hardware store — hanging on fishline so that it cast a shadow. Kit wanted the strip red.

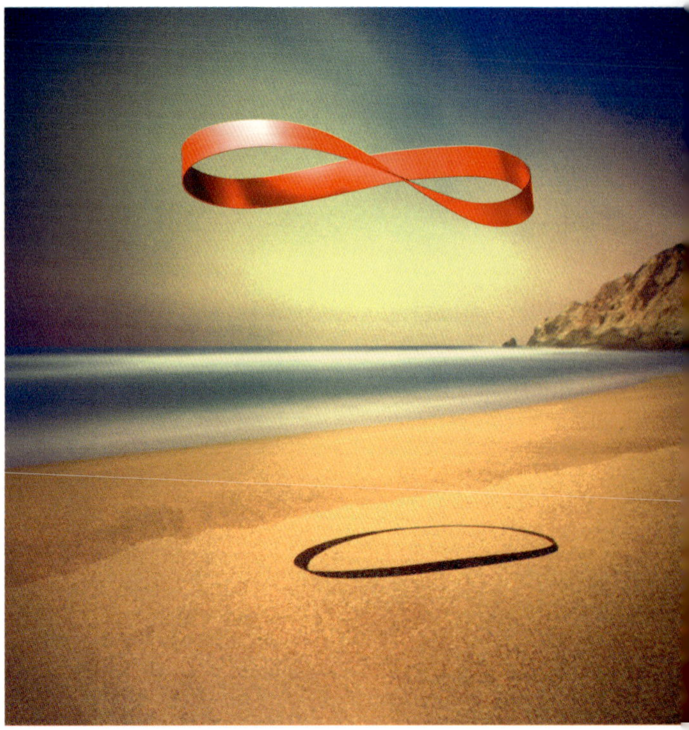

1.

Well, the time exposures produced some pretty strange colors. But there was a soft, weird quality to them that I liked. So I scanned them in and I was able to change the color of the background. I isolated the sand and made it really yellow; made the sea a deep blue; altered the sky from the ghastly green color we got with the exposures. I used the colorize controls — the Hue and Saturation — for the strip, and made it red. And the picture came out even cooler looking than I'd expected.

Then Michael Vanderbyl called with a job for Rucker-Fuller, an office furniture company. He wanted some pictures involving their furniture. I showed him the Simpson picture I had just done, and explained what I thought I could do using the computer. He was excited, so I did some sketches which the client approved. The first one I did was the chair floating over the beach.

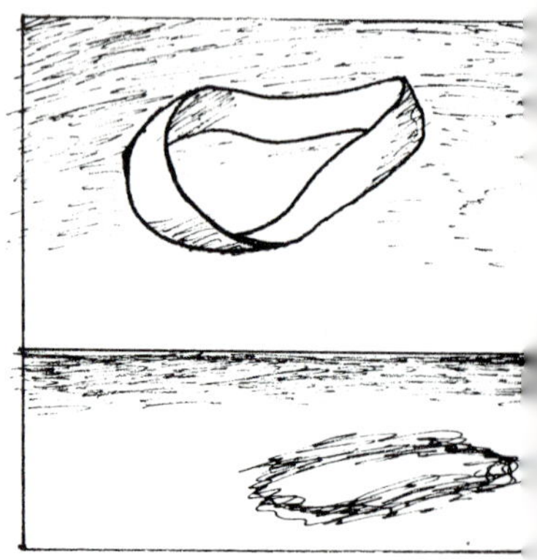

2.

I made an attachment for a light stand to support the chair. First we shot the background, which was empty. Then we set up the chair with the light stand, and photographed the chair. So we had two pictures: the background and the chair, but with the stand still in the shot. So, in the computer I outlined the chair with its shadow, and took it out of the one picture and placed it in the background shot. I realized this was a much better way of working. It was fun and also reduced the location work because we didn't have to spend hours trying to figure out how to support the chair without showing the supports.

What are the advantages of the computer for creating images, and for working with clients?

The benefits for creating pictures are legion. There are so many pictures you can do with the computer that would otherwise be impossible for most client's budgets. For example, the picture for the Silicon Graphics Indy poster. They wanted the machine

1. Red Ring
   Client: Simpson Paper Company
   Designer: Kit Hinrichs, Pentagram
2. Red Ring (sketch)
3. Phone in Bottle
   Client: Computer Sciences Corporation
   Art Director (in-house): Tony Salerno

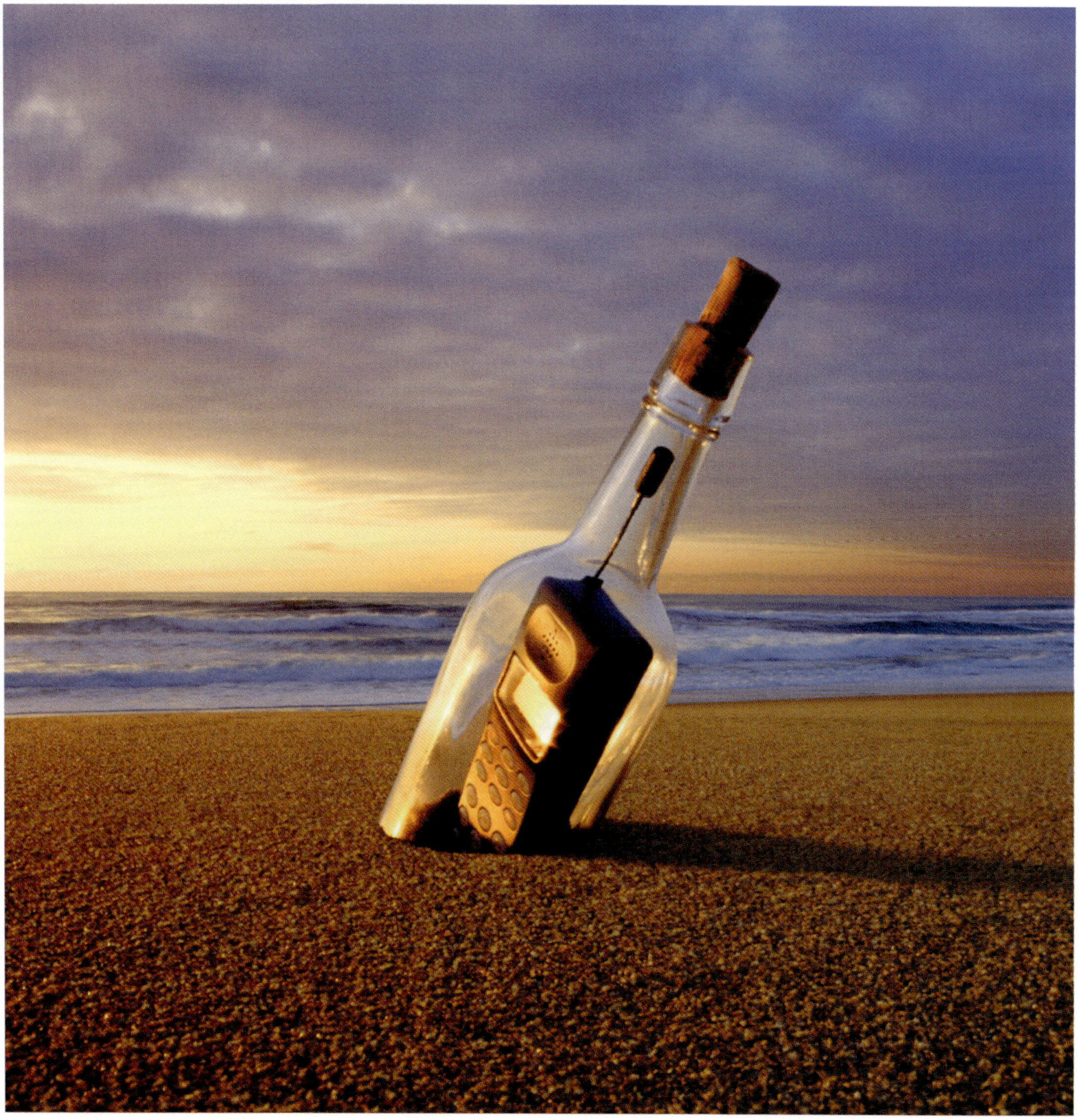

3.

photographed in a strange landscape. They also gave me a tight deadline. And they could only give me one dummy machine when the picture demanded a lot of those machines.

So we went out to shoot the background at Mono Lake. Then we shot the computer in the studio. We shot this one computer from different viewpoints. The column the computer was shot on was originally box-shaped, but later I sliced off the sides in Photoshop so that the machine looked like it was balanced on a point. It took maybe twenty hours of computer work, plus a couple of days at Mono Lake. You just could not do that without the computer.

Clients are happy with the computer work, because you can reassure them that if they agree to the idea, you will be able to carry it off. And if later, they want to, say, change the color of the ground for whatever reason, then we would be able to do that as well.

But that brings us to a problem. Once people understand something about the computer work, they do have a propensity to interfere. They think it's easy for you to change things. So they start demanding changes. But if they agree to pay more money for the changes, that's fine.

It is reassuring to know that if something does go wrong, you can probably fix it fairly easily, and without spending a lot of money. In some cases, you don't even have to go out and photograph at all. Now, you can make up the background from stock, photograph the object you need, and put it all together. There are so many advantages, that I can't imagine being in the business of doing photography and not using a computer.

I heard that you start from a hand-drawn sketch. Could you tell us briefly about your work method and techniques from that point through the finished print?

I started by using the sketches because it was an easier means of showing someone what the photograph might look like than describing it in words. So I would sit down and draw out the

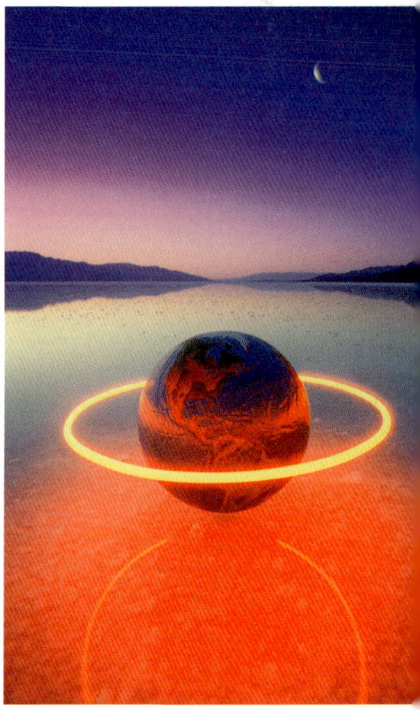

4.

4. Globe & Ring (pre-computer image)
   Client: Computer Sciences Corporation
   Designer: Larry Long/Runyan Hinsche Associates
5. Boxes
   Client: Computer Sciences Corporation
   Art Director (in-house): Tony Salerno

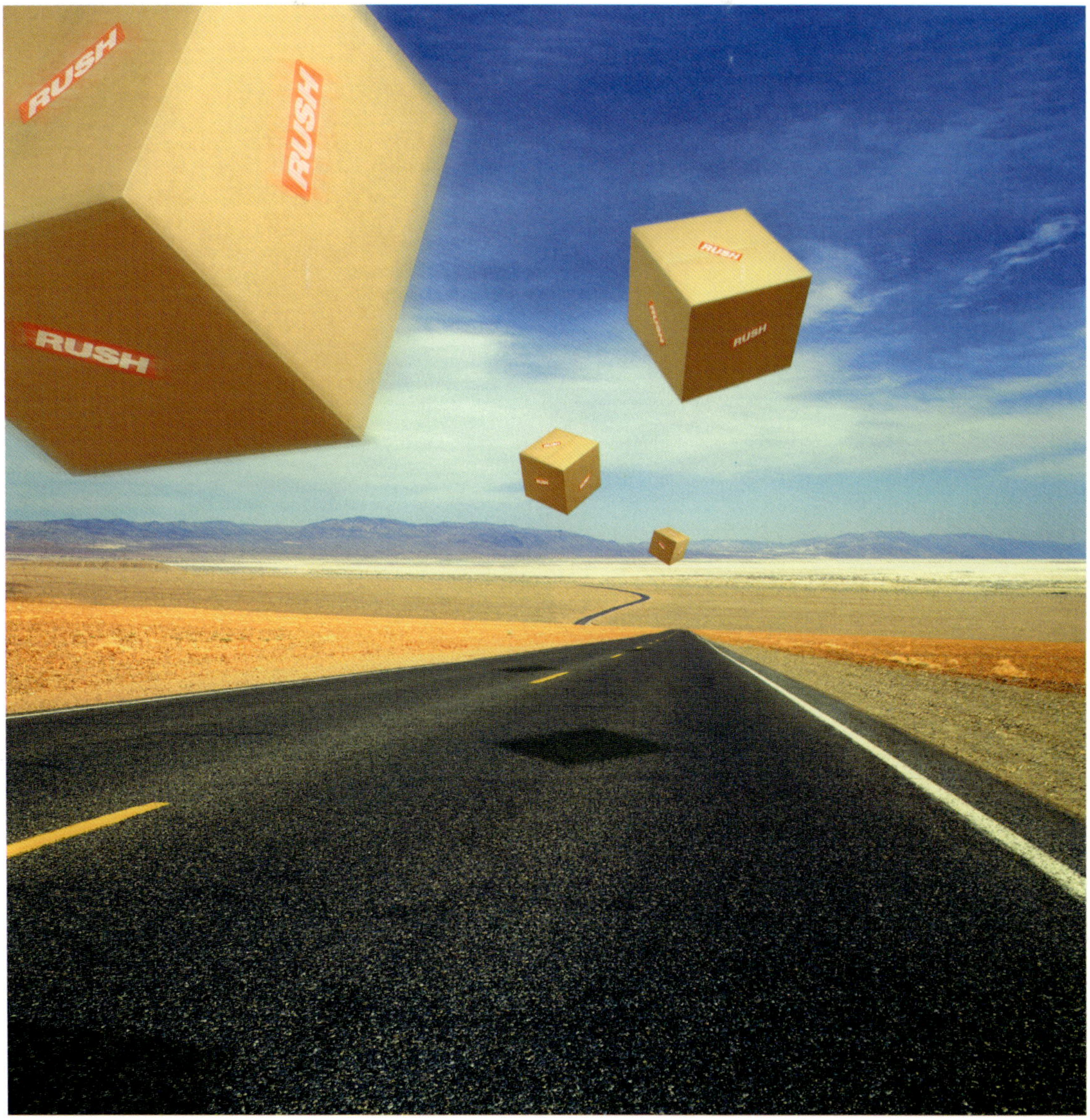

5.

Charly Franklin

6. Opposite: Man with Balloons
Client: Computer Sciences Corporation
Art Director (in-house): Tony Salerno

picture. I'd make several sketches. Eventually I'd hit on one that looked right. Then I could fax the sketch to the client and get a reply back immediately.

And while I'm doing the drawing I'm also thinking about the method I will use to make the photograph. What kind of background will look right and so on. Sketching enables me to get my thoughts straight.

I try to make the sketches specific, but at the same time I leave a margin of vagueness. So then I'm not tied down to one exact rendition. But I get the basic composition down in the drawing. I spend a lot of time doing this, because if I go out to shoot something, and I haven't gone through the drawing stage, basically I won't know what I'm going to do.

After getting the drawing down, I put it to one side. Then it's just a matter of dealing with the reality of what the photo will look like.

DTP has shortened the process of commercial work. How do you see commercial photography changing in the future due to digital technology?

I have noticed that people think everything is easier to do these days. Five years ago, they would never have asked for some of the things they're asking for now. Back then, they were put off because they knew we'd have to use the expensive machines. But now they come along with plans for images that can be pretty outlandish. And many of the people making these plans have no idea about what is possible and what's not. Or even what will look good and what won't.

I don't know about other photographers, but these days, I'm able to do a lot of work virtually without leaving the building...work that in the past would have involved extensive travel, difficulties and expense.

All this has shortened my work process because I don't have do each picture as an original piece, where everything is in plac and complete. It doesn't have to be done like that anymore.

But essentially, no matter how the photograph is produced, the seems to be an increasing demand for "pictures." So there's demand for the kind of people who can produce them, regardles of the kind of technology that's used.

I don't think we are all going to move into multimedia. I mea they've been predicting the decline of print ever since the invented TV. But it's still around. And there's still a strong demar for it.

Could you explain the philosophy behind your work?

Well...I think you should keep the picture as simple as possibl The best photographs, to my mind, are the ones where you get version of the idea right away — as soon as you look at th picture. Where you don't have to go through this long proces over why this object has been put in here, or that object ther and so on. Either the picture works the instant you see it, or doesn't.

I don't think you can put across a specific message in a goo photograph — one that cannot be misinterpreted. And yo don't really want to. I'm a great believer in letting people us their imaginations. The point is to produce something th people may have slightly different reactions to, but whic hopefully, they will like.

But ultimately, it's myself that I try to please. I can't say I'm eve completely satisfied with the work. While you are producing you are always tearing the thing to pieces in your head, an worrying about whether it will work or not. But after a few month or so, when you come back and look at the finished work agai you can be surprised and find that it really worked out well. The you forget all the aggravation and hassle you went through get the picture.

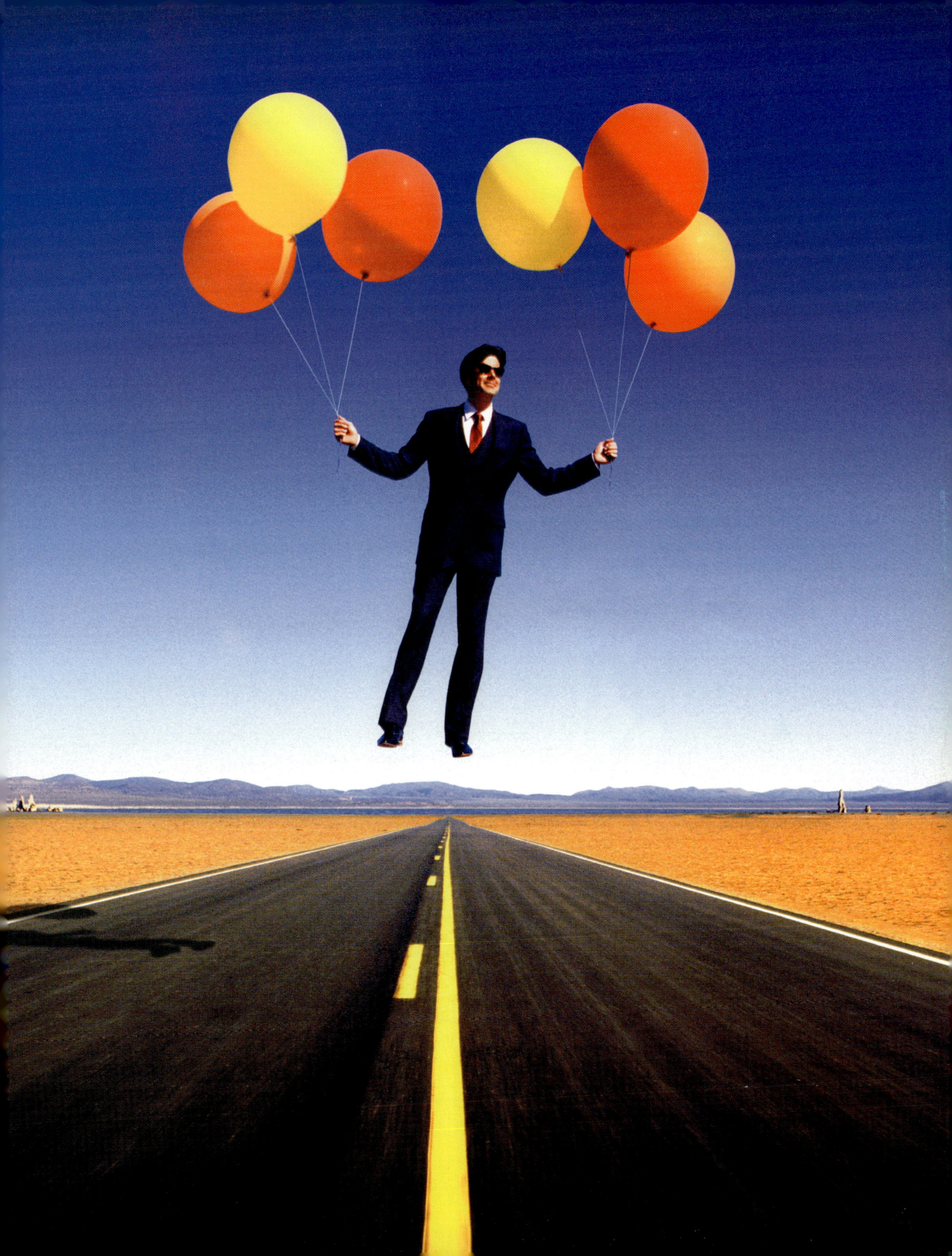

Charly Franklin

How do you get your inspiration?

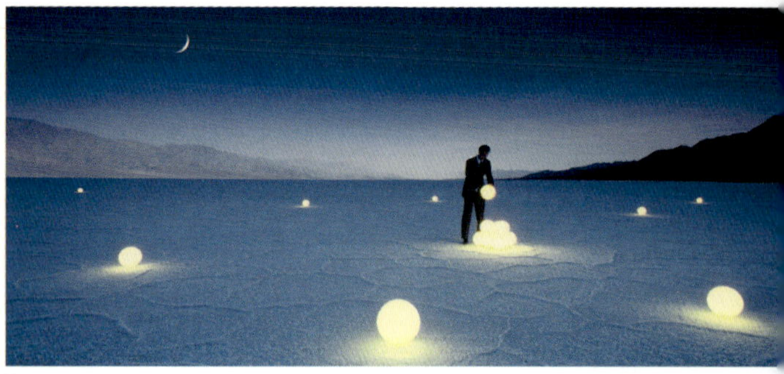

7.

Back in the mid-seventies I started doing some studies of rooms in black and white. That turned into a whole series of grainy pictures of corners of rooms, where you just got these intersecting planes, with whatever light was happening. The light had to be interesting, otherwise I wouldn't have photographed it. But really, there was nothing else in the pictures. And I shot in all kinds of odd spots. I thought the results were fabulous. But unfortunately, not many other people did.

Some of the inspiration might come from the landscapes I use. I love empty places — deserts and great stretches of beach — where you don't have a lot of things going on. I don't like a busy background because I want to focus attention on the subject. You need a clear space to place these subjects.

Could you tell us about the projects you are working on now?

Next up, I have some things to do for Pentagram: five pictures with an environmental theme. It looks like an interesting project. I might be doing another poster for Silicon Graphics.

What is your vision of the future?

I'd like to continue working, make money, retire to Hawaii maybe (laughs).

It's going to be exciting. I remember thinking, years ago, when I was struggling in the darkroom — how wonderful it would be if you could do all this work without having to deal with pieces of paper, chemicals and enlargers. How great it would be if you could just look at it on TV, press a button and change it there on the screen. Then print it out perfect. That would be a whole lot better than using these complicated methods in the darkroom, where half the time it doesn't work anyway.

Now, of course, all that is happening. I never thought it would, but amazingly it is. Look at what we've got compared with ten years ago. It's amazing when you think about what we can expect

7. Salt Flat/Man with Spheres
Client: AT&T
Designer: Stacy Rogers/Rogers & Company
8. Dinosaur

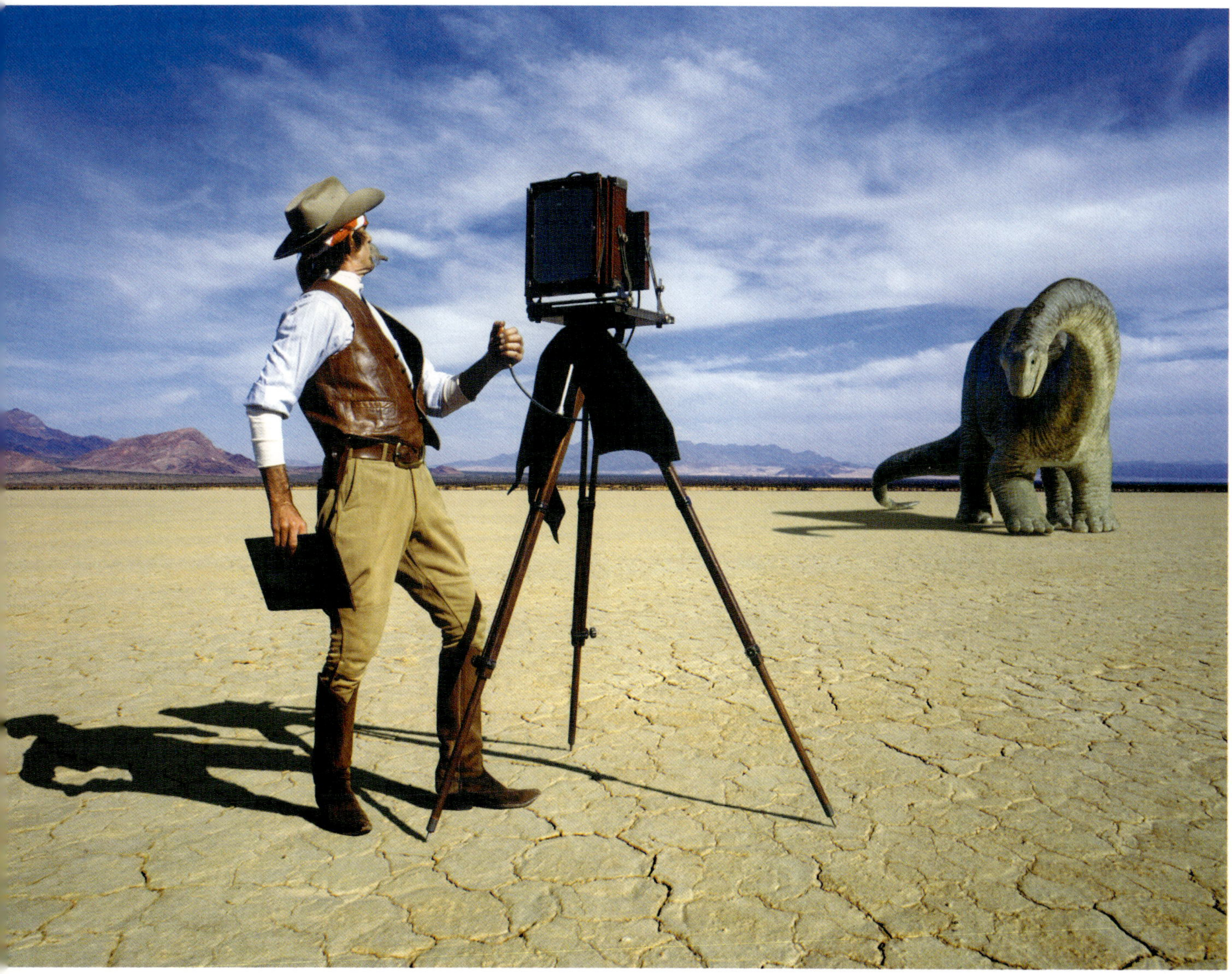

from the next ten years. You can buy these printers now that produce 18 x 12 dye subs. And they only cost around $3,500. It's incredible, the development of the hardware, and the software, too. And the better platforms we get the better the programs can become.

But aside from all the technology — which is all very exciting, of course — I'm just hoping I don't run out of ideas. Because without the ideas, all the technology in the world isn't going to help you one bit.

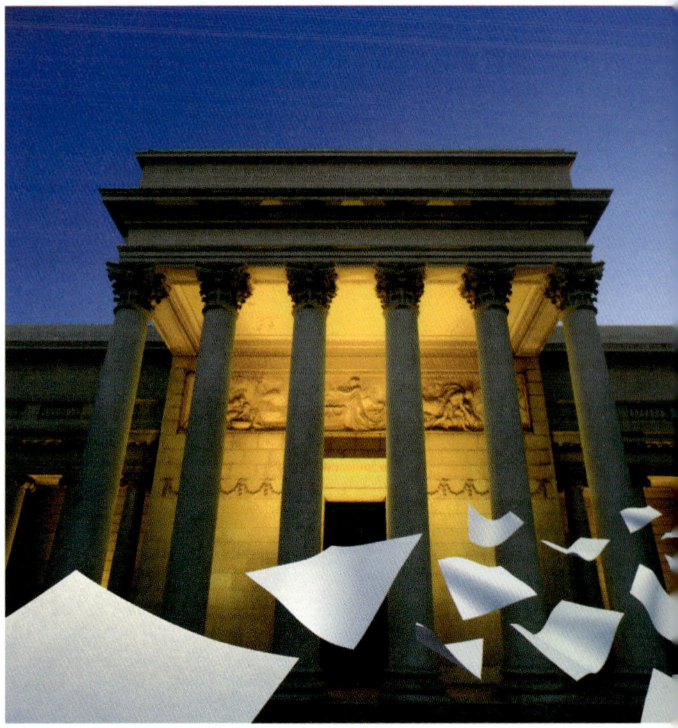

9.

9. Paper & Building
Client: Computer Sciences Corporation
Art Director (in-house): Tony Salerno

10. Opposite: Airplanes
Client: The New York Times Magazine
Art Director: Kathy Ryan

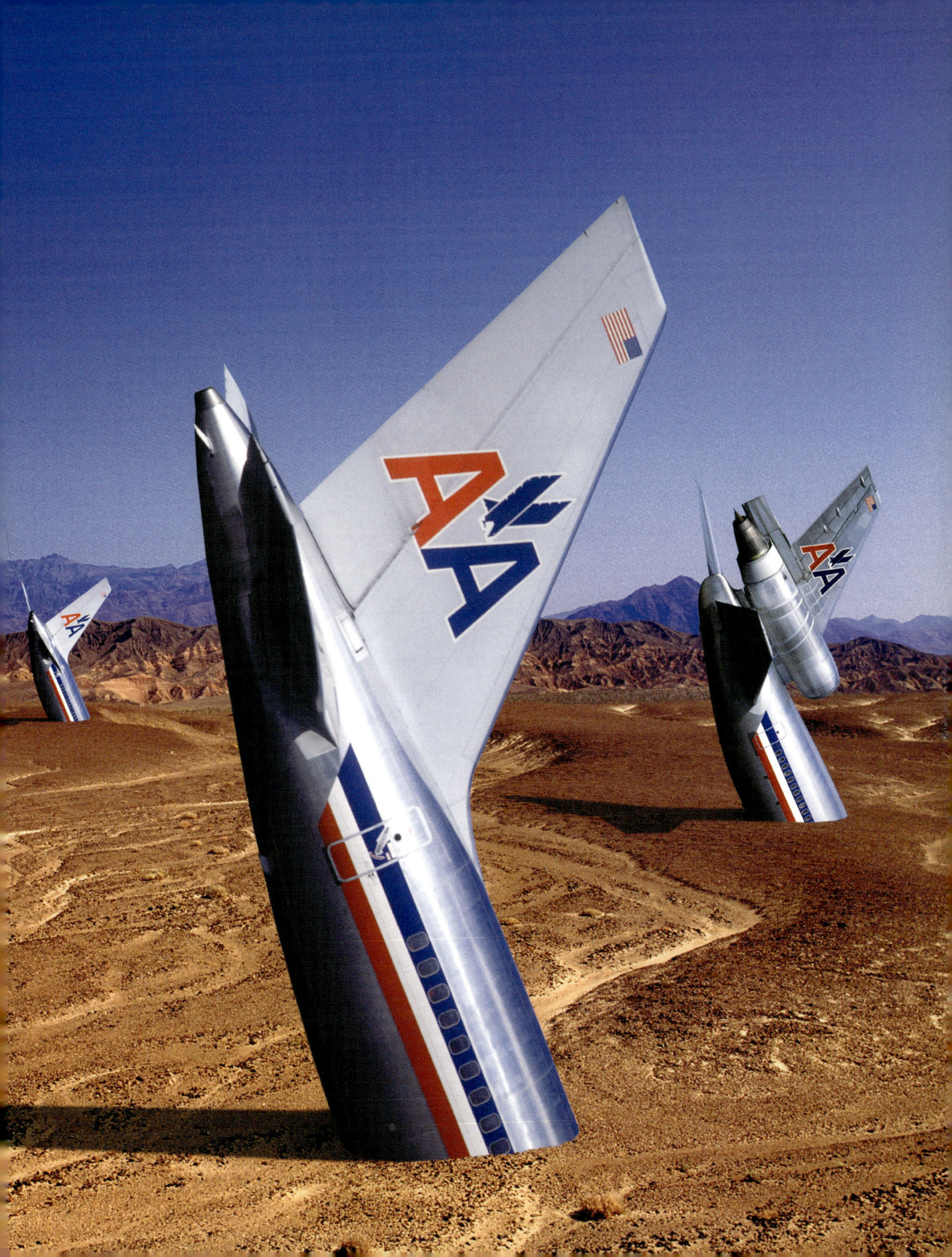
AA

Charly Franklin

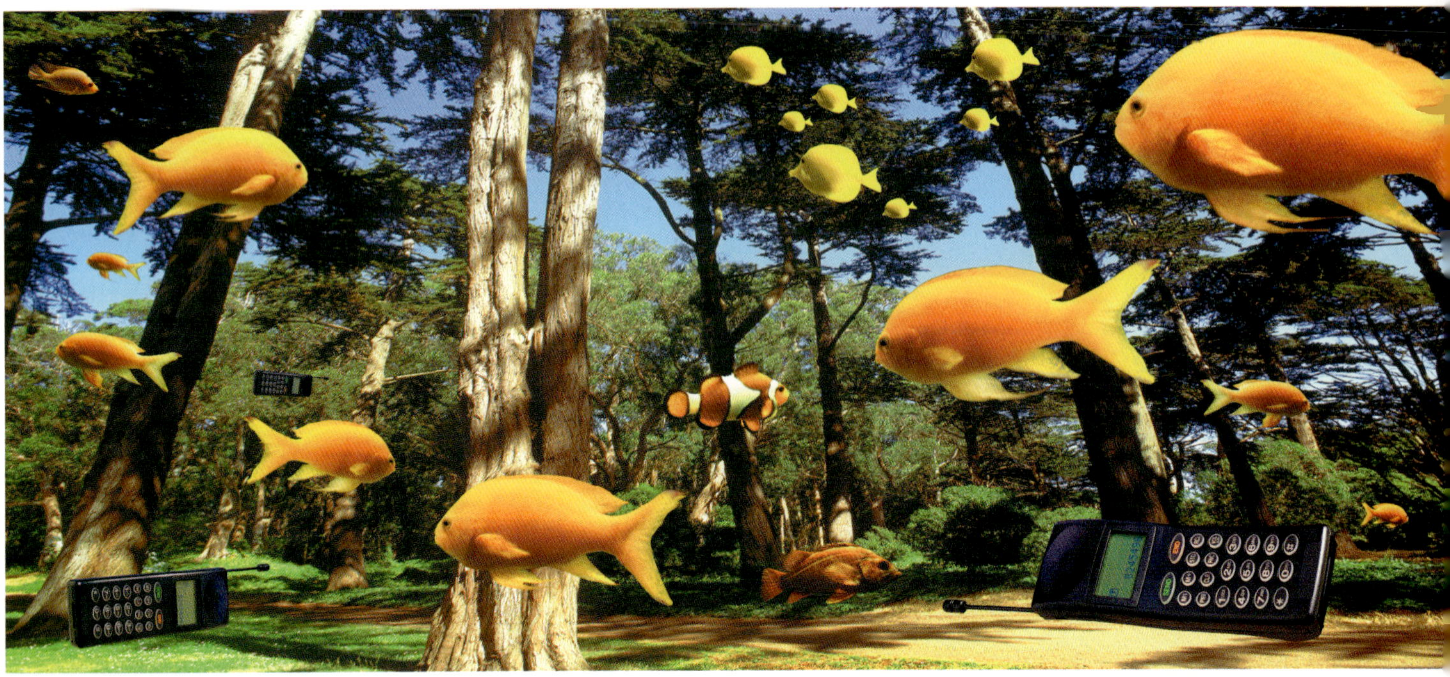

11.

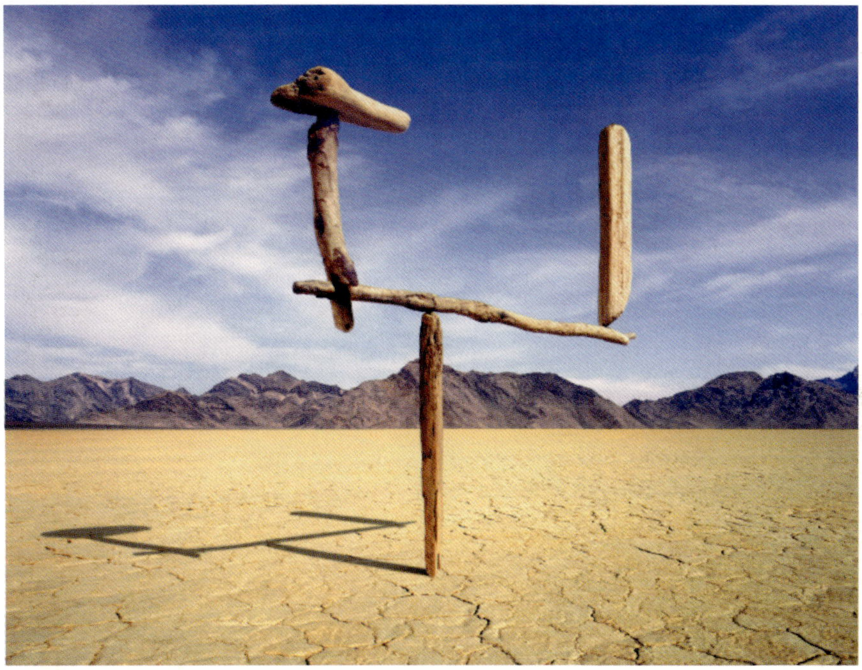

12.

11. Fish in Forest
    Client: British Columbia Telephone
    Art Director: David Tennant
    Agency: McKIM BAKER LOVICK BBDO, Vancouver, BC
12. Driftwood
    Client: First Data Technologies
    Designer: Jeff Stone, Stone Design, Massachusetts

Charly Franklin

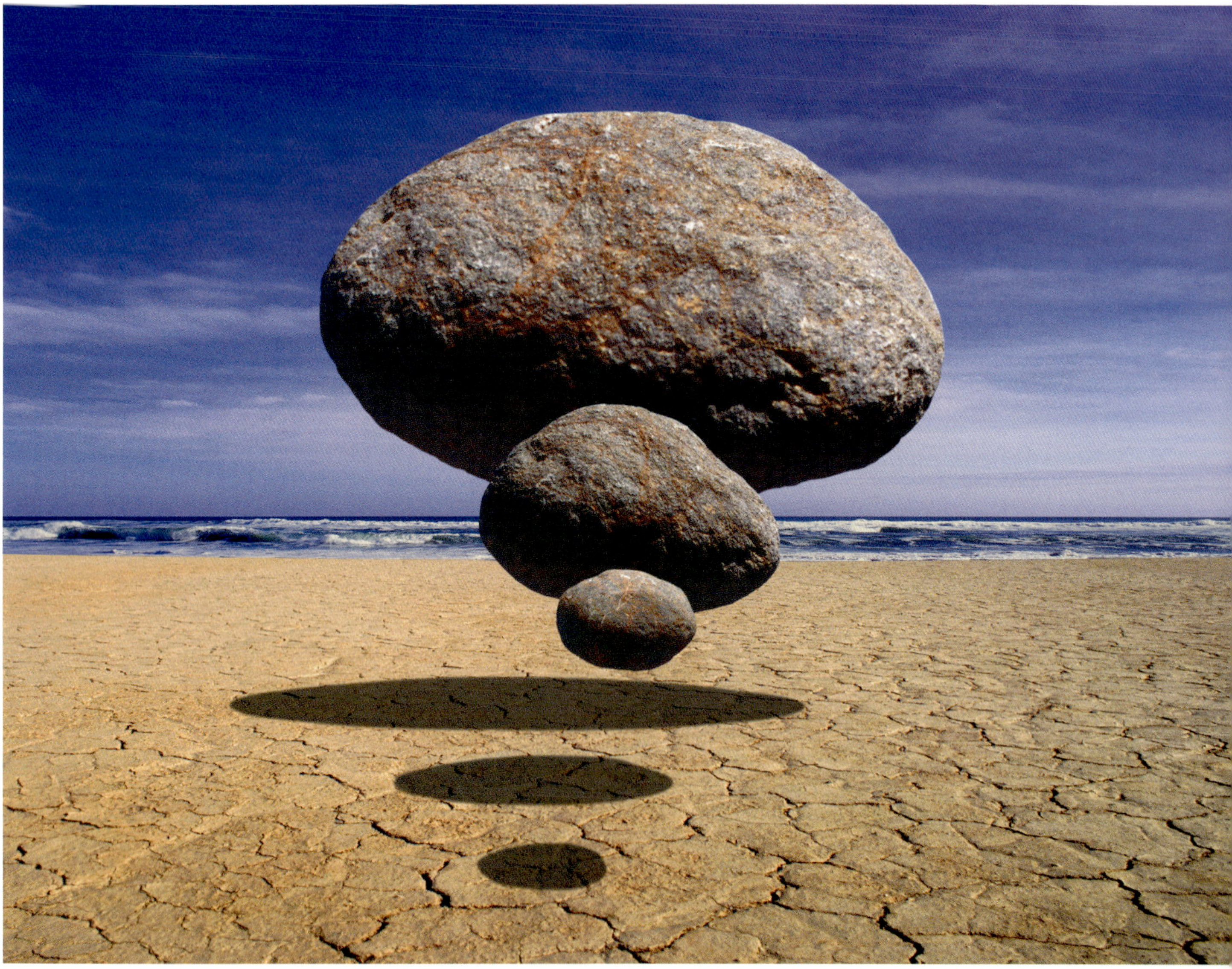

13.

13. 3 Rocks
Client: First Data Technologies
Designer: Jeff Stone, Stone Design, Massachusetts
14. Plant in Desert
Client: First Data Technologies
Designer: Jeff Stone, Stone Design, Massachusetts

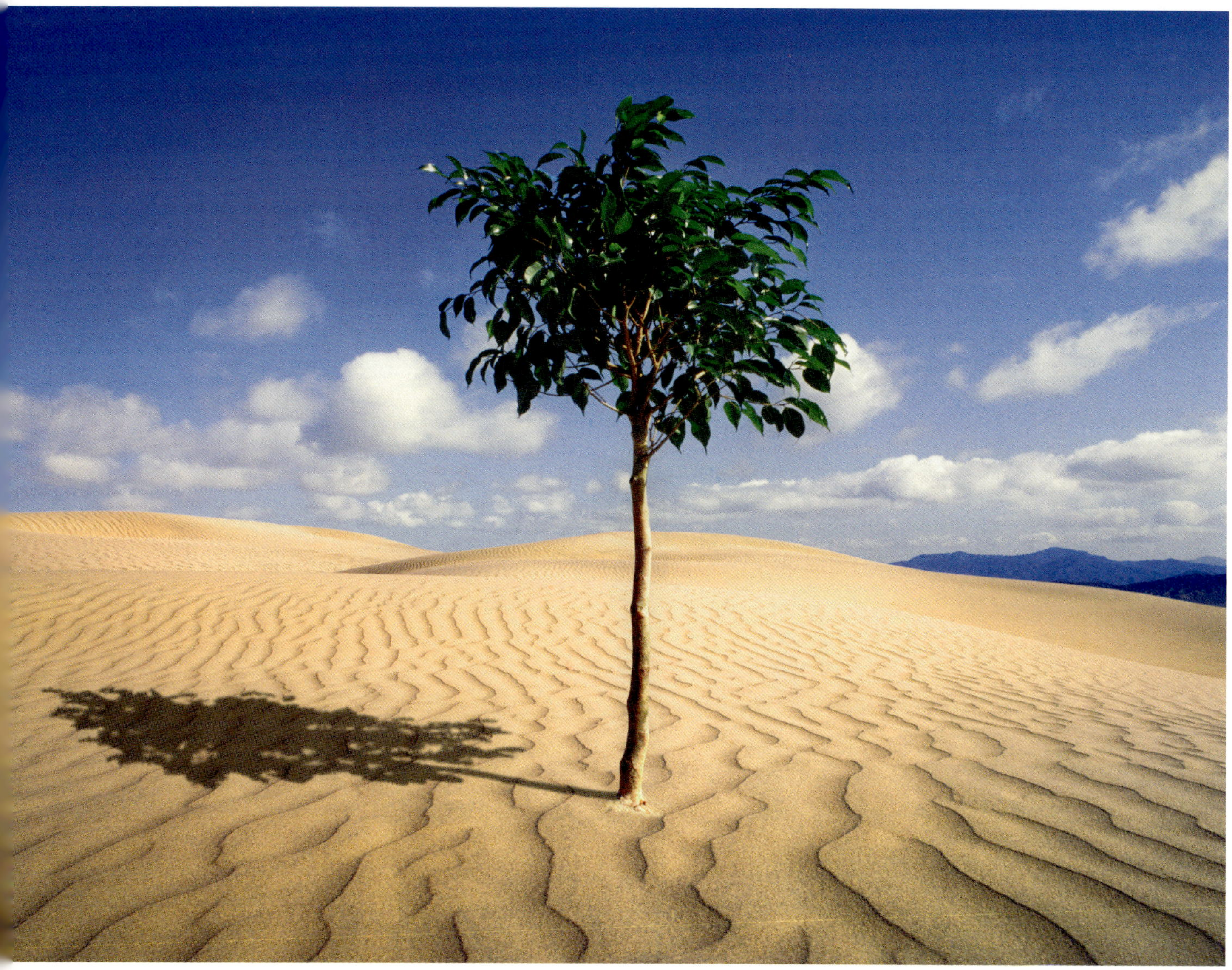

Charly Franklin

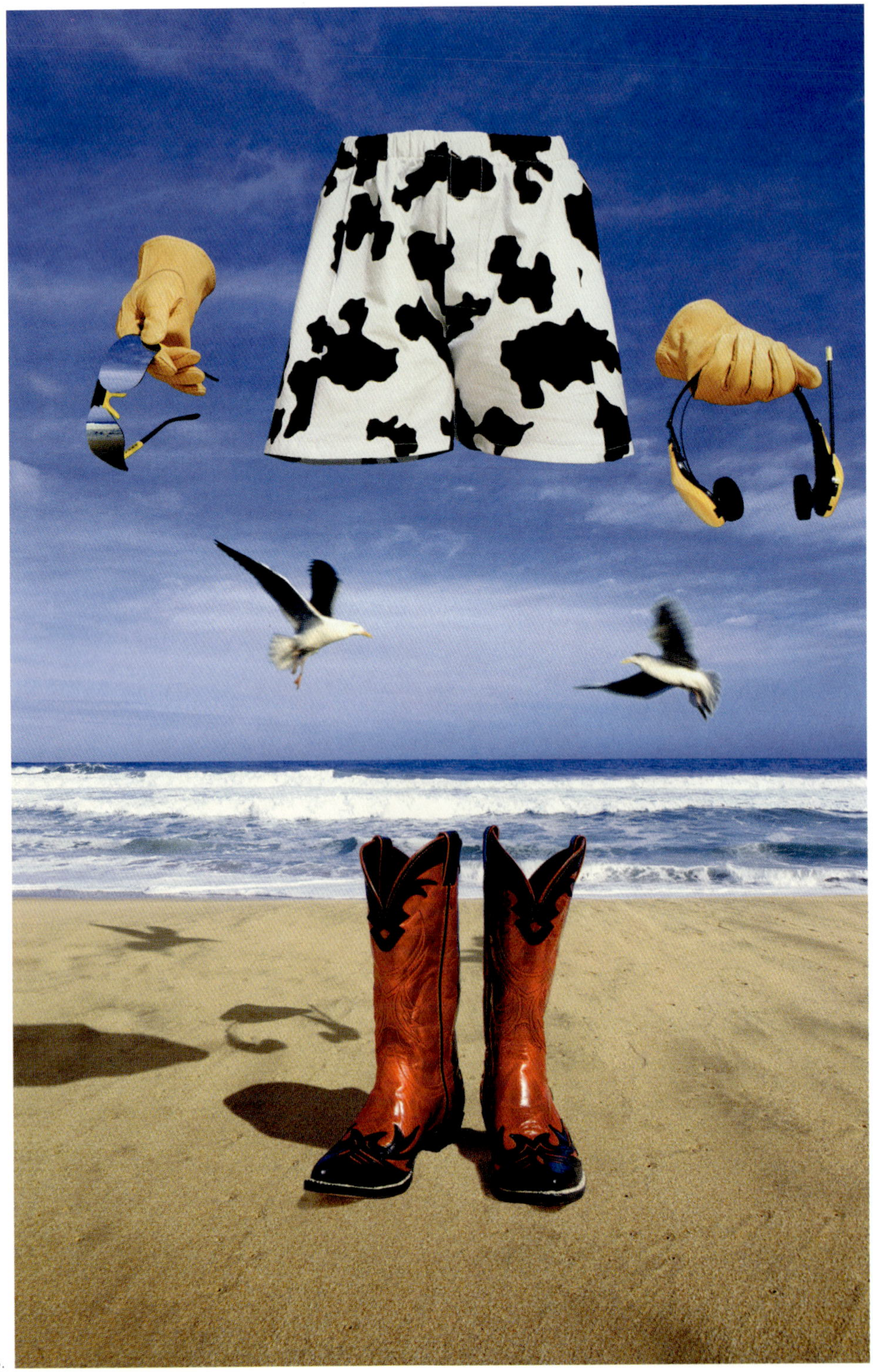

15.

15. Pairs
    Client: SuperMac
    Designer: Gary Bolen, Los Gatos
16. Man on Ladder
    Client: Computer Sciences Corporation
    Art Director (in-house): Tony Salerno

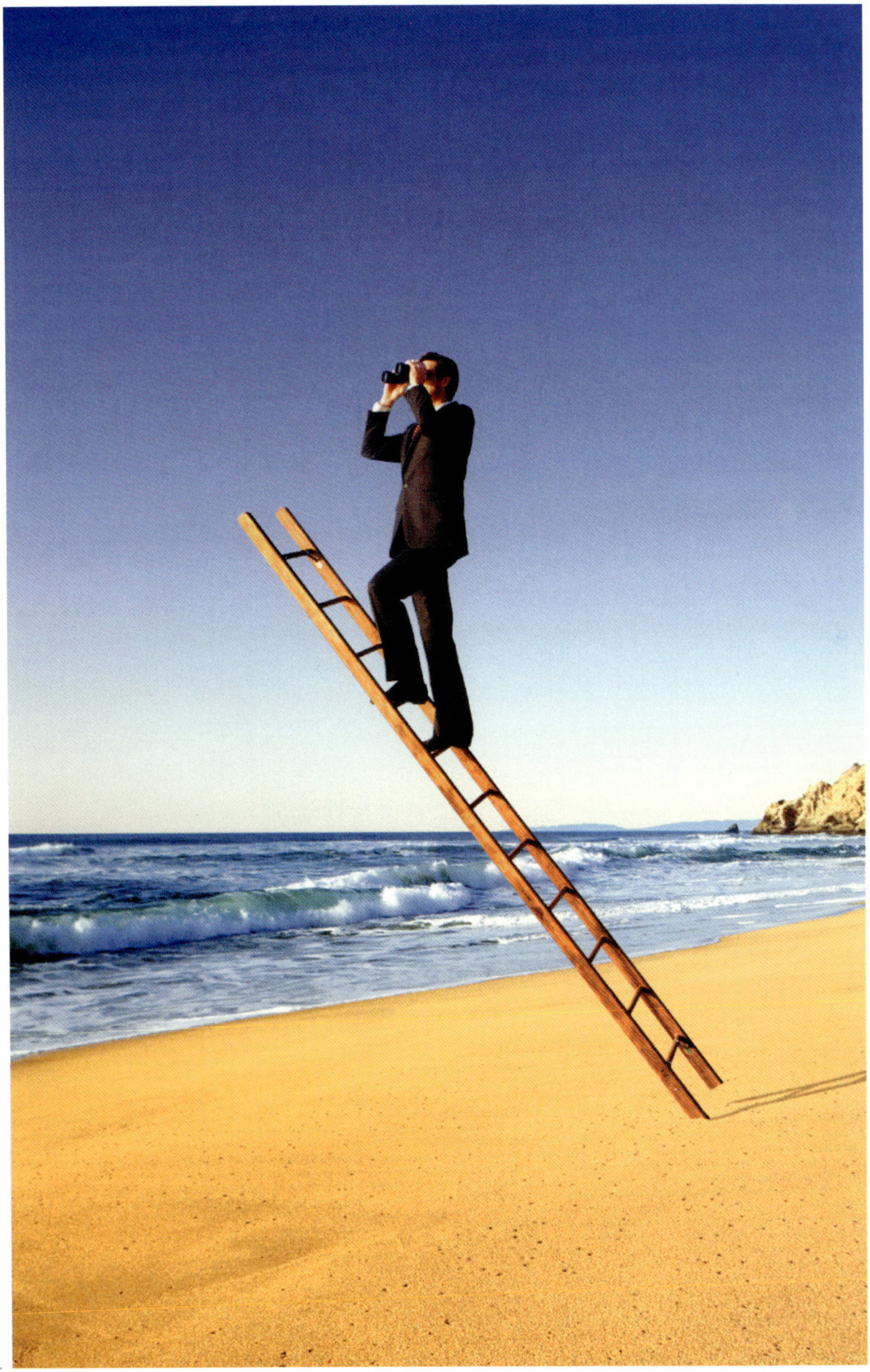

16.

Charly Franklin

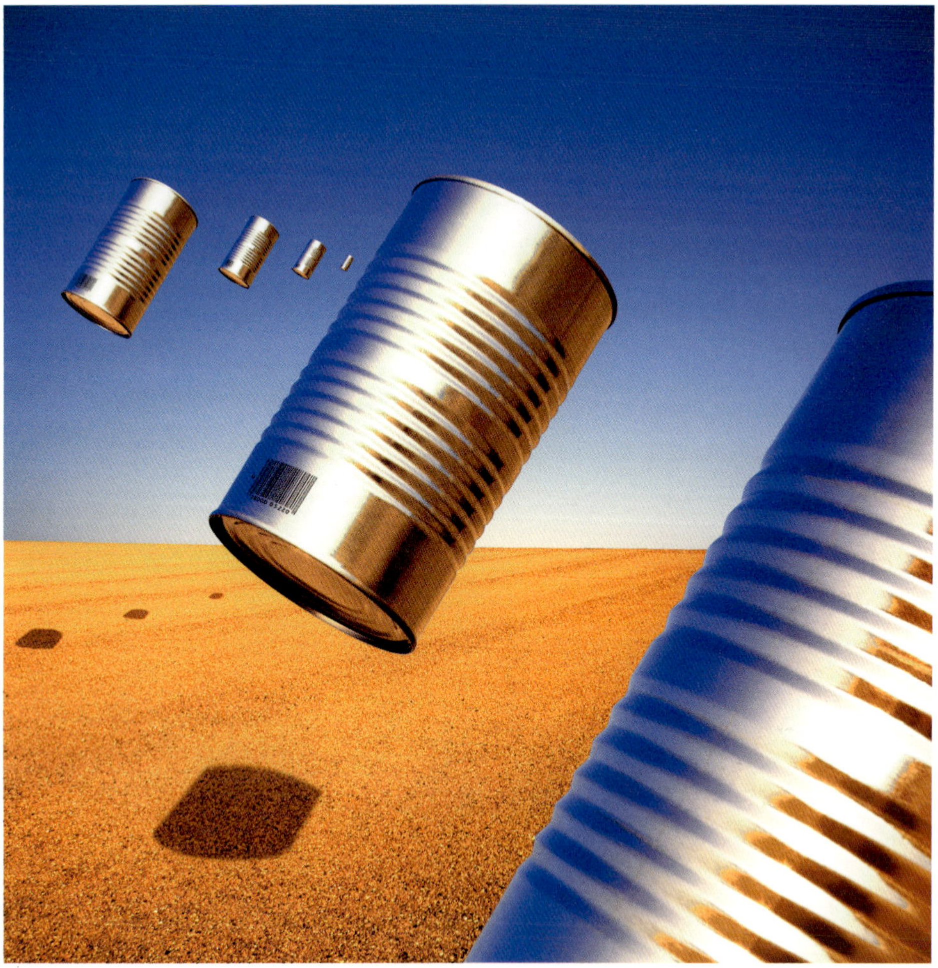

17.

17. Tin Cans
Client: Computer Sciences Corporation
Art Director (in-house): Tony Salerno

18. Nuts & Bolts
Client: Computer Sciences Corporation
Art Director (in-house): Tony Salerno

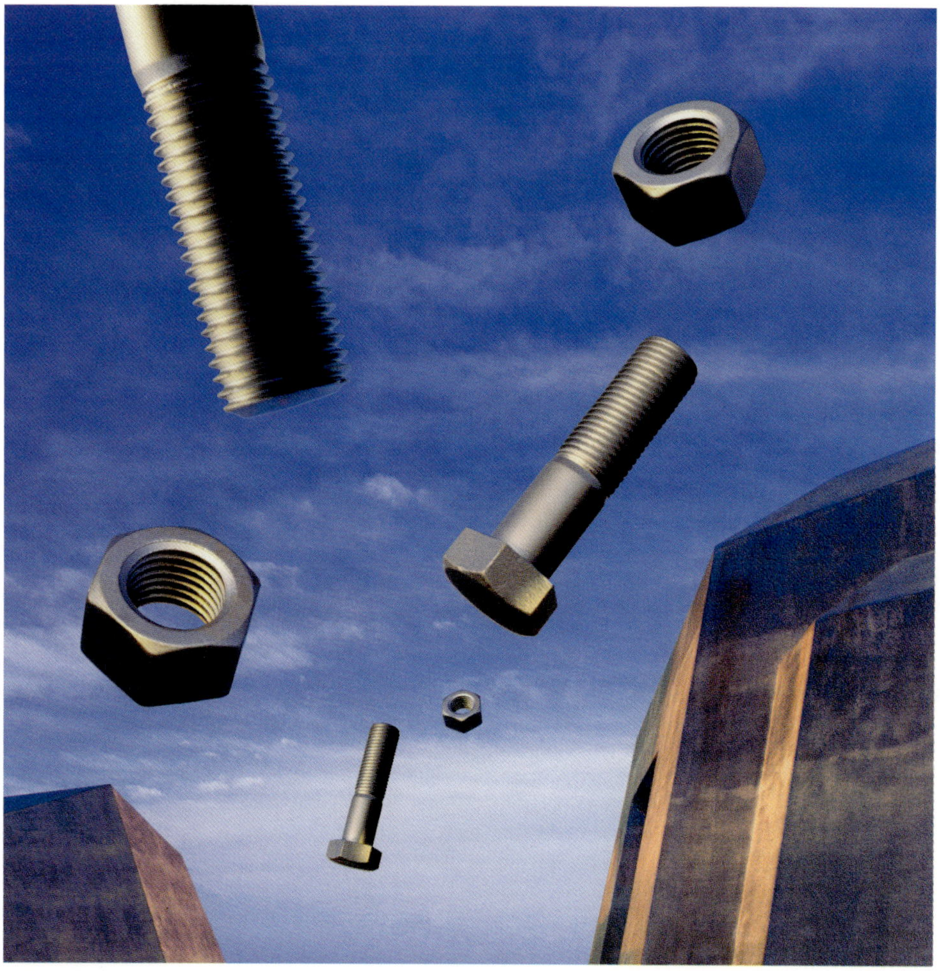

18.

Charly Franklin

19. Ergonomic Chair
Client: Rucker-Fuller
Designer: Michael Vanderbyl, Vanderbyl Design

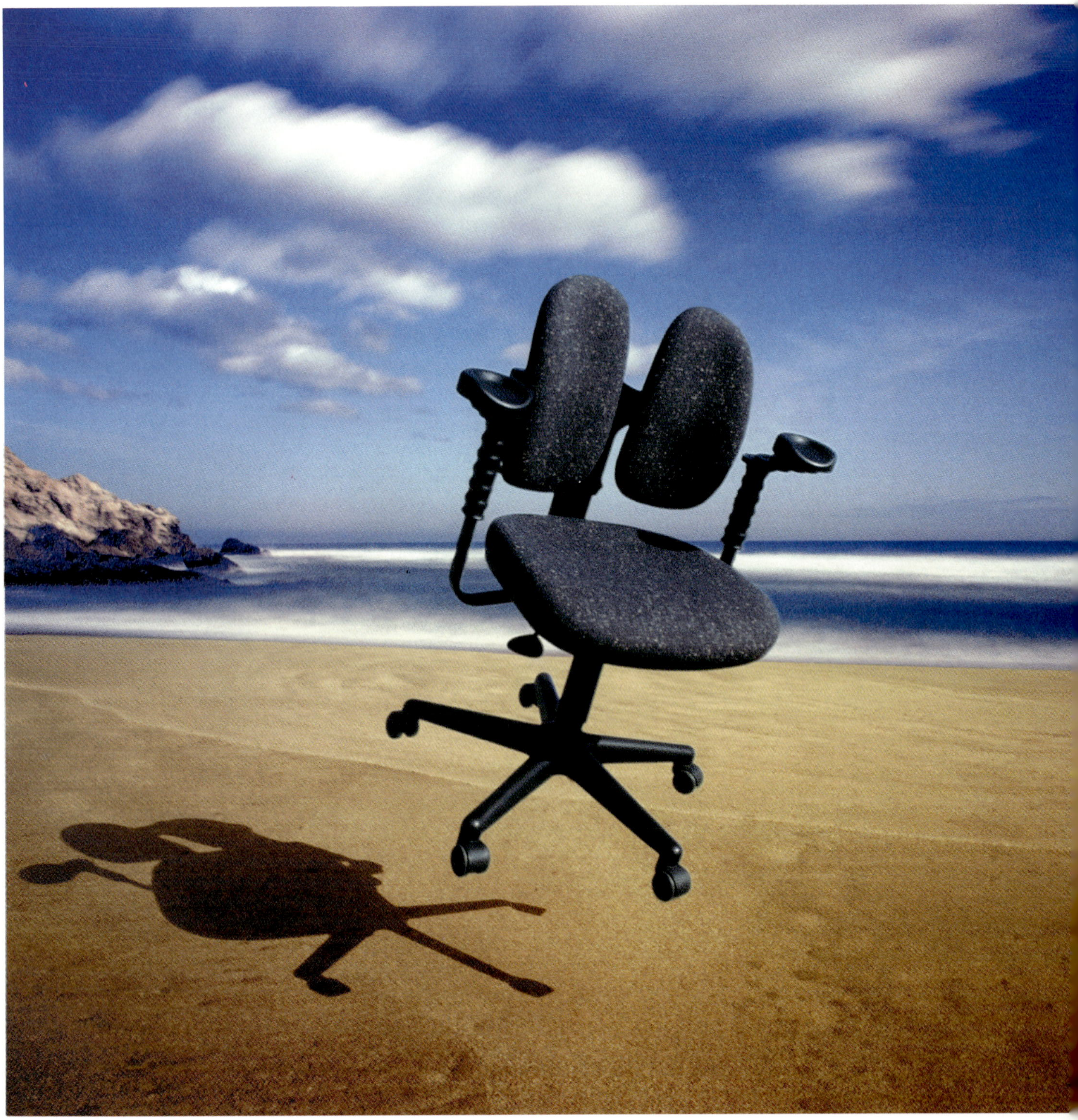

19.

Douglas Kirkland

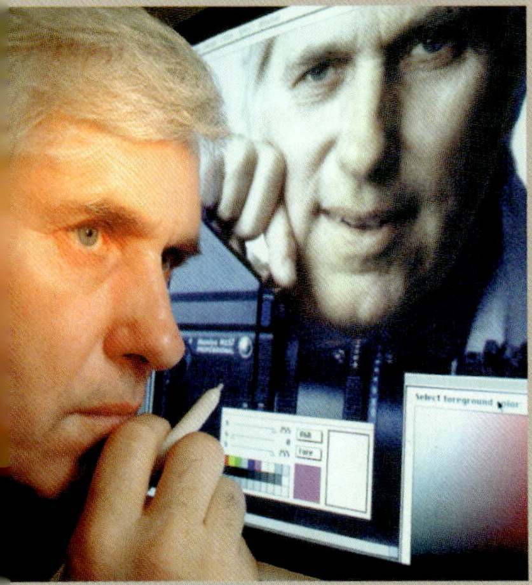

Douglas Kirkland was born in Toronto, Canada, and spent much of his early professional life working in New York, before relocating to Los Angeles in the mid '70s.

After apprenticing with Irving Penn in the late '50s, Kirkland established himself with *Look* and then *Life* magazine in the '60s and '70s. His early photo essays on Greece and Lebanon were followed by fashion and celebrity photography of Marilyn Monroe, Judy Garland, Marlene Dietrich and Elizabeth Taylor, among others.

A book of Kirkland's work, *Light Years,* was published by Thames and Hudson in 1989. His first computer artwork was showcased in a book entitled *ICONS,* in which Kirkland digitally recreated many of his original celebrity shots, including studies of Dustin Hoffman, Kim Basinger, Sean Connery, Robert De Niro and Dr. Stephen Hawking. His next book, which is scheduled to appear in late 1996, is a collection of nude photographs entitled *Body Stories.*

Kirkland's work has been widely exhibited in Asia, Europe and the United States, and he is a highly sought after commercial photographer. Within the last few years, he has lectured at the Smithsonian Institute in Washington D.C., the American Film Institute in Hawaii, the Art Center of Design in Pasadena and Apple Computer Centers in New York and Los Angeles, as well as Kodak Centers in Hong Kong, Singapore and Taiwan. Douglas Kirkland is represented by Imperial Press in Tokyo, Sygma in Paris and New York, Graza Neri in Milan, and Marni Hall in Los Angeles.

Douglas Kirkland

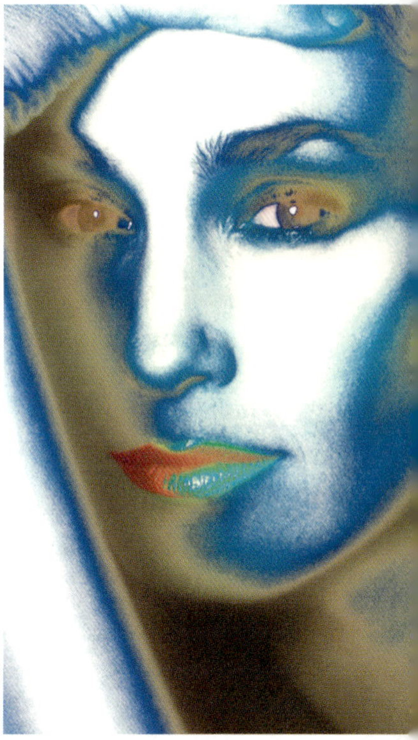

1.

Could you tell us about your success story, and how you got into this field?

I started photographing celebrities in 1960. Among the people who gave me the opportunity to photograph them was Elizabeth Taylor. She was the very first celebrity I photographed. At the end of an interview Elizabeth had done for *Look* magazine, I asked her if she knew what it would mean to my career if I were given the chance to photograph her. She thought for a moment, and the idea seemed to appeal to her. So I got the opportunity to photograph her, and the shots were used for *Look* magazine and covers all over the world.

You have to remember that Elizabeth Taylor was an ultrasuperstar at the time. She's still very prominent today, of course, but back then the world could not get enough of her. She was young and very pretty. She was widowed from Mike Todd. There was so much about her life that everyone wanted to know. That was the beginning of the great fixation the world has developed for celebrities.

Later on I got to photograph people like Judy Garland and Marilyn Monroe, and my career was off and rolling.

How has the field of celebrity photography changed over the years?

I got started working for large magazines that could, in those days, give a great deal of publicity to a young star or starlet. But all that has changed these days, because the magazines represent a different world. They used to say in the sixties that one out of every five Americans saw *Look* magazine. Back then, a photograph on the cover of *Look,* with an article on the person, could essentially have made someone's career. But as time went by, the magazines became less important to the celebrities. Their agents, lawyers and press agents became more significant in their lives. So now my importance as a photographer for celebrities is much less. These days I go more on the basis of friendship. It would not be as easy to get started in celebrity photography today.

1. Jessica Lange
2. Opposite: Dustin Hoffman

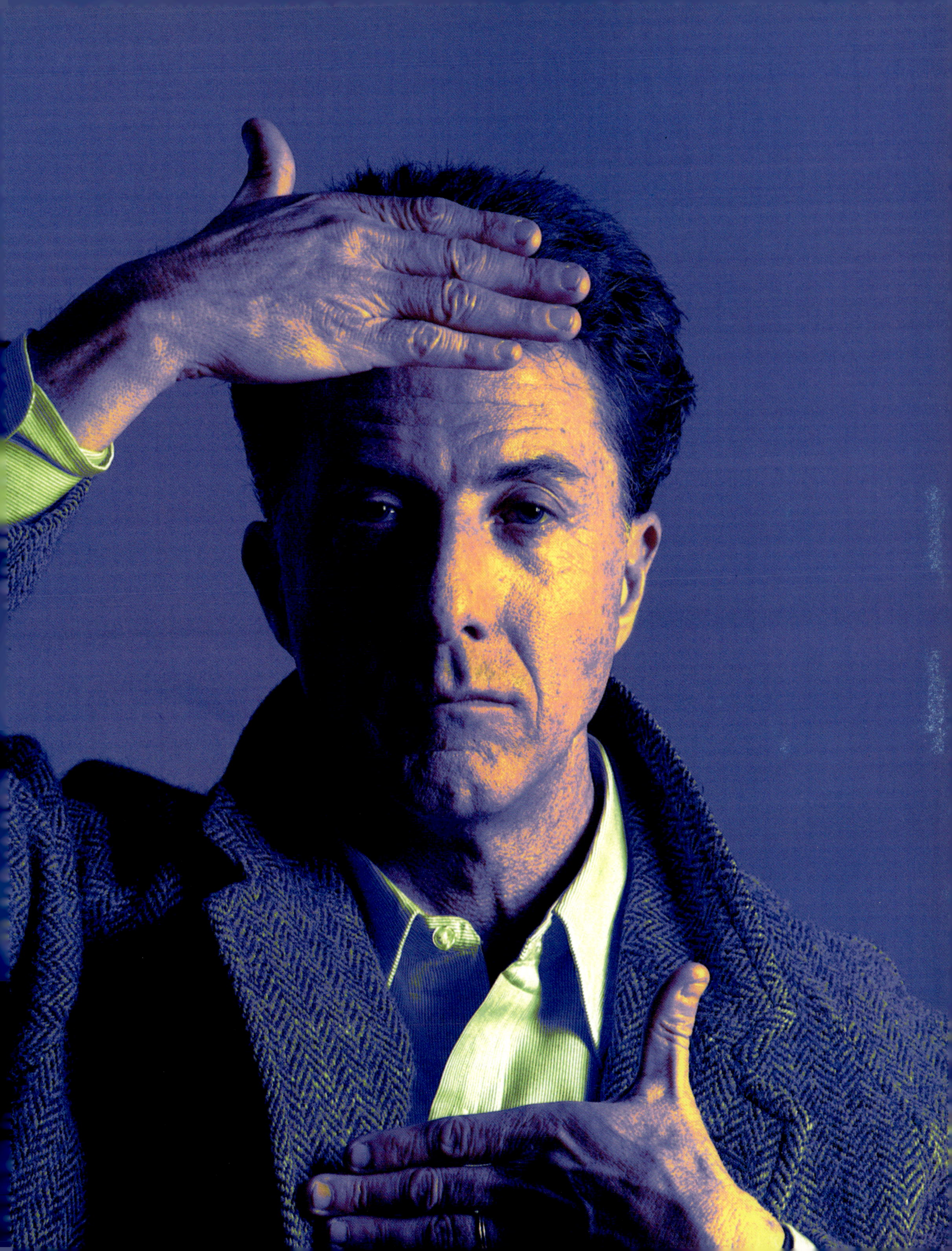

Douglas Kirkland

What are the most important aspects of portraiture?

In simple terms, you have to give your subject your undivided attention. You must have all your equipment working correctly.... You have to be technically proficient enough so that when you come to take the photograph, all of your attention is focused on the subject, not the equipment. This is out of respect for the subject. After all, they don't want to be distracted by a photographer who seems preoccupied by his equipment.

Then, when the photographer is looking through the camera, he or she should do whatever they can — on the strength of this technical background — to talk to the subject. You can talk about almost anything that the person is interested in. And on most occasions you can find something that you share an interest in. While you are talking, of course, another side of you is checking the exposure.... You are reckoning on whether you should be closer to the subject, or further away. Or whether some object in the field of view is doing something strange to the picture.... You should have a severe critic inside you, demanding that you do not violate the rules you have learned.

What it boils down to is that you should have sufficient technical competence not to let the technology get between you and your subject. I mean, the subject doesn't want to know about the technical aspects of the shoot.

Do you find it easier to work with actors?

It varies. Some actors don't like being photographed as themselves. Certain actors say it is easier for them to assume a role. Because when you are in a role, you are less exposed.... You are not revealing yourself to anybody. But in a situation where you are taking a portrait, you have to be yourself. And that's where the talk comes in. I have had some experience of film making, worked with cinematographers on a variety of projects. I know a lot about the life on movie sets. So I am able to talk about that field with some confidence. I can draw on all of that experience to keep a discussion going with the subject while I'm photographing.

But there are no cookie cutters as to what you should get fr your subjects. For instance, if you are with a beautiful wom who is very sensual, you are obviously going to be talking i different manner than you would if you were with, say, a six year-old man. Each portrait situation is unique.... You re differently, depending on the individual you are photographi There isn't any simple and consistent rule about how to do t work. Whether it is with the computer or the camera, you sho always be asking the question, "How can I treat this subject the best possible way and make the most dynamic image?"

When did you start to produce digital images?

The first time I was exposed to the world of digital imaging w in May 1991. I was in Camden, Maine, where Kodak was open its creative imaging center. They held a very special week, a invited a lot of people, including myself. I spent most of the we signing posters of my work from the book *Light Years.* Then, the last day, I finally got the chance to work for three hours o computer.

Prior to that I had never used the computer for imaging becau I didn't know it was possible to make prints. Making prints i critical element in the entire photographic process. So I could believe that simply being able to view images on a compu monitor — where the image might appear just like a TV image would have much value for me. But this introduction to t Macintosh and Photoshop showed me that I had every possibi of doing what I'd been doing in the darkroom, but even m effectively — and with much more control.

I was ignited with excitement. I decided then and there tha wanted to do everything I could to master this technology. An wanted this to be the process with which I did my next bo which became *Icons.*

Have you had any formal training in digital imaging?

No, I was basically self-taught. I just read every word ab Photoshop that I could get hold of. When I ran into problem

3. Arnold Schwarzenegger

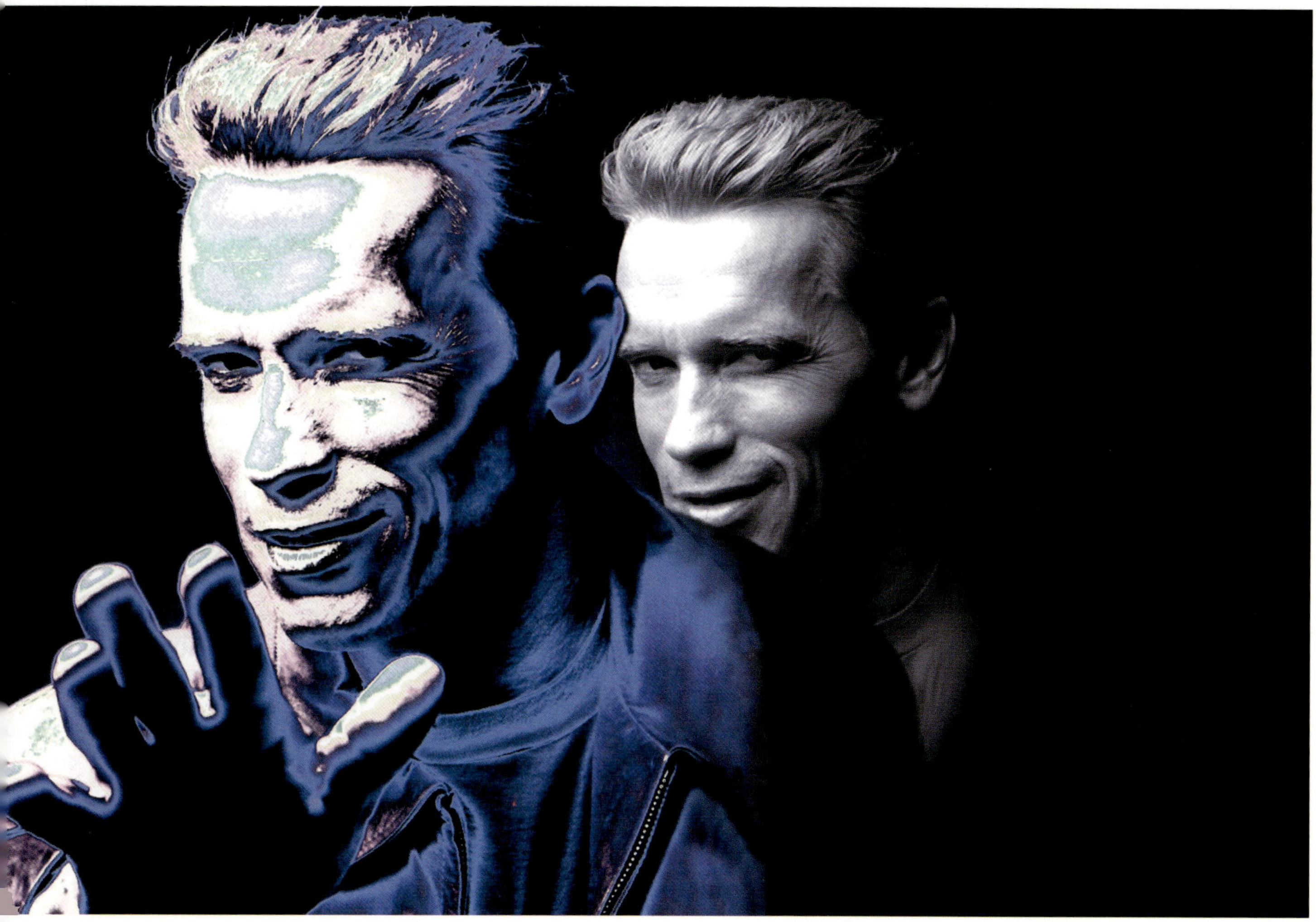

was fortunate enough to find people who knew the answers to them.

Some people find this technology more difficult than others, and consequently find it hard to believe that I was self-taught. But for me, if I dive into something with passion, within reason, I can learn anything. And this technology was so significant to me. It seemed like a major turning point from all the photography I'd done since I was thirteen years old. It simply permitted me to do things that I had seen in my mind, that my equipment prior to the computer could not reach. I used to have to paint on my pictures. I learned the basic skills of watercolor and oil painting. But now I can do all that much better using the computer.

Could you tell us how you came to produce the book Icons?

Icons was very much a learning process for me. I decided that a celebrity book would be a good one to work on. So I went into my celebrity files and did the pieces that became the Grace Jones, the Cindy Crawford, Dustin Hoffman images and so on. I put in a lot of hours on that project. But just as a pianist has to put in so much time to learn the instrument, so I had to devote a lot of time and energy to this digital imaging process.

Once I'd finished the project, I suddenly went into a kind of withdrawal. Suddenly, I had nothing to do.... So I ended up going back and doing some more material on Tom Cruise, Jessica Lange, and Sting.... And, I found that I couldn't stop the momentum that had built up. Those images weren't for *Icons.* They were distributed through my agency Sygma in Paris.

After that, I started on a book of nude studies entitled *Body Stories.* It's very strange to me, but I was told by my publisher, that the kind of books which are the most successful in the art field are photographs, drawings and paintings of nudes. I didn't think it would be easy to get subjects for the work, but in fact it turned out to be just the opposite. People were just lined up down the block to have me photograph them.

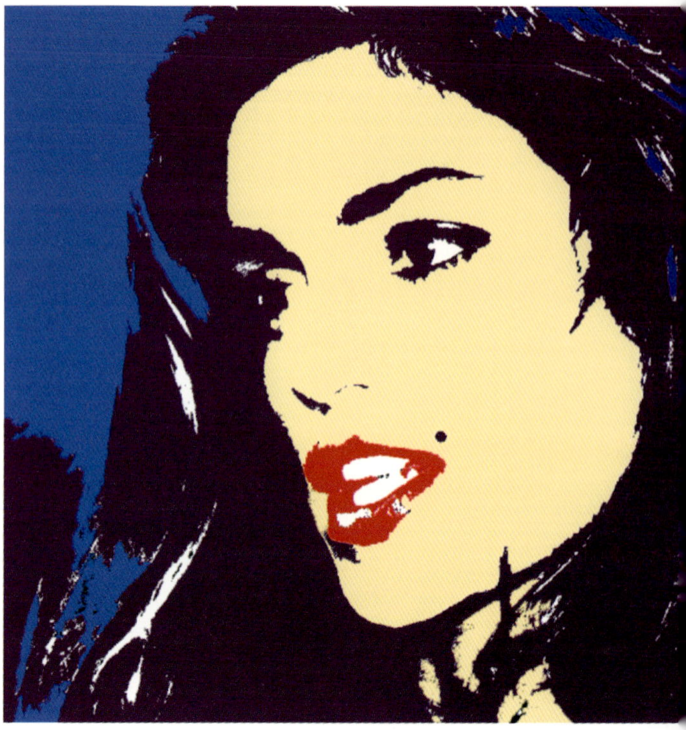

4.

4. Cindy Crawford
5. Rome

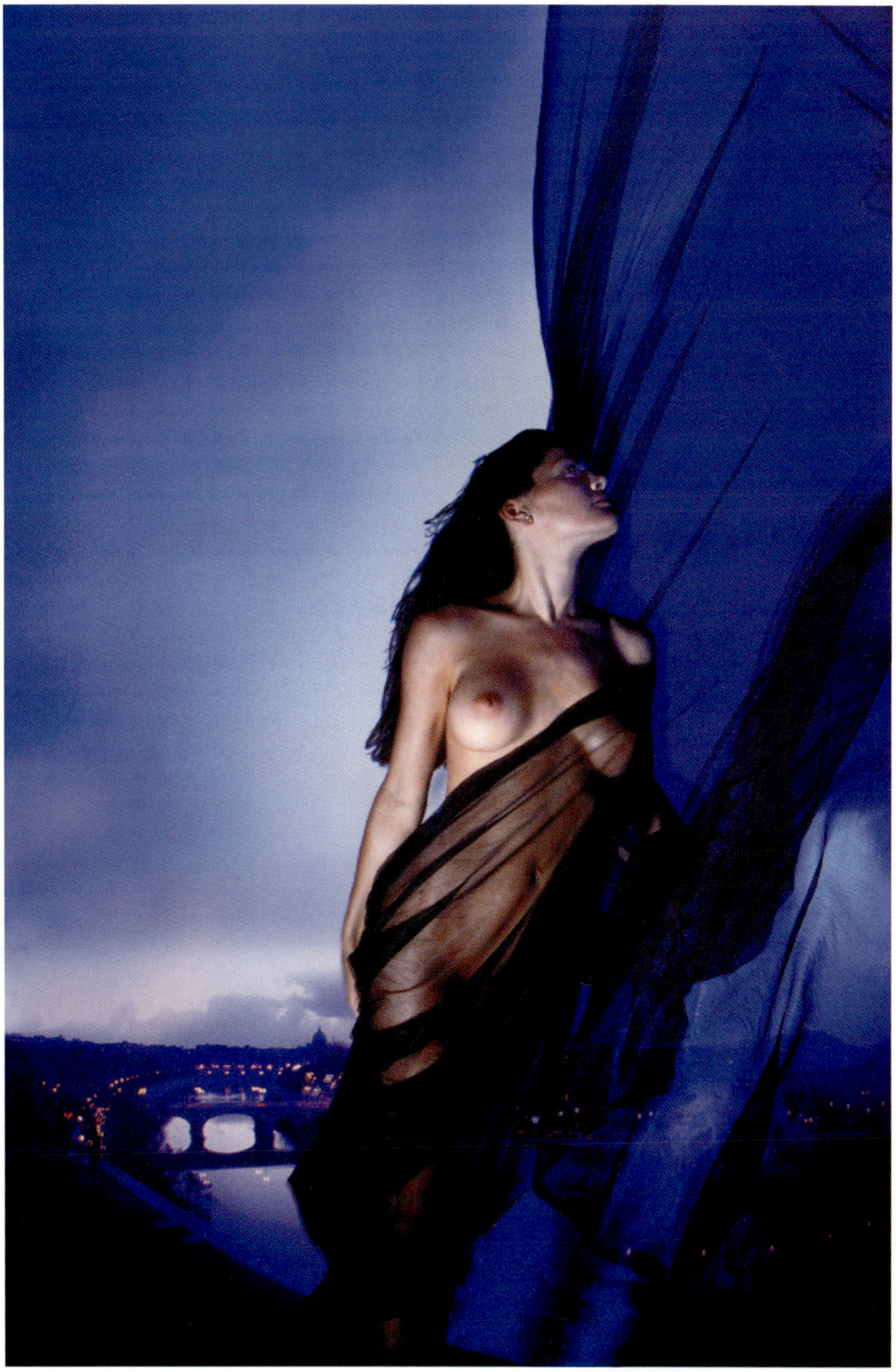

5.

Douglas Kirkland

6. Sting

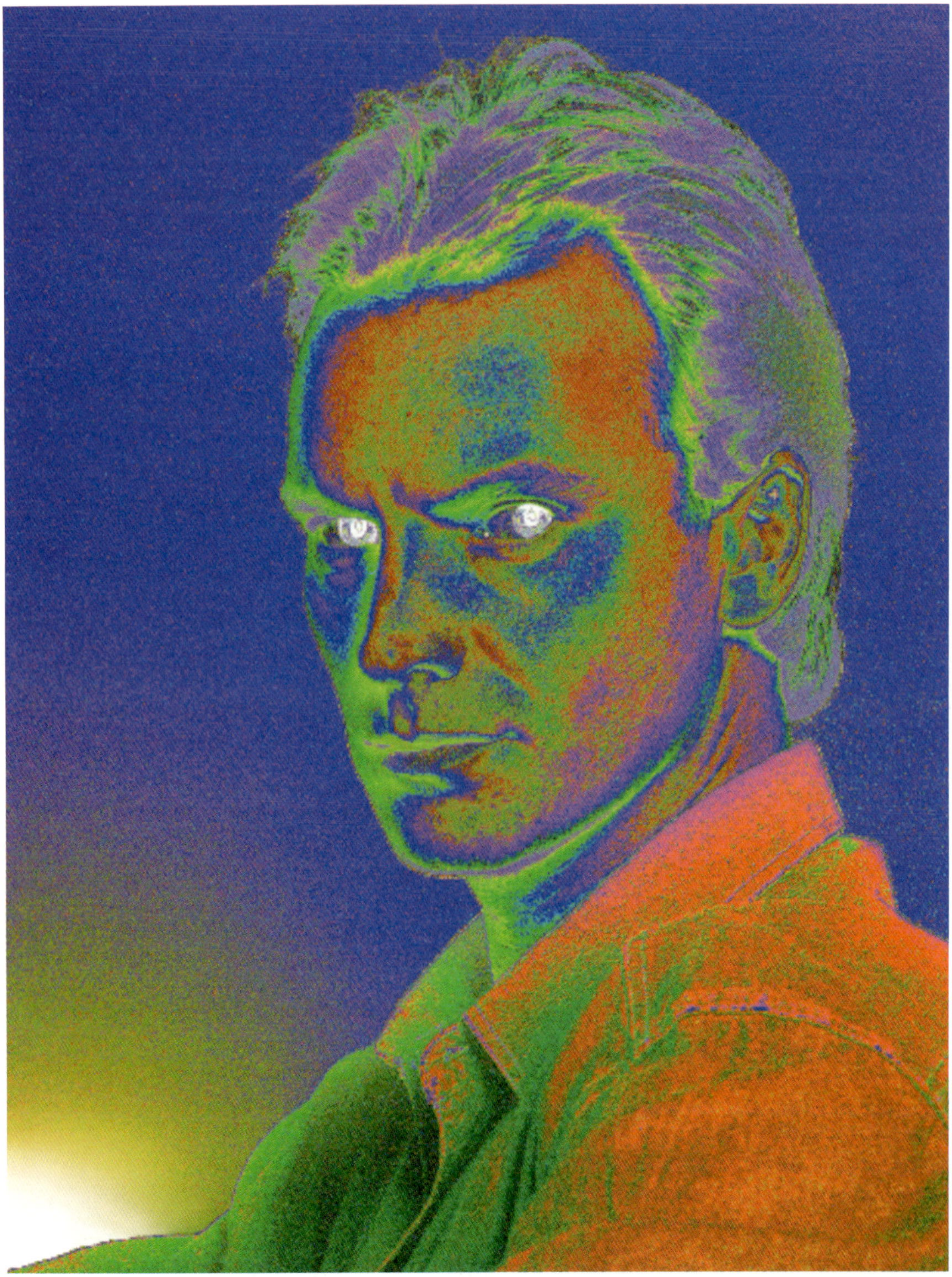

6.

Sanjay Kothari

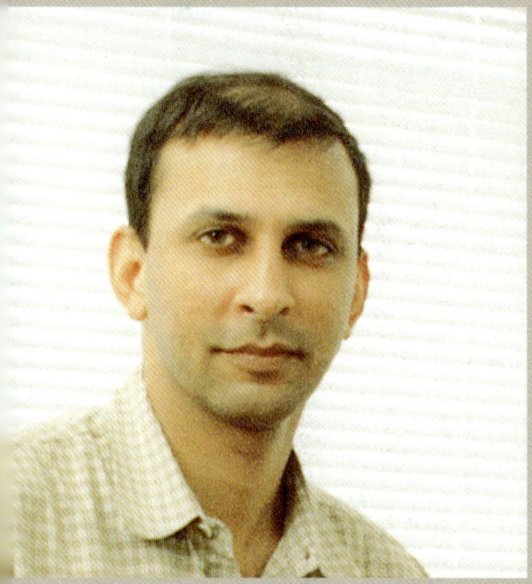

Sanjay Kothari was born in Poona, India, in 1960. Upon earning his degree in engineering at Mysore University, India, Kothari changed course and pursued his strong interest in the visual arts by attending The New England School of Photography in Boston. In 1984 he discovered photomontage.

In 1993, Kothari joined the Color Center (Boston), offering his capabalities as a photographer for the classes and equipment. For one year he experimented with Photoshop. Three entries in ASMP's Big Picture Show won him two silver awards and one bronze. *Confetti Magazine* subsequently conferred on him their Gold award for the Photography / Imaging category and he promptly found himself freelancing for clients such as Lotus, *The Boston Globe Sunday Magazine* and *The Atlantic Monthly.*

Relocating to New York, he set up a studio in Manhattan's Chelsea district, and produced work for myriad clients: *The New York Times Sunday Magazine,* Adobe Systems, Dell Computers, Polygram Records, Atlantic Records, Estée Lauder and Lotus Inc.

As a photographer, Kothari found montage to be at the edge of the photographic process. In its digital equivalent, he believes the new edge to be at the intersection of photomontage and painting.

Sanjay Kothari

Could you tell us about your philosophy of photography?

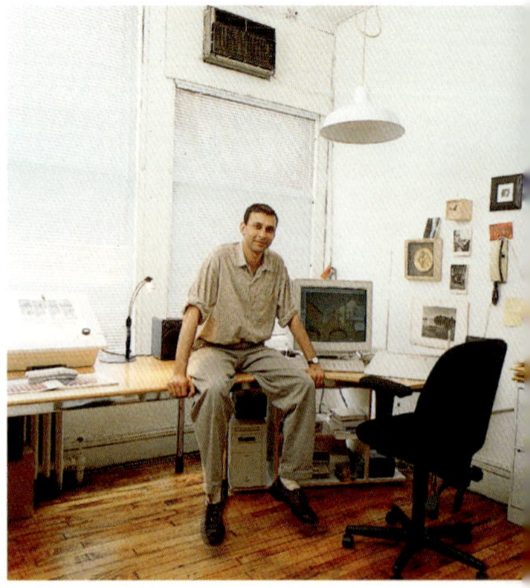
Sanjay in His Studio

There are two distinct trends in photography. One is "straight photography," which can be defined in terms of a natural transformation of physical reality from three dimensions to two. The other is photographic manipulation, which implies any alteration in this correspondence with physical reality.

In the case of straight photography, the photographer is limited by the possible, the feasible and the immediate physical world. These limitations govern the photography. However, the imagination is independent of these restrictions. As an artistic medium, straight photography is very restricting.

To get around this problem photographers can manipulate the medium. This allows us to transcend what is possible. You can make things happen which otherwise could not happen in reality.

For example, if you have a landscape photograph, there is a direct correspondence in the color, and in the gray scale of the image to the physical reality. Now, if you burn or dodge that image, you are interrupting that correspondence. That process is manipulation.

We manipulate in this way because we want to affect an area independently of the laws of nature. For instance, if I use a wide-angle lens, the image obviously looks different from the way we see it under normal circumstances. It becomes distorted. Now, if one portion of the image is distorted, the viewer will know immediately, because that one portion would not correspond with the physical reality of everything else in the picture. That's how we know the image has been manipulated. It is also how we come to know the photographer's intention.

Manipulation is a means that allows the artistic photographer to communicate his intention. Any picture is trying to say something, however abstract that something might be. But with a straight photograph, there is a confusion between what is intended and what simply exists. With manipulation, the manipulation becomes, in itself, the language by which the artist can communicate.

a. Wave
b. Sky
c. Sky and Water

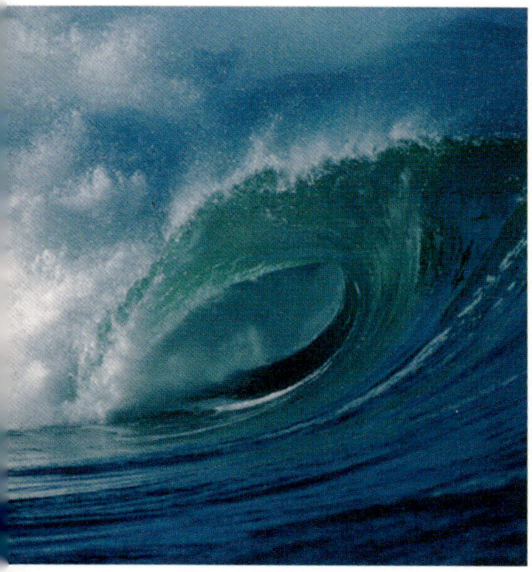

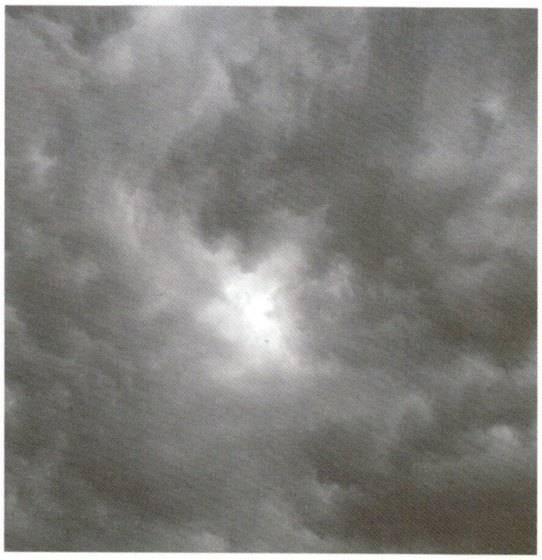

b.

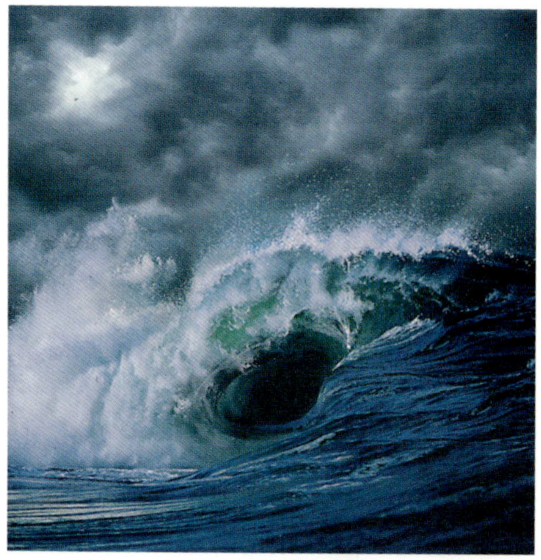

c.

›rbie Hancock's: "Dis is de Drum"

.e project began with Herbie's ideas about the um having a supernatural force or power and ›as about creation. Initially, we focused on ding an "interesting" drum to photograph as r starting point. Having spent a lot of time ›king for the right drum, anxiety started to ›ep in. I needed something in the drum that ›uld make it totally distinctive.

decided to wander around the Musical struments and African Art sections of the ›tropolitan Museum. I walked around soaking the sculptural richness of African masks and ıking mental notes of the ornamental styles and ›tifs. As I wandered out of the African section, ıl not clear how I would proceed, I saw Alicia, security officer at the Metropolitan with a autiful and serene face and I realized that her ›e would make the drum come alive.

a-c. I began with creating the "environment" that the drum would occupy. The water photograph (a) was by Jeff Divine and the stormy sky (b) was by Steve Shields.

I flopped the underbelly of the wave to create the cavity. And the new Color Range tool enabled me to isolate the droplets as I montaged the water and sky images. I used Curves to match the color and contrast of the sky and water elements (c).

Sanjay Kothari

With manipulation you can also transform the normal identity of the objects in the picture. For example, I can take a photograph of grass and transform that grass into, say, a chair, or a rope. So the viewer no longer sees the object as grass, but as something radically different.

You can do this to some degree with conventional photography by using close-up techniques, for example. But you cannot change the actual form in the way I just described. Maybe the close-up makes for an abstract picture, but you are still bound by the physical limitations of the medium.

One of the things a digital artist working with Photoshop wants to do is remove the original identity of physical objects, and give them any identity he wants.

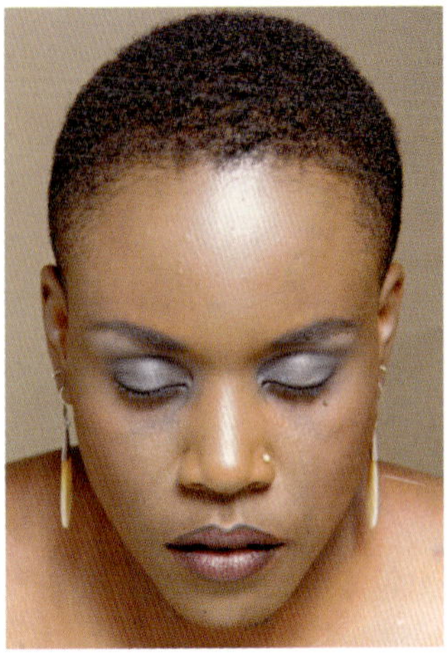

d.

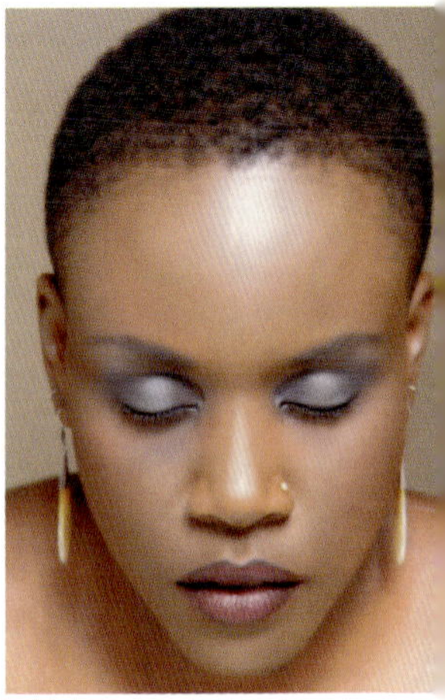

e.

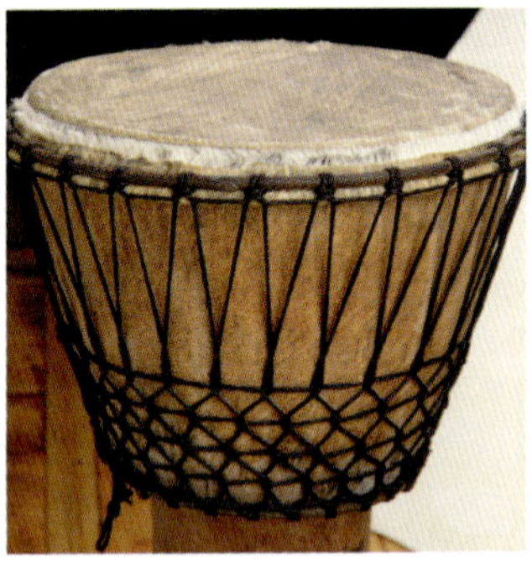

f.

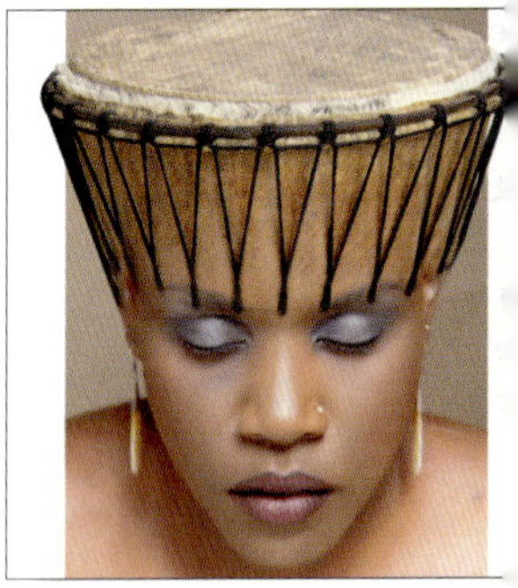

g.

d. Alicia's Picture
e. Alicia's Picture
f. Drum Picture
g. Alicia
h. Alicia
i. Textures in Channels
j. Drum

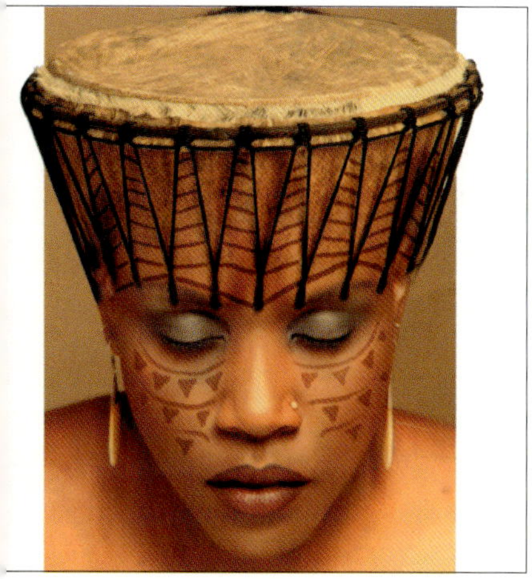

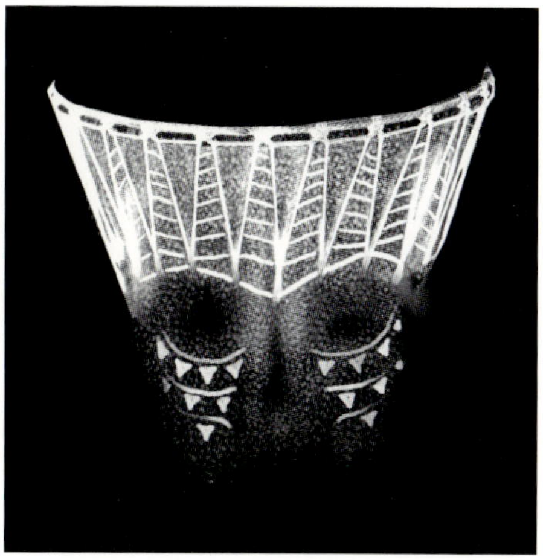

i.

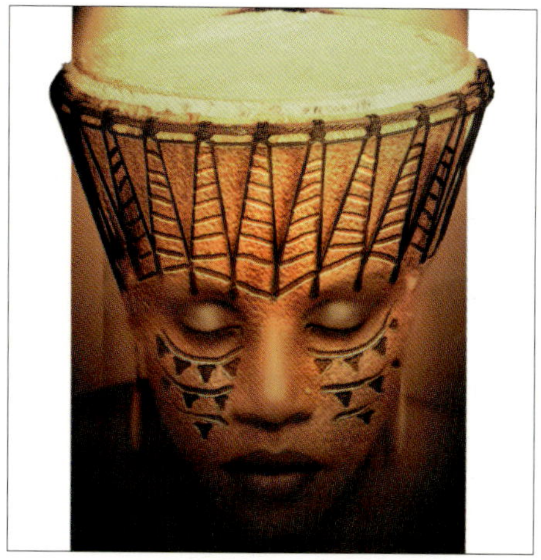

j.

e. I next worked with Alicia's picture (d) eaking the highlights and making the skin lose textural detail, using the Rubber Stamp and brush (e).

. I next combined her face with the image of drum (f) placing the two on different layers d using the layer mask to control the transition (g).

h-i. To unify the drum and face further, I would transform the color and texture. I next used curves to warm up the drum composite, painting in African motifs (h) and painted in textures in channels that I would use to transform and unify the textures of the face and drum (i).

j. I wanted a heavier texture where her forehead became the drum and a finer texture on the face and none on the nose or lips. I then applied color and brightness changes.

Sanjay Kothari

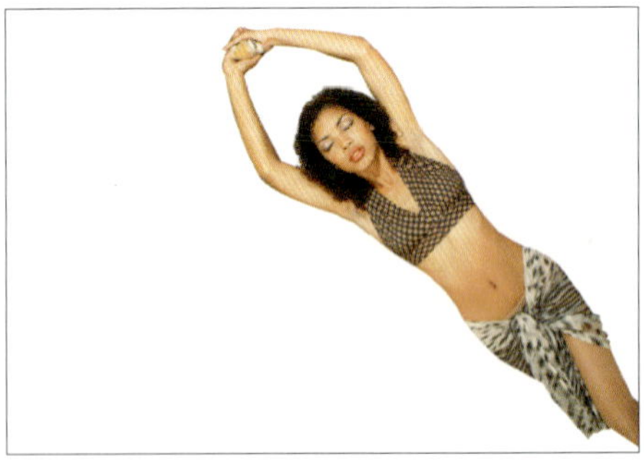

k.

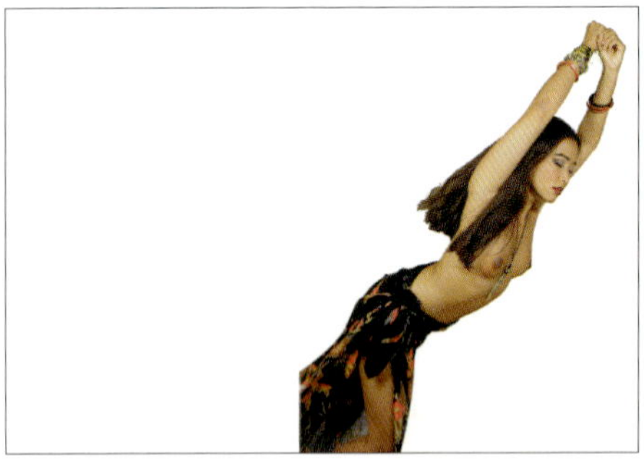

l.

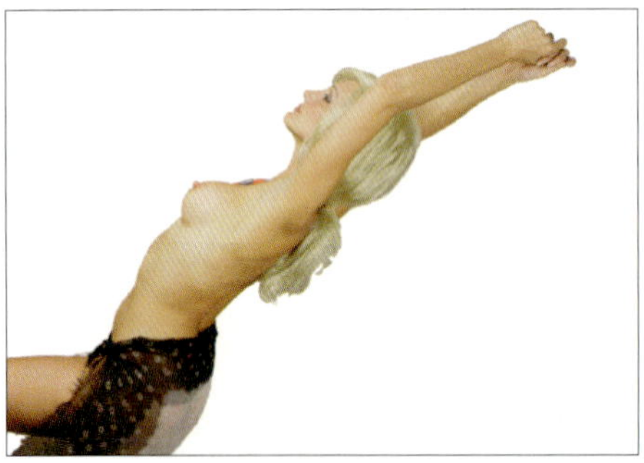

m.

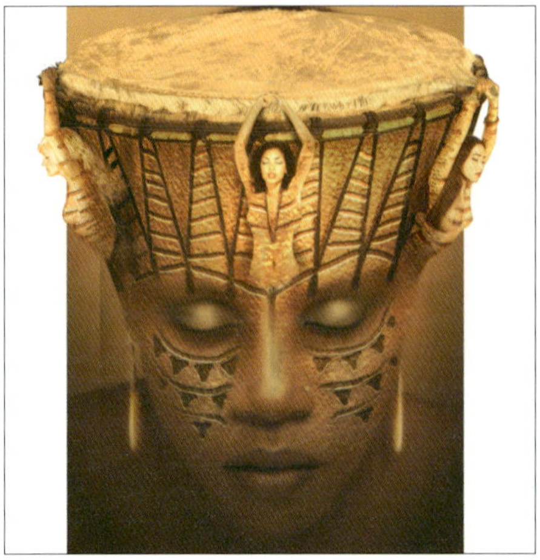

n.

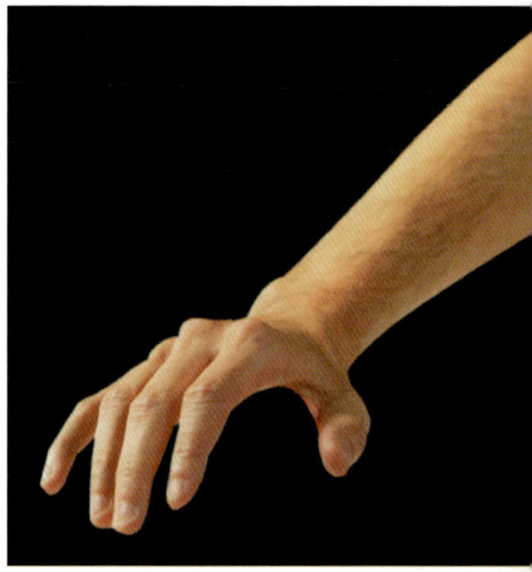

o.

k-m. I worked separately on the 3 female figures, using same techniques of lighting and channels to create those textures. For the central figure I just used some of the texture that was behind her.

n. I used the smudge tool and the Rubber Stamp to make the figures look as though they were pulling the skin of the drum, and used the layer mask to combine the figures into the drum composite.

The drum composite was then pasted into the "environment" again using the layer mask to smooth edges and fade the lower part of her face into the swirling water.

o. The last element being the hand, I phot graphed the hand after the rest of the imag had been composited, using a template guide in composition. I then used the har image as a channel, and pasted the entire s image into it, moving the element till I liked t way it blended with the area around it. I us the Rubber Stamp to finish and blend it in.

k-m. Female Figures
n. Drum with Figures
o. Hand
p. Dis is de Drum

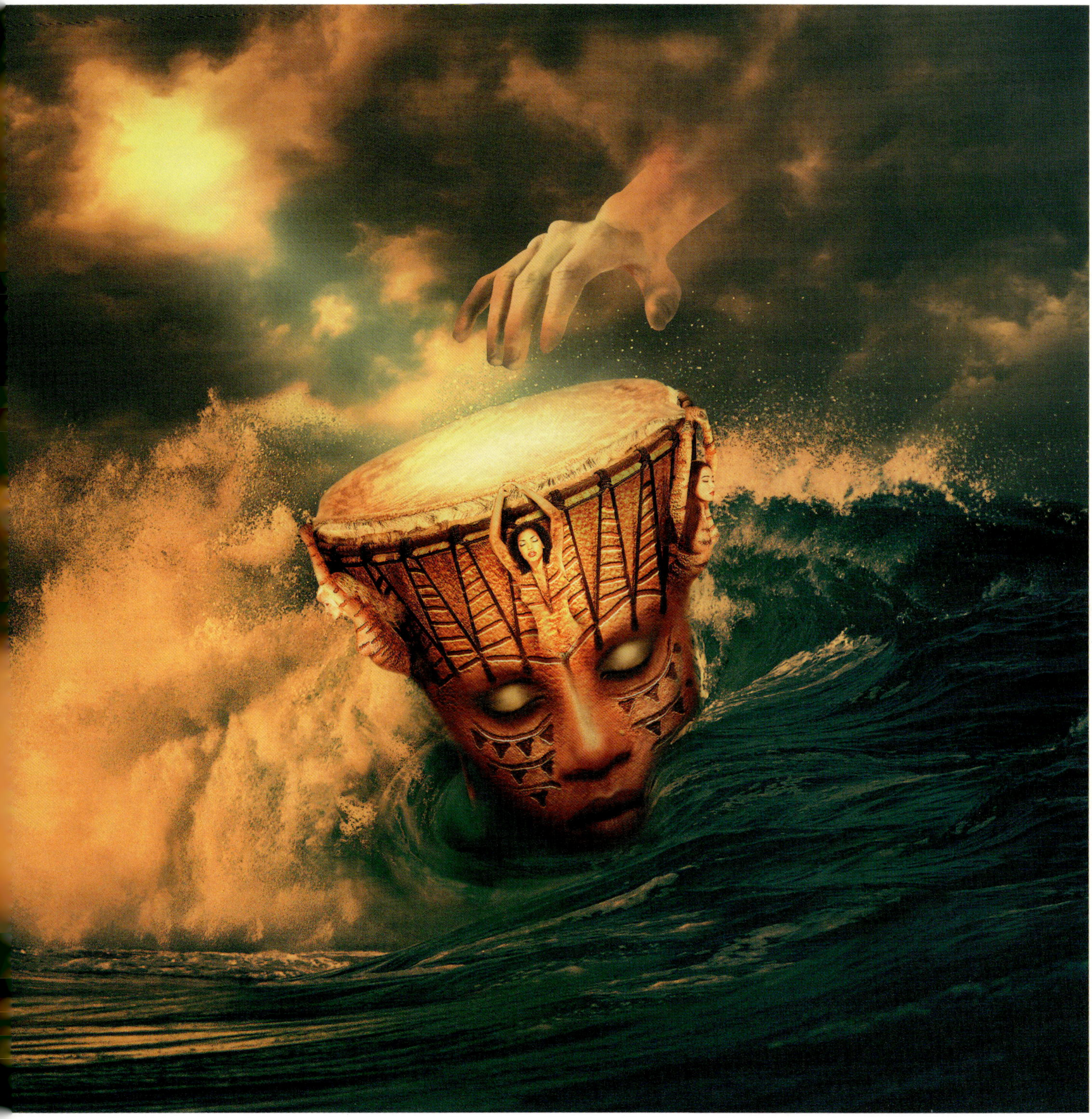

Sanjay Kothari

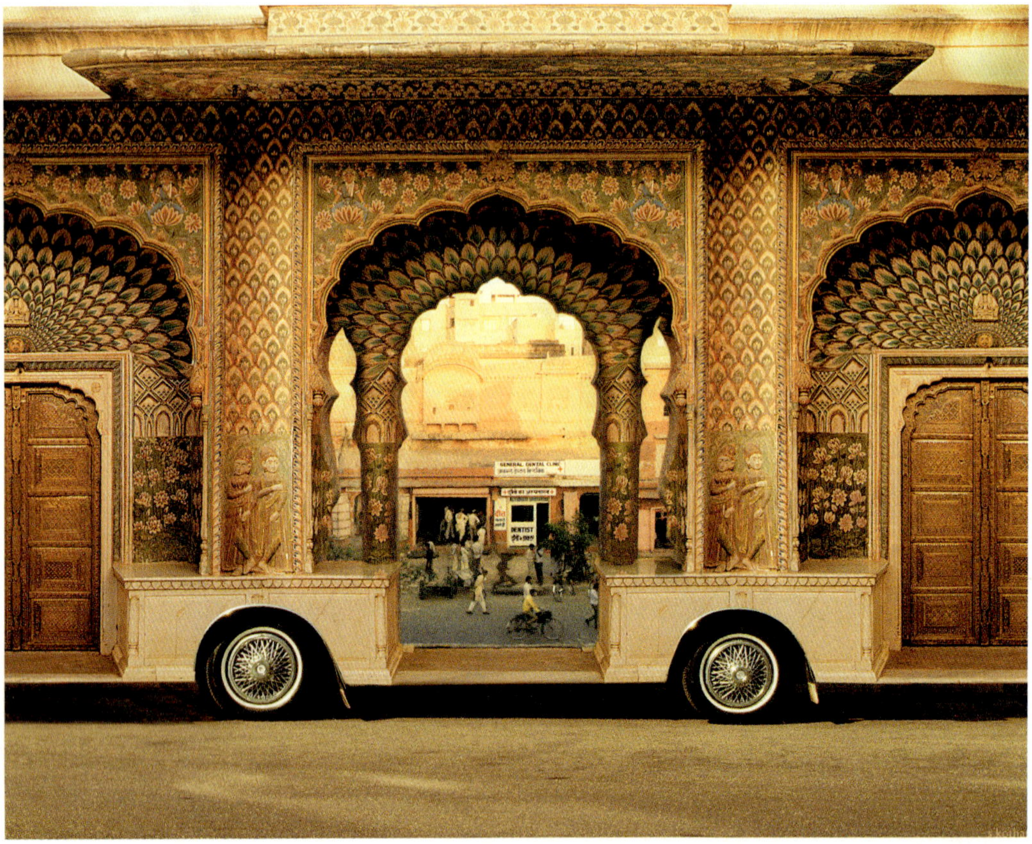

1.

1. Wheels
2. Opposite: Face

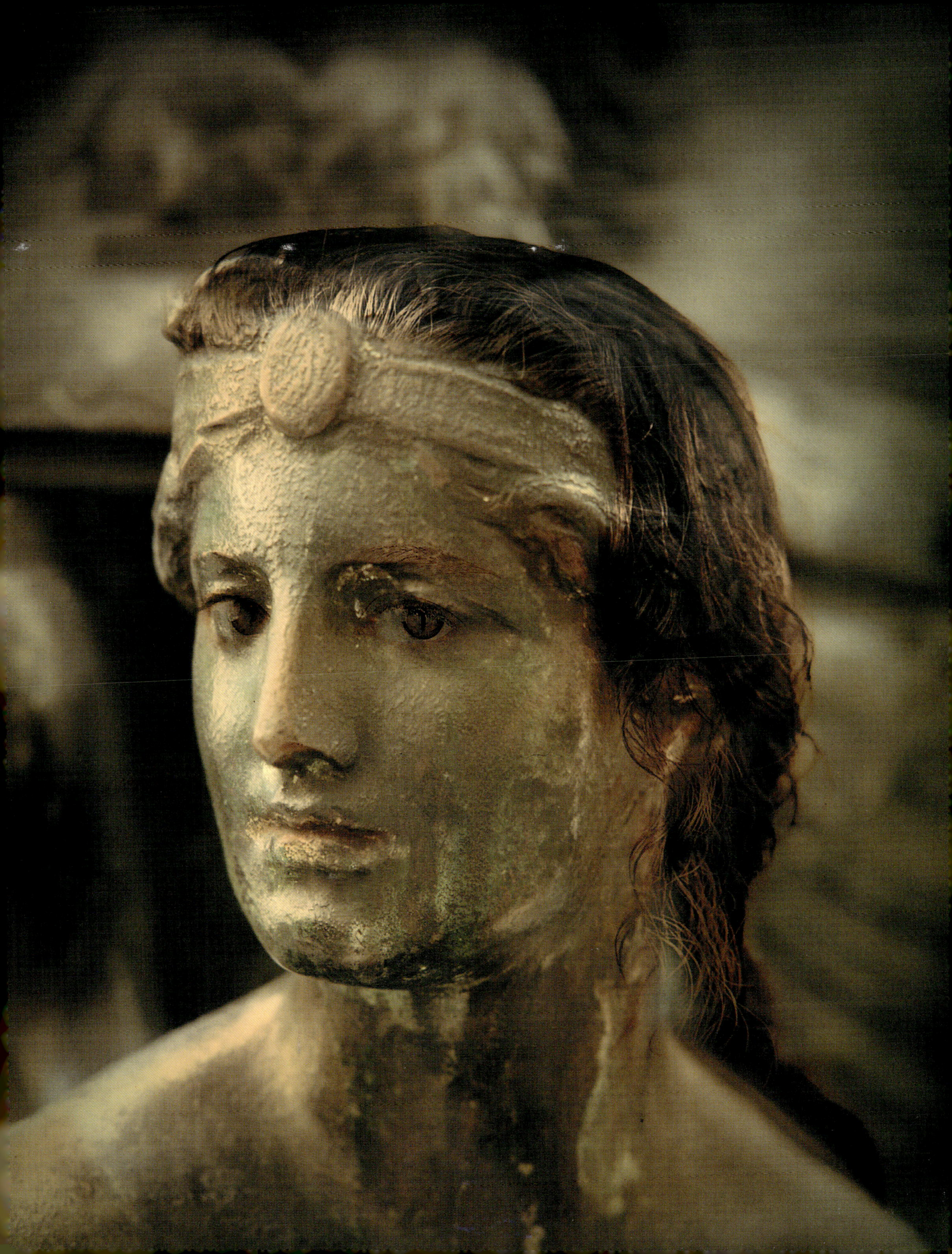

Sanjay Kothari

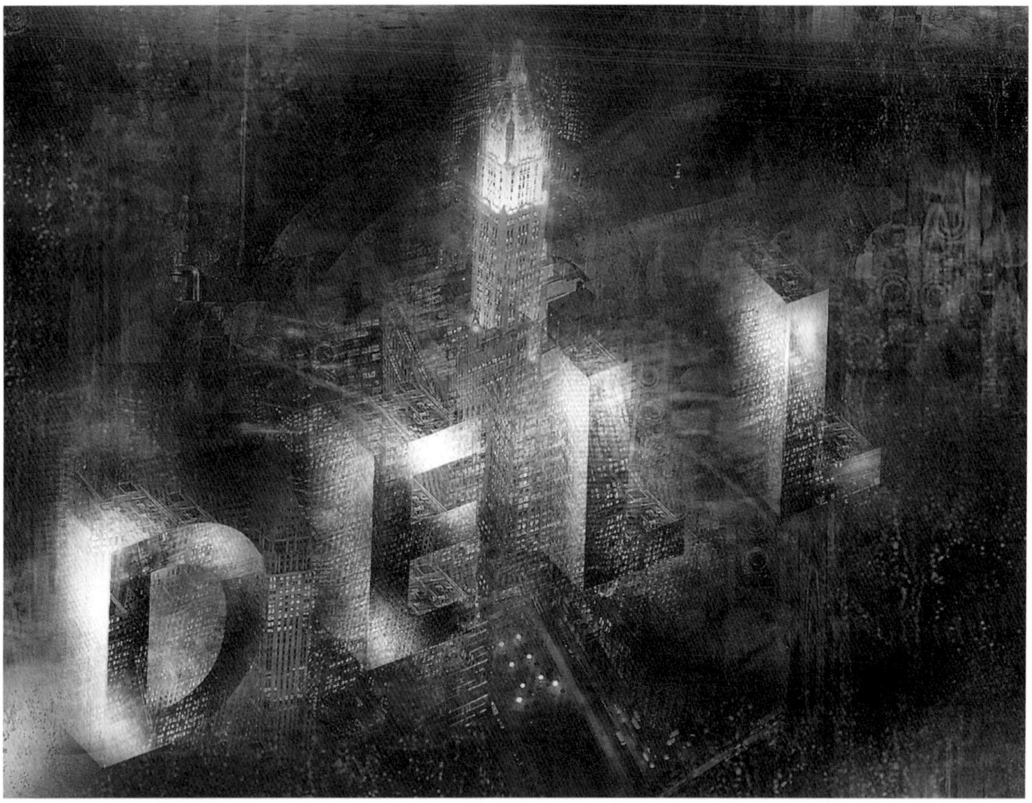

3.

3. Dell Series / Building withType
4. Dell Series / Machine

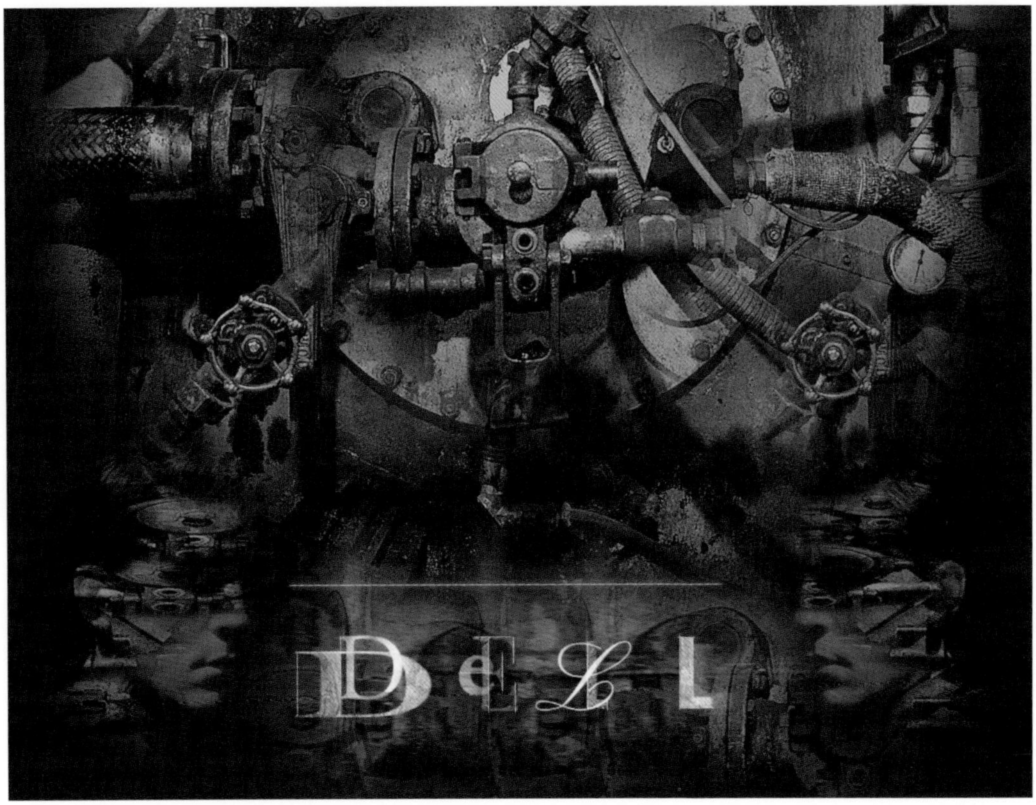

4.

Sanjay Kothari

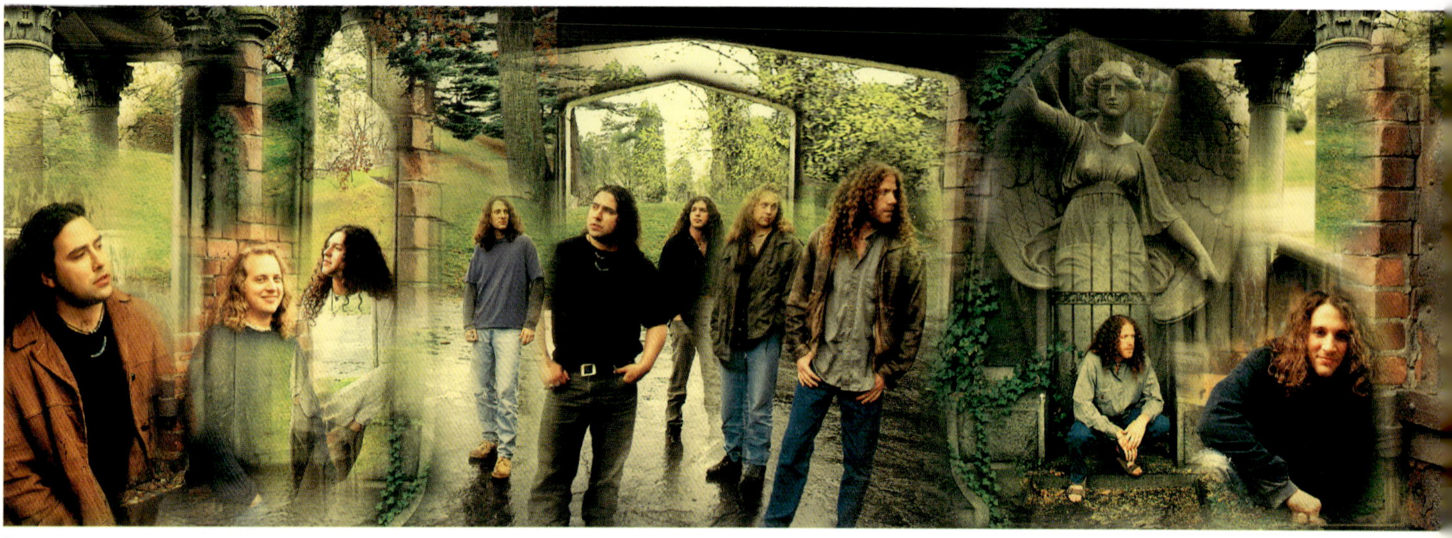

5.

5. Hatters (Panel)
6. Mobile

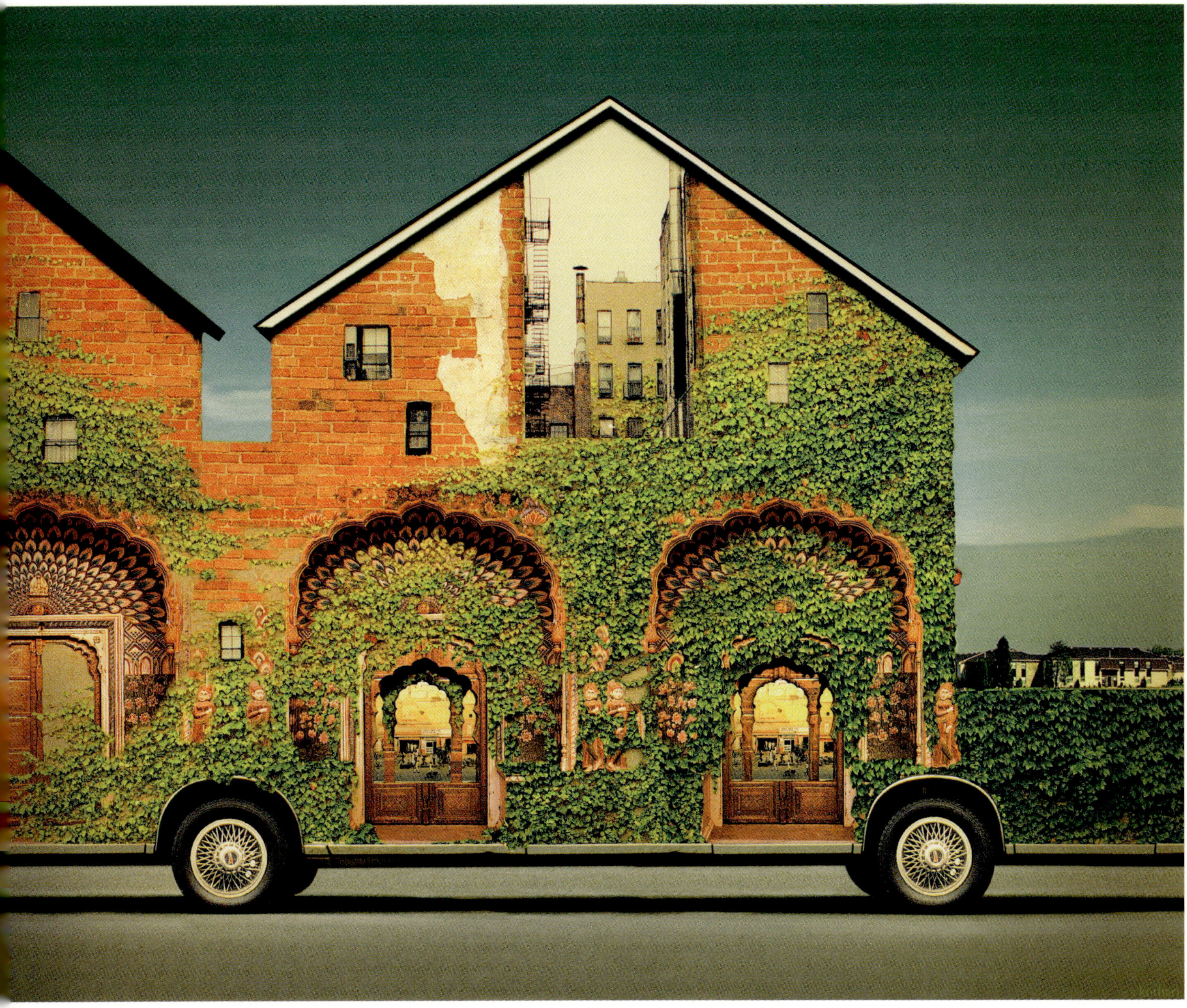

Sanjay Kothari

7.

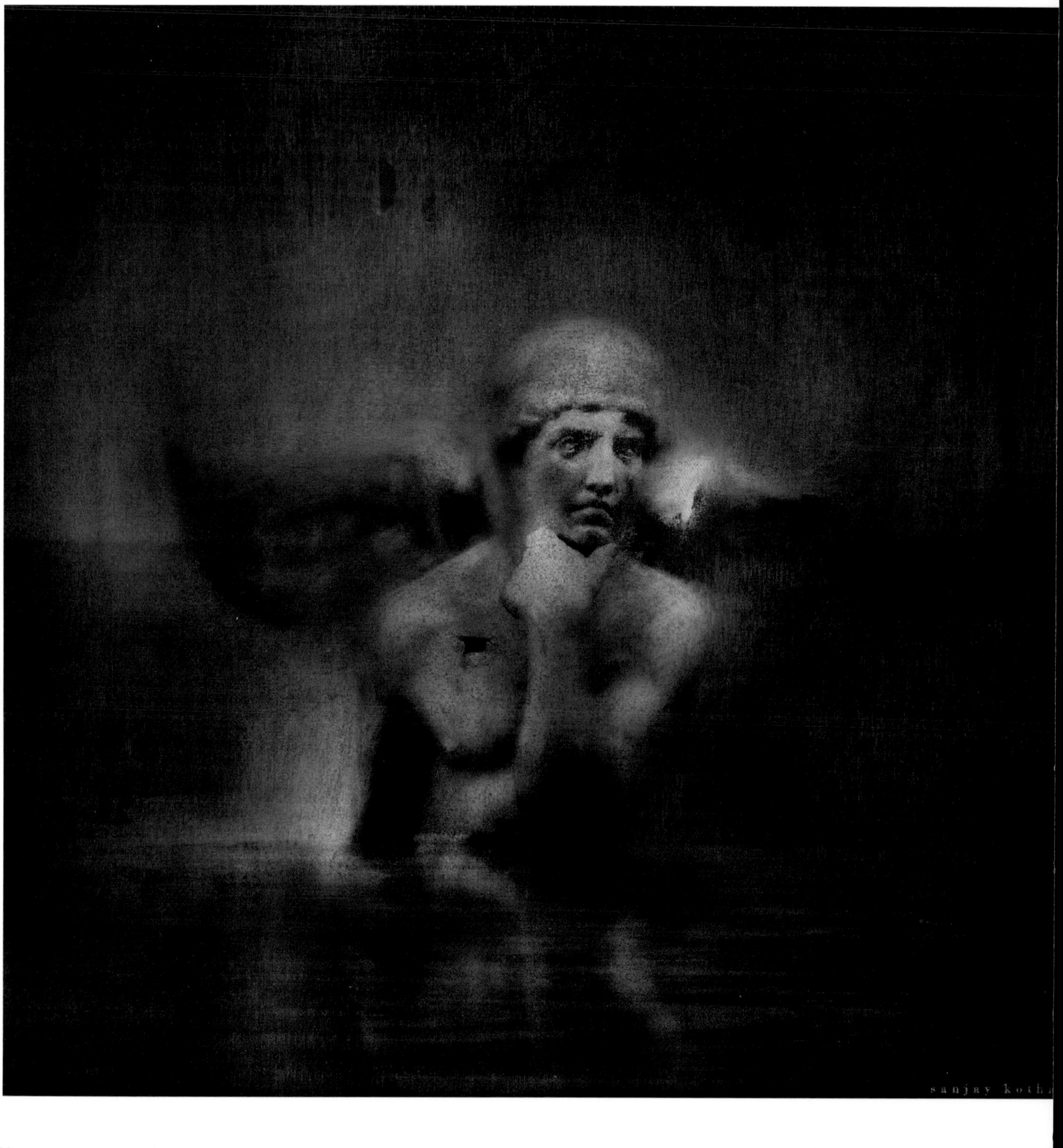

7. Thinker
8. Hatters (Single)

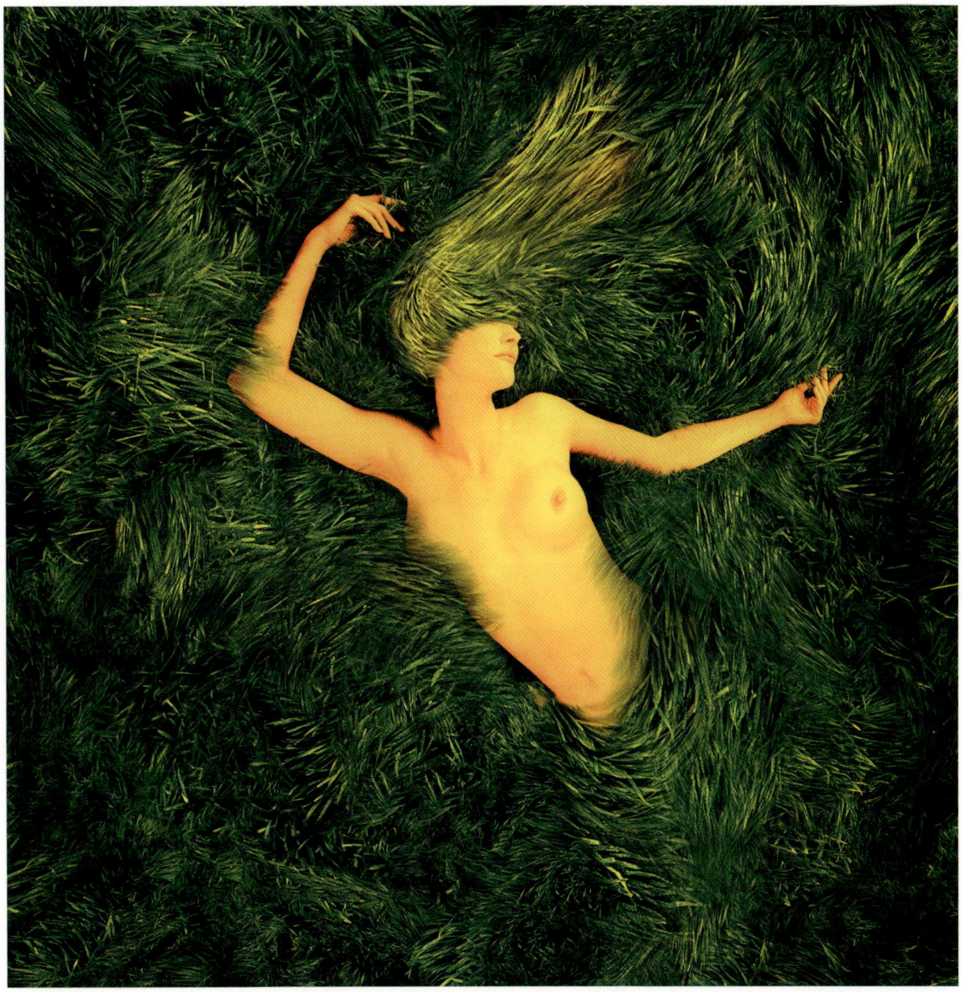

8.

Sanjay Kothari

9. Gearface

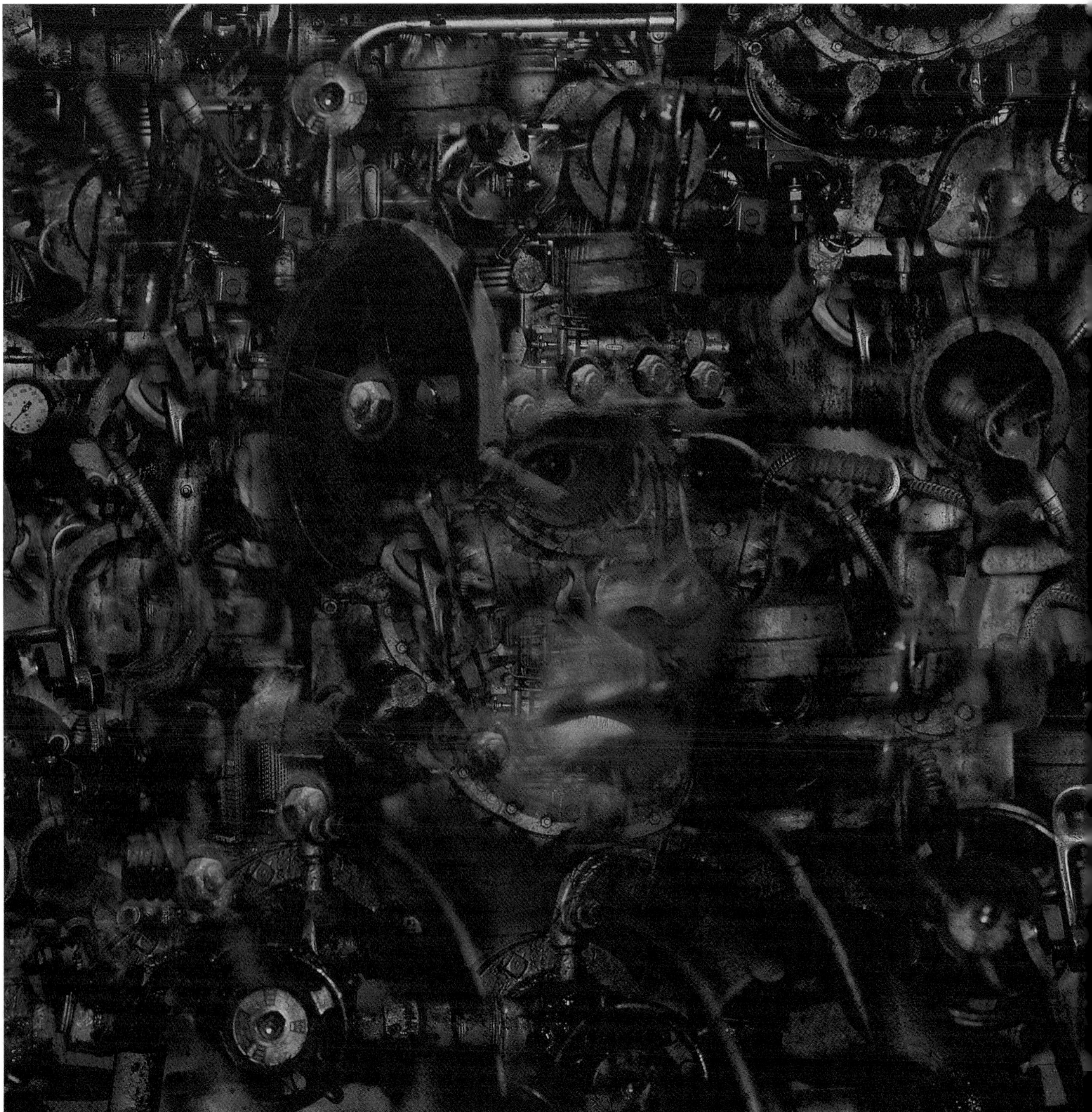

9.

Daniel Lee

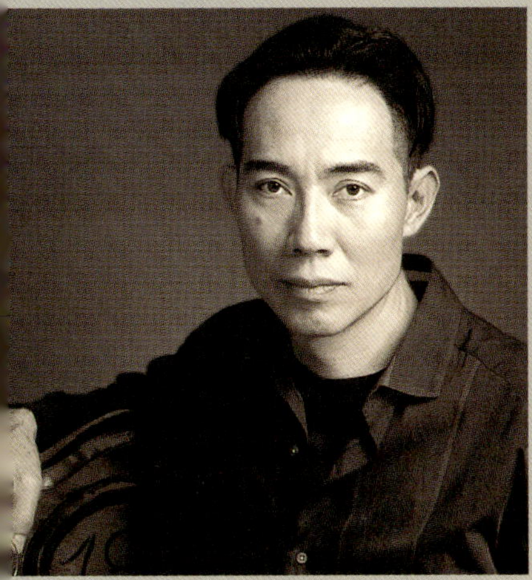

The disturbingly powerful digital images of photographer and computer artist Daniel Lee have earned him international recognition. Beginning from stark portraits photographed with a large-format camera, Daniel Lee submits his pictorial subjects to the digital wringer, provoking their unsettling metamorphoses into animal-like forms, inspired by the Chinese zodiac and mythological characters from Buddhism. He appropriately entitled these series "Manimals" and "Judgment," initially shown at OK HARRIS Works of Art Gallery in New York in 1993. Publications and exhibition venues around the world quickly took notice.

The resulting phantasmagoric man-beast images are intuitive renditions in which he uses his imagination to make uncanny yet strangely convincing transformations.

Known as Lee Siaojing in Chinese, born in China and raised in Taiwan, Lee moved to the United States to take his MFA and currently lives in New York. He began his professional career as an art director in New York, and switched to photography in the late seventies. Recent computer technology allowed him to combine his various drawing, photographic and fine art skills in one medium.

Daniel Lee

Developments in computer technology have had an enormous impact on photography. How is the photographer's situation changing spiritually and materially because of this?

To me, it's like a revolution. It's almost like when movies began to take the place of the theater and the opera. This computer technology is a very big step forward for photography. It supports your work, helps you to develop ideas, gives you strong visual results and lets you use your imagination. It goes beyond illustration and painting for me. And it overcomes the shortcomings of photography, too.

I had been watching the technology changing very carefully. Then three years ago, when I saw the computer being used by a photographer, I knew that some very important changes were going on. And I found it very exciting when I saw that a computer image could be as fine as a photo image. High-resolution images produced on the monitor could be output as pictures of the same quality.

So, after I saw these things, I knew I would have to get involved in computer imaging. It is a very big advantage for a photographer today to move into computer technology. The entire process, from taking the photo to retouching the image and rearranging image to be pre-press ready; all of it gives the photographer more control. I always used to complain to the printers because they would change my work. Now I can control most of the steps up to the final stage. With the new computer technology, a photographer can have much more control over the entire process.

I think that traditional photography will continue to exist side-by-side with digital. What is your opinion?

Well, I had been working in traditional photography since 1976. I put in a tremendous amount of work, and spent a lot of time trying to do photography very seriously. I think traditional photography will always be there. But the future will be digital imaging because it avoids the waste of labor and time in the

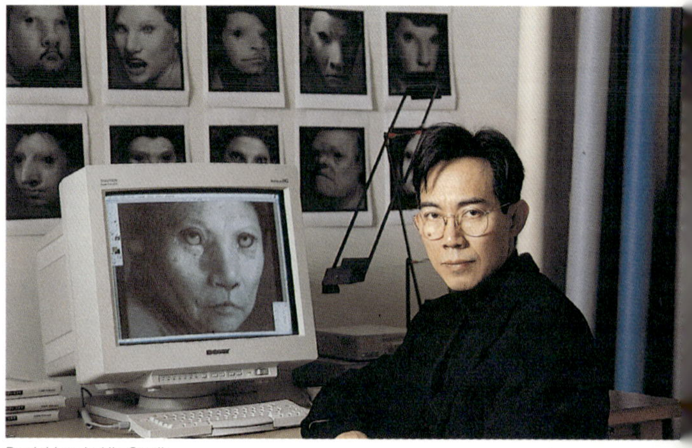

Daniel Lee in His Studio

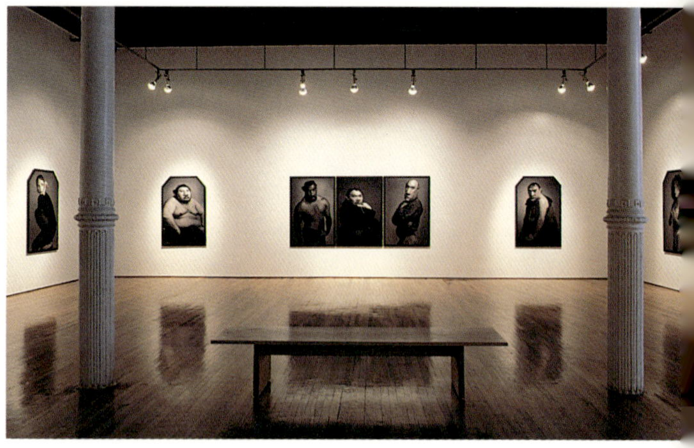

Exhibition Space: OK HARRIS Gallery

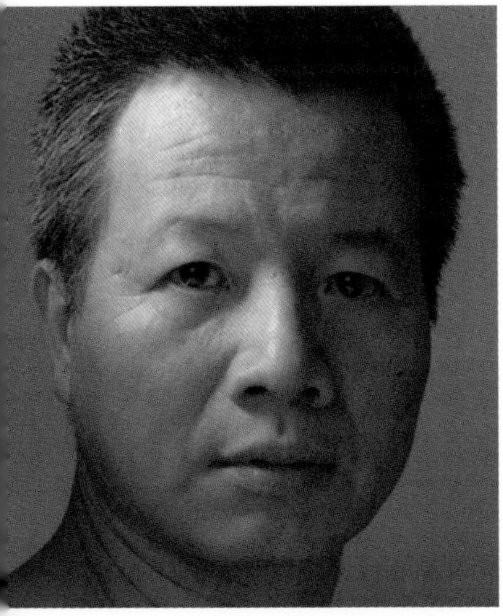

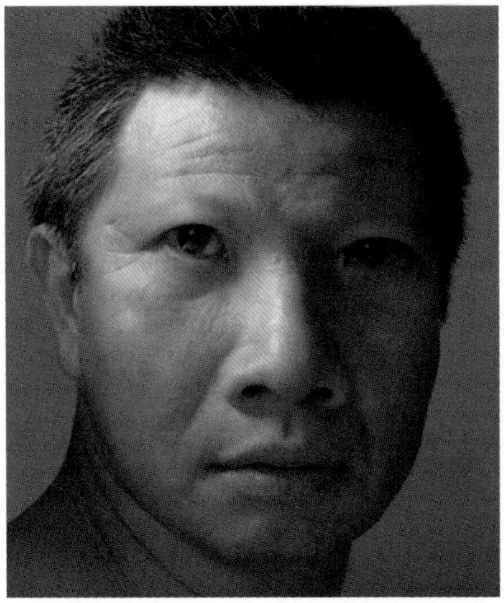

c.

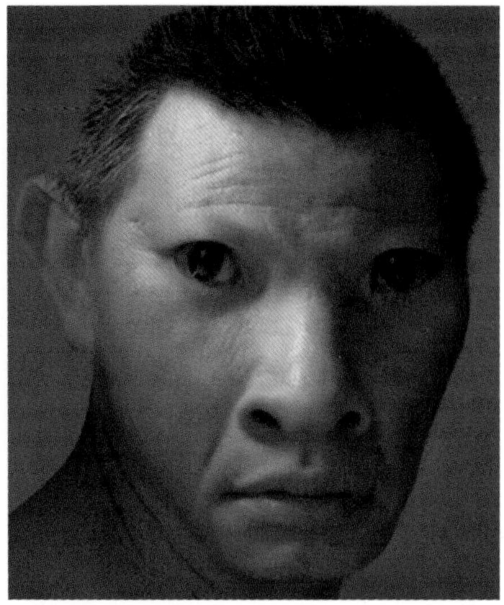

e.

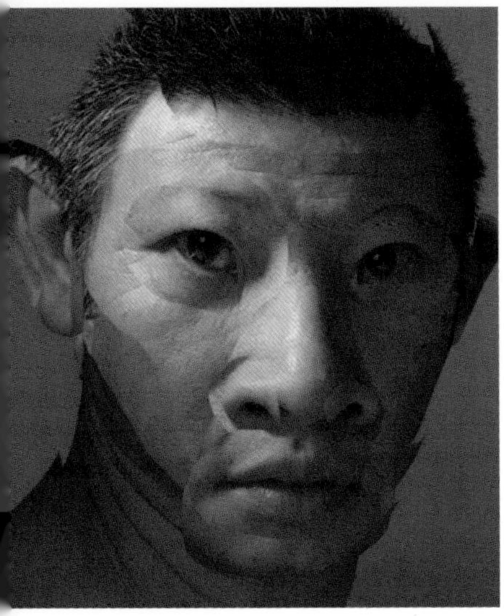

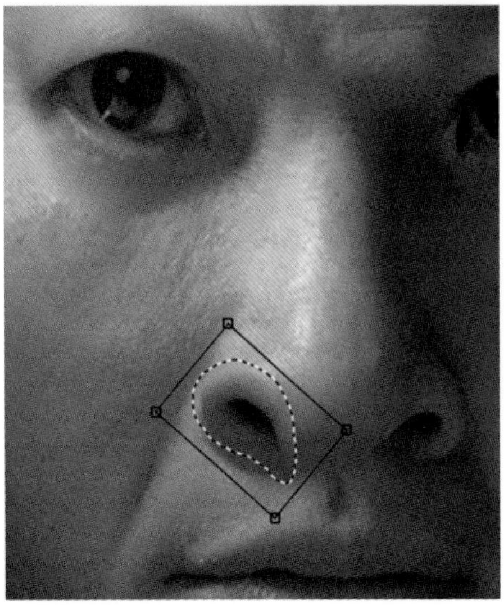

d.

. Original photograph

photographed the model with a $2^1/_4$ x $2^1/_4$ format amera using Ektachrome 100 Plus film. Then I canned the image onto a Kodak Pro Photo-CD. 'he image size at this stage is 3.5 x 4.5 inches vith a resolution of 240 pixels/cm.

b. Rough composition and altering the color

I selected a low Feather to move, scale and rotate most sections of the face to give a general impression of a man who resembles an ox.

I changed the colors of the original photo using the Hue /Saturation tool. First I reduced the color by 75%. Then I used the Color Balance tool to add color and get the mood I was looking for.

c. Manipulating the facial features

Working from the rough composition, I began to reshape the forehead, further separate the eyes and scale up the nose. The Feather selection was between 9 and 14 pixels.

d. The details

I zoomed in to check the details while reshaping or rotating each part of the image. The Layer tool in Adobe Photoshop 3.0 is perfect for making these moves.

e. Final steps

I went through many versions of the image before I was satisfied.

Daniel Lee

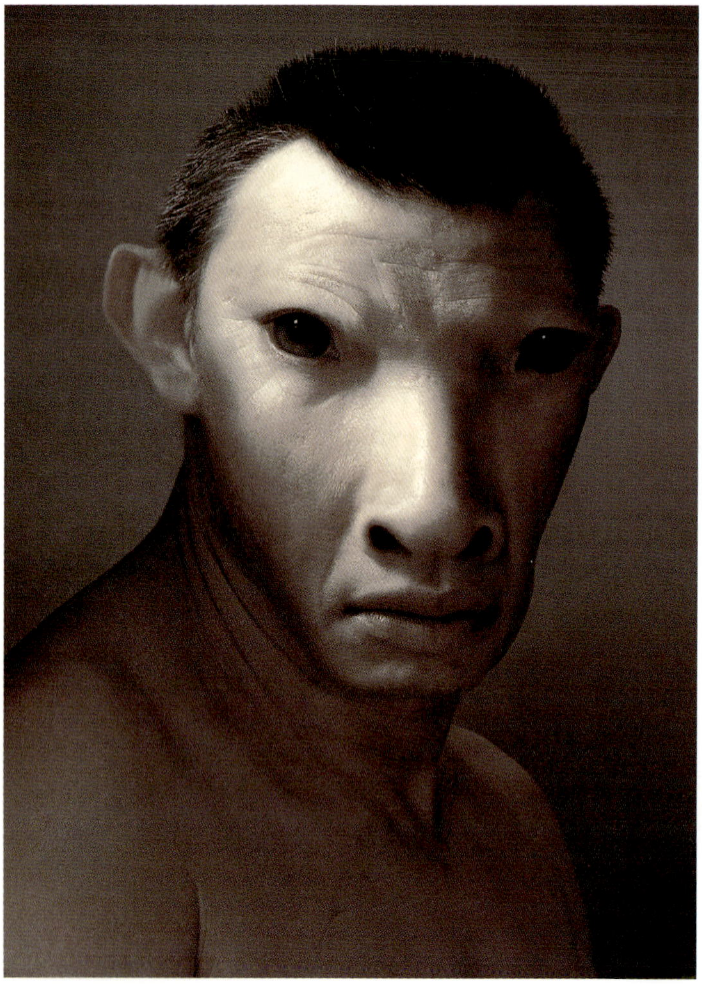

f.

f. Finished art
I output to LVT 4 x 5 transparency and printed with the Laser Master 24 x 40 inkjet printer. I entitled this piece "Year of the Ox."

industry; it also provides the photographer with more freedom t develop ideas than traditional photography.

In the future, I think most photographers are going to use digita imaging to complement their work. The concept of th "photograph" will be changed by electronic imaging. Instead o using film, we will be transferring our images for photofinishin via the computer networks. Digital photography is not only mor efficient, it is also suited to the future, since it is readily accessibl for telecommunications purposes.

Since the need for traditional photography is going to be limited it will not continue side by side with digital. I think people will b using traditional means in some specific areas, like classica artwork, amateur or family photos.

With traditional photography there was such a thing as th "original print." But with digital work it is more difficult to defin original print. Do you say that the enlarged print is your own original

First of all, I think that in traditional photography, we can sa that there are original prints, or original artwork. In black an white photography, the naked film could be construed as th original artwork. In color photography the original could be th transparency. In digital photography, however, you might hav to call the computer file the original artwork. The work itself i actually a file. You can open it, you can manipulate it. But it i not something you can see as a material. I think if we have t define "original" in digital photography, then the computer file is it

The artist controls his own file, and then the printer can use tha file to make a printout. Then the first printing can be called th artist's proof or the first copy. Then with the second print yo can, for example, make it a little darker, or open up the shadov details. You can use color correction. These things can all b changed immediately. So then you can't call the print an origina print any more.

Digital technology certainly has changed our thinking about wha the original work is. But I choose to think that everything tha omes out in the photographer's work — the first step — should e regarded as the original. I think that for the artist the original s really the exhibition or presentation. The whole presentation is he original art. And everything shown in this one-time resentation is the original work. The same presentation shown gain somewhere else, in a different setting, would be something ew again. The artist should have this kind of freedom — and eep an open mind for presentation.

hat is why the original as such is not that important any more. he only reason I still sign my work is for limited editions. It tresses the value of those prints among other work. That value s for collectors only. For me, if I can show some work in a nagazine, that's a presentation to me also. I show my work in ooks. This is also a presentation. And then we have to keep ne piece as the original, which has value, like a masterpiece? I on't really think we need to do that.

n a sense, the role of photography is widening: from recording he world we see to expressing the artist's vision of the world. ow do you consider this as an artist?

Vell, I had training in fine art, both in undergraduate and graduate chool. I think the reason I switched from painting to photography s because I preferred the more modern medium. Photography is omething I can use to express myself more directly than with ther media.

s an artist I enjoy very much being a photographer because hotography allows us to work in so many different areas. From ecording the world as seen in photojournalism, to art and ommercial photography. There is such a diversity of subjects or the photographer to choose from.

hotography, of course, is very technical. I have spent around wenty years working on the techniques. But right now, the omputer is giving the photographer so much more leeway. It's lmost like the saying in Chinese about giving a pair of wings to tiger. The tiger was a very powerful beast to begin with. But iving the tiger wings enables it to do almost anything. So it is with photography. There was a time when photography was kind of limited. But the computer has given photography unlimited power.

I've done different things at different stages in my career. To me, the photographer has some kind of job to do which is different from a painter. Before, I was thinking, what is the most important thing a photographer should do? And the answer was to capture life. That is why I went to China. I went to the minority areas between China and Burma, and I took photographs of minority people there in an attempt to capture their way of life. I tried to preserve something of their way of life on film because it might be disappearing someday.

But later on I became dissatisfied with simply trying to capture things. I have this kind of mind driving me that wants to create. It's not that creating things is more important than capturing things with the camera. I wouldn't say that. But I was trained as an artist in the first place. If I stopped creating things I would probably start feeling sorry for myself. That's why, this year, in my work I was trying to create new images. Something that people have had no experience of in the past. The computer has allowed me, as an artist, to do this...to express my imagination, to share things with other people. At this moment these are the kinds of images that are important to me. And for the moment, using photography to record or capture life is less important than the creative work I'm doing on the computer.

What is the meaning of "Manimals"? Where do you get your image concepts?

"Manimals" is a conflation of "man" and "animals." Actually, a very good friend of mine, Ken Thompson, suggested this word to me to describe these images I was working on.

Originally, making these animal-like portraits came from my idea that man and animals are really not a whole lot different. If we look at our evolutionary history, for example, the emergence of man from the beasts is like yesterday. We still have a lot of animal-like thinking and behavior in us. We can be vicious. We still have

Daniel Lee

this ugly, uncivilized part of us beneath the surface.

This idea of the similarity between man and beasts is the philosophy behind the work. I took the twelve animal signs of the Chinese zodiac — the year of the tiger, year of the pig, etc. — and used them as a reference. I would first take the portrait of a person, and if that person was born, say, in the year of the tiger, I transform the portrait so that it comes to resemble a tiger. The person comes to have some identifiable tigerlike characteristics. I do not superimpose a tiger picture on a human's. That, for me, would be too ordinary. It's still a portrait of a person, but after I've scanned the image in and worked on it in Photoshop, the person winds up looking uncannily like a tiger.

The "Manimals" prints for the exhibition were very large. What is the size of those prints, and where and how did you print them out?

This work has already been shown twice in the last three years in New York. The first show was of the 12 "Manimals" and the second show was called "Judgment." The prints in those two shows were of different sizes and different materials. The "Manimals" were C-prints. I made internegatives from the original 8 x 10 transparency output. The 8 x 10s are a product called LVT from Kodak. It has a very high resolution. From these I made the internegatives. And then I made the enlarged prints.

The images for the second show, "Judgment," are supposed to be characters in a kind of underworld courthouse. The idea is really about Judgment Day when we are judged on our lives. If we are judged sinners, we are turned into animals. If we are judged otherwise, we will become human beings again in the next reincarnation. The characters are from Chinese mythology.

The images for that series were direct digital output. I was dissatisfied with the output for the first series, so I decided on digital for the second. I used Laser Master inkjet prints for the second series. The printer is similar to the Iris. I would even say that Laser Master is better than Iris. The trouble with

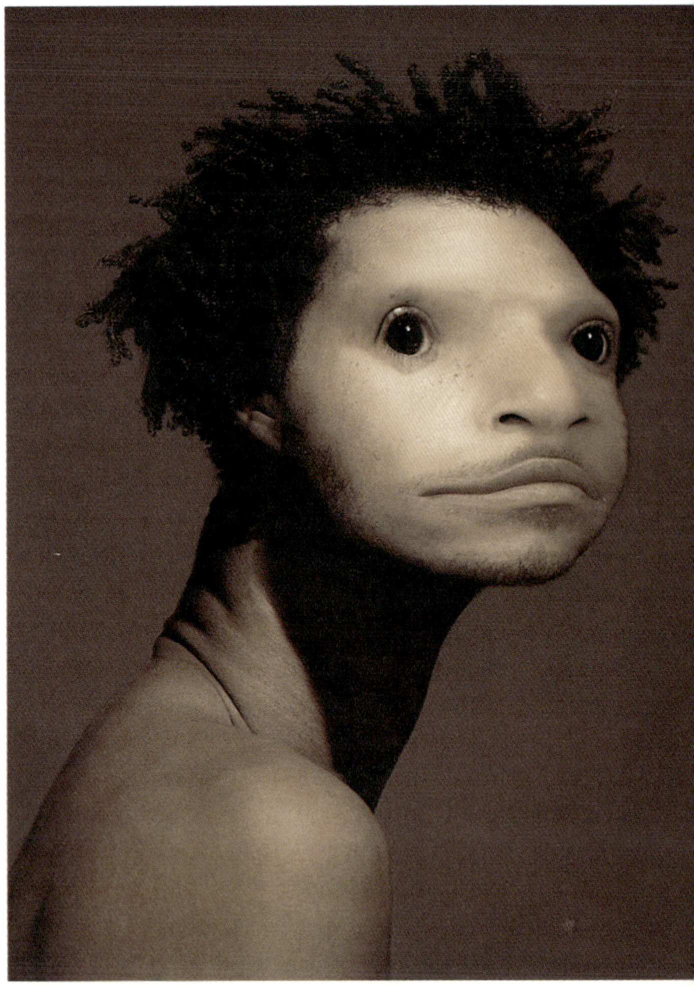

1.

1. Year of the Snake
2. Year of the Tiger
3. Year of the Tiger (before)

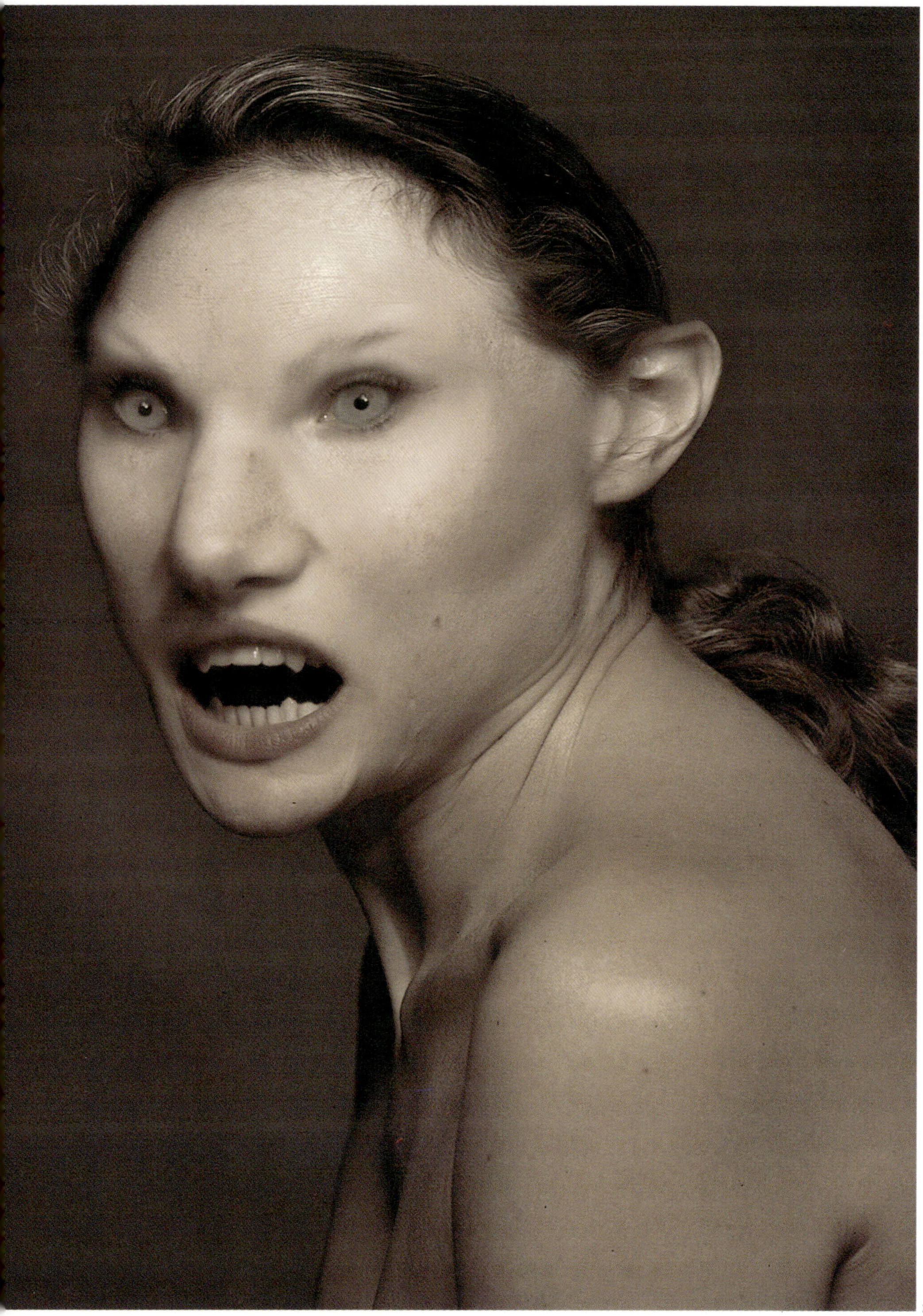
2.

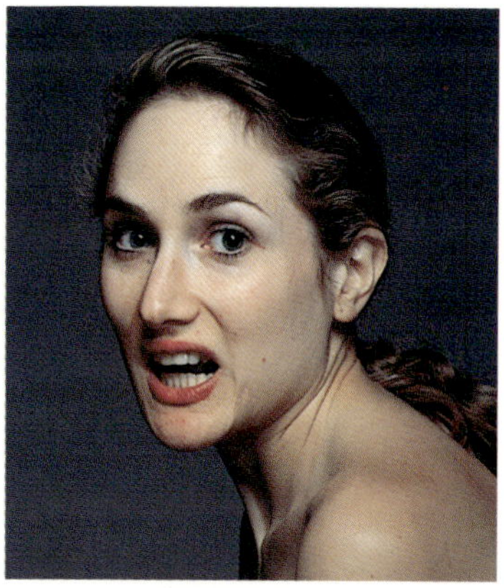
3.

Iris prints is that they are limited in size. They can only go to 30 x 40. Laser Master lets you go as big as 50 x 80. Also the price is a little bit less than Iris.

I heard that your last solo exhibition was very successful at OK HARRIS Gallery in New York. Could you tell us about the exhibition?

My first computer-generated images were shown at OK HARRIS at the end of 1993. I got a very good response for the work in that show. Then I worked on the second theme, "Judgment," which was shown at OK HARRIS towards the end of 1994. I took the Judge of Dead, his two guards and eleven other characters from the underworld courtroom of Chinese mythology. I grew up with these mythical characters in comic form. I wanted to see them again, today, as photolikenesses.

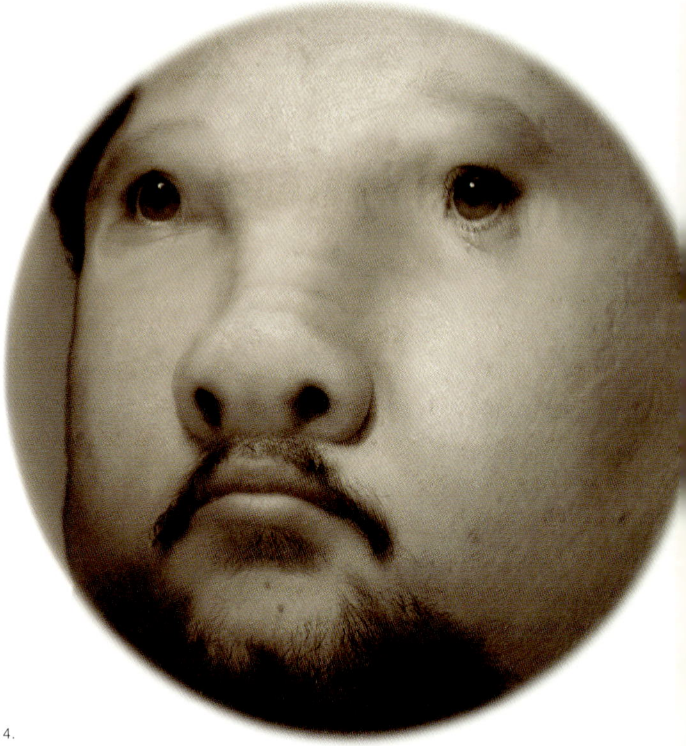

4.

People found the images disturbing because they look so strange, but at the same time realistic. A lot of people appreciated these images, perhaps because they bring a new kind of experience to the photographic portrait. So reviews came in very quickly from many magazines and papers, including *American Photo, Creative Technology* (England), *ZOOM, Photographer International, A Venir* and *Newlook* (France) and other publications from Hong Kong, Taiwan, Canada, Greece and Brazil, etc. I am also planning exhibitions in Italy, France, as well as in Japan, Taiwan and Slovakia.

I was very lucky to have this kind of success which happened in a short period after I picked up the computer technology. I think this is mainly because I use computer just like a new tool, to extend the photography I have been working in for a long time.

What advice would you give to emerging artists who want to work in digital imaging?

First I would like to impress on them that the future of photography lies in digital imaging. I hope that they spend a lot of time studying and practicing digital imaging. Because right now people are

4. 12/108 of the 108 Looks
5. Untitled Nude 9501

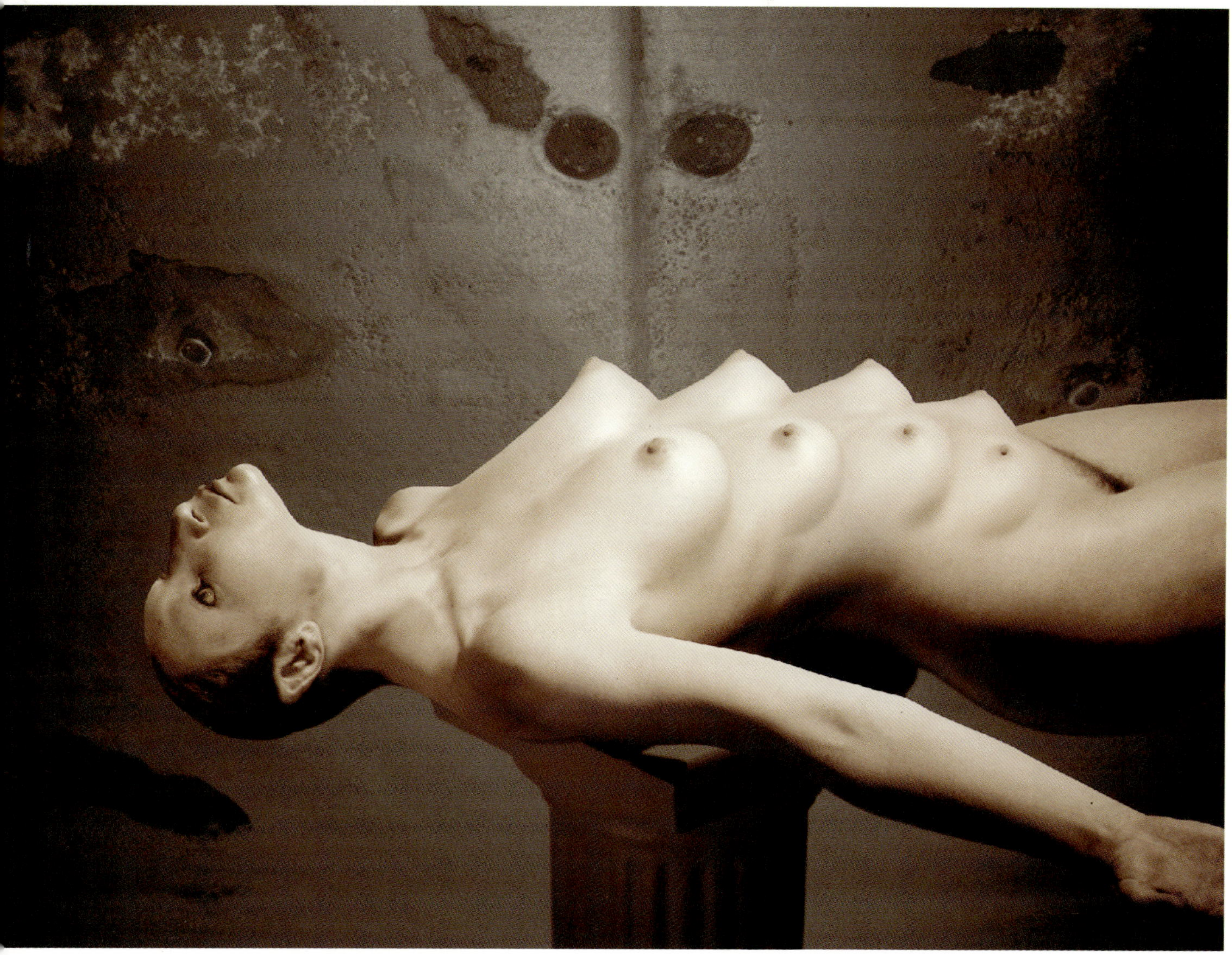

Daniel Lee

6. Juror no. 9
7. Juror no. 9 (before)
8. Opposite: Year of the Cock

taking this work very seriously. They can see the potential in the power of the computer. Other people are wary of the technology, and think they'd never be able to use the computer very well. And in the worst case, there are people who are dead set against digital imaging. They are of the opinion that computer-generated images cannot be compared with traditional photographs...and that computer art work can never be fine art. Those people are too conservative in my opinion. We should all try to keep an open mind about this technology. We should always be ready to discover new media. Nowadays, a lot of the technology is available to almost everyone. Eventually, everything — education, communication, broadcasting, print media and so on — will be linked together with these high-tech communication media. And as a professional, if you don't get used to the technologies, you may very well be left behind.

So I think that today's students should take more time to familiarize themselves with the computer. For photographers, this technology is so much more convenient. It lets you control the colors and contrast a whole lot better. And it eliminates all that hard darkroom work we had to do. So instead of shying away from the technology, they should take positive advantage of it.

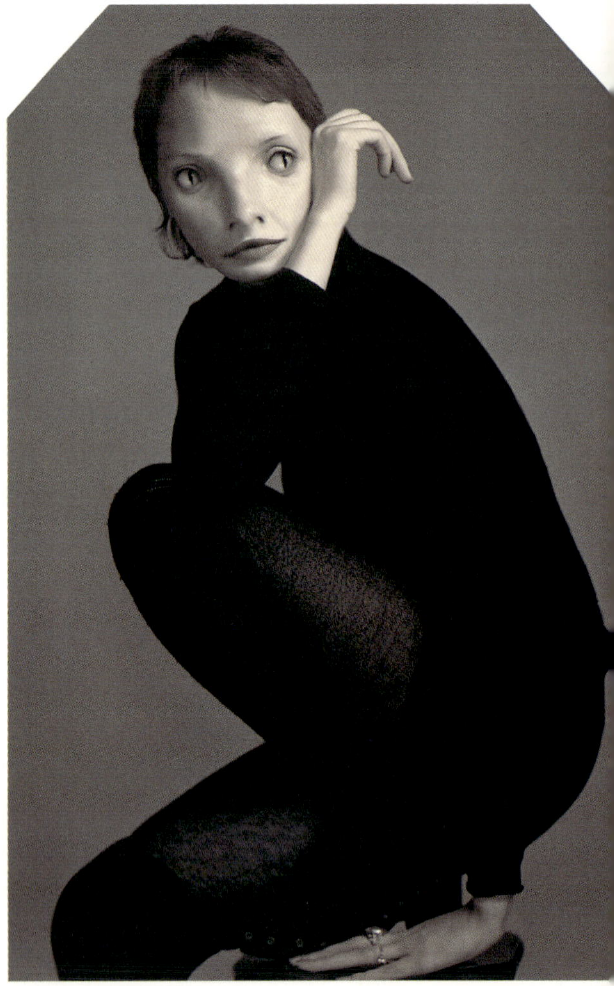

6.

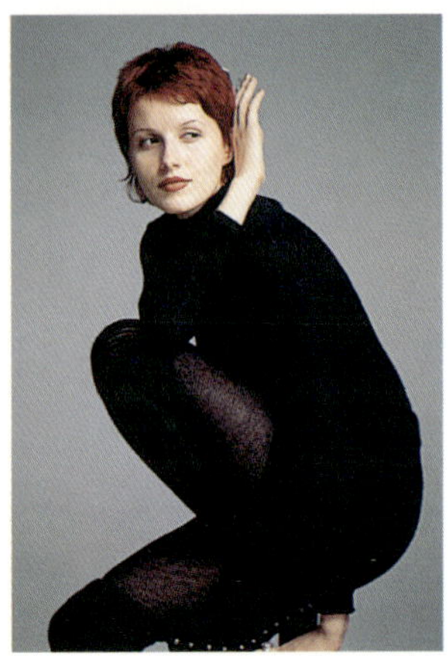

7.

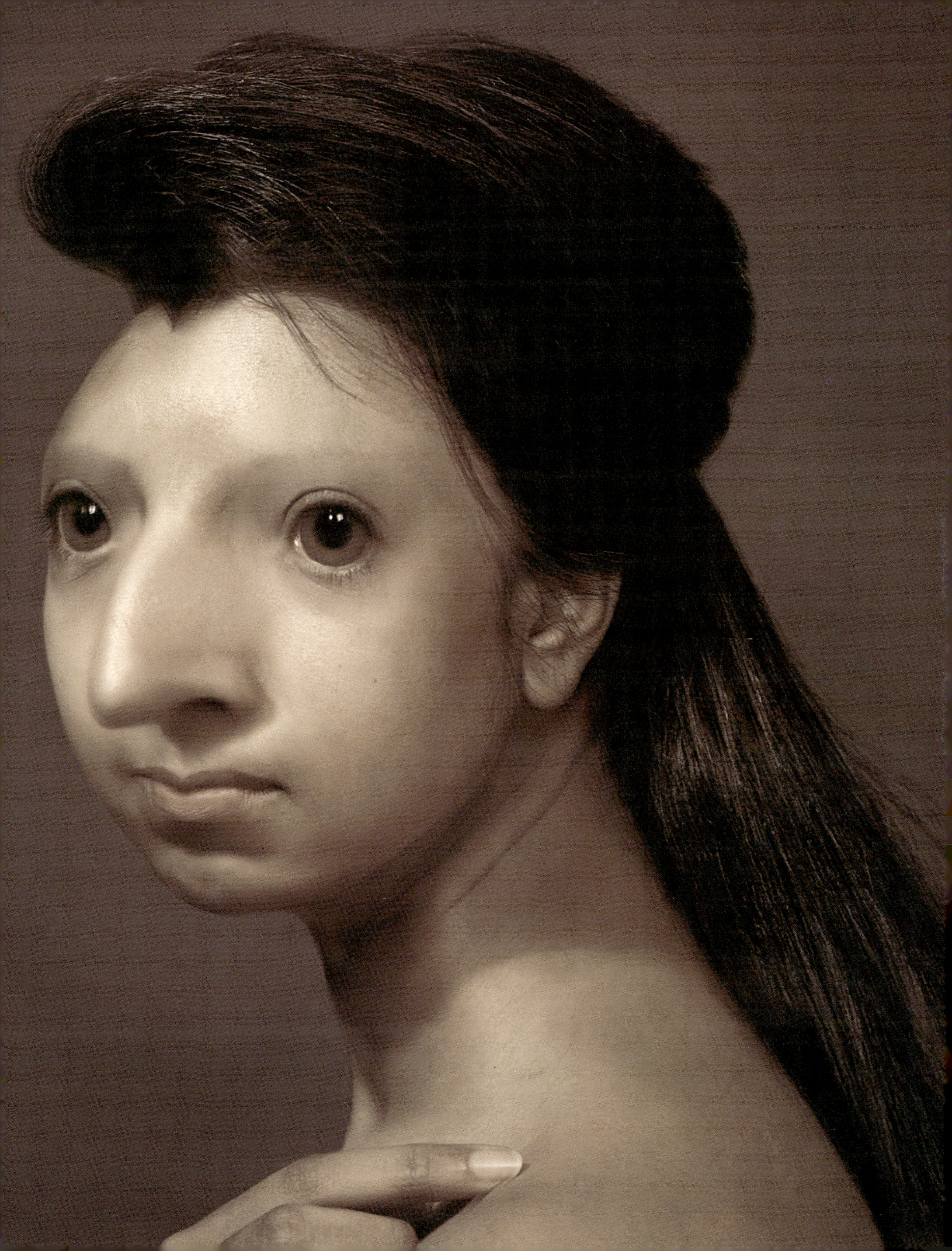

Daniel Lee

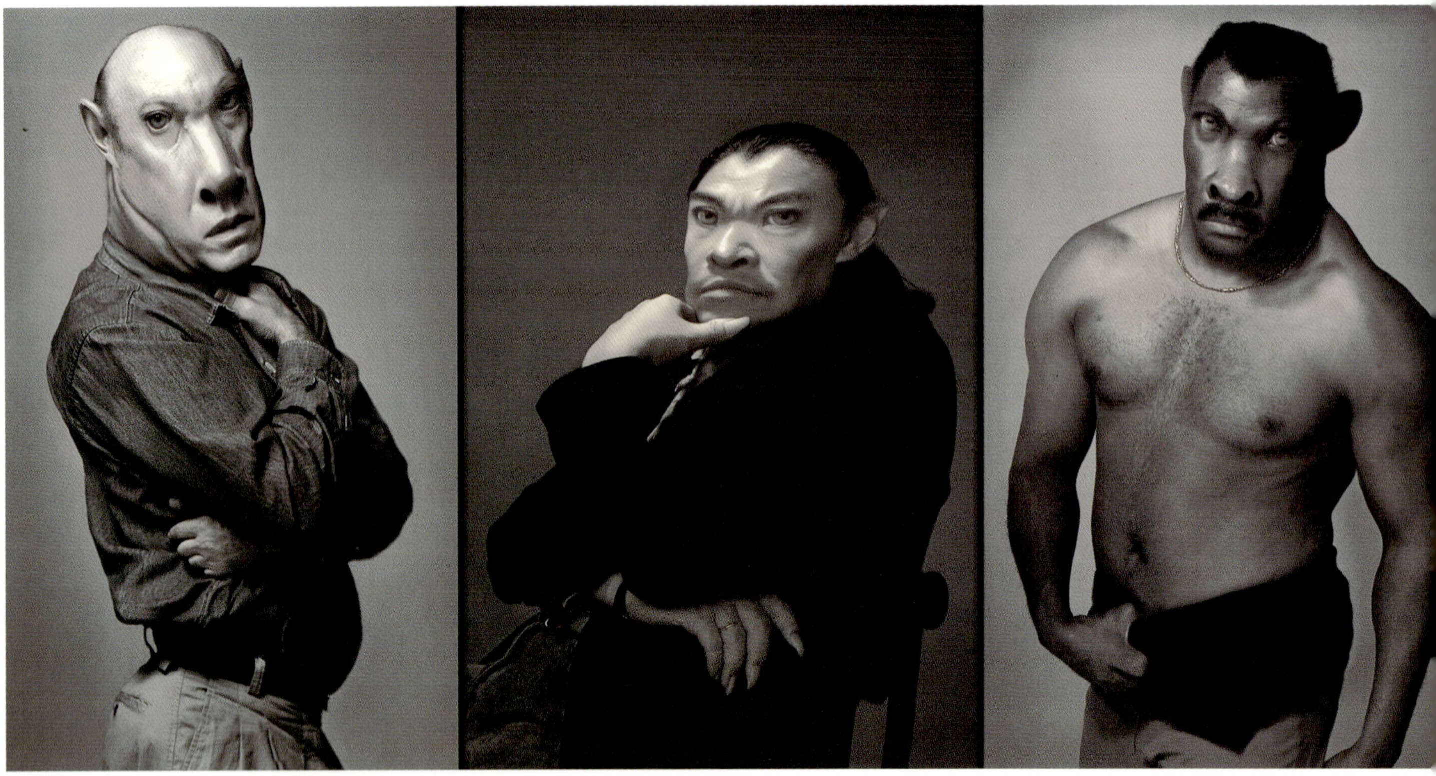

9.

9. Judge of Dead & His Guards
10. Juror no.10

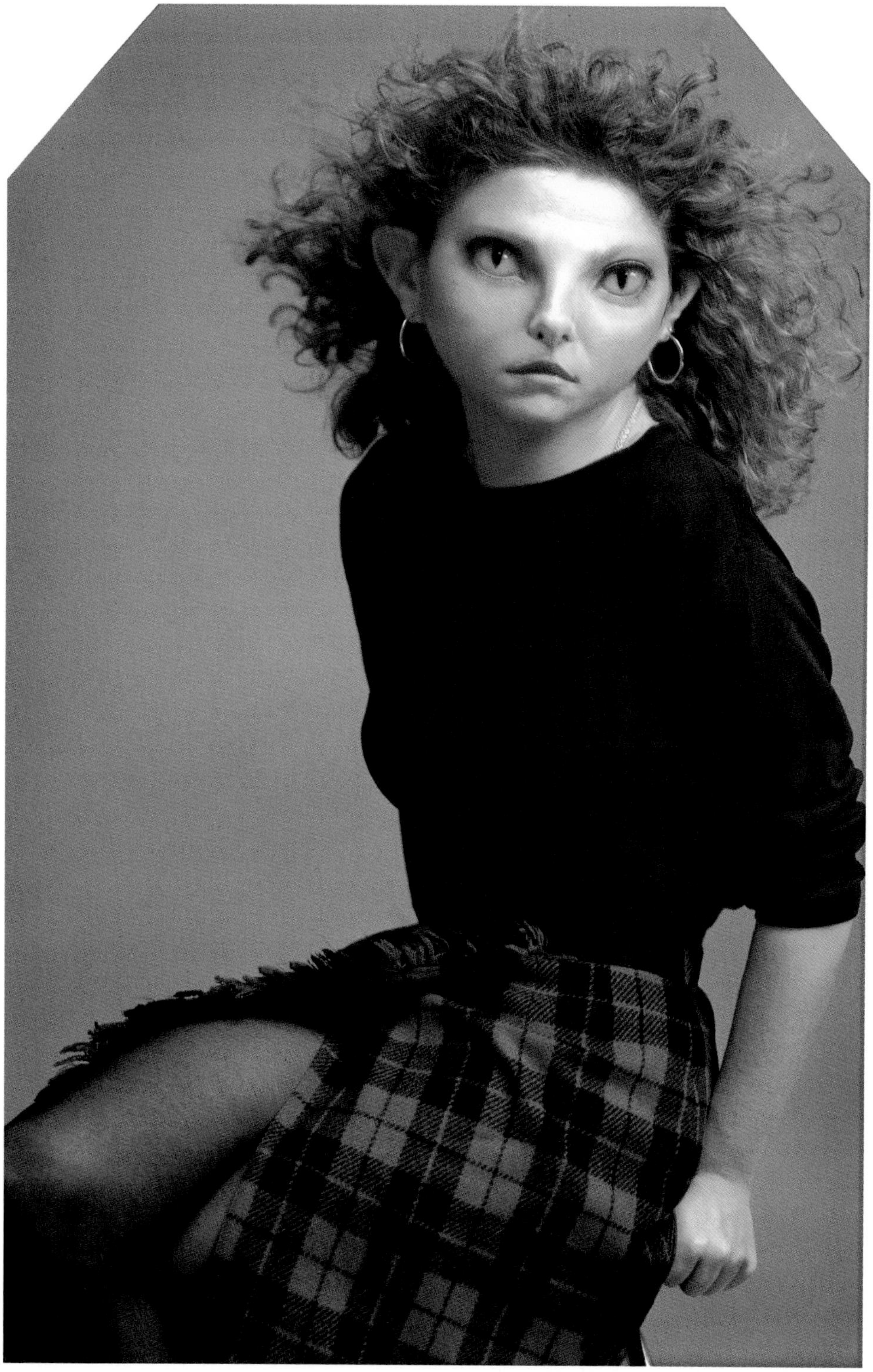

10.

Daniel Lee

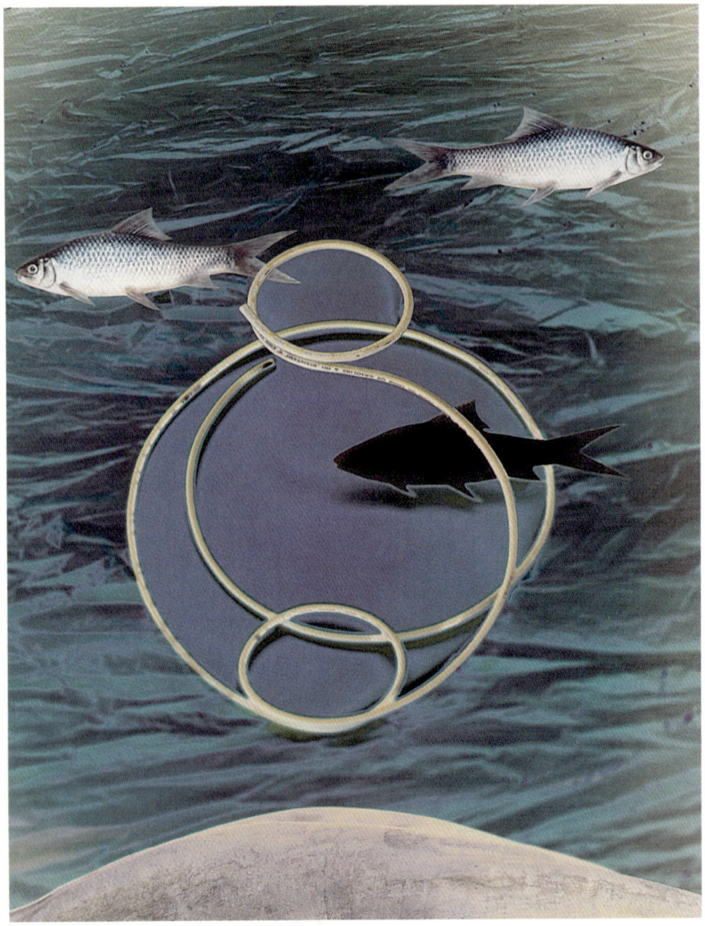

11.

11. Fish and Bowl
12. Juror no.7

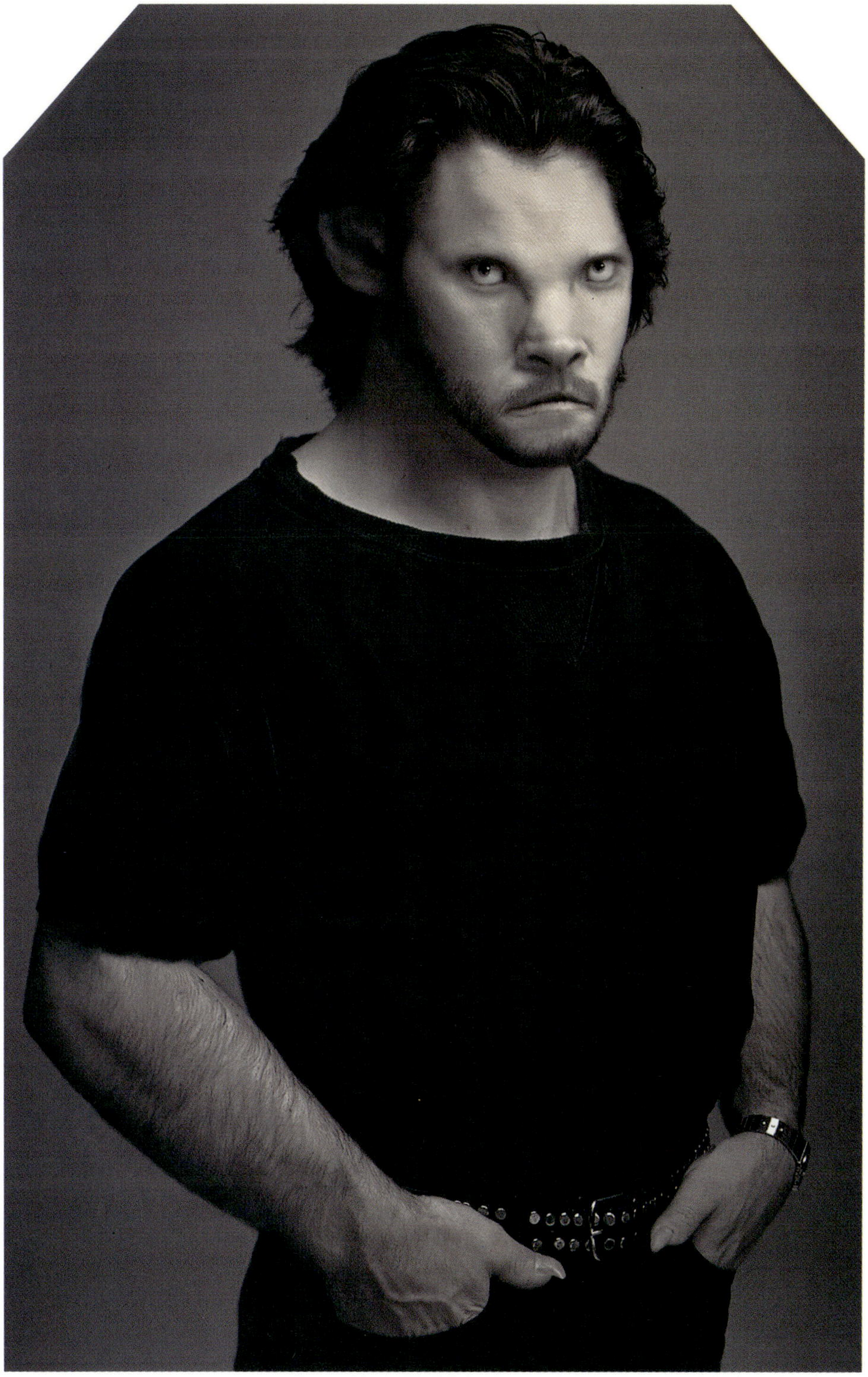

12.

Daniel Lee

13. Juror no. 6

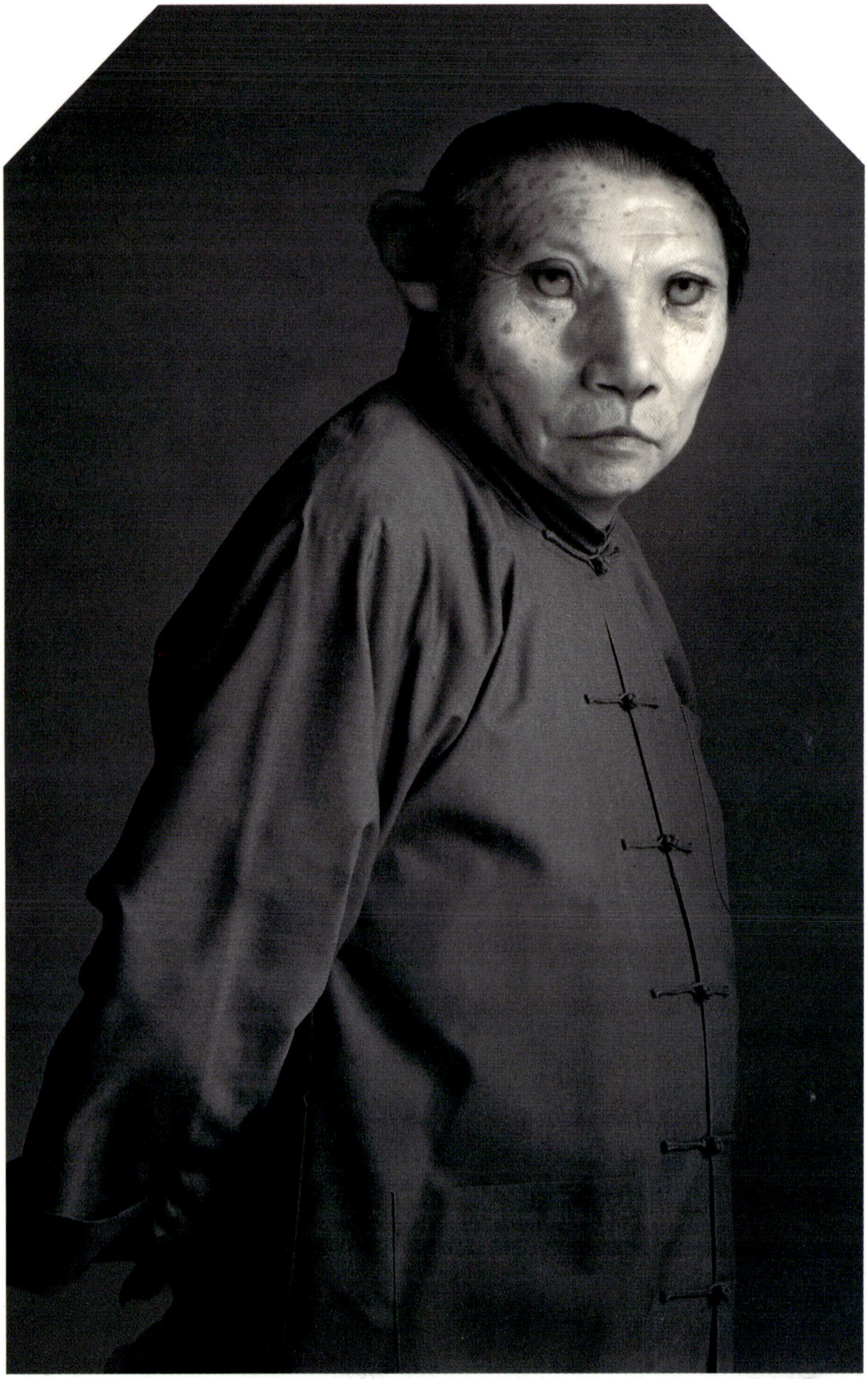

13.

Joyce Neimanas

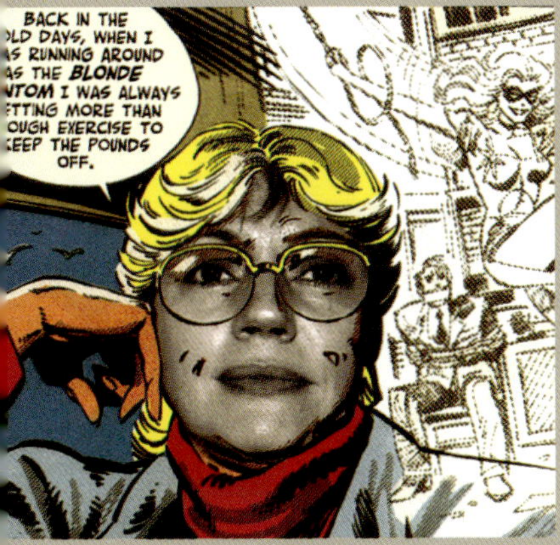

Joyce Neimanas draws her images from a multitude of sources. She also has little regard for the notion of media purity, even using negatives she did not take herself, manipulating the images and making elaborate collages of Polaroid SX-70 prints. Rather than treating the photograph as a precious object, she uses it as a tool to examine questions of representation, reality and artistic expression through media.

In 1992, a grant from Apple Computer gave her the opportunity to take her media exploration into the computer realm. Her first computer art production was the "Heroicomic" series. This was followed by her "Legends of the Powerless" exhibition, printed as Iris Prints in 1993. She now takes her work to Nash Editions for Iris printing because she feels that the staff there are most accommodating to her needs as an artist.

Joyce Neimanas has been a faculty member at the School of the Art Institute of Chicago since 1973. Her work has been exhibited in the Museum of Contemporary Art, Chicago, the San Francisco Museum of Modern Art, the California Museum of Photography and other institutions.

Joyce Neimanas

When did you start to use the computer? Could you tell us about the transition from your early work to the work you've been doing recently?

I received a computer from Macintosh Apple Corporation in 1992. It was part of a program they had for artists. After I'd received the machine, I just left it sitting in my office for about six months and didn't touch it. Computers all seemed too difficult for me. Apparently, the same kind of thing happened to many of the artists they gave their machines to. So Apple decided to organize a workshop for us in Camden, Maine. That really made a big difference for me.

Then, someone told me about this guy in Los Angeles named Jonathan Reff. He's wonderful, a really great teacher. He knew that I wanted to know just enough about the computer to be able to make some art. He could work with me in that way. We worked together for about a month. That was enough time for me to learn how to use the computer for the work I was doing. I still call him when I run into problems, but these days that's only about once a month. In the beginning I used to call him every day.

So those two things — going to Camden, Maine, and meeting with Jonathan Reff — were what really got me started using the computer.

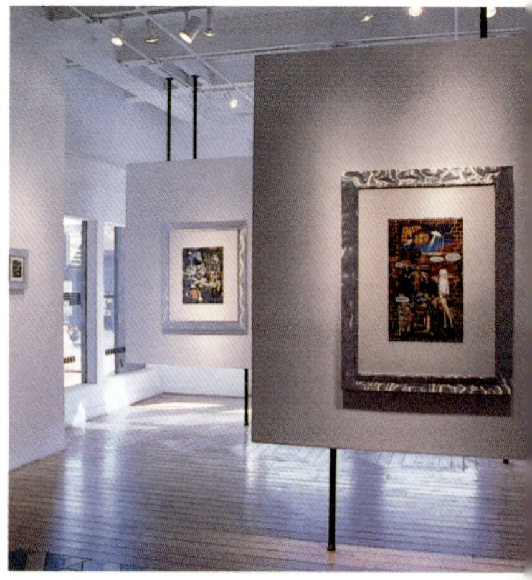

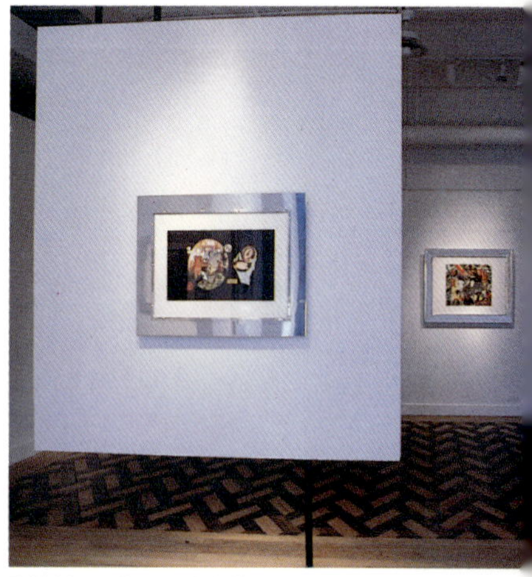

Exhibition at Vernon Ezell Gallery, Chicago, Illinois

My early work consisted of collages. They involved putting things together that aren't necessarily associated. The only bad part about the computer for me is looking at the image at such a reduced scale. I'm so used to working with the material at its actual size. That's why I always like to make a proof print. So I can get an idea of the actual scale of the thing.

Please tell us about the themes of your work.

The work is really about the dilemma of being a person in the world who lives an ordinary life but is expecting something extraordinary to happen. In this connection, I was thinking of the Dada period in art. My work is very much connected with the

a. Dolls
b. Doll Scan
c. Boy Figure Scan
d. Background

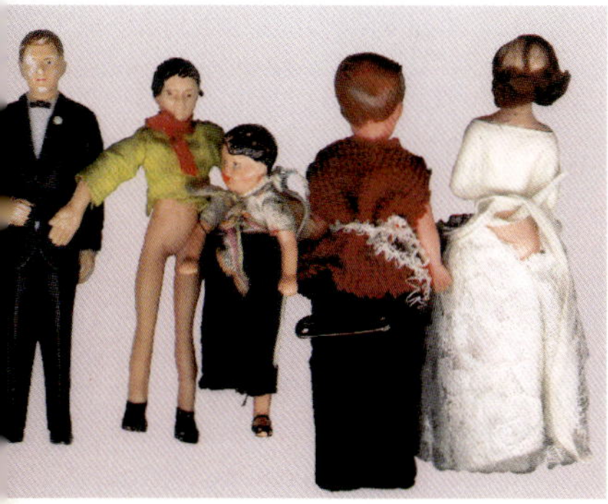

My niece chose these dolls for me. She thought ould like them. As you can see, they all have nething wrong with them.

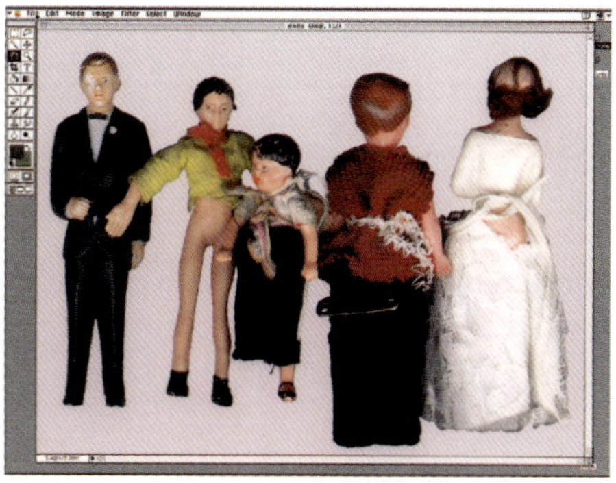

b.

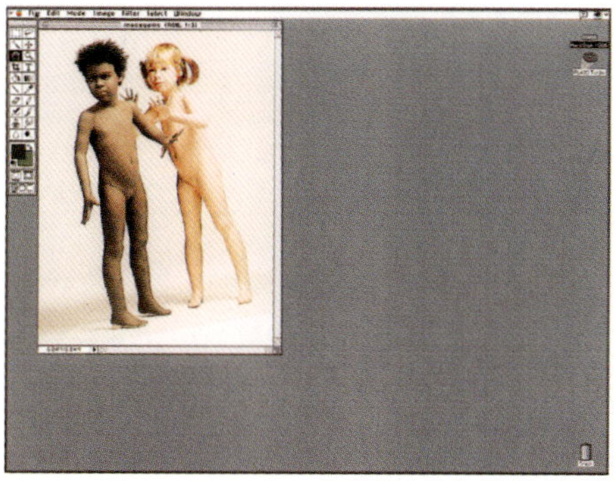

c.

b. I scanned in the photograph I took of the dolls.

c. Then I scanned in this figure of a boy that I had taken from a catalog.

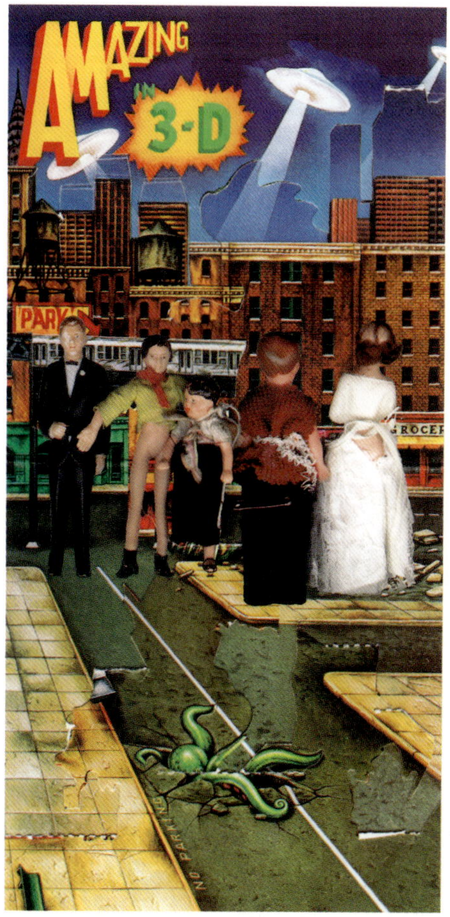

d.

d. The background comes from a postcard.

Joyce Neimanas

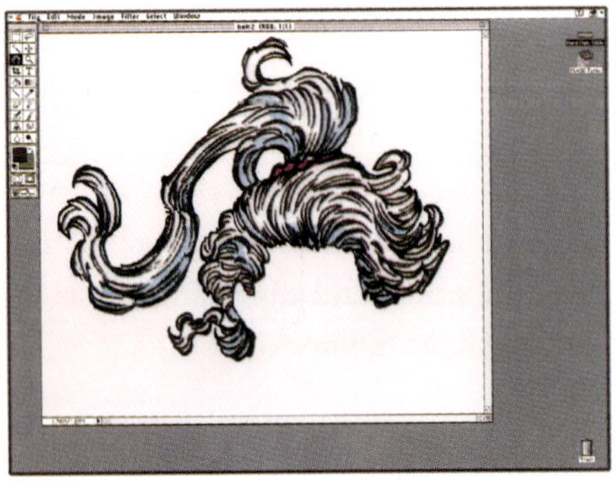

e.

e. I took this hair and placed it on the primitive figure.

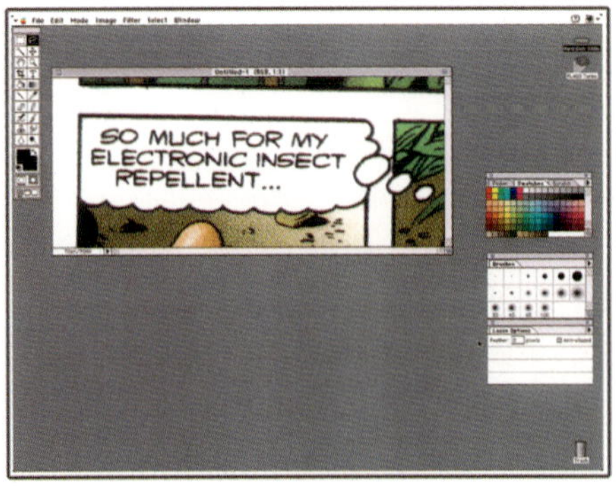

f.

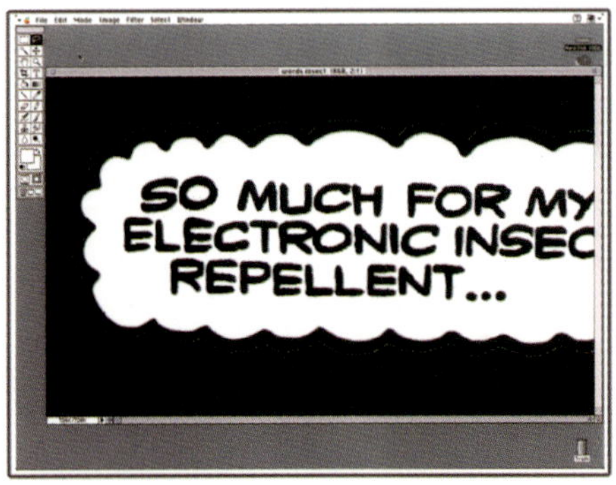

g.

f. I scanned in the captions from a cartoon.

g. I retouched each letter, then I pasted in the word balloon. I always put the words in last.

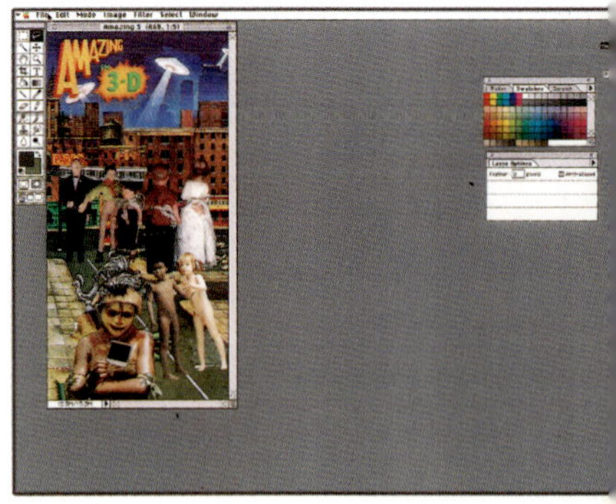

h.

h. I arranged all the elements as I wanted th in the picture. Then, I used the color palet selected the colors I wanted, and made hue a saturation adjustments.

i. (Opposite) And this is the finished picture.

e. Progress
f. Captions
g. Captions (progress)
h. Progress
i. Amazing
24" x 15"

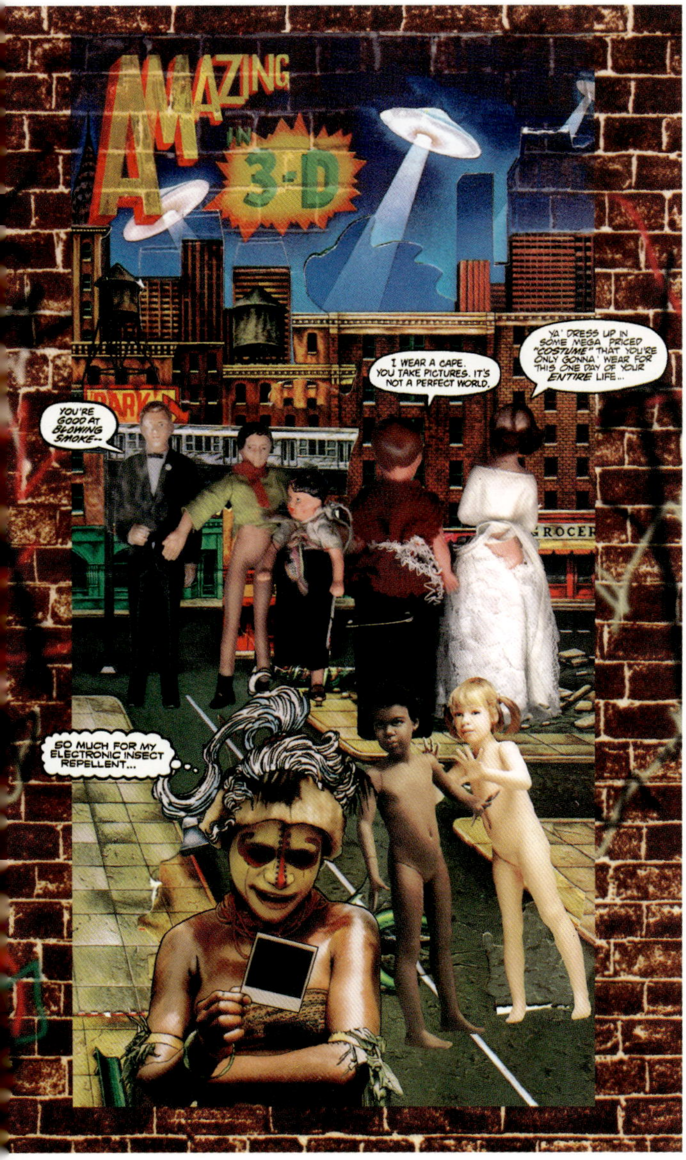

Dada spirit. I'm looking for the unpredictable and extraordinary things that can happen to someone, in ordinary life.

I usually have ideas about what I will work on, but I don't draw them out ahead of time because I like the element of the unpredictable to enter into the work. And the computer is so logical. It doesn't like illogic. So I have to think of ways of working with the computer that avoid all that logic. It's an interesting dilemma for me.

In the earlier work I actually did sketches beforehand. But again, I would let the drawings grow as I was making them. You have to be constantly aware of change. As the piece grows, I want it to make me think of something else. Because I'm not a designer I can allow that to happen. Designers have to know exactly what the end product is going to be. I like to have much more freedom than that.

I can get ideas for the words in my pictures by going around the city on the public transportation. On the train or the bus I can overhear conversations, and I can put them together to make a story. I get the image made first. Then I look for the words to fit the image. The conversations I hear are supposedly logical, but when you put them together they make a kind of nonsense. I like that.

The color you get with the computer is seductive. I have to pay attention to the color. Prior to the computer I did a little color work, but basically I worked in monotone. I have a background in painting and drawing. It's my nature to collage and draw things. Working with the computer is like painting in a way. You can work on several pieces at the same time. You can work on one image a little bit at a time. But when you do photography you have to set up your whole lab, and get everything ready, and decide that you are going to go ahead and print. So that really makes you do the work in different time slots — one is the photographing stage and the other is the printing stage. With the computer you can work on something for maybe half and hour, then put it away and work on it the next day.

Joyce Neimanas

Where do you get your inspiration?

Usually, I get the inspiration from real life experiences. The characters in the pictures are not real. The situation is real. It is something I have experienced. The work is really like a documentary photograph of my life. It's not just an image I can get from the lens in one click.

This picture, for instance, from Legends, is of a woman who is a model and a mother...and inside her brain is this screaming maniac. But she looks perfectly calm. The caption says, "When you shriek like that it goes in here and comes out there and kills brain cells. Know that?" Inside her is this raging human being, but on the outside she has a little hand over her mouth and she looks really calm.

Many of the characters in the pictures have double personalities...multiple personalities, even. That is something you can do with this medium. You can give a person more than one personality.

Are the characters happy about the different personalities, or do they experience any conflict?

No, I think that this is the way people are anyway. You have all these different ways of dealing with your life, otherwise you are not going to get along living in the world as it is.

But at the same time this woman has a screaming maniac inside her?

Yes, that's okay (laughs). I'm like that. You can scream on the inside.

So how do you vent that energy?

I make these pictures (laughs). I mean, some commit murder when they get into this state.

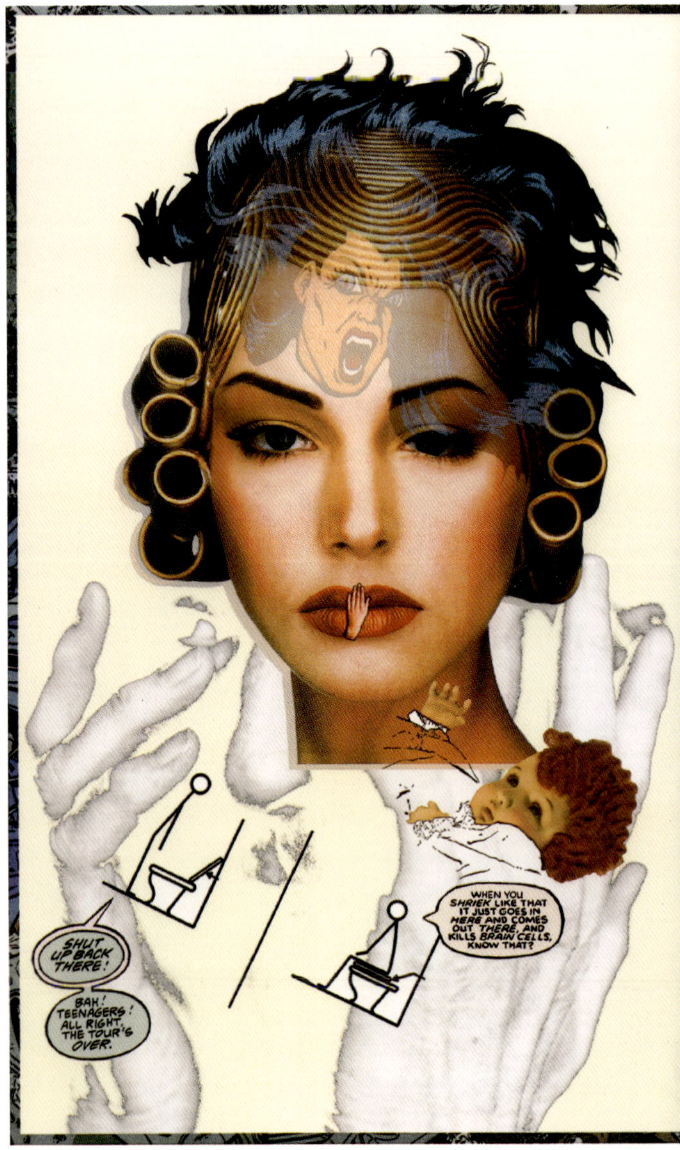

1.

1. Duchamp
39 1/2" x 24 3/4"
2. Casino Curtain
10 1/2" x 7 1/2"

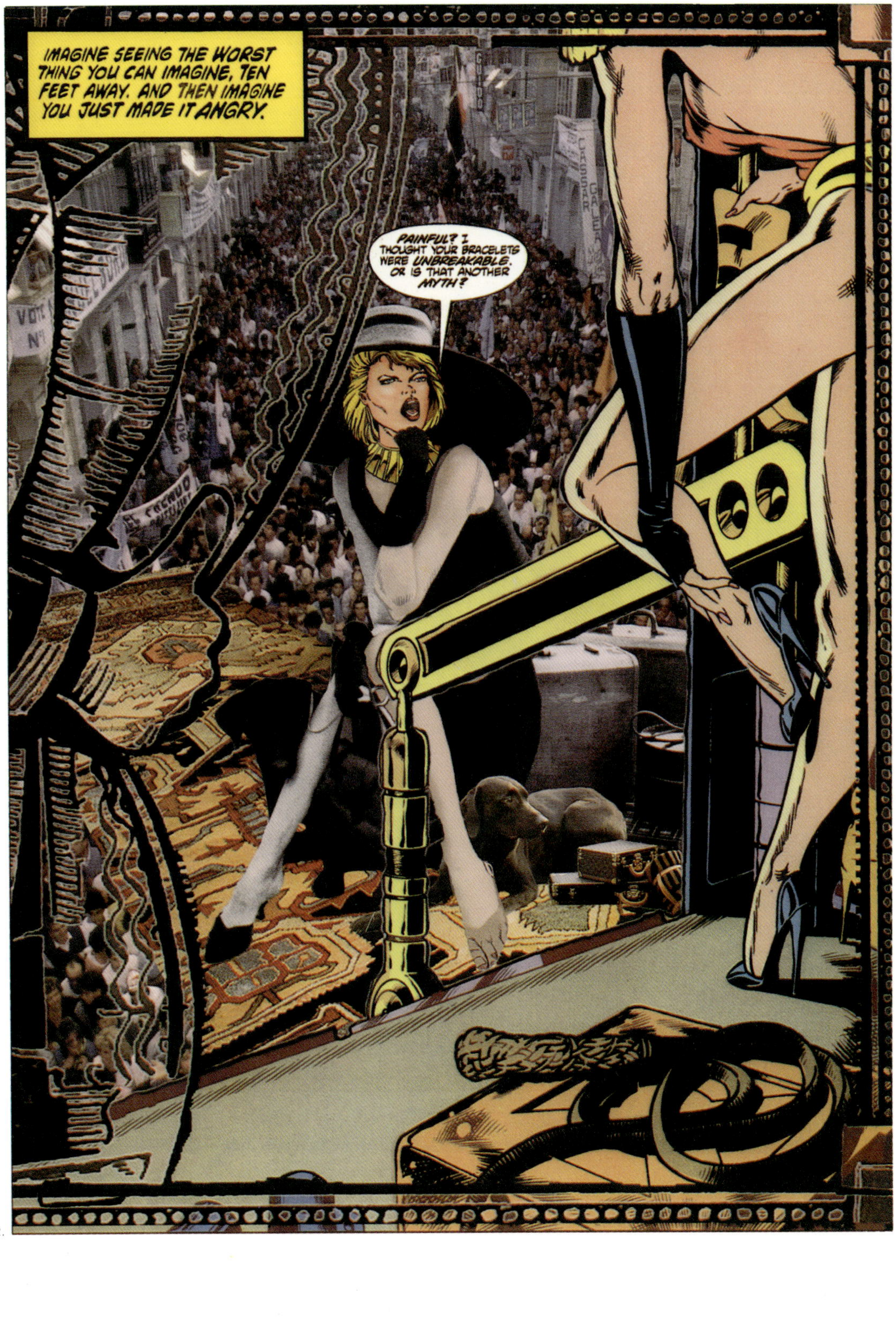

2.

Joyce Neimanas

Was that one of the reasons you became an artist in the first place? To have a means of releasing these strong emotions without necessarily harming others?

Partly that...and also to have a way of dealing with my fantasies. Let me mention Diane Arbus in this regard. She had a way of seeing the unusual, the odd, the fantastic in the world around her. I don't just mean the "freak" pictures, either. She did some landscapes that were so bizarre. You can look at those pictures and not be able to believe that that kind of landscape exists. It's just incredible.

In my case, I see things and make them happen in my head. I create them there. They are fictions based on facts. I did try "straight photography" for a time, but I realized I was trying to emulate people who I admired, like Diane Arbus, rather than simply be inspired by them while I pursued my own kind of work.

For almost the whole of my career I have been making collages. In fact, the very first picture I did was woven. I should have known right then that collage was what I was going to pursue forever.

So don't you see yourself mainly as an illustrator, rather than a photographer?

I'm neither of those. Photography is interesting in that you can use the photograph in a variety of ways. I don't even have to use a lens. A lot of my work was done with photograms. You can look at photography as you would other media, for example painting. There are so many styles — photorealistic, abstract, surrealist, postmodernist ... There are so many possibilities within the medium. Photography also has that, but mostly what people see who are not involved in the art world — are photographs that are reproduced in magazines. Usually they are documentary or fashion photos. But there are lots more positions within the field. I think it would be a detriment to the field if photography were defined too narrowly. I prefer to have things open.

Though I wouldn't call myself an illustrator. A painter, perhaps, would be a more appropriate word for me. This work is more like painting to me because you begin with the blank canvas, or t blank computer screen in this case. A blank canvas is the wor thing imaginable for me. I have to start filling it up immediate When I look at the blank screen, it's the same feeling.

Now, the very first thing you put down on the screen or canvas the key to the picture. It could disappear by the end of the pictur but it is the initial spark that sets the whole picture in motio The objects in there are open to a variety of interpretations. I a not trying to deliberately play games with the audience, or tryi to mislead them. But the meaning of the picture cannot alwa be understood immediately. If I could do pictures that peop immediately "got," I would be more of an illustrator or a cor mercial photographer. I don't think I'd be very good at commerc photography. I think that kind of work is very creative, but it's n something I can do very well.

Do you have a definition for creativity?

I can recognize creative people. Usually, creative people a putting out something I have never even imagined yet. When th occurs, it is something completely extraordinary. Even some commercials on TV have this. To put all that into a 30-second can be astonishing.

Although photography is a reproducible medium, wi traditional film photography there is the concept of the "origin print." How has the meaning of "original print" changed wi the advent of digital imaging?

Well, I don't really fit within the photographic tradition. Mo photographers can reproduce the same negative over and ov again. But in my case, I made unique images which were painte collaged or photograms. Because there was so much handwo involved, they weren't editioned.

It doesn't interest me to make a lot of copies because once I' made the picture I don't want to make another one. I don't wa to waste my time and energy doing reproductions. So the situati I have now is very advantageous. Once I've made one picture

3. Waste War
10 1/2" x 7 1/2"

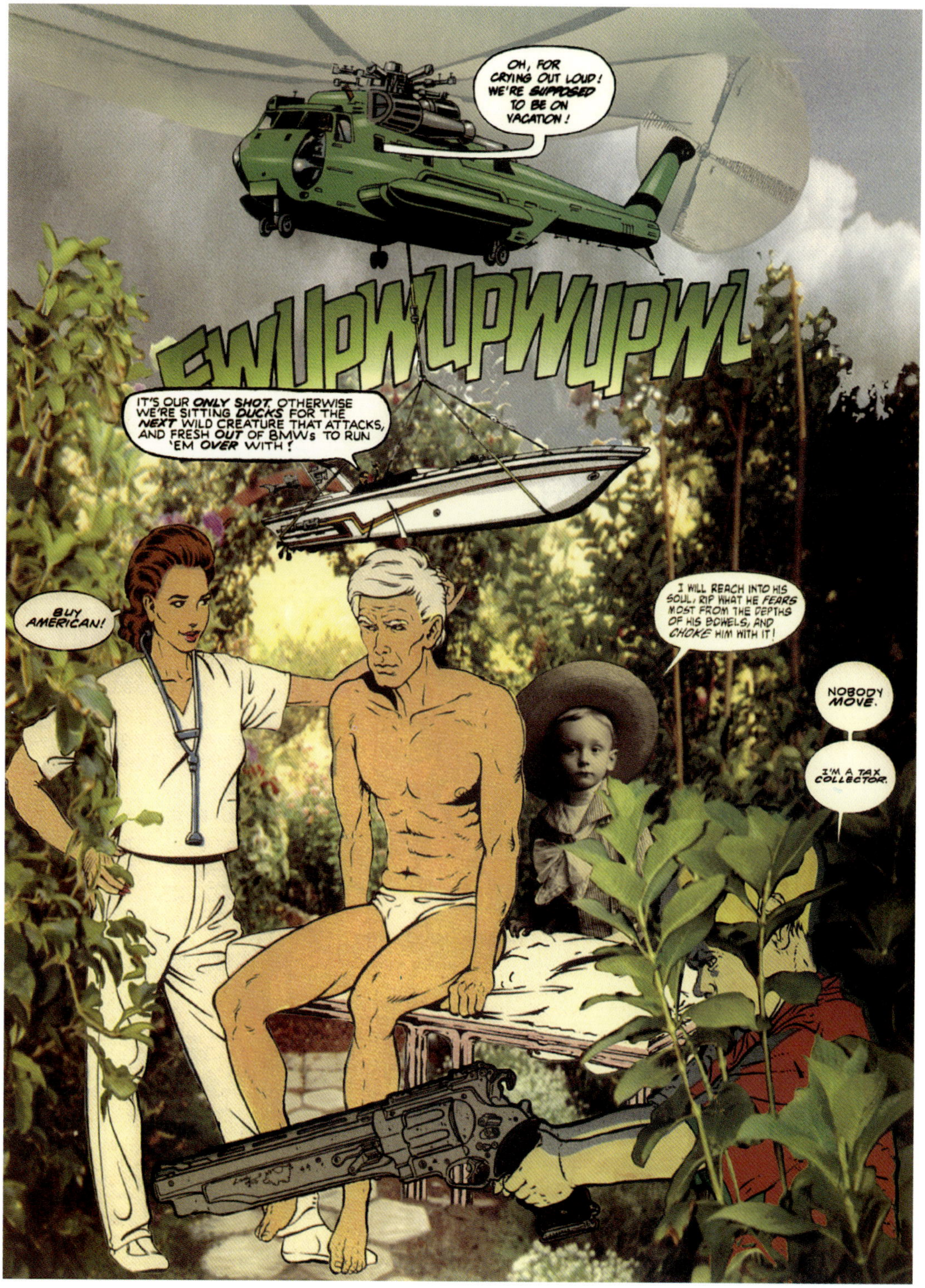

3.

can send it off to Nash Editions, and have them make another one if it's needed. But if I had to print them myself, I would probably just make one. I love the darkroom because every time I make something I want it to look different. But I'm not the kind of photographer who takes a negative, puts it in the enlarger, and prints it many times over. That would be boring for me. I want to use my energy creatively.

How has digital photography brought you closer to the images you want to express?

If somebody hadn't given me the computer, I wouldn't have said I absolutely needed it in my work. I'm not the kind of person who goes out and buys every piece of new hardware and software they can lay their hands on. That's all too distracting to me. But if I came across a piece of software by accident, and saw that it had potential, then I would use it. But to me, digital photography is really just a tool — like the telephone. If we didn't have the telephone we wouldn't know that we needed one.

Could you describe the tools that you have?

I have a dye-sub printer and a Hewlett-Packard scanner. I also have a Syquest. I use DAT tapes for backup. I also have a modem, but it's not connected. I have another computer that I use for my office work. I have a line conditioner. That keeps the electric power at an even level. It blew up the other day, actually. There must have been a big fluctuation in current or something. I don't know exactly what happened. But fortunately nothing broke. These things are especially useful in places like L.A. where you get a lot of power fluctuations and brownouts.

What advice would you give to the young generation who are working with electronic imaging? What are the important points for the photographer?

The first thing is that the person should have in mind what kind of photographs they want to produce. That depends on the photographer. Some photographers really adore being out on the street. They like the challenge of getting certain subjects, like

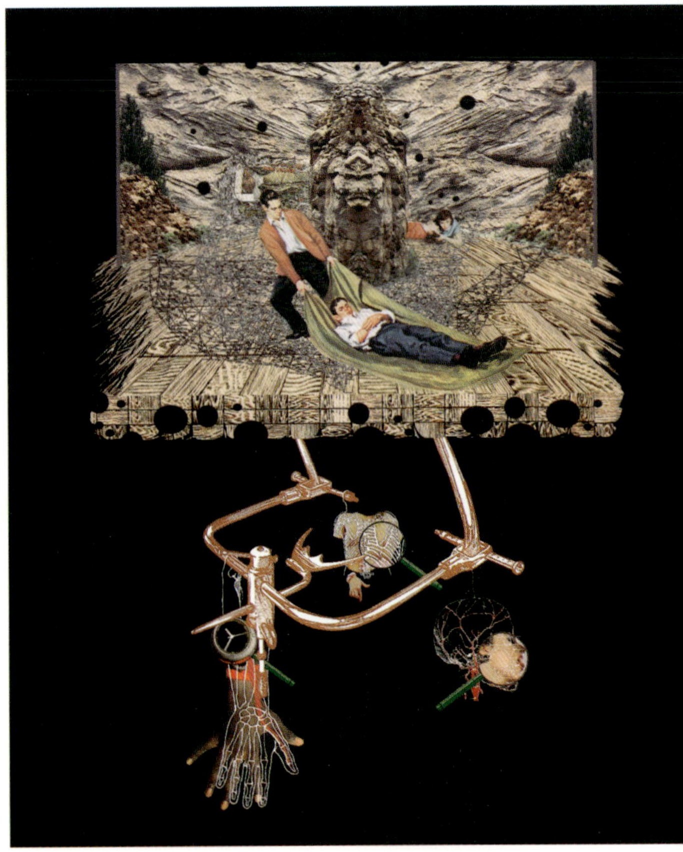

4.

4. Natural Targets
28" x 24"

5. The Village People
10 1/2" x 7 1/2"

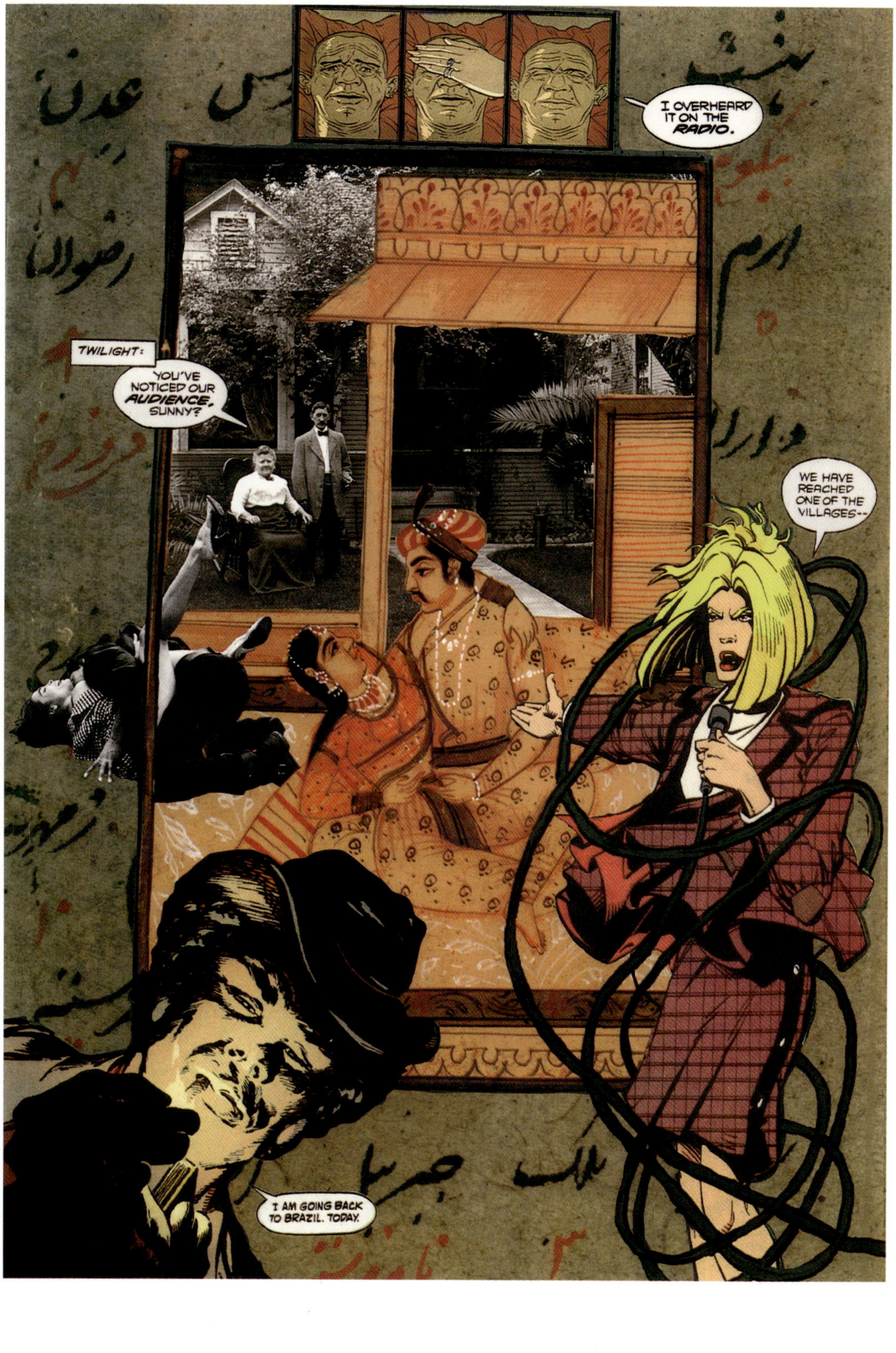

5.

Joyce Neimanas

Diane Arbus. Sometimes she would be so absorbed in the subjects themselves that she would forget her camera. But photography was the medium she used to get next to those people she portrayed.

Other photographers might prefer to use photography as a tool, like a paint brush. Moholy-Nagy was one of those. However, Arbus was as inspirational to me as Moholy-Nagy in terms of their work. I don't have to imitate an artist's life style or work in order to be inspired by them.

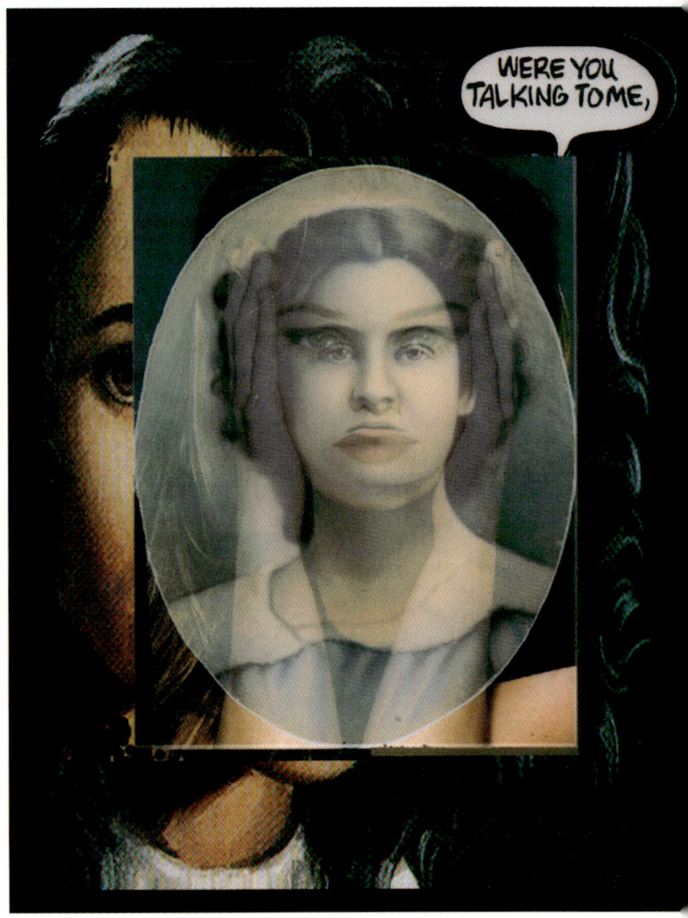

6,

6. Face Lift
10" x 8"
7. Signals
20 1/2" x 36 1/4"

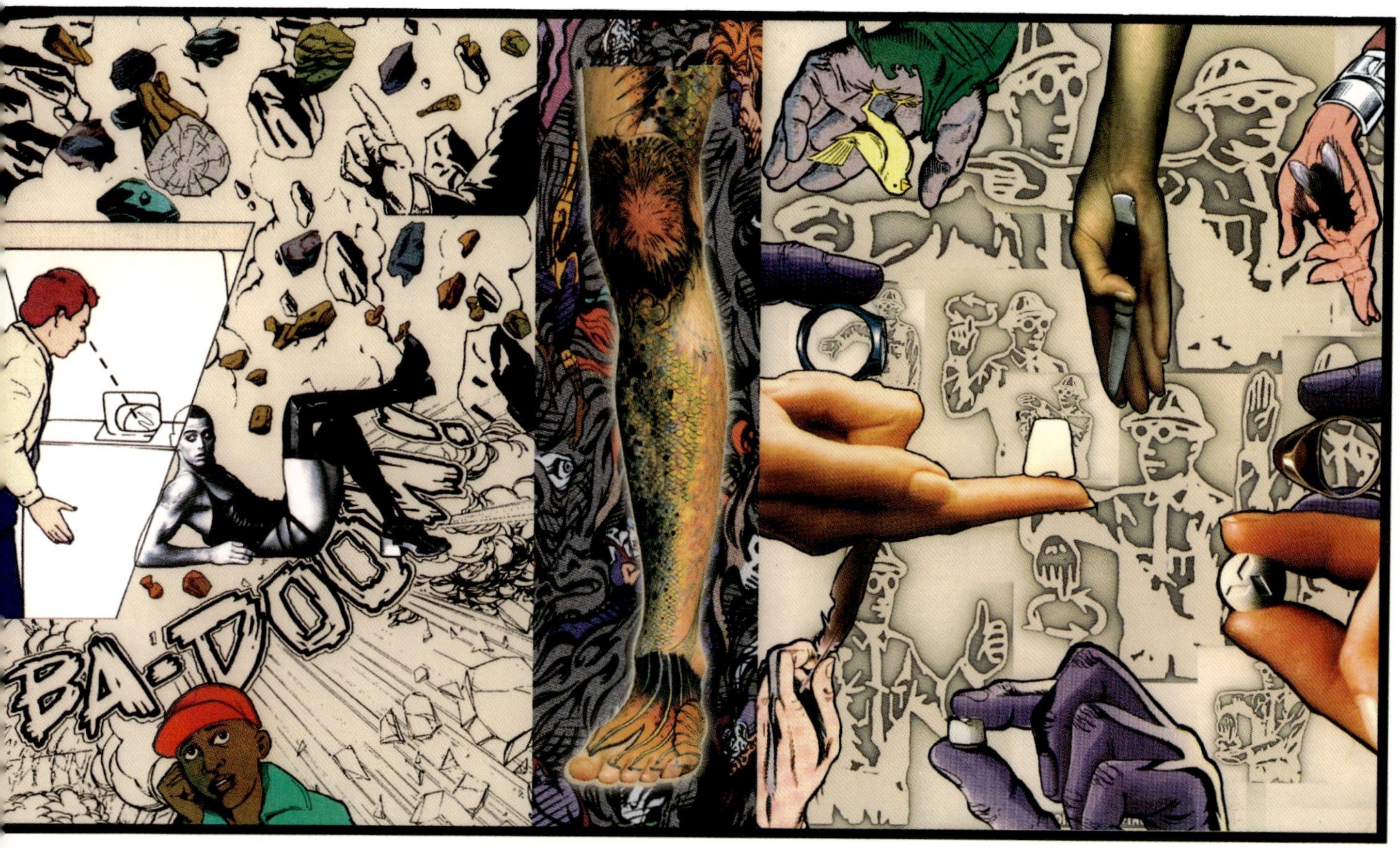

Joyce Neimanas

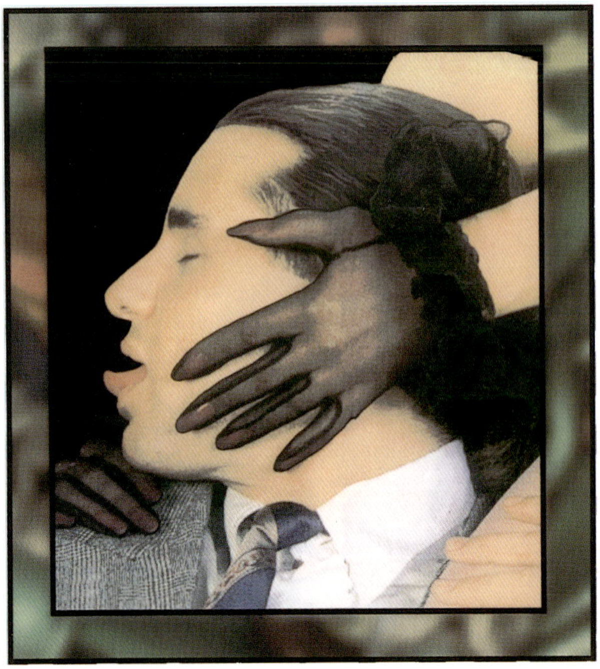

8.

8. My Gloves
   $3\ ^1/_2$" x $3\ ^1/_2$"
9. Opposite: Adam and Eve
   $10\ ^1/_2$" x $7\ ^1/_2$"

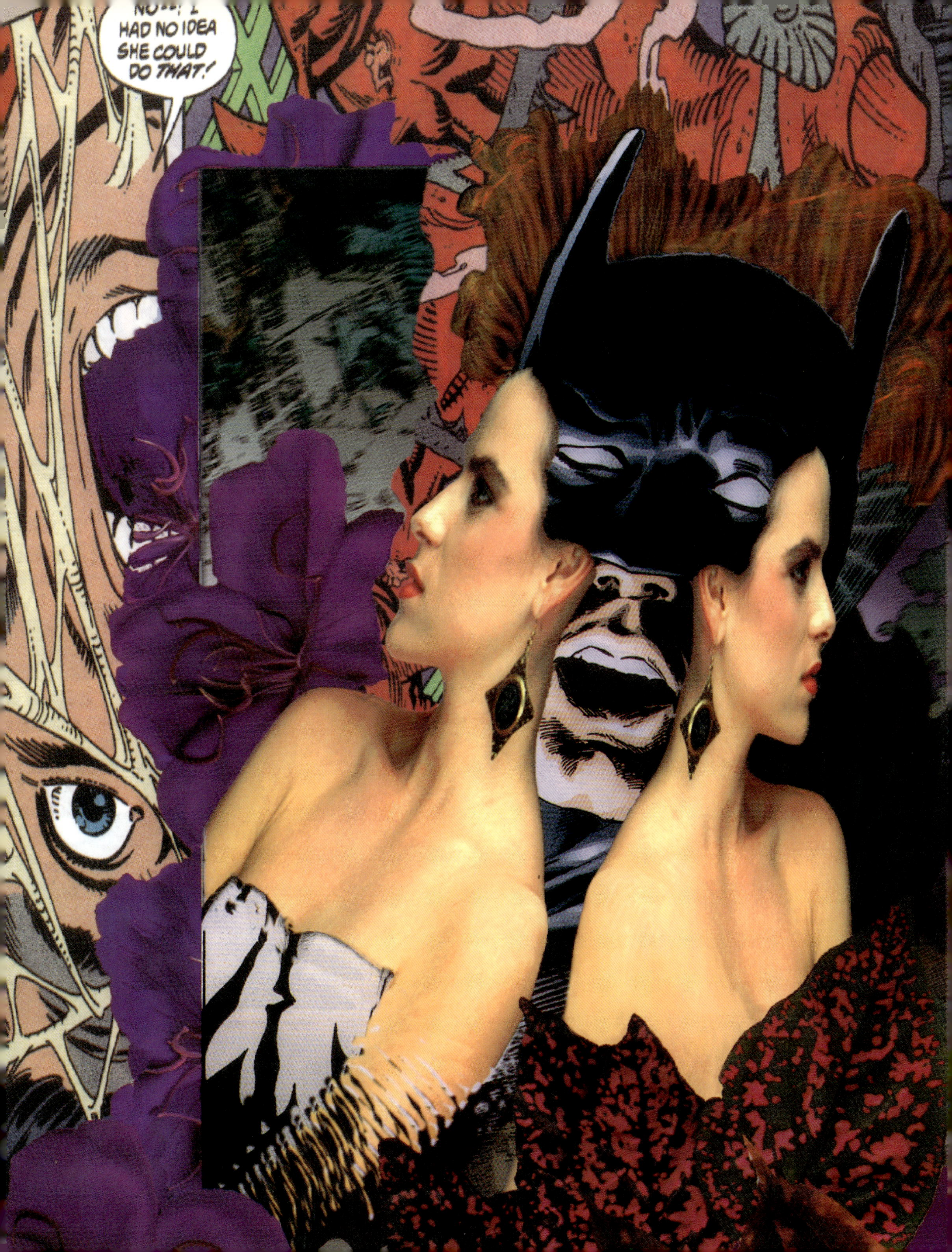
NO--! I HAD NO IDEA SHE COULD DO THAT!

Joyce Neimanas

10. Dear Diary
22" x 15"

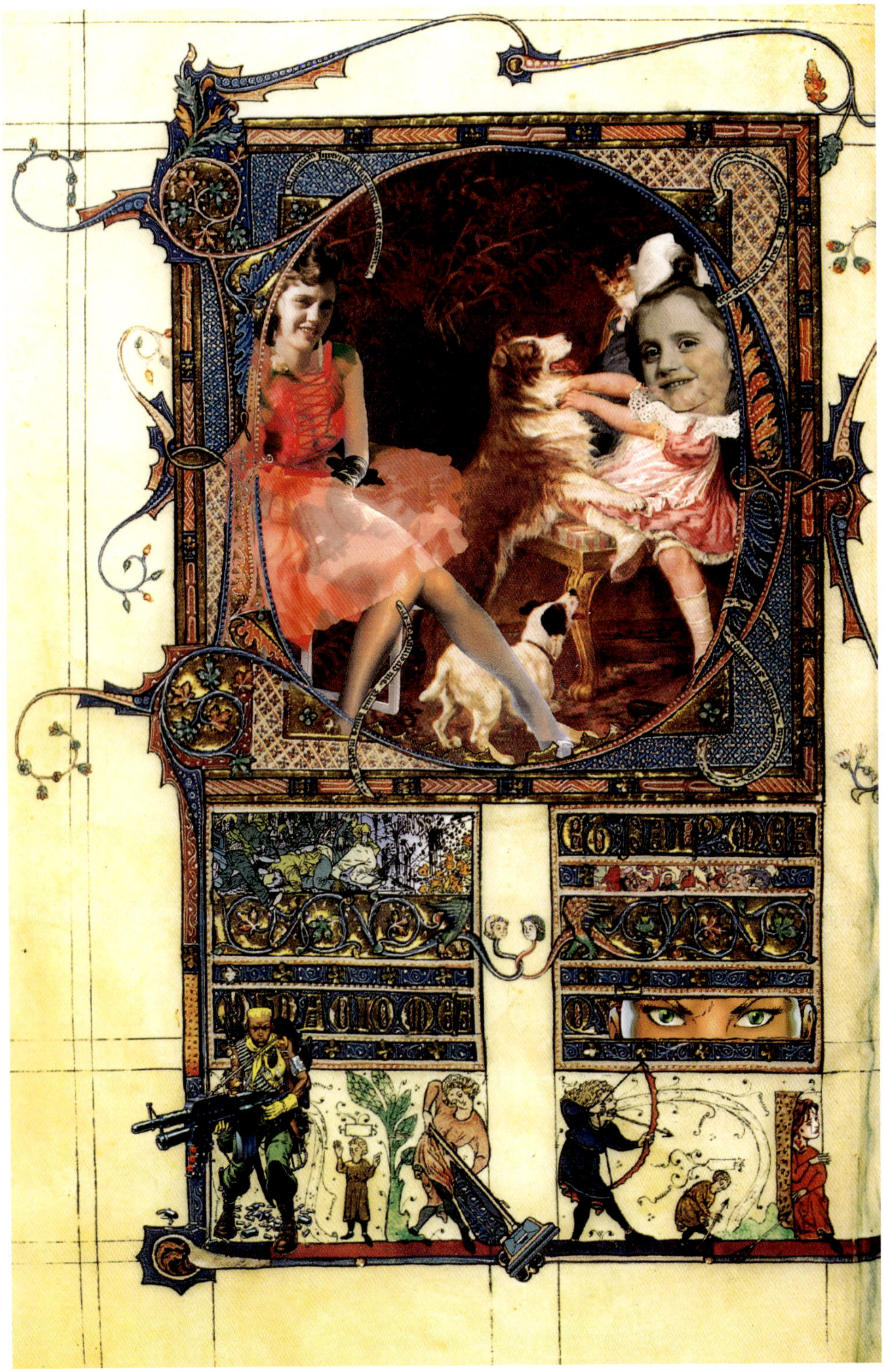

10.

Editor's Note

The idea for this book came out of conversations I had with Takenobu Igarashi in June, 1994. At that time I had been writing magazine articles on digital photography and was becoming extremely interested in the subject. In the U.S., various photographic journals were featuring articles on digital photography, indicating that this new technology represented a turning point with major consequences for the world of design and photography.

I immediately started to do some research with a view to publishing the book. Unfortunately, there was very little information available at the time, and I had no list of photographers who were involved in the digital medium. Eventually, I tracked down some relevant photographers, had them send me their portfolios, and went along to meet with them. I also visited VISCOMM (The Visual Communications Expo), held twice a year, once in New York and once in San Francisco. VISCOMM takes as its themes photography together with multimedia and design. At VISCOMM in New York last October there were many digital cameras on show, as well as other new products from various companies, and numerous seminars and workshops were held.

With the aim of assembling this book with highly finished and rewarding photographic works, I visited a host of photographers across the United States. Unfortunately, for the most part, they were not kind of photographers I expected to meet. Some of them seemed unduly carried away by the technology Itself, and had little in the way of artistic sensibility. Others were relying on stock photographs to produce their images, and thus far had put together only a meager body of work. I suppose this situation was inevitable since digital photography has been around for only a short period, and getting suitably equipped to work in this medium is forbiddingly expensive. I realized I had a long way to go before I found the right photographers to include in a book such as this.

The photographers represented here are radical exemplars of the field, and exhibit both artistic sensibility and technical competence in high measure. After selecting these photographers, I made the transition from my previous research to actually gathering material for the book in June, 1995. I travele to New York, Chicago, Dallas and San Francisco to interview th photographers, received examples of their work and had the boo manuscript finished in just three months.

To keep all of the photographic information in digital format un the final printing stage, the photographers provided their wo as digital files. We also employed hard copy in addition to th digital format. For instance, Iris prints were provided to give u an idea of texture. However, we took the digital route at the tim of printing in accordance with the artists' intentions.

If one uses the digital camera for shooting, and prints usin DTP, then the process is completely digital. However, a present, there are few photographers who use the digit camera for all their finished work. Resolution and shutt speed still leave much room for improvement. The digit camera must make three separate exposures for red, gree and blue data in sequence, and this takes time. But befo this book goes to print, perhaps some company will hav introduced a new digital camera that shoots with a sing shutter action at high speed and with a resolution goo enough to satisfy the professional photographer. As regard computers, Macintosh is the machine of choice fo photographers, as it is with designers. If the Mac prove insufficient for certain tasks, then usually the photograph will employ the Silicon Graphics Indy. The preferred displa device is the 20-inch monitor.

Jody Dole, a commercial photographer with the latest, mo powerful equipment, owns a CD-ROM writer, and was kin enough to present his work recorded on CD-ROM. The beau of the recorded images is outstanding, and they perfect reproduce the simple yet precise atmosphere that is characterist of Jody Dole's work. The images contained an enormous amou of information, and were written to disk in CMYK mode, so RGB to-CMYK conversion was not required at the printing stage. Th majority of computer owners these days own a CD-ROM driv allowing them easy access to digitally recorded images. CD-RO cartridges come at the reasonable price of $10 to $20. For thos o do not own a CD-ROM writer, a service bureau will scan images you want and write them to your CD-ROM cartridges. ubtless, with the widespread use of CD-ROM drives, the nber of people choosing to have photographs on CD-ROM increase enormously from now on.

oert Bowen and Sanjay Kothari provided their work on DAT e. The compact (5.5 x 7.5 cm) DAT cartridge can hold up to out 1 GB of data. Again, the price is moderate at $10 to $20 cartridge. As a precaution against the possibility of tape nage, the photographers also provided backup tapes. Both otographers stated that the desired colors could not be fully ained with RGB-to-CMYK conversion on a desktop system, they stored their files as RGB data. An RGB file contains color ormation as a combination of the primary colors, red, green d blue. This is the system of display on the computer's color nitor. CMYK (cyan, magenta, yellow and black) is the color tem used in printing. The closer one gets to accurate color roduction, the wider the gap between what the individual can with his or her equipment and what a company with more pensive equipment can accomplish.

niel Lee provided his samples on 3.5-inch magneto-optical ks, and Charly Franklin stored his work on 5-inch MO disks. Carroll and Douglas Kirkland used Syquest. Syquest is used ensively by professional photographers and designers in the . Syquest drives can be bought fairly cheaply these days. wever, for several digital photographs requiring a huge amount data, the storage capacity of Syquest disks, at 88 MB or even MB, is still insufficient. Syquest cartridges are also expensive, d as things stand, the future demand for Syquest is likely to cline.

hel Tcherevkoff and Elle Schuster provided positive film output n digital data. Despite the use of top-of-the-line Macintosh SGI machines, since film output was in conventional positive color, the photographers did not feel comfortable with the ult unless they could check it personally. This is because there no objective standards of judging color and picture quality n digital data. The characteristics of the computer monitor have a decisive influence on color and picture quality, and matching the colors of the photographer's monitor on monitors at the printing house is next to impossible. In this regard, you get to know how exacting professional photographers can be when it comes to color reproduction.

Nash Editions provided examples of the work of seven artists as Iris prints. The finished quality of the prints is up to the standard demanded for display in art galleries. The depth of color and textural quality of the Iris prints is phenomenal. Nash Editions accepts work from its artist-clients for processing in any format. The company takes great pains over color correction, repeating the process many times before they are satisfied with the result. This is the kind of work that can only be done by artists. In the age of electronic reproduction, Nash Editions is creating what they call new editions in multiple form.

From Joyce Neimanas we received dye-sublimation prints. When Joyce is ready to print her finished work she usually relies on Nash Editions, but for this project she used her own dye-sublimation printer. The dye-sublimation printer delivers a close approximation of the image projected on screen. The output has a quality close to color prints from conventional film, and Joyce's prints were good enough, considering the character of the work, to use as originals.

As I have mentioned, we received photographic originals through digital technology in various formats. Although convenient and compact on the one hand, there are still problems remaining to be solved with this technology. The sheer variety of formats can be a headache for editors, since they must match all the different cartridges received with the appropriate drives. The editing and design work for this book was done in the U.S.. At the editing and layout stage, hard copy was needed for verification purposes. As a precaution, the data was dropped to low resolution, and copies were made on Syquest and HD floppy diskettes for easy access. The most widely used removable disk format varies from country to country, but in Japan the magneto-optical disk is the mainstream storage device. When it comes to the printing stage, immeasurable problems are caused if the required data files cannot be accessed. Meticulous care was therefore taken in this area. Another area in need of attention was size. Although a little enlargement and reduction were permissible, in observance of the intentions of the artists as to the size of print, we could go no further than 120% enlargement or 80% reduction of the original dimensions.

Taking 300 to 350 DPI as a mean standard, one could set several original sizes for an image. There was concern, however, that this would cause severe restrictions for designers at the layout stage. At present, it is difficult to say whether it would be better to digitally integrate all procedures from the photographer's production process through to final printing, or to continue with the conventional method of photo-engraving from positive film or prints, and go back and forth between analog and digital. In the near future it would be desirable to have a simple, large capacity removable disk that the majority of computer users could own, and which was used uniformly in all countries.

For myself, the most interesting part of the assignment was interviewing the photographers. I was thoroughly impressed by their sheer energy and strength of character. What they all shared was a grasp of the essence of photography, as well as sound ideas as their source of artistic expression, and a willingness to pursue the unknown. Each had a philosophy underpinning what they wanted to express, and a keen visual sensitivity. These photographers developed their own styles during the analog era, and had already established themselves as professionals by the time digital photography came along. No matter how the technology progresses in the future, there should be no reason for them to be perturbed. For them, the technology will always be regarded as a tool — solely another means of realizing their vision. Perhaps this is something we should all bear in mind as we live through these fast-changing times.

The presentation of the work steps as a kind of manual was avoided. Instead we have incorporated the photographers' comments on the aims behind the works in a format suited to each. Before the end of another year, new computer models will be introduced with double the power of the machine I am currently using, and application software will again be upgraded. But e with these changes going on, I hope that the details of manipulation methods described in the work steps will at le help the reader grasp the essentials of the digital photogra process. I must express my gratitude to the photographers taking the time and effort to put together the materials requi for these valuable pages.

I called on the services of two translators, David Howarth Chiaki Hikasa, to ensure that the substance of the photograph discourses was rendered accurately, word for word. During course of the assignment I was actively involved with th translators, both in person and via e-mail. In the U.S., Ame Online and CompuServe are the popular providers of netw services. I myself used America Online to transmit and rece large volumes of text, but found a severe handicap in not be able to exchange Japanese text via e-mail. There are several w around this problem, but the quickest method was to sign with Nifty-Serve in Japan. Once I had the Nifty-Serve communications between Tokyo and Los Angeles were ope to me via a local access point here in Los Angeles. Of cou the final text for layout went to the printer also as a digital fil is possible to take even further advantage of toda telecommunications networks by sending the photograp material as a compressed file to the printer.

Having access in this way to all this equipment makes the w go a lot faster. Just as we all became used to live satellite broadcasts, so we are now routinely using the computer telecommunications to do our work simultaneously, even tho we are situated at opposite sides of the world. That toda communications technology makes use of the characteristic digital images is a key point in speeding up the work proces I would like to take up this theme in a future project.

This book would not have been brought to completion wit the use of digital technology and the cooperation of a great m people. The editor-in-chief and book designer, Takenobu Igara was instrumental in giving appropriate advice whene necessary. The translators, David Howarth and Chiaki Hik nderstood the intentions of this writer completely, and followed ıe project closely between Japanese and English. I would also ke to express my gratitude to the person in charge of editing at iraphic-sha, Seiki Okuda, for his strict attention to the details.

ust as digital photography transformed into reality what was a nly dream a few years ago, so we can expect big changes to ome over the next five or ten years. Digital technology is affecting ot only photography and design, but bringing about changes in reas peripheral to these fields. We must also consider the ounger generation, the first to grow up with the digital camera. very much look forward to seeing the kind of work that those oung people will be doing when they come of age.

isaka Kojima
os Angeles, August 1995